KING JOHN

BOOKS BY ALAN LLOYD

Biography

KING JOHN

THE WICKEDEST AGE

FRANCO

History

THE SPANISH CENTURIES

THE MAKING of the KING 1066

THE ZULU WAR

THE DRUMS OF KUMASI

Fiction

THE EIGHTEENTH CONCUBINE

KING JOHN

ALAN LLOYD

DAVID & CHARLES : NEWTON ABBOT

0 7153 5915 0

© 1973 by Alan Lloyd

All rights reserved. No part of this
publication may be reproduced, stored
in a retrieval system, or transmitted,
in any form or by any means, electronic,
mechanical, photocopying, recording or
otherwise, without the prior permission
of David & Charles (Holdings) Limited

To Simon, whose tournaments

are fought on other greens.

Printed in Great Britain by
Redwood Press Limited, Trowbridge, Wiltshire
for David & Charles (Holdings) Limited
South Devon House Newton Abbot Devon

CONTENTS

List of Illustrations   vii

Prologue   xi

Part 1 THE CROWN

Chapter	1 The Devil's Brood	3
	2 Lord of Ireland	19
	3 John versus Longchamp	37
	4 The Decade of the Lion's Heart	57
	5 King John	79
	6 Isabelle of Angoulême	99

Part 2 POPE AND EMPIRE

7 The Disappearance of the Young Duke	121
8 Good-bye Normandy; Come Back Poitou	142
9 John and the Pope	163
10 Serfs, Celts and Spectres	183
11 The Pope's Man	208
12 The Grand Design	228

Part 3 THE BARONS

13 Rebellion	251
14 A Kind of Peace	271
15 Magna Carta	292
16 Demise of a Settlement	313
17 The King Strikes	332
18 England Invaded	353
19 The Long Ride	374
Epilogue	393
Select Bibliography	396
Index	407

LIST OF ILLUSTRATIONS

	facing page
A map of England by Matthew Paris (*British Museum*)	52
Coins minted during John's reign (*R A Gardner*)	53
The Battle of Gisors (*British Museum*)	68
Lismore Castle, Ireland (*Irish Tourist Board*)	69
Bamborough and Alnwick Castles (*Aerofilms Ltd*)	196
Seals of Richard I and John (*British Museum*)	197
Part of the *Itinerary to the Holy Land by Matthew Paris* (British Museum)	212
Beaulieu Abbey and Chinon Castle (*J Allan Cash*)	213
Winchester Cathedral (*A F Kersting*)	308
Rochester Castle (*Royal Commission on Historical Monuments*)	309
Effigies of Eleanor of Aquitaine and Richard I (*French Tourist Office*)	324
The Bull of Innocent III (*British Museum*)	325
An Exemplification of Magna Carta (*British Museum*)	356
Corfe Castle (*Royal Commission on Historical Monuments*)	357
The Effigy of William Marshal (*A F Kersting*)	372
Pembroke Castle (*A F Kersting*)	372
Dover Castle (*Royal Commission on Historical Monuments*)	373

Be not righteous over much—
Ecclesiastes 7:16

PROLOGUE

In days of old, when knights, if not invariably bold, were commonly rapacious, the humble peasant was regarded as expendable. Medieval noblemen fought for the hell of it, exchanging blows at breakfast-time, making up over supper. For them, war was to some extent a game governed by strict rules of conduct. When they were getting the worst of it, they could retire to the relative safety of their castles and sit it out. It was the peasant who suffered. It was the peasant's hovel which was burnt down, the peasant's womenfolk who were ravaged, the peasant's crops which were trampled or plundered. The noble might hunt all day on his wide domains; the peasant who killed a rabbit on the same land could be hanged for it. No nobleman would be without his falcons, he even took them to church, yet the peasant who kept a stray falcon for himself was obliged, under ancient law, to feed the bird with six ounces of his own flesh unless he could pay a heavy fine to the owner and a special bonus to the king.

The lowliest in rank could not escape their oppressors. The law prevented their packing their meagre possessions and leaving a cruel master without his permission. Their daughters could not marry outside his dominions. Regional lords held their own courts of justice and were sometimes only too willing to execute sentence with their own swords. Gibbets towered wherever commoners were accustomed to congregate.

It is not surprising, therefore, that popular stories should have evolved connecting the nobility with devilry. One which gained wide currency by the twelfth century told of a certain Count of Anjou, in the kingdom of France, who returned from a distant land with a beautiful woman, whom he presently married. The countess settled well enough with her husband, and gave him four children, but there was something strange about her. She appeared to have no relatives, her parentage was obscure, she seldom entered a church and she never heard Mass. For some reason or another, she always left before the Consecration. At length, the count, worried by this eccentricity, detailed four knights to make sure that next time the countess entered chapel she remained to the end of the service. When the day arrived, and the Consecration was approaching, the knights discreetly but firmly trod on the hem of the lady's cloak.

As the priest raised the Host, the countess gave a scream as though in agony, tore the fastening from her cloak, and, still shrieking, flew out of the window. With her, she carried two of her children, who had been standing beside her. The other two remained behind in the chapel. The countess, it transpired, was Mélusine, the daughter of Satan, and could not bear to gaze on the Body of Christ. From the two remaining children, so the legend asserted, were descended all the later counts of Anjou, and, in due course, the Angevin Kings of England, Henry II, Richard I and John. All three were widely hated in their own time, for they were hard men in a hard age, and possessed demon tempers. But Henry and Richard fared better posthumously. Henry was remembered justly for his law and order, the discipline he imposed on his predatory minions and his tireless and beneficial administrative efforts. Richard, less deservedly, was glamorised by posterity as the heroic crusader, gallant and lionhearted.

John alone of the "devil's brood" survived in popular mythology as the irredeemably bad man, cynical, irascible, ruthless and cowardly, the oppressor of the Church and people, the insatiable extorter of money, the murderer of his rivals, the seducer of his subjects' daughters and sisters, unstable, unfaithful, a true product of Mélusine. "Foul as it is," wrote one historian, "Hell itself is defiled by the fouler presence of King John." Generations have seen him as England's most evil king. The prologue to his reign begins a century before his birth.

In January 1066, the long and peaceful reign of the childless English king, Edward the Confessor, ended with his death at Westminster Palace, and the country awaited the violence which customarily attended contested successions. In Norway, Harald Hardrada, rugged, hirsute and reputedly the greatest fighting monarch of the North, advised his Russian queen, Elizabeth, and his mistress, Thora, that the green lands of England would soon be his. His claim to the island throne was based somewhat remotely on an arrangement between his predecessor, Magnus, and the former king of England and Denmark, Harthacnut. It was backed, however, by the formidable reputation of the soldiers who followed him under the Land-Waster, the notorious black raven banner of the Vikings.

Immediately across the Channel, in Normandy, Edward's cousin, the towering Duke William, a fighter and administrator of great panache, was equally intent on receiving the crown at Westminster. William was related to the Confessor in the female line, but he was illegitimate, a technical drawback. His strongest argument was the claim that he had once been named as Edward's heir by the king himself. In England, the most powerful of the Anglo-Saxon earls, Harold Godwinson, a cleanjowled man with long, fair locks, was the most crucially situated of the power-seekers. Virtually Edward's deputy, and a tested general, he was at once a likely man to hold the country together and defend it against foreign invaders. According to Harold's supporters, it was Edward's dying wish that this strong son of England should succeed to the throne.

If so, the Confessor's spirit was swiftly gratified, for Harold, backed by the majority of men on the spot, contrived his election and crowning almost before the dead king was buried. His rivals might bluster and pontify; a *fait accompli* was, after all, the most positive argument. Hardrada and William of Normandy spent the summer assembling fleets to ferry their avenging armies to England. In September, the bearded Norwegian king landed in Yorkshire and, having beaten the regional army at Fulford, near York, was challenged by Harold Godwinson at nearby Stamford Bridge. Thanks to a celebrated forced march from London, Harold was able to take the Scandinavians by surprise. They had scarcely buried their dead from Fulford and tended their many wounds, when the English king hit them. Harald Hardrada was killed and his army routed. "Diversely they perished," reported one chronicler, "until there were few survivors." Of three hundred-odd ships which had carried Hardrada's force to England, twenty-four were sufficient to take the remainder home.

Stamford Bridge marked the failure of the last Scandinavian invasion in English history. Three days later, William's army splashed ashore on the south coast. It is interesting to speculate that had William's invasion preceded that of Hardrada, their fortunes might have been reversed, for the medieval armies of the time had neither the logistical sophistication nor the reserves to fight great battles in quick succession, and the fresh side had a notable advantage. In that case, a Scandinavian king would have sat at Westminster and the Angevins might never have ruled England. As it was, it became Harold's turn to take the field with his best men weary and battle-torn. The ensuing engagement at Hastings ran true to pattern.

In the early morning of Saturday, 14 October, William of Normandy's knights, their kite-shaped shields daubed with brightly coloured birds, dragons and wild beasts, jogged over a ridge some seven miles inland of the Sussex coast and saw Harold's army positioned on a grassy, peninsula-shaped hill later known as Senlac. From the outset, the English king fought a defensive battle, deploying his men on foot and depending on the so-called wall of shields formed by his select troops to repel the Norman cavalry. For many hours, and against many charges, the English wall held firm, but by mid-afternoon it was breached in several places and the scene on the hill was a confusion of hand-to-hand fighting. Harold resisted, wrote the monk Florence of Worcester, from the third hour of day until nightfall, displaying such courage that, almost to the end, the invaders despaired of taking his life. Around him stood the last of his nobles and house guards, bloody and exhausted, still fighting shoulder to shoulder.

In the waning light of that fateful autumnal day, Harold Godwinson, the last Anglo-Saxon ruler of England, was smashed down by an unknown assailant and his body trampled to anonymity in the soft turf of the Sussex downs. The winner of Hastings was the winner of the English throne. In a few brief hours of fighting, a polyglot band of some five thousand continental adventurers, led by an austere and daring Norman general, had decided the future of a nation. William was crowned on Christmas morning in London's West Minster, where the grave of Edward the Confessor was not yet a year old. The approaches were thick with Norman horsemen. Others patrolled the streets of the city. Inside, the surviving lords of England and Normandy, whose blood was to mingle henceforth in the history of the country, kept uneasily in their own divisions. For the English aristocracy of the period, the Norman conquest was a disaster of the utmost magnitude. Many left the country to take their chances abroad as soldiers of fortune rather than stay where, as the northern poet Thorkil Skallason put it, "Cold heart and bloody hand now rule the English land." Indeed, by the end of William's reign almost every magnate with any power in England was a foreigner.

When William the Conqueror died in 1087, his sons inherited their major problem not in the disaffection of the English people but the ambitious and independent nature of the baronage. The English monk Orderic, who lived for years in Normandy, found the nobility there a brash and aggressive one. "The race of Normans," he wrote, "is unconquered and ready for any wild deed unless restrained by a strong ruler. In whatever gathering they find themselves they always seek to dominate, and in the heat of their ambition they are often led to violate their agreements." Orderic's contemporary, Geoffrey Malaterra, described them as "eager for gain and eager for power . . . unbridled unless held down firmly by the yoke of justice." The Conqueror had spent much of his life subduing the Norman barons, suppressing the feuding, plundering and mayhem which had divided the duchy, before harnessing their dynamism to the capture of the English crown. On his death, the rebellious tendencies of the barons burst forth again.

William bequeathed Normandy to his eldest and smallest son, Robert, an easy-going, self-indulgent fellow who not only allowed the barons of the duchy to do as they pleased, but encouraged those in England to do the same. The second of the Conqueror's sons, William Rufus, so called for his red hair, inherited the English throne. Soon, Robert and Rufus were engaged in a struggle for the whole of their father's domain. William Rufus was a cynical and licentious tyrant who preferred bribing his enemies to fighting them. In 1096 he was offered a fine chance. Robert wished to take part in the crusades, but, being impecunious, agreed to pledge Normandy to William for three years in return for having his expenses paid. The taxes Rufus extorted from his English subjects to raise the money, and the oppressive methods he used to subdue the Norman barons, made him equally unpopular on both sides of the Channel. In August 1100, he was killed while hunting, struck by a stray arrow of remarkable accuracy.

By now, Robert was on his way home from the Holy Land with sufficient money to redeem his duchy from pledge. On hearing of his brother's demise, he pronounced his claim to the throne of England. But the third and youngest of the Conqueror's sons, Henry, was already in England and, like Harold before him, made the most of his proximity to the action. Seizing the treasury, Henry had himself crowned at Westminster three days after William's death and bought off the furious Robert with the promise of a sizeable annuity. He also renounced any claim to Normandy. Henry I was energetic and mercenary, a shrewd businessman with his father's flair for administrative efficiency. Under him, the Anglo-Norman monarchy was to establish a degree of organisation which would render it momentarily secure from the barons and bring England peace for a generation.

Meanwhile, Normandy, under Robert, had relapsed once more into anarchy. Bloody private wars raged amongst the nobles in which innocent people, as usual, bore the brunt of the violence. A number fled to the court of King Henry, who was begged to rescue the oppressed, especially the churches, in his brother's land. Armed with the excuse to break his pledge to Robert, Henry promptly set about the conquest of Normandy. The wheel had turned full circle since the conquest of England, and the battle of Tinchebrai, fought in September 1106, the fortieth anniversary of the Conqueror's landing in England, proved to be Henry's Hastings. It was a tribute to the English resistance at that earlier conflict that many of the Anglo-Norman knights, and indeed Henry himself, dismounted and fought on foot in the Anglo-Saxon style. The duke's army was swiftly and decisively vanquished, Robert was captured, and Henry proceeded to restore law and order to the duchy.

For the remaining twenty-nine years of his long reign, Henry I, King of England and Duke of Normandy, held his own against numerous continental enemies and the rebellions of his lusty subjects, and it seemed likely that his one legitimate son, William, would succeed him. Then William was drowned in a shipwreck off Barfleur, and the future of the Norman dynasty was thrown open. Henry had twenty-one known children, but only two had been born in wedlock, and the survivor of those two was a daughter, Matilda. In 1109, with the intention of establishing an alliance between England and Germany, Henry had approved the betrothal of Matilda to the Emperor Henry V. Unless England and Normandy were to become German states, the empress could hardly be considered heir to her father's dominions. As it happened, however, the emperor died before the King of England, and in 1125 Matilda, an imperious young woman of twenty-two, was free to inherit.

Two years later, Henry's barons assembled at his bidding to acknowledge Matilda as their future ruler. They did so with forebodings. The prospect of taking orders from a female was both novel and distasteful.

Medieval France—fertile, temperate, a land of cherries, raspberries and wood strawberries growing wild for the picking; of grapes and plums, spread to dry in the sun, shrivelling aromatically on the terraces; of herring, porpoise, dogfish and whale hung in salted strips in the markets—cradle of the gastronome, where pork was the standard meat, and most French families reared and fattened a pig, or pigs: coarse, hairy creatures which hunted the woods for acorns or roamed the towns freely eating garbage and getting under horses' feet. Here, hedgehog, squirrel and crow were devoured as delicacies, goose flesh was especially favoured and flocks of geese were driven to the grasslands like sheep. Cheese was also popular. One ancient anecdote greatly enjoyed by the initiated held that Charlemagne, on first eating green cheese, had cut out the green part in the belief that it was bad. In some provinces, they relished *serat,* a liquor made from buttermilk, garlic and onions.

Good living, however, was largely reserved for the nobility, and exploitation of the lower orders by their predatory lords was rife. Most peasants held their land from a master, either as serfs or as free tenants, both classes possessing their plots on a hereditary basis in return for service, money or kind. The burdens put on them were onerous. Everything was a source of privilege for the nobles. They had a thousand pretexts for establishing taxes on their peasants, who were generally considered "taxable and to be worked at will." Fines, tolls and tributes were levied everywhere, and endlessly, to meet the exigencies and avarice of the ruling classes, and if a man was so impoverished or simple as to be incapable of exploitation in any other way, he was driven to some absurd task to satisfy the facetiousness or sadism of his master. He might be reduced to such humiliating occupations as beating the castle moat to keep the frogs quiet, hopping about the hall on one leg, kissing the latch of the castle gate, making some drunken play in his master's presence, or singing a bawdy song before the lady.

Higher up the social scale, fiefs, or land originally granted by lord to vassal on condition of fidelity, gradually became hereditary, much like the smaller tenures of the peasants: that is, the rights and obligations of both lord and vassal were inherited by their successors. These might involve, among other things, military duties for so many days a year within a certain radius of the suzerain's castle on the part of the vassal, and, reciprocally, protection for the vassal by his lord in time of attack.

Theoretically, the duke or count held title by the grace of the king, the barons by grace of the duke or count, the knights from the barons, and so on. Almost everyone, to use a classic description of such relationships, was the man of someone else. In practice, the changing fortunes of noble families introduced complications. As generations passed, a vassal might find himself as powerful as, or even more powerful than, his lord. From the time of the Conqueror, for instance, the dukes of Normandy were stronger than the King of France, whose capacity to control his vassals was limited. In fact, the king enjoyed real control of no more than the Ile de France, the area immediately surrounding his capital, Paris. Nevertheless, the oath of homage remained an important political gesture, and carried much moral weight.

Count Geoffrey of Anjou, the earliest of the "devil's brood" to be encountered in this story, was still a boy when Matilda was named as her father's successor, but already held three fiefs on the continent. For Anjou and Maine he did homage to the King of France, and for Touraine to his neighbour the Count of Blois. Since Anjou, Maine and Touraine formed an important bloc immediately to the south of Normandy, the disposition of their ruler was of more than ordinary interest to Henry I, who conceived the strategically sound notion of marrying Geoffrey with Matilda. In human terms, the idea had less merit. Superficially, Geoffrey was appealing: handsome, sportive and devoted to hunting. To thicken the forests of Anjou and provide better cover for the game there, he instructed his servants to plant broom, or genet, from which derived his surname Plantagenet. He was a fine horseman, skilled at jousting and attracted the women.

But beneath the dressing, he was vain, autocratic and possessed of a cruel streak. When the chapter of Séez met to choose a new bishop without consulting him, Geoffrey Plantagenet ordered the canons and the bishop-elect to be castrated. Those who poached on his estates were shown no mercy. The combination of this self-willed Angevin and the haughty, tactless and quick-tempered Matilda was unpromising. Nor was the disparity in their ages more hopeful. When they married at Le Mans in June 1128, Matilda was twenty-five and Geoffrey fifteen. If the youthful count had landed an impressive prize in the empress, as Matilda insisted on calling herself, the clash of temperaments soon proved too much for him. A little more than a year after the wedding, he packed her back to her father, who was then at Rouen, with the message that she was too quarrelsome. Soon afterwards, thanks to the efforts of diplomats on both sides, he resigned himself to being nagged and took her back again. In 1133, their first son was born, and named after his grandfather, Henry.

The birth of Henry Plantagenet seemed to clinch the succession, and the ageing king hurried from England to France to mark the advent of his grandson. He never returned. In November 1135, he fell ill with food poisoning. On December 1, he died. With some excuse, for Matilda had already been meddling in Normandy, and had not bothered to visit her dying father, the English magnates now repudiated their oaths of homage to the empress and accepted Henry's nephew, Stephen of Blois, a grandson of the Conqueror, as their new king. Stephen had spent most of his life in England and Normandy, where he held large estates, and was liked for his generous, open manner. He had other traits which appealed to a baronage fed up with being held on short reins by a firm and determined king. Stephen was indecisive and irresolute.

When the pope, Innocent II, confirmed Stephen's coronation, Matilda was livid. At first she pursued her claims in Normandy, where she won over a number of strongholds on the southern border. Then, warming to her task, she switched to England, joining her bastard half brother Earl Robert of Gloucester, who had risen to champion her cause in the West Country. In the long and bitter civil war which followed, punctuated with the customary sieges and counter-sieges, Robert and the barons who followed him were never quite strong enough to overthrow Stephen, who, in turn, was insufficiently resolute to put down his enemies. At one stage, his forces had Matilda cornered at Arundel, Sussex, but Stephen chivalrously provided her with an escort to rejoin her brother at the Angevin headquarters in Bristol.

Perhaps there was more behind the gesture than good manners, for Matilda's persistent arrogance and lack of tact were a contributing factor to the failure of her own cause. When her fortunes were at their highest, after Stephen's defeat in a pitched battle at Lincoln, and London was at her feet, her high-handed manner so upset the citizens that they rose spontaneously against her and drove her from the city gates. It was not the only time she had to fly for her life. The indomitable granddaughter of the Conqueror was an accomplished survivor of setbacks. During a rout of her forces at Winchester, she remained with her brother at the rear of the fleeing army until the enemy was so close that she had to hitch up her skirts and escape astride a borrowed charger. Again, surrounded in Oxford, she climbed down the castle wall on a winter's night and struggled over snow and ice through the lines of the besiegers to safety. By the time she gave up the fight, in 1148, she was loved by few but at least grudgingly respected by many.

While Matilda was campaigning against Stephen, Normandy, like much of England, had sunk once more to anarchy. Geoffrey was not slow to grasp his opportunity. Though the Normans had little love for the Angevin, neither did they raise any affection for Stephen of Blois, who was, after all, just another Frenchman, and one who could not maintain order from the throne he had usurped. If they had to choose a duke from between the two, then Geoffrey's candidature had the merit of uniting Normandy with her southern neighbours and protecting a vulnerable portion of her border. When, in 1141, Geoffrey embarked on the task of taking over the northern state, he was able to win large areas with very little bloodshed. Three years later, he took Rouen and proclaimed himself duke. The title was ratified by Louis VII of France, who received him in Paris, and Geoffrey did homage for the duchy.

Prudently, Geoffrey governed the duchy as regent for his son, who had a legal title through his mother, rather than as duke by right of conquest. In 1150, when young Henry Plantagenet came of age, his father took him to Paris to do homage in turn, and Henry became Duke of Normandy in his own right. At seventeen, the new duke was a stocky, red-haired youth endowed with the ambition and energy of his redoubtable mother plus a calculating charm and cunning which Matilda lacked. He had been well educated, enjoyed reading and was never idle. Indeed, his restlessness verged on the neurotic. He seldom sat down except to eat, loved to travel, and found it hard to keep still even in church, where he paced up and down the nave during services. His reaction to frustration was violent. Thwarted, Henry was capable of screaming like a madman, tearing up bedclothes and chewing rushes from the floor in his fury. At such times, awed spectators remembered his legendary ancestry and slipped away until the temper had abated. Since the age of fourteen, Henry had made several expeditions to England in support of his mother, designating himself "the rightful heir of England and Normandy." It soon became clear that this would not be enough for him.

It was Geoffrey's wish that his second son, another Geoffrey, should inherit the ancestral fiefs of the family, and Henry at first swore to uphold his younger brother in these bequests. On Count Geoffrey's death in 1151, however, Henry promptly broke his promise and, taking advantage of his brother's youthfulness, took over Anjou, Maine and Touraine, leaving the young Geoffrey only three castles, at Chinon, Loudon and Mirebeau. Characteristically, Henry acted behind a veneer of respectability, arranging for a discreetly selected group of Anjou's vassals to beg him to rule them. He also did a voluntary penance for his sin of perjury. It was a small price to pay for the great domain he now held north of the river Loire. Before the year was out he would have acquired an even greater one to the south—and a wife every bit as remarkable as his mother.

South of the Loire, stretching from the border of Anjou to the Pyrenees, lay the great duchy of Aquitaine, whose people, gayer and more passionate than those of the North, spoke a language of their own, langue d'Oc, reflecting a culture more akin to that of the sunny Mediterranean than the bleak English Channel. When Duke William IX of Aquitaine died in 1137, his granddaughter Eleanor, then fifteen, became duchess in her own right. Eleanor was a true daughter of the South, black of hair, dark of eye and with a loveliness in feature and figure which captivated everyone. Knights sighed for her, gallants followed her in legion, troubadors composed *aubades* in her honour. Spirited, witty and romantic, Eleanor loved the fuss. But a girl could not handle the practical side of ruling. She needed a husband to master her barons and lead her armed forces. Eleanor found a fitting one in the heir to the French throne, who, within weeks of their marriage in July 1137, became Louis VII of France.

For several years it seemed a perfect match. Louis was entranced by his gay wife and eager to learn the fashionable game of courtly love as practiced by the sophisticated knights and damsels of the South. Then a disaster occurred which profoundly changed the king's outlook. Intoxicated by the cult of romantic love, Eleanor's younger sister Petronilla eloped with a brother of King Louis, the Count of Vermandois, who was married to a sister of the Count of Champagne. This powerful lord, whose lands bordered those of the French royal house on the eastern side, took up his sister's cause, and, when Eleanor persuaded her husband to support Petronilla, it came to a war in which Champagne was worsted. In the course of hostilities, the king's mercenaries ran amuck and burned down the cathedral of Vitry, in which hundreds of women and children were sheltering. The unfortunate refugees perished.

Louis, appalled by the atrocity for which he felt responsible, decided to atone by making a crusade to the Holy Land. Each spring, hundreds of Christians trekked east to fight the infidel. The French king who now joined them with his army was a new man. Gone was the light-hearted gallant Eleanor had married, and in his place was a sombre and devout prince who cut his hair short like a monk and spent his spare time not diverting his wife but quietly praying. Left to her own devices, Eleanor resolved to make entertainment. She and the ladies of her court, she decided, would join the crusaders. They would wear armour, ride chargers and generally fulfil the role of twelfth-century Amazons. Horrified, the French knights refused to joust with these female warriors, but the queen was not to be deflected from her purpose. Throughout the pilgrimage, she made herself a thorough nuisance to her husband.

On one occasion, while riding with the vanguard of the crusading army through hills infested with Turks, she countermanded Louis' order to hold a pass until the baggage party had gone through, and herself commanded the captain of the van to press on. As a result, the baggage party was ambushed by the enemy and the column suffered heavy losses. At Christian Antioch she flirted so outrageously with her uncle Raymond, the reigning prince, that their relationship became a public scandal. By the time the French crusaders reached Italy on the return journey, in 1149, Louis was as disenchanted by his wife as she by him. It was not only her unseemly behaviour which distressed him. More important, eleven years had passed since their marriage and Eleanor had failed to produce a son to succeed him.

At Tusculum, near Rome, the pope, Eugenius III, took a hand in the matter. It was said that he personally tucked the king and queen in bed together and gave them his blessing. If so, he scored a near miss. A royal baby was born the next year, but the child was a girl. Louis now determined to conclude his marriage to Eleanor and try elsewhere for a son and heir. Throughout their fourteen years together, the king's behaviour to the queen had been tolerant and considerate, and it remained so at the end. Though many urged him to charge Eleanor with adultery, which might not have been difficult, he had the marriage annulled instead on the ground that he was Eleanor's cousin in the fourth degree, and therefore within the bounds of consanguinity appertaining in the twelfth century.

On Palm Sunday 1152, Eleanor ceased to be Queen of France and became once more the Duchess of Aquitaine in need of a protector. Such a man would have to be of sufficient rank to uphold the ducal dignity and sufficiently strong in his own right to impress her factious vassals. There was little choice beyond Henry Plantagenet. He was eleven years younger than she, but he had proved a successful Duke of Normandy and had a reputation for boldness and intelligence. When Eleanor appealed to his chivalry, Henry came running. Even had she been ugly he would scarcely have refused the opportunity of getting his hands on Aquitaine, a duchy more valuable even than Normandy. At Pentecost, they were married in the cathedral at Poitiers.

Henry was now lord of two thirds of France. He could ride from the English Channel to the border of Spain without leaving his territories. Not only was he Count of Anjou and Maine, lord of Touraine and Duke of Aquitaine and Normandy, he even had a tenuous claim to the homage of Toulouse and Auvergne through his wife, while the dukes of Normandy had a similar claim with respect to Brittany. There was one more prize, England. In 1153, Henry was able to conclude a treaty with Stephen whereby the English king recognised Henry as his heir in return for Henry's help in bringing order to the island. The following year, Stephen died and Henry and Eleanor were crowned king and queen at Westminster. The "devil's brood" had come to the throne of England.

Part 1
THE CROWN

Chapter 1
THE DEVIL'S BROOD

Whereby God, to punish King Henry, raised up against him his own flesh and blood.

Roger of Wendover

A hundred years after Hastings, England was still a land of great forests. The three largest—the Weald of Sussex and Kent, the great Essex-Chiltern belt, which survives in fragments as the forests of Epping and Hainault, and the Bruneswald, which covered much of Huntingdonshire and Northamptonshire—were prized for their timber, their game and their excellent swine pasturage: feared for the outlaws who sheltered in them. The fens also provided refuge for the fugitive and recluse. In the east, from Cambridge to York and beyond, there was more marshland than forest. Vast watery wastes stretched for hundreds of square miles, treacherous in summer, impassable, except by boat, in winter, when the unbanked rivers spread unchecked across the lowlands. Places bordered by marshland, such as Ely, Peterborough, Ramsey and Crowland, attracted monastic communities, their subsistence guaranteed by the abundance of waterfowl, fish and eels.

Between woodland and waste, the large majority of the people depended for their existence on farming. In the hill country, the rhythm of life seesawed from the high pastures in summer to winter feeding in the valleys and enclosures, the main concern being for cattle, sheep and honey bees. On more workable lands, the farming was mixed. Rye and wheat for bread, and barley and oats for beer, porridge and animal foods, were the principal crops. Oxen were kept as plough and wagon beasts, horses for lighter draught work and riding, while milk was obtained from cows, goats and sheep. Poultry and pigs were kept for eating.

Of the towns, London was by far the largest. In the first year of Stephen's reign, a great fire had demolished most of the old wooden buildings from London Bridge to St. Clement Danes, and a new city, some of it constructed in stone and tiles, had arisen on the ashes. With its thirteen monasteries, 126 parish churches, its markets, stalls and cookshops, it was a busy and prosperous place, already spreading beyond the wall which had contained it since Roman times. Elsewhere, villages were developing into administrative and trading centres roughly corresponding in size to the lesser market towns of modern proportions. Richard of Devizes, the Winchester monk and writer who flourished in the twelfth century, presented a jaundiced view of English towns through the eyes of one of his characters. London, he reported, was full of druggists, lustful persons, extortioners, common beggars, buffoons and tatterdemalions; in Canterbury, people were dying in the streets for want of bread and employment.

> Rochester and Chichester are mere villages, and they possess nothing for which they should be called cities, but the sees of their bishops. Oxford scarcely, I will not say satisfies, but sus-

tains its clerks. Exeter supports men and beasts with the same grain. Bath is placed, or rather buried, in the lowest parts of the valleys, in a very dense atmosphere and sulphury vapour, as it were at the gates of hell. Nor will you select your habitation in the northern cities, Worcester, Chester, Hereford, on account of the desperate Welshmen. York abounds in Scots, vile and faithless men, or rather rascals. The town of Ely is always putrefied by the surrounding marshes. In Durham, Norwich or Lincoln . . . you will never hear any one speak French. At Bristol there is nobody who is not, or has not been, a soap-maker.

For the most part, people still lived in villages and hamlets, housed, with a minimal concept of privacy, in daub and wattle dwellings where the family cooked, sheltered and slept in a single room. The heat came from a smouldering fire in an open grate, and the light from the single aperture that served as doorway and window, and supplemented a hole in the roof by way of ventilation. Here the peasantry was born without ceremony, matured rapidly, mated robustly and died early, probably diseased and hungry.

John, the eighth child of Henry II and Queen Eleanor, was born in Oxford on Christmas Eve, 1167, one hundred and one years after Hastings—probably in the palace of Beaumont. The word palace has since acquired lavish connotations. At the time of John's birth it was a place of most austere grandeur, a place where, despite the rich tapestries and drapes, mother and child had little comfort. The solid wooden furniture was not upholstered, draughts gusted everywhere and there must have been times when even the hounds in the hall preferred the wind itself to the billowing smoke from the open fire. In this spartan atmosphere, Eleanor had produced children for her second husband with exhausting regularity. In 1153 there had been a son, William, who had died at the age of three; in 1155, Henry, the oldest surviving son; in 1156, the first daughter, Matilda; in 1157, Richard; in 1158, Geoffrey; in 1162, Eleanor; and in 1165, Joanna.

To the chroniclers of the day, a fourth son, even of a king, aroused no great excitement, and almost nothing was recorded of John's early days. Soon after his birth, he would have been handed over to a wet nurse who would suckle and wean him. "She chews up his food first and by chewing it makes it ready for the toothless boy so that he can swallow better," wrote a medieval writer of the nurse's duties. "When the boy is asleep she soothes him with whistlings and lullabies. She binds up his limbs with splints and rags while they are young and corrects them so that the little one does not contract ugly bandiness. She cherishes the little one's flesh with bath and ointments."

In his second year, John was placed in the care of the abbey at Fontevrault, Anjou, possibly with the intention that he should devote his life to the Church. If so, the intent proved abortive, for before long, the youngster turned up in the household of his eldest brother, Henry, riding his first ponies, learning to handle a sword and lance and experiencing the thrills of the hunting field. While John was a small child for his age, brother Henry was tall, good-looking and full of gay irreverence with a charm which made up for his empty-headedness. He was very much his mother's son, and his light-hearted affability stimulated poets and songsters to dwell romantically on his character. John's academic education was placed in the hands of Ranulf Glanville, a high and trusted officer of the king's establishment in England.

In those early days, John can have seen little of his parents. His mother was in her forty-fifth year at his birth, her last confinement, and still a strong and good-looking woman. But her relationship with the thirty-four-year-old king was growing strained. In contrast to her first husband, whose monkish traits had so frustrated her, Henry II was generous with his affections and kept several concubines. He was also businesslike and hard-working. The administration of his vast domains left little time for entertaining his wife, whose sympathies turned increasingly towards her elder sons. Since the death of Stephen, Henry had worked tirelessly to bring the English barons to heel, making his own courts supreme in the land, suppressing private warfare and destroying the castles of those who defied his authority. In a few short years, he had returned law and order to a land surfeited with anarchy, and the king's peace meant something once more in England.

With so much to do, Henry had no zest for frivolity. The one touch of lightness attributed to him was his introduction of a new clothes fashion to the wealthier classes of his island kingdom, and that was fortuitous. Until the arrival of the new king, English men and women of substance had worn their robes to the ankle, gathered at the waist by a belt or girdle. They also wore an over-mantle of the same length, caught at the throat or shoulder by a large brooch. Brooches and belt buckles, wrought in many shapes and sometimes precious metals, were an important feature of medieval costume. Henry wore his mantle in the style of Anjou, that is, reaching only to the knees. He was nicknamed "Curtmantle," and the fashion spread quickly in England. It was a short-lived diversion. There was little talk of chivalry at the court of this intense king, and Henry discouraged tournaments. Eleanor was increasingly deprived of her pleasures.

Though he ruled through his justiciar in England, and his seneschals on the Continent, Henry was aware of the dangers of delegating responsibility in that turbulent age, and he dragged his court at whirlwind pace across England and France to keep in touch with developments. He seldom stayed anywhere more than a few days, and when the king moved the entire paraphernalia of government moved with him: his treasure, his chancellor, clerks and business documents, and the multifarious staff of his household, including his chamberlain, tailor, butler, ewerer (bath preparer), the keeper of his hounds, his mews, and so on. This method of travelling, common to the kings of the period, not only allowed them to dispense justice throughout their lands, but meant that the court was able to consume the produce of the widespread royal estates on the spot, instead of it having to be hauled long distances to the city palaces.

Walter Map, a courtier and wit of Henry's day, found the king sober, modest, careful and generous. "On the other hand, he was always on the move, travelling in unbearably long stages, like a post, and in this respect merciless beyond measure to the household that accompanied him . . . Whatever way he goes, he is seized upon by the crowds and pulled hither and thither, pushed wither he would not, and surprising to say, listens to each man, though assaulted by all with shouts and pullings."

In an age of itinerant princes, none was more restless or impetuous than Henry. "If the king promised to remain in a place for a day," wrote Peter of Blois, who was for a time his secretary, "he is sure to upset all the arrangements by departing early in the morning. As a result you see men dashing around as if they were mad, beating their packhorses, running their carts into one another—in short, giving a lively imitation of hell." While the royal baggage wagons struggled down rutted lanes and forded unbridged rivers, laden with everything from the royal crown to the royal urinal, the king and his courtiers hunted the surrounding countryside, or rode off to take refreshment at some nearby manor.

It was a very different way of life to languishing in the warmth and flattery of a southern court, and, shortly after the birth of John, Eleanor retired from England to Poitou, leaving Henry to replace her with a well-born mistress named Rosamund Clifford. There was talk of a divorce, but nothing came of it. Perhaps Henry was too busy.

The Devil's Brood

One subject of recurring concern to him was the apportioning of his domains among his sons. Henry had seen enough of violently contested succession in his youth to wish something better for his own boys, whom he held in great affection. It was best, he reasoned, that their prospects were decided in his own lifetime, so that they could grow up to a settled future. Besides, if each were responsible for a part of his empire, the task of administration and law-keeping would be eased in his old age. By the time John was born, his father had already resolved the division of his territories. His eldest son and namesake would take England, Normandy and the continental lands the king had inherited from his own father, Geoffrey of Anjou. Richard was to have Aquitaine and the rest of his mother's lands. Geoffrey was eventually provided for by his betrothal to Constance, daughter and heiress of Duke Conan of Brittany, who died shortly after the arrangement was effected. This accounted for everyone and everything, except John. By the time he arrived, the cake had been shared out. Henry coined a name for his last-born: *Jean sans terre,* or John Lackland. The name stuck.

So anxious was Henry that his plans should not be upset that in June 1170, when the young Henry was fifteen, his father had him crowned at Westminster as King of the English. This unprecedented step, creating two kings of England (contemporaries called them the Young King and the Old King), produced a chain of dramatic reactions. The right to crown the Kings of England belonged properly to the Archbishop of Canterbury, then Thomas à Becket, a vain and obstinate man who had once been Henry's chancellor and constant companion. But Henry and Becket had become estranged in a long and complicated argument involving the right of lay courts to try members of the clergy who committed crimes. Henry held that the Church should not protect criminous clerks; Becket, that they should not be tried by the royal officers like laymen. The outcome was that the uncompromising archbishop had flounced off to France to sulk in self-imposed exile, and young Henry had been crowned by the Archbishop of York, Roger of Pont l'Evêque, assisted by the Bishops of London, York, Rochester, Durham and Salisbury. Further inflamed by this insult to his station, Becket complained to the pope, Alexander III, who promptly excommunicated Roger and the assisting bishops.

Another man who took exception to the crowning was Eleanor's former husband, Louis VII of France. When young Henry was still a toddler, he had been betrothed to Margaret, the eldest daughter of Louis by his second wife, Constance of Castile. As tradition demanded, Margaret, then an infant, had been handed over to her future father-in-law for safekeeping. This was an important political compact, for it not only created a bond between the kings of France and England, but brought to Henry II as the little bride's dowry a strip of much-disputed territory on the Norman border known as the Vexin. When Louis received the news of young Henry's coronation, he demanded to know why his daughter had not been crowned at the same time, and, fearing some deceit on the part of the elder Henry, threatened Normandy with his army. The English king immediately hurried to the duchy to placate his French counterpart with the promise that Margaret would be crowned along with her young husband in the near future, a promise that was fulfilled two years later at Winchester.

Meanwhile, Thomas Becket had returned to Canterbury in December 1170, still inveighing against Roger of York and the offending bishops, whom he publicly denounced from his pulpit on Christmas day. Three of the bishops, those of London, York and Salisbury, now presented themselves before Henry in Normandy with complaints of Becket's behaviour. Henry had recently recovered from a serious illness and was in no mood to be troubled by anyone. In a characteristic outburst of fury, he is said to have raged: "What a parcel of fools and dastards have I nourished in my house, that not one of them will avenge me of this upstart clerk!" Four knights of the household, Reginald FitzUrse, Hugh of Morville, William of Tracy and Richard the Breton, without waiting for the king to regain his composure, set off for England, where they burst into the cathedral at Canterbury. Edward Grim, an eyewitness to what ensued, concluded the violent tale.

"Where is Thomas Becket, traitor to the king and realm?" roared the vengeful knights. "Where is the archbishop?"

Replied Becket in a clear voice: "I am here, no traitor to the king, but a priest, ready to suffer in His name who redeemed me by His blood. Be it far from me to flee your swords."

At first, the knights tried to drag him outside, to kill him away from the cathedral, but Becket clung to a pillar. Fearing he might be rescued if they delayed too long, one of the knights swung his sword at the crown of Becket's head. "Then he received a second blow on the head but still stood firm. At the third blow he fell on his knees and elbows, offering himself a living victim, and saying in a low voice, 'For the name of Jesus and the protection of the Church I am ready to embrace death.' Then the third knight inflicted a terrible wound as he lay, by which the sword was broken against the pavement, and the crown which was large was separated from the head so that the blood white with the brain and the brain red with blood dyed the surface of the virgin mother Church . . . the fourth knight prevented any from interfering so that the others might freely perpetrate the murder."

Becket's murder shocked the whole of Christendom, and must have been among the earliest memories of young John. Everywhere, the archbishop was proclaimed a martyr, and it was not long before he was canonised. Henry was in a position of great embarrassment. Though he quickly disclaimed responsibility for the act, the pope refused to see his envoys, threatening instead to place all Henry's lands under an interdict and to excommunicate the king himself. Prudently, Henry embarked for Ireland before the pope's legates could reach him, and here rough weather in the Irish Channel isolated him for six months from the reproaches of the Christian world. When he returned, the first high passions of his opponents had abated and he was able to negotiate a reconciliation with the Church on reasonable terms. Among other things, he was obliged to maintain two hundred knights in the defence of Jerusalem for a year, to found three monasteries, and to make restitution to any who had suffered as a result of their support for Thomas Becket.

For some time, Henry had been concerned about providing for his son John, and at Christmas 1172 a deal was completed with one Count Humbert III of Maurienne which seemed very favourable to the English king. Humbert's fiefs stretched from Grenoble in France to Turin in Italy, being of special strategic importance since they included the Alpine passes between these countries. Humbert, both impoverished and lacking a male heir, was anxious to raise money on his eldest daughter, Alice. The bargain agreed was that John should marry Alice, that Humbert should acknowledge John as his heir, and that Henry should pay the count five thousand marks, a mark being worth thirteen shillings and fourpence. At a time when a sheep was worth about sixpence, and a foot soldier was paid twopence a day, that was a large sum of money. On second thoughts, however, Humbert decided it was not large enough to balance the dominions which would pass from his family to the Plantagenets on his death. Two months later, at Limoges, where Henry was staying with his eldest sons, the count enquired what part of the king's dominion he intended to settle on John by way of matching Alice's endowment.

It was an awkward question, since the king's lands had already been promised to his other sons. Seemingly caught off guard, Henry replied that John would have the castles of Chinon, Loudon and Mirebeau, north of Poitiers, the traditional holdings of younger sons of the Angevin counts. The dubious wisdom of his earlier promises now became manifest. Since reaching the age of political consciousness, the young Henry, now eighteen, had been demanding the right actually to govern some part of his inheritance instead of being a king and lord in name only. His father had always refused him. This time, incensed by the assignment of the castles, part of his own inheritance, to his brother John, the young Henry resolved on a showdown. Angevin tempers flared on both sides as young Henry refused to countenance the transfer of the castles and pressed again for direct rule of Anjou, Normandy or England. The elder Henry upheld his position.

To a father who seems to have doted on his offspring, it was perhaps hard to believe that they should regard his plans for them with less than gratitude. The events which followed can only have surprised and disappointed Henry. A few days after their quarrel, his eldest son left him without warning and made speed to his father-in-law, the King of France. Louis, only too eager to embarrass his rival, the King of England, promised the young man his assistance in a war against Henry II. From Poitiers, where Eleanor was now the toast of a court dedicated to chivalry and romantic love, the resentful queen saw her chance to oust her second husband from the Continent. Having encouraged Richard and Geoffrey to join their elder brother, she attempted to follow them disguised in male attire to elude her husband's officers. She was captured and consigned to imprisonment at Winchester. By summer 1173, what started as a family squabble had exploded into a general rebellion in which a host of the most powerful barons on both sides of the Channel saw their opportunity to throw off the yoke of the king who had reduced them to orderly subjection.

Co-ordinated by a skilful generalissimo, the revolt must have swamped the English king and swept away the Angevin empire, for the risings were so widespread that even Henry would have found it impossible to have coped with them. As it was, his sons were young and inexperienced campaigners (Richard was not yet sixteen; Geoffrey, a year younger) and Louis was unable to impose any overall plan of action on the rebels. On the whole, the Church remained loyal to Henry II, as did his administrative officers and the business and lower classes. They had gained the most from his reign of law and order. For his own part, Henry remained cool, switching his attentions with remarkable swiftness from one part of his dominions to another, from crisis to crisis, throughout the twelve months or so that the rebellion continued.

He appears to have attributed the disloyalty of his sons to divine retribution for his part in the murder of Becket, and at one stage he did penance at the martyr's tomb in Canterbury. "St. Thomas guard my kingdom," he is said to have muttered. "To you I declare myself guilty of that for which others bear the blame." His sons took themselves less seriously. According to the chronicler Gerald of Wales, those who reproved them for their belligerence were told laughingly: "Don't deprive us of our heritage; we cannot help acting like devils!"

Alone of Henry's four boys, John, now aged six, remained with his father through much of the rebellion. He must have been bemused by the almost superhuman activity of the tireless king. Now Henry was in Normandy repelling an invasion by Louis, now in Brittany capturing the castle of Dol, now in England facing an opportunist invasion from Scotland, then back across the Channel to repel Louis once more and bring his son Richard to submission in Poitou. By Michaelmas 1174,

The Devil's Brood

Henry's remarkable efforts had entirely succeeded; his enemies were beaten on all fronts. He treated his wayward sons with undeserved generosity. Under an armistice made at Montlouis, near Tours, in September, the situation was more or less restored to that appertaining before the rebellion.

One exceptional point involved Prince John. Henry had now grown closer to his youngest son, the only member of the brood who had not offended him, and both policy and affection urged him to promote the boy's career as a balance to that of his eldest son. Unfortunately, little Alice of Maurienne had died, and John's prospects of a southern realm had gone with her. Instead, as part of the peace settlement, the Old King required his heir to provide for John out of his inheritance. From each part of his proposed dominions, the Young King was to hand over one or more castles and their honours. In England, John was to have the castle and county of Nottingham and the castle and lordship of Marlborough, together with a thousand pounds a year from the royal estates; in Normandy, two castles and a revenue of a thousand pounds Angevin (worth a quarter of its English counterpart); in Anjou, one castle and the same amount of money, and one castle each in Touraine and Maine.

Soon afterwards, the large estates of the Earl of Cornwall reverted to the crown on the earl's death, and these too were set aside for John. In 1176, the boy's prospects were enlarged by an even greater lordship, the earldom of Gloucester. William, the current earl, had been implicated in the recent rebellion and now bought his peace with the king by making John heir to all his land in return for the prince's betrothal to his daughter Isabel, John's second cousin. At Oxford, in May 1177, Henry bestowed on his youngest son the titular sovereignty of the unruly frontier lands of Ireland, obliging the barons who held fiefs in that country to do homage to John as well as to himself. Not yet ten years old, John was no longer "Lackland," and could look forward to being among the richest and most powerful men in England. Nevertheless, he still ran a poor fourth in terms of ruling power to his brothers.

The rebellion had not altered the frustrating position of the young Henry, a king in name, but in reality little more than a cypher. On the other hand, Richard and Geoffrey had been given an increasingly free hand in their duchies by their father, who was pleased to leave them to the job of controlling their fractious barons. In Aquitaine especially, confusion and unrest had not ceased with the peace of Montlouis, and Richard tackled the troublemakers vigorously. Energetic and ruthless, already a precociously skilful soldier, Henry's second son waged a ceaseless battle against all disturbers of the peace, destroying their castles and exacting stern punishments. Smarting under his harsh rule, the rebellious barons of Aquitaine invoked the aid of the discontented young Henry, and his brother Geoffrey, a vicious and deceitful fellow. So considerable had become their jealousy of Richard, that both were now prepared to make war on him.

Again, Angevin power was imperilled by family disunity. Hostilities had reached no decisive stage, however, when the young Henry died of dysentery. It was June 1183. Richard now became heir to England, Normandy and Anjou, theoretically releasing Aquitaine for his brother John. In fact, the purposeful Richard had no intention of doing so. He had made Aquitaine his own by eight years of relentless warfare against its headstrong magnates. He liked the South, its warmth and its colour. Why give it up for the merely nominal titles held by his late brother? As long as he lived, he told his father forcibly, he alone would rule Aquitaine. In one of his bursts of rage, Henry is said to have told John that the duchy was his if he could win it by force. Since John, now sixteen, had neither the army nor the experience to challenge so redoubtable a warrior as Richard, maybe the king was not expecting to be taken literally. At all events, he must quickly have regretted the outburst, for Geoffrey of Brittany was only too willing to have another go at Richard, and together the brothers marched, burning and ravishing, into Poitou. Richard retaliated by harrying Brittany.

John, though well proportioned, was developing into a small man of some five feet five inches, shorter in stature than his father, who was of medium height, and far shorter than Richard, who was tall. From the only surviving likeness, an effigy in Worcester Cathedral (which may or may not be accurate; it was carved two decades after John's death), he appears to have had an oval face, wide-set eyes and not unhandsome features, with hair worn long to the neck as was the custom of the times. As a man, he sported a moustache and a trim beard, but at sixteen was most likely clean-shaven. Geoffrey, nine years older than John, about the same height, and noted for his persuasive eloquence, was well equipped to mislead an impressionable youngster. "He would have been among the most sagacious of men had he not been so given to deceiving others," wrote Gerald of Wales, who knew the brothers. "In his deepest soul there was more bitterness than sweetness, but outwardly he was ever ready with a flow of words smoother than oil."

Though John fell momentarily under Geoffrey's influence, their characters were very different. Geoffrey was a vicious young man who spent what remained of his life in aimless looting and killing. John, as Gerald had it, was not fond of warfare. His tastes were more refined. In time, the self-discipline and administrative urge of his father would be imposed within him upon the imagination and love of things sensuous bequeathed him by his mother. As a youth, he was "given to the fancy of the moment, to the impulses of nature," preferring ease and enjoyment to hardship and endurance.

He was, by contemporary judgement, obedient to his parents,

and was probably the first to accede when Henry, hearing what his hasty words had started, called the three brothers to England. That December of 1184, Henry persuaded his sons to make peace, and Richard and Geoffrey soon returned to their continental territories. For all their troublesomeness, the two elder brothers were still valuable to the king as tamers of large and turbulent areas of his empire. It remained to find a job for John. The prospect of his taking over Aquitaine had faded. But Henry had not forgotten Ireland, and now decided that the subjection of that wild and unruly corner of his dominions should be the task of his youngest son. It was a singularly unappealing one, and, in the following January, John saw a chance to get out of it.

Early in the new year, Henry received a visit from the patriarch of Jerusalem, one Heraclius. The patriarch implored the king's help. The ruler of the Holy Land, Baldwin IV, was dying of leprosy and the only male heir in his line was a small child. Since Henry was not only outstanding among Christian monarchs, but well endowed with sons, the patriarch looked to him to provide a successor. This was doubly appropriate in view of the fact that Baldwin's line was a junior offshoot of the house of Anjou. By substituting the elder line in the person of one of Henry's offspring, "the seed royal might be raised up and spring into new life." So moving was the appeal of Heraclius that his audience at the English court was in tears by the time his tale ended.

Henry, however, was too shrewd to be influenced by pathos. He saw no political future in the Holy Land; moreover, he needed his sons for his own purposes. When John jumped at the opportunity of exchanging the uninviting prospect of Ireland for the warmth and romance of the Middle East, Henry forbade it. John pleaded on bended knees, but his father was adamant. Soon after the patriarch departed, Henry announced that his son would sail at once for Ireland.

Chapter 2
LORD OF IRELAND

There is no doubt, as Your Highness recognises, that Ireland and all the islands upon which Christ, the Sun of Justice, has shone, belong to the jurisdiction of the Blessed Peter and the holy Roman Church.

Bull *Laudabiliter*

Isolated by adverse shipping winds and a widespread concept that the civilised world ended at England, Ireland had remained unvisited by the social developments of other parts of Europe in the eleventh and twelfth centuries. The last settlers had been the Norsemen, known in Ireland as Ostmen, who had built the towns of Dublin, Waterford, Wexford and Cork on the east and southeast coasts, and Limerick by the Shannon. But the Ostmen had made little impression on Ireland beyond the immediate surroundings of their settlements. Elsewhere in this island of hills, lakes and bogs, the people still built their dwellings of mud, lived pastorally, trading hides and wool for their simple needs, cultivating few grain crops and possessing few fruit trees. Cattle products, and small quantities of gold, produced in Ireland from perhaps as early as 2000 B.C., were the only currency outside the districts of the Ostmen.

Irish society was still organised on a primitive basis. There were no regular administrative assemblies, no laws beyond the ties of ancient custom and no appeal against injustice except to the drawn sword. Of kings and tribal lords there were plenty. Each of the main provinces, Ulster, Leinster, Munster, Meath and Connaught, had its own king, with a high-king theoretically above them all. The relationship between these princes, as between the lesser lords, was one of rumbustious rivalry. According to an Irish writer, "they battled like bulls for the mastery of the herd . . . a normal Irish king had to clear his way through the provinces, battle-axe in hand, gathering hostages by the strength of his arm." The Irish fought without armour, protected only by the coarse plaid or blanket, trimmed with fringes, which hung from their shoulders. The chief weapons were axes and slings, and those who rode pony-back controlled their mounts with no more than a rope bit and switch. "The natives," wrote one who encountered them, "from the constant state of warfare in which they are engaged, and whose manners are formed by the habit of war, are bold and active, skilful on horseback, quick on foot, not nice as to their diet, and ever prepared when necessity requires to abstain both from food and wine."

Story had it that William Rufus had once stood on the shores of Pembrokeshire and bragged that he would span the Irish channel with a bridge of boats, and add Ireland to his kingdom. If so, he did nothing about it. It was not until 1155 that an English monarch again raised the matter. In that year, Henry II, then young and relatively inexperienced, put forward the idea of the conquest of Ireland at a Michaelmas council meeting in Winchester. His mother, Matilda, whose views on foreign policy were respected by Henry, opposed the project on the grounds that her son had sufficient to do on the

Continent. For the moment, the king took her advice. Nevertheless, he did send an envoy to Rome to sound the pope on the subject.

At this time, the Church in Ireland reflected the generally backward state of that country. There was no central control, such power as existed residing in the hands of hereditary abbots, not infrequently married men. In many places, the endowments of the Church had been appropriated by lay lords, and the clergy was largely dependent on the fees and donations of its poor flocks. Not only had it failed to eliminate polyandry, and other scandalous customs rife among the populace, but the behaviour of its own members was far from exemplary. One commentator noted that while the Irish priesthood made a great show of fasting by day, it put in some pretty hard drinking at night.

Informed of this state of affairs, the pope, then Adrian IV, himself an Englishman, authorised the conquest of Ireland by Henry "in order to extend the boundaries of the Church, to restrain the attacks of evil, to improve the morals and foster virtue, and to increase the Christian religion." Together with his permission (contained in the so-called Bull *Laudabiliter,* named after its opening: "Laudably and profitably does Your Magnificence contemplate spreading your glorious name on earth"), the pope sent an emerald ring to Henry with which to invest the ruler of Ireland.

For a decade and more, Henry was too busy to return to the Irish project. Meanwhile, events in Ireland were themselves preparing the way for English intervention. In 1152, the King of Leinster, a huge and cruel man named Dermot McMurrough, had abducted the wife of Tiernan O'Rourke, lord of Meath, while O'Rourke was away on a pilgrimage. The rape of his rival's wife, whose name was Dervorgil, was all too typical of McMurrough's social ethic. He had already carried off an abbess in Kildare, murdering the monks who tried to stop him, and burning their monastery. He was also noted for discouraging his opponents by blinding them. At length, Dervorgil was returned to her husband, but O'Rourke did not forget the insult. In 1166 the high-king of Ireland died and the ruler of Connaught, Roderick (Rory) O'Connor, took his place, winning the support of the Ostmen of Dublin and the princes of the South.

O'Connor and O'Rourke were allies. They now set about driving big Dermot McMurrough from Ireland, enthusiastically assisted by many of the tyrant's own subjects.

In August, McMurrough sailed from Cork to Bristol to seek English help in regaining his kingdom. Leaving a son behind in Ireland to uphold his battered interests, he took with him perhaps his brightest asset, his daughter Eva, a colleen of captivating loveliness. Henry was in France at the time. When the Irishman eventually reached him there, he found the English king too preoccupied with his dispute with Becket, and other affairs, to bother much about Ireland. Henry did, however, accept McMurrough's fealty, giving the Irishman in return permission to recruit supporters in England, Wales or Scotland. McMurrough plumped for Wales, the nearest to his homeland, and the adopted country of barons who had become accustomed to holding their possessions by armed force against intransigent natives. Here, supported by the charms of the beautiful Eva, he gained the interest of a canny adventurer named Richard FitzGilbert, Earl of Pembroke and Strigul, who was to become known in Ireland as Strongbow. A deal was arranged by which Strongbow was promised the hand of Eva, and seemingly the succession of Leinster, in return for providing military aid to McMurrough.

McMurrough also gained pledges of support from a number of Strongbow's vassals, Robert FitzStephen, Maurice FitzGerald, Raymond of Carew, and others, sons or grandsons of a former mistress of Henry I, the celebrated Welsh princess

Nesta. Bolstered by these promises, McMurrough returned to Ireland, where his son had been holding out for him, and came to terms with O'Rourke by paying him a hundred ounces of gold as reparation for abducting his wife. Having thus bought time in which to lay his wider plans, he sent word to his Anglo-Welsh allies to hasten to his side and help vanquish his enemies.

Strongbow, in no hurry to commit himself to the perils of a strange land, allowed his vassals the privilege of sailing first. Successive landings in Ireland were now made by FitzGerald, FitzStephen and Carew, none of whom brought with him more than four hundred men. Outnumbered though they were, the invaders scored rapid successes. The Irish were no match in the open for armoured knights, and the arrows of the Welsh archers filled them with terror. Later, the natives learned to use their knowledge of the terrain more effectively, fighting from the hills, the bogs and forests, but the first encounters were a triumph for the sons of Nesta and McMurrough.

After Wexford had been captured and given to FitzGerald, McMurrough struck a treaty with the high-king. McMurrough was conceded the whole of his kingdom against his undertaking not to bring further invaders to Ireland. As a token of his good faith, the high-king retained McMurrough's son as a hostage. But the big king of Leinster had no intention of keeping the bargain. Inspired by dreams of conquering all Ireland and toppling O'Connor from the high throne, he wrote again to Strongbow for reinforcements, regardless of the consequences to his hostage son. This time the cautious earl himself responded, landing near Waterford in August 1170 with the strongest body of troops yet to arrive in Ireland, twelve hundred men. Waterford was quickly captured, and, soon afterwards, Dublin, already the most important of the Irish towns. Having received Eva in marriage as promised, Strongbow joined his new father-in-law in the invasion of Meath, north of Leinster, the land of Tiernan O'Rourke.

At this point, developments were confounded by two deaths. As retribution for continued invasions, McMurrough's son was executed by the high-king. Not long afterwards, in May 1171, McMurrough himself died—"of an insufferable and unknown disease, for he became putrid while living"—and Strongbow inherited Leinster. This was too much for the Irish. Uniting under O'Connor, they drove the invaders back on Dublin and Wexford, holding them in siege throughout much of the summer. By this time, Henry II had become concerned with the Irish scene. Alarmed at the prospect of an independent state emerging under the Anglo-Welsh barons, he commanded them to return home. When they failed to do so, he first cut off their line of reinforcement, and then set about raising an army of his own to go to Ireland.

The hard-pressed Strongbow was now caught between two fires. Cutting his way out of Dublin in a daring sally which destroyed the Irish encampment, he reasserted his authority over much of Leinster before hastening to England to make peace with Henry. The king reserved Dublin, Waterford and Wexford, with their adjoining lands, for himself, and allowed Strongbow to do homage for Leinster. Then, armed with the papal bull, he sailed with a great armada for Waterford to impress the Irish with the true source of English strength. It was said that his fleet numbered four hundred ships and carried some four thousand men, of whom perhaps five hundred were knights.

When it is remembered that William the Conqueror won Hastings with probably not more than five thousand men, it is clear that Henry regarded the prospect of opposition seriously. When the Conqueror landed in England, English armies were composed largely of reservists and levies (the so-called select fyrd and great fyrd), both of which classes owed service for a

Lord of Ireland

strictly limited period. Indeed, members of the great fyrd, or peasants' army, expected to return home at night. Such forces were organised primarily for defensive wars, and when English kings started to venture abroad to fight they came to depend increasingly on mercenaries. So did their barons. Some of the first troops to land in Ireland under the sons of Nesta were neither Welsh nor English but hailed from the Flemish district of Ros.

In the case of knights, the elite striking power of the army, recruiting methods varied. Many landless knights, especially on the Continent, hired out their services, either for cash payment or a territorial share in a profitable enterprise. Landed knights owed service in respect of their holdings. Most of the barons and bishops of England held their estates by knight's service: that is, each undertook to provide the king with a given number of knights when he called for them, the number being related roughly to the size of the lord's estate. The lord either employed his knights in his household, or, more commonly as time passed, settled them on a portion of his land. This was the knight's fee, in return for which the knight was required to present himself, mounted and equipped with mail, shield, helmet and lance, for a period of service in the royal army at his own cost. The period seems likely to have been forty days in the case of peace-time training, and two months in time of war. The knight could, however, commute his service by a money payment, known as shield money, or scutage. On the other hand, if the king wished his knights to remain in the field more than two months, he had to pay them for the extra time.

Henry brought his knights and archers to Ireland, he was careful to give out, not to suppress the natives but to regularise the activities of the adventuring barons, and to guarantee his protection to those native princes who acknowledged his authority. For the moment, his diplomacy paid off. There was no armed opposition, and many Irish chiefs arrived at the coast to pay homage. Henry spent the winter entertaining them sumptuously in Dublin, where he had a palace built for him in the style of the Irish kings. Importantly for him, since it went some way towards offsetting the disgrace he had incurred by the murder of Becket, the Church leaders of Ireland followed the example of the princes, and a number of reforms were agreed at a council held early in 1172, the synod of Cashel, at which it was declared: "Divine offices shall be celebrated according to the forms of the Church of England, for it is just and right that as Ireland has received her lord and king from England, she should accept reformation from the same source."

Among other things, it was agreed that Irishmen should cease to mate with female relatives, that children should be baptised in church, and that Church property should be free from all secular exactions. In due course, Pope Alexander III conveyed his approval of Henry's conduct in Ireland and addressed letters to the Irish princes and bishops instructing them to remain faithful to the King of England.

With the arrival of spring, Henry left Ireland, to all appearances an acknowledged overlord who had set things to rights in a firm but entirely peaceful manner. Unfortunately for the English monarch, appearances were deceptive, the blarney illusory. Fickle by nature, the Irish princes were as quick to repudiate their undertakings as they had been to enter into them. Nor were the Anglo-Welsh barons much better. The first were eager to regain their old powers and possessions; the second, to extend the lands they had settled on. To complicate matters, intermarriage between the two elements produced Anglo-Irish families, who might fight with one side or the other, or simply for themselves. From the first English landings, a proportion of the invaders had gone over to the enemy. Now old feuds and new feuds were pursued with vehemence.

Two men stand out in the free-for-all that followed. One was

Lord of Ireland

John of Courcy, the conqueror of Ulster, Ireland's most northerly province. Tall, blond and tenacious, Courcy set out from Dublin in 1177 with an almost pitifully small force, and by dint of his personal courage and audacity, won battle after battle against heavy odds to subdue most of the northern state. The other was Hugh of Lacy, a small, dark and hairy man who had come to Ireland with Henry. Distrustful of Strongbow's intentions, Henry had granted Lacy the territory of Meath before leaving, appointing him ruler of Ireland in the king's name. His first task was to defeat O'Rourke, who did not take kindly to his kingdom being given to a foreigner. Hugh of Lacy silenced his objections by impaling his head on a Dublin gate. A stroke of fate disposed of Lacy's other rival. In 1176, Strongbow perished from a poisoned leg. On the whole, Lacy's administration was characterised by tact and moderation. In 1181, he married the daughter of Rory O'Connor, still nominally high-king, further endearing himself to the natives by protecting them against the greed of the barons.

Hugh of Lacy's good relationship with the Irish worried Henry. The viceroy's enemies accused him of cultivating the friendship of the natives in the hope of becoming an independent sovereign. His marriage, they noted, had been contracted "according to the manner of the country," and without Henry's wayleave. Several times, the king called Lacy to England for questioning, then sent him back. He was deprived of the custody of Dublin, and then reinstated. Still, suspicion nagged Henry's mind. The king determined to send his son John to Ireland as soon as he was old enough. In 1185, when the youth had been titular Lord of Ireland for eight years, his time came.

On the last day of March that year, when John was seventeen, he was knighted by Henry at Windsor Castle. There were two modes of conferring knighthood at the time. In one, the accolade constituted the bulk of the ceremony. This was commonly used during war, when a number of knights was created before and after battle. In this case, the candidate kneeled before the chief of the army, or some other high lord, who struck him three times with the flat of a sword, pronouncing a brief formula, which varied at the creator's will. On grander occasions, a more elaborate ritual was observed. This often included the ceremonial bathing of the candidate, a night of vigil beside his armour, and the gift of costly robes from his creator. The more intricate formula would certainly have applied in the case of Prince John. Now, with the sword of knighthood girded about his waist, he was fully fledged as a warrior. In April, he set sail for Ireland, landing at Waterford on the twenty-fifth.

It is a pity that the ensuing eight months John spent in that unruly realm, his first recorded adventure in public life, were scantily reported, and that the main source of evidence, Gerald of Wales, is not entirely above doubt as an impartial witness. Gerald, then approaching the fortieth year of his life, was a chaplain at Henry's court. He was sent by the king on John's expedition because he was one of the few men in England who knew Ireland. In fact, as a grandson of the Welsh princess Nesta, he had close connections among the survivors and representatives of the original Anglo-Welsh settlers. In such circles, intrusion from England, especially by a callow youth, was unwelcome, and it may or may not be that Gerald sympathised with his relatives. At all events, the story handed down cast John in a dismal light. According to one historian, "his criminal folly" was a characteristic beginning to John's career.

On landing, it seems that the king's son received a friendly welcome from the local Irish chiefs, but a distinctly half-hearted one from the families of the original settlers. Unfortunately, so the tale has it, the nobles of John's suite, young and inexperienced braves like himself, failed to conceal their amusement at the costume and manners of the Irishmen, sportively tugging at the beards which they wore long in the custom of the country. So incensed were the other kings and princes of Ireland to learn of this insulting behaviour, it appears, that they promptly buried their time-honoured animosities and pledged themselves in amity to oppose the English prince. John built castles at Lismore, Tibraghny and Ardfinnan to defend the Waterford area, and made grants of land to his young friends to counterpoise the independence of the Anglo-Welsh settlers— a move regarded by the established barons as blatant favouritism.

Gerald described John's courtiers as boasters, lechers, liars and cowards, who, instead of taking steps against a threatening Irish coalition, spent their time in high living on the coast. His condemnations were sweeping. When John's soldiers demanded their wages, the prince refused to pay out. Apparently he had frittered away too much money indulging his favourites. The garrisons of Ardfinnan and Tibraghny, seeking to enrich themselves by plundering in Munster, were defeated with heavy losses by a native king, Donell O'Brien. More of John's troops went over to the Irish. In short, John's expedition was far from successful. On the other hand, so, in enduring results, had been his father's. In remaining on the coast, entertaining lavishly and eschewing military action, John was following his father's precedent. Nor were troop desertions in Ireland unique to John's expedition. It is interesting that the prince was sent to Ireland with a considerably smaller army than the one Henry took—probably less than three thousand men in all, against the four thousand with Henry.

On the whole, John's detractors were perhaps overvehement. Henry had sent two trusted men to Ireland to help John. One was the archbishop John Cumin, a confidant of the king, who had preceded the expedition to prepare for its arrival.

The other was Ranulf Glanville, who had supervised John's education, the wise and experienced Justiciar of England. One wonders what they were doing during the eight months in Ireland if John failed so entirely to take their advice. Finally, there was the question of Hugh of Lacy. When John returned to England in September, he complained that Lacy had exacerbated the Irish situation by plotting with the Irish against him. This was to be widely regarded as a lame excuse. Yet Lacy had been humiliated repeatedly by Henry and permanently deprived of the custody of Dublin before the expedition. John's charge did not fly in the face of human nature.

At all events, Henry now raised John of Courcy to viceroy in Ireland and, within two months of John's return, was sending to Rome for the pope's permission to crown his son king of that island—an extraordinary step, even for a fond father, if he had reason to share fully the views of the prince's detractors. Eventually, he received the pope's blessing, together with a crown of peacock's feathers set in gold. Meanwhile, Lacy had been murdered in Ireland, his head severed from his body by an axe while he was supervising the building of a castle at Durrow. Henry told John to return to Ireland and take possession of Lacy's estates. Destiny, however, was pointing elsewhere. Before the youth could sail, news arrived of his brother Geoffrey's death in France, probably from a wound inflicted in a tournament. Both the crowning and the journey were put off. There were more urgent matters awaiting on the Continent.

Louis VII of France had died in 1180, and his successor, Philip II, known as Philip Augustus, had little in common with his devout and gentlemanly father. Philip was shrewd, eager for power, and an unscrupulous politician. Though contentious, he was not an outstanding warrior, his talent revealing itself less in battle than in the subtle exploitation of the weaknesses of his enemies. In the early years of his reign he was still a

Lord of Ireland 31

youth, but already involved in bitter disputes with the lords of Champagne, Blois and Flanders—disputes in which he was glad to count Henry II as an ally. By the age of twenty, Philip had extricated himself from his youthful quarrels and could turn his attention to the major ambition of his life: the destruction of the Angevin empire and the submission of its components to his direct rule. So much for his gratitude to Henry!

When Geoffrey of Brittany died in 1186, he left a daughter, Eleanor, and an unborn son, who, in due course, was christened Arthur. As overlord, Philip claimed the wardship of Arthur. He also claimed the Vexin. When the young Henry had died, the Vexin, his wife's dowry, had passed by agreement to Philip's other sister, Alice, who had been betrothed to Richard since 1169. During the intervening years, she had remained in King Henry's household. Henry seemed loath to part with her; Richard showed no desire for marriage. Now Philip demanded that both Alice and the Vexin should be returned to him. The seeds were sown for the conflict.

Henry would have preferred to negotiate. There is a further suggestion that John had not disgraced himself as thoroughly as some would have had it in the fact that the king now sent him to Philip to prepare a conference between the two monarchs. Moreover, when the conference broke down and the inevitable war commenced, John was given command of one of four divisions of the Angevin forces. Richard commanded another of the divisions, and, together with their father, the brothers were soon marching to the relief of Châteauroux, southeast of Tours, to which Philip had laid siege at the outset of hostilities. Siege warfare was more characteristic of the twelfth century than pitched battles, and could prove a very protracted business due to the general invulnerability of castles. Frequently, the defenders had to be starved out.

The eleventh-century castle had commonly been made of wood, and, often of necessity, thrown up relatively quickly. A tall blockhouse of timber was built on a man-made mound, or *motte*, which had been prepared from earth displaced in the creation of a moat. The ground floor of the stronghold, used as a well for stores and prisoners, had no direct access to the outside. Instead, entrance was effected across a steeply inclined drawbridge descending from the second storey of the blockhouse to the far side of the moat, this bridge being cleated to give footing to horses. In the Conqueror's time, these cramped and comfortless structures, with few rooms, fewer windows and often ladders rather than stairways, served as the homes of noblemen and their families. From here the knights clattered forth to harry or ambush their rivals, or organised their defence when their own territory was attacked.

The wooden structure, however, was vulnerable to fire, and to the heavy battering-rams which were designed to invade it. Gradually wood was replaced by masonry. Since the artificial mound was insufficiently stable to bear the weight of stone stuctures, the engineers of the twelfth century placed their foundations on solid ground enclosing within an outer wall a massive rectangular keep. This was impervious to fire and battering, but had its own weaknesses. The corners of the stonework invited under-mining, and the field of fire from any one side was limited. The next stage, therefore, was the cylindrical keep with a uniform curved surface, after which the emphasis was switched to the outer defences. The single wall was superseded by two, even three walls, in which might be placed additional defensive towers. Such castles were formidable obstacles, and few commanders tried to overwhelm them by direct assault.

At the approach of Henry and his sons, Philip raised the siege of Châteauroux, and, in June 1187, a truce was arranged with the help of clerics on both sides. Alarmed at this conflict between Christian princes at a time when their aid was sorely needed in the Holy Land, the pope called for peace. In

Palestine, disaster was impending. Heraclius the patriarch had returned East after his vain endeavours at the English court to find Baldwin V, the young nephew of the now deceased Baldwin IV, established on the throne of Jerusalem. When Baldwin V shortly died, the crown devolved of his mother's husband, Guy of Lusignan. A truce with Saladin, the Sultan of Egypt, now seemed to augur a period of tranquility, but a foolhardy Christian lord, Reginald of Châtillon, pillaged a Moslem caravan and Saladin prepared for war. In two days of fighting near Tiberias, on the western shore of the Sea of Galilee, Guy and his Christians were defeated, most of their leaders beheaded, and, in October 1187, the Holy City fell. Urgently, the pope called for a new crusading effort.

Meanwhile, Philip's ingenuity had been at work. Under cover of the truce with Henry, he called Richard to him and showed him a letter purporting to be from Henry. The letter contained the proposal that Alice should marry John instead of Richard, and that John should succeed to the whole of the Angevin empire except England and Normandy, which would be Richard's inheritance. Enraged by this further attempt to remove him from Aquitaine, Richard drew closer to Philip. At Bonmoulins in November 1188, he was present at a confrontation of the two kings. When Richard, seconded by Philip, challenged Henry to acknowledge him his rightful heir, Henry was evasive. Inferring that his father was planning to supplant him by his younger brother, Richard immediately turned to Philip and, falling on one knee, paid homage to the King of France.

Once more, Henry, now an old and weary man, prepared for battle. Once more, the pope's servants pressed for a settlement in the interests of the crusade. Once more, the rival kings faced each other in conference. At La Ferté-Bernard in June 1189, Philip demanded that Henry should give up Alice so that Richard could marry her. Henry's reluctance to part with

Philip's sister had already been rationalized by his enemies into the story that he had made Alice his mistress. Richard, who was anxious to be crusading, joined Philip in the further demand that John should accompany him. Henry refused his assent in both instances, countering openly now with the proposal that John should marry Alice.

John's part in all this is obscure. He was not mentioned as being present at the conferences, and seems to have been alone among the principals in desisting from demands and claims. If he was willing, or even eager, to go crusading, as he had been earlier, he must have deferred to his father's wishes —as, indeed, he appears to have done all his life to this date. In the final stages of the war which flared again, this time with Richard on Philip's side, John was with his father. The old king, grey-haired, portly and bandy from a lifetime of riding, was no match for the cunning of Philip and the generalship of Richard. His powers were waning and his barons were deserting him. Relentlessly, his enemies marched west towards Le Mans, where Henry had been born, and to which he now retreated. As Philip prepared to attack the city, one of Henry's officers set fire to the suburbs facing the enemy. Suddenly, the wind changed and the city centre went up in flames. Despairingly, Henry evacuated what remained of his army, riding north on the Alençon road toward Normandy.

John was still at his father's side at Le Mans on June 12. Before fleeing the city, the old king sent his son—"whom he loved and in whom he greatly trusted," according to the recorder of the incident—on a reconnaissance. From this moment, to the fast-approaching end of his father's life, John's movements are a mystery. Twenty miles out from Le Mans, Henry seems to have changed his mind about seeking the safety of Normandy and, for some reason, decided on the hazardous course of doubling back to Anjou. Before doing so, he ordered the greater part of his army to continue north, making its commanders swear on oath that if anything should happen to him they should deliver the castles of Normandy to John and John alone. Skirting Le Mans to the west, Henry made for Chinon. Here, he collapsed with a fever.

Tours fell to Philip and Richard on July 3. Further resistance on Henry's part was impossible. Next day, the sick and defeated king attended a meeting near that city to capitulate to the victorious Philip. So broken was the once tireless ruler of the Angevin empire that he had to be supported on his horse by attendants. Amidst the dramatic effects of an electric storm, Henry agreed to hand over Alice, to recognise Richard as heir to all his dominions and to pay Philip an indemnity of twenty thousand marks. As a final humiliation, he was obliged to give Richard the kiss of peace. The thunder rumbled. As the two men drew apart, Henry muttered: "May God grant me not to die until I have revenged myself." The wish was not granted. On July 6, his fever heightened by the anguish of defeat, Henry died at Chinon. During his last hours he repeatedly murmured, "Shame on a beaten king; shame on a beaten king."

Following a well-established medieval precedent, his attendants looted what treasures remained with the dead king, stripped the corpse and made off leaving the body lying naked.

One more anecdote has survived of Henry's tragic passing. Before he died, the old king was provided by the victors with a list of lords who had deserted him in the conflict to transfer their allegiance to Richard. At the head of the list was the name of his dearest son, John. The shock was too much for him. Raising himself on his bed, Henry is said to have exclaimed: "Is it true that John, my heart, whom I have loved above all, whose advancement has cost the disaster which has overtaken me, has forsaken me? Forget everything. I care no more for this world." It is a poignant story and held, like the tale of John's folly in Ireland, to set the pace of his evil reputation. Yet there is certainly room to doubt John's desertion. No evidence survives beyond the reported black list. If he did go over to Richard, he must have been one of the last to do so, for he was with Henry at Le Mans three weeks from the end.

It is not inconceivable that Richard placed John's name on the list as a precaution against his father's recovery and further alliance with his younger son. It is the sort of ploy Philip would have relished, and might even have devised. One fact is worth pondering. When Richard came to power, he dismissed from his service the men who had deserted Henry, asserting that as traitors they deserved no reward from him. To those who had remained loyal to his father, he offered friendship and favour. Pre-eminent among those favoured by Richard was his brother John.

Chapter 3
JOHN VERSUS LONGCHAMP

Truly, had it been the time of the Caesars, he would with Tiberius have had himself styled the living God.

Roger of Howden
quoting the Bishop of Conventry on Longchamp

A troubador once asked, "What more can kings desire than the right to save themselves from Hell-flames by puissant deeds of arms?" The statesmanlike Henry II would have scoffed at the sentiment. His son Richard, the patron of troubadors, probably would not. The great passion of Richard's life was the crusade, to which he was pledged at the time of his father's death. Among the least of his passions seems to have been England, which he was to visit for no more than six months in the ten years of his reign. Both in appearance, and literally, Richard was a striking man. If the effigy on his tomb can be taken as accurate, his features were not dissimilar to those of his brother John. His nose was straight and delicately pointed, he had a somewhat protruding and pugnacious underlip, a trim beard and moustache and hair swept back behind small ears. There his resemblance to the stocky John ended. In the words of a contemporary, Richard "was tall of stature, graceful in figure; his hair between red and auburn; his limbs were straight and flexible; his arms rather long, not to be matched for wielding the sword and striking with it; and his long legs suited the rest of his frame."

Richard provoked strong reactions in those who knew him. To some he was a hero, to others a villain. He has been described variously as vicious yet forgiving, hot-tempered yet good-natured, arrogant yet trusting, grasping yet generous. Unlike his father, he loved fine dress and pageantry. Above all, and indisputably, he was a talented and accomplished soldier.

On July 8, 1189, Richard was present at his father's funeral, after which he lost little time in winning over the barons who had remained loyal to his father during the hostilities. He seems to have held them in genuine respect. One of the first to receive his pardon was William Marshal, an impecunious knight who had not only stood beside Henry to the bitter end, but had also come very near to killing Richard in a skirmish. By giving Marshal in marriage to the daughter and heiress of the deceased Earl of Pembroke and Strigul, Strongbow, Richard was to confer on the grateful knight estates beyond his dreams in England, Wales and Ireland.

But first, Marshal was despatched from France to England with Richard's orders that his mother, Eleanor, should be released from detention at Winchester with authority to act as regent until her son could be with her. Elated by the turn of events, Eleanor, "even now unwearied by any task and provoking wonder at her stamina," proceeded on a regal tour of England, exacting oaths of allegiance to Richard, and celebrating her freedom by throwing open the prisons of the country.

Her role as oath exactor was important. Oaths, though not infrequently broken in medieval times, were regarded with

John versus Longchamp

solemnity and seldom revoked without the assertion of some equally solemn excuse. Belief in miraculous earthly retribution, or supernatural retribution beyond the grave, was a very real deterrent to perjury. One of the most famous of medieval oaths was that supposedly sworn by Harold of England to William of Normandy when the two men were together before the conquest of England. The Bayeux tapestry portrays Harold swearing an oath, possibly of fealty to William, whilst touching two coffers containing religious relics. Oaths sworn on such relics were deemed doubly potent. Supporters of Harold would later claim the oath inadmissible due to being sworn under duress. Others would hold that Harold's defeat at Hastings was divine retribution for perjury. At all events, throughout Christendom the oath was held binding and sacrosanct.

John had not been present at the funeral of his father, his whereabouts uncertain, but another member of the family had. Richard had received the king's seal from Geoffrey Plantagenet, the only one of Henry's illegitimate offspring to make an impact on history. Geoffrey had been born in England at about the middle of the century, to a mother now unknown, and intended for the Church while still a small child. For some reason, Henry favoured Geoffrey above his other natural children, publicly acknowledging the lad his son and allowing him to grow up with Eleanor's brood. Though inclined to be quarrelsome, with flashes of his father's hot temper, Geoffrey had never been disloyal to the king. He had fought energetically for Henry in the North of England during the great revolt of 1173-74, prompting the king to contrast him with his rebellious sons. "You are my true son," Henry is said to have told Geoffrey. "They are the bastards."

At about the age of twenty, Geoffrey had been elected Bishop of Lincoln. Since 1182, he had been chancellor. During the final conflict with Philip, he had remained faithfully at Henry's side, and had been the only member of the family present when his father died. Now, in his late thirties, Geoffrey was rewarded by Richard with the archbishopric of York, which had been vacant for some years.

On July 20, Richard was installed as Duke of Normandy in the cathedral at Rouen. Two days later, he met Philip at Gisors, north of Paris, where both men pledged themselves anew to set off for the Holy Land next spring. Some time between the funeral and this date, Richard and John had come together, probably in Normandy. If John had been apprehensive about his fate in the hands of his triumphant brother, he was soon reassured. Richard was almost overwhelming in his generosity toward John. To begin, he confirmed the prince in his existing possessions and titles, which included the castles of Nottingham and Marlborough, the estates of his uncle the Earl of Cornwall, and the lordship of Ireland. He also invested his younger brother with the lofty Norman title of Count of Mortain, and sanctioned his marriage to Isabel, heiress of the Earl of Gloucester, thus assuring him of more wide domains. Before the year was out, Richard had added to John's possessions numerous castles and manors in England, together with the entire counties of Dorset, Somerset and Cornwall in the west, and Derby, Nottingham and Lancaster to the north.

While Richard retained control of some castles in these counties, the revenues from them (estimated at £4000 a year) went to John instead of, as normal, to the royal exchequer. John was allowed to rule his lands as he chose. Not only was he his brother's richest and most powerful subject, he was practically a king within his own kingdom, accountable to no one but Richard himself.

At the end of August, John was married to Isabel at his castle of Malborough, Wiltshire. Marriages of the time were not always accompanied by the reverence the Church would have wished for them. Many were celebrated in none too sober fashion in taverns or at public drinking parties. People of the

John versus Longchamp

lower classes sometimes engaged in mock marriages; thus, early in the next century, a bishop would feel constrained to announce: "Let no man place a ring made of rushes or of any worthless or precious material on the hand of a woman in jest that he may more readily gain her favours." John's marriage was celebrated with due solemnity, but the honeymoon was broken five days later when the groom attended his brother's coronation at Westminster.

"At the coronation," wrote one who was present, "were John, his mother Eleanor, counts and barons, and an immense crowd of men and soldiers; and the kingdom was confirmed to the hands of King Richard. On the 3rd day of September, in the year of our Lord 1189, Richard was anointed king, on a Sunday in the year after leap year. Many were the conjectures made, because the day above that was marked unlucky in the calendar; and in truth it was unlucky, and very much so to the Jews in London." The Jews, who had settled in England at the time of William the Conqueror, and who had flourished under successive kings, had gathered in the capital to present a gift to the newly crowned Richard. At this period, the considerable wealth amassed by the talented Jews, together with their individualistic religious practices and their success as money-lenders, had aroused envy and dislike among the general populace. Richard had ordered that no member of their persuasion should attend the coronation banquet.

When a number of Jews tried to break in on the banquet to make their presentation, they were man-handled by the doorkeepers. Seeing the Jews expelled, the crowd outside took up the anti-Semitic theme, and soon mobs were rampaging through the city, murdering Jews, burning their houses and desecrating their synagogues. Throughout the night, while the banquet guests consumed nearly two thousand chickens, the slaughter and destruction of the Jews continued, with no great attempt on Richard's part to prevent it. During the early months of his reign, similar atrocities were enacted in other towns of England. In York, 150 Jews were trapped in the castle, to perish at the hands of irate citizens.

Before leaving on his crusade, Richard turned his attention to the Welsh and Scottish borders. The warrior princes of Wales, with their predilection for plundering across the frontier from their strongholds in the mountains, had made trouble for English kings since Saxon times. Like the Irish, the Welsh were accomplished at what a later age would term guerrilla warfare. "They make use of light arms, which do not impede their agility, small coats of mail, bundles of arrows, and long lances, helmets and shields," wrote Gerald of Wales. "The upper class go to war mounted on swift steeds, which their country produces, but the greater part of the people fight on foot . . . in peacetime, the young men, by penetrating the depths of the woods and climbing to the mountain peaks, learn to endure fatigue through day and night, pondering war during peace and inuring themselves to hard exercise."

Henry II had dealt with this problem by taking the most powerful of Welsh chieftains, Rhys ap Gruffyd, Prince of South Wales, into his confidence and favour. In return for handsome treatment from Henry, Rhys kept the lesser chieftains in order, and the country had been relatively peaceful for some time. During this period, the Welsh celebrated at Cardigan, where Rhys had a castle, the first Eisteddfod on record. There were prizes for the best poet and musician in the country. Gerald noted the hospitality in Welsh homes. "No one of this nation ever begs, for the houses are common to everyone, and they regard liberality and hospitality among the greatest virtues. It is neither overtly offered nor requested. On entering a house, travellers merely deliver up their arms to be received as guests." Young warriors seeking shelter in Welsh homes were entertained by the conversation of the daughters of the family,

John versus Longchamp

and by harp music, the entire family eventually lying down to sleep in their day-clothes on a bed of rushes on the floor.

Welshmen wore their hair in fringes to their eyes, and shaved their beards. The women wore large white veils on their heads. Gerald was much taken by the whiteness of their teeth. "Both sexes exceed any other nation in attention to their teeth, which they render like ivory by constantly rubbing them with green hazel and wiping with a woollen cloth."

On the death of Henry, affairs in Wales had been disturbed by more strife, and it is noteworthy that Richard placed enough trust in his younger brother to place him at the head of an English army assigned to obtain the homage of the Welsh princes. John, now twenty-two, handled the expedition with an efficiency remote from his earlier excursion in Ireland. Arranging a peace treaty with most of the Welsh princes, he persuaded Rhys to return with him to Oxford to pay homage to Richard in person. It was not John's fault that the king, busy with his crusade preparations, refused to meet the Welshman, who returned to his homeland bitterly offended, and spent the last decade of his life in rebellion.

With equal casualness, Richard next proceeded to turn England's relations with Scotland upside down. The Scottish clansmen were traditionally feared by the English, who had little good to say for them. Wrote one twelfth-century Sassenach: "It [Scotland] has inhabitants that are barbarous and filthy, oblivious of great cold or extreme hunger, putting their faith in speed of movement and light equipment. In their own country, they scorn death; among foreigners they surpass all in cruelty." The King of Scotland, a redoubtable warrior named William the Lion, had invaded northern England during the revolution of 1173–74. His best soldiers, travelling quickly on sturdy highland ponies, and living off the land, were formidable opponents. Reinforced by Flemish and Norman mercenaries, they had laid siege to many English castles until the invasion had been cut short by the capture of the Scottish king. William was attacking Alnwick, Northumberland, when an English army under Ranulf Glanville had surprised him in thick mist. William's horse was killed and the king, trapped beneath it, had been taken prisoner by Glanville. As the price of his release, William had been obliged to do homage to Henry II. Since then, Scotland had been dependent on England. Richard now offered the Scottish king the independence of his country in return for ten thousand marks towards the crusade. The bargain was agreed at Canterbury, and witnessed by John. As it happened, Richard and William got on well together, and for many years the two countries lived at peace.

William's ten thousand marks was the largest single contribution to Richard's crusade fund, but the English king did not stop at selling Scotland's freedom. Henry had left the coffers of the treasury well filled, but Philip had to be paid a high price for his part in the late war, and crusading was a very expensive business. Richard embarked on a gigantic clearance sale. "Everything could be bought," declared a contemporary, "powers, lordships, earldoms, shrievalties [sheriffs' offices], castles, towns, manors and suchlike." At the top of the scale, the Bishop of Winchester purchased two royal manors for three thousand pounds. More modestly, the Bishop of Coventry bought the priory of Coventry for three hundred marks. The disposal of sheriffs' offices showed a two-fold profit, the new officers paying for admission, the outgoing ones being fined for supposed misdemeanours. Another fund-raising ploy, the sale of dispensations from crusading vows, did brisk business. Many men who had taken vows on the impulse of the moment had had second thoughts. They were prepared to pay well for a let-out. "I would sell London if I could find a buyer," asserted Richard.

Lastly, before setting off for the East, Richard made arrangements for the government of England in his absence. It

John versus Longchamp

would have been asking too much of brotherly affection that he should leave John in the tempting position of regent. Instead, the king divided the government of the country between two justiciars, Hugh Puiset, Bishop of Durham, in the North, and William Longchamp, Chancellor and Bishop of Ely, in the South. The old justicier, Glanville, was relieved of his post, and died later on crusade. Hugh Puiset had bought Northumberland from Richard for two thousand marks. He was a fighting bishop of the old school who had held military commands in the days of King Stephen. Cultured, aristocratic and eloquent, Puiset was "a man of commanding presence and grand looks."

William Longchamp could scarcely have been more different. Small and unprepossessing, his head and feet too large for his body, he walked with a limp and, according to one who knew him, possessed the face of a dog. His enemies, of whom he had many, maintained that Longchamp was the grandson of two fugitive peasants. More likely, he was the product of a middle-class Norman family, and had achieved promotion by hard work, lack of scruple and loyalty to Richard, whom he had served in Aquitaine. In contemporary writing, he emerges as a domineering, ambitious man, with an unconcealed scorn for all things English, including the language, which he never bothered to learn. Longchamp was said to have purchased the chancellorship from Richard for three thousand pounds. His first objective on finding himself justiciar of the southern half of England was to add the northern half to his jurisdiction.

Richard had left England in December 1189. The following May, Longchamp marched north with a sizeable armed force to punish York for the massacre of the Jews there. This was properly Puiset's business, not Longchamp's. But when Puiset protested, the diminutive Norman lured him to a meeting, forcibly arrested him and carried him to London. Here, the old bishop was compelled to surrender all the lands he had purchased from Richard. Allowed free for a few short days, he was re-arrested by Longchamp's men on his way home and detained indefinitely. Thus rid of his co-justiciar, Longchamp proceeded on a grand tour of the country, surrounded by a crowd of Norman and Fleming henchmen, impoverishing the houses in which he quartered his retinue and exacting vast sums of money everywhere to meet his own needs and the continuing demands of his absent master, Richard.

"He moved pompously along," wrote an outraged observer, "a sneer in his nostrils, a grin on his face, derision in his eyes and haughty indifference on his brow." Clergy and laity alike were enraged by his overbearing conduct. Both found him "an intolerable tyrant."

For six months or more, Longchamp lorded it over England, with no one of sufficient stature to rally opposition. John and Geoffrey were in France, where Eleanor was preparing to follow Richard to the Middle East. Before leaving, Richard seems to have had some qualms about his munificent treatment of his younger brother. Mindful of the power he had bestowed on John, the king took two steps toward preventing its abuse. He named his young nephew Arthur of Brittany as his heir in the event of his dying childless. And he made John swear not to return to England for three years. At Eleanor's behest, however, he later released his brother from this oath.

So far, John had never lacked for a champion when he needed one. In Eleanor's intercession on his behalf, in Richard's generosity toward him, and the affection in which his father had held him, there is a suggestion of something more appealing in John's make-up than early pen-pictures admit. Dapper and quick-witted, with the sense of humour that enabled the Angevin princes to laugh at the fables told against them, he was probably very good company. At all events, when he returned to England at the end of 1190 (or possibly the beginning of 1191), he found himself one of the most popular men in the country. Here at last was a rallying point against Longchamp. Men of rank and wealth paid their respects to the king's brother, and were treated to the splendours of his housekeeping.

John had been born in England, he had spent much of his life there, he held territories in that country which amounted to a palatinate, moreover he was the only surviving full brother of the absent king. It would have been surprising had he stood idly aside and watched Longchamp, an upstart Norman and despiser of Englishmen, ruling the land like an overweening monarch. As winter and spring passed, men with grudges against the chancellor turned increasingly to John for support. Midsummer saw the first collision between John and Longchamp. The constable of Lincoln Castle, one Gerard of Camville, had purchased the title of sheriff of the county of Lincolnshire from Richard. Longchamp, wishing to give Camville's offices to one of his favourites, deprived Camville of his sheriffdom and called upon him to hand over the castle. Camville was accused of harbouring men who had attacked the Jews. His reply was to declare himself a liegeman of John, and to call on the prince for assistance.

John and Longchamp now mustered their forces. The chancellor called out levies and sent abroad for mercenaries. John raised an army of rugged Welshmen. When Longchamp laid siege to Lincoln Castle, John took over the royal castles of Nottingham and Tickhill, which offered no resistance, warning the chancellor that if he did not raise the siege of Lincoln he, John, would "come and visit him with a rod of iron and such a host as he could not withstand." Longchamp responded by ordering John to give up the royal castles and answer to the king's court for his behaviour. This was more than the prince could tolerate. He erupted in a burst of fury that would have done justice to his father. "His whole body was so contorted with rage," reported an observer, "as to be scarcely recognisable; fury furrowed his brow, his eyes flashed fire, his colour became livid and I know not what would have happened to the chancellor had he fallen into John's hands."

At this juncture, a new figure entered the drama. Walter of Coutances, Archbishop of Rouen, one-time Bishop of Lincoln and a native of Cornwall, had been sent from Messina, where Richard had received messages of complaint against Longchamp. The archbishop was armed with the king's authority either to govern in concert with Longchamp or to replace the chancellor altogether, depending on the prevailing situation in England. In all matters, Richard had directed, Coutances was to act in consultation with a council of prominent barons, including William Marshal, William Bruyere, Hugh Bardolph and Geoffrey FitzPeter. The Archbishop of Rouen, a cautious and scholarly man, listened carefully to both sides of the argument, then, with the backing of the council, arranged a reconciliation under which Longchamp reinstated Camville in his sheriffdom while John surrendered Nottingham and Tickhill castles to Coutances on behalf of the king. The position thus reverted more or less to its former state.

But tempers were still hot, and Longchamp, emboldened by the arrival of reinforcements to his mercenaries, quickly repudiated the agreement, proclaiming that there would be no peace until either he or John was driven from the country. Towards the end of that summer, 1191, a connection of the chancellor's by marriage, Roger of Lacy, Constable of Chester and the new overseer of the disputed castles, hanged two of the officers who had handed them over to John. When an attendant of one of the executed men had the temerity to drive the crows from his master's hanging corpse, Lacy promptly strung up the attendant. John avenged the three victims by ravaging Lacy's lands and confiscating those which lay within his own palatinate.

John versus Longchamp

In August or September, arbitration was again arranged between John and Longchamp, this time not by Coutances but by a committee representing the two parties in equal numbers and presided over by three bishops. The terms arrived at were very much in John's favour. The castles should still be held for the king, but now under the control of two of John's partisans. Among other decisions, by far the most important was a resolution that should Richard die on the crusade—an eventuality perhaps considered more a probability than a possibility—Longchamp was to uphold John as successor to the throne against Arthur. In this pronouncement, the arbitrators were expressing the feelings of the great mass of Englishmen, who held the king's English-born brother a more fitting heir to the throne than his dead brother's son, a child and a foreigner. They were, however, ignoring the wishes of the king himself.

Again, the peace did not last long. The terms had scarcely been agreed when Longchamp, his authority already undermined by the presence of Coutances, was faced with a further threat in the person of John's half brother Geoffrey, the former chancellor. Geoffrey, like John, had sworn to Richard to keep out of England for three years, but, like John, had been released from the oath shortly afterward. His promotion to the see of York had been confirmed by the pope in May, and in August he had been consecrated in Tours. John had urged him to come to England and take up his appointment. As soon as he learned of Geoffrey's intention to do so, Longchamp instructed the sheriffs of the south coast to prevent the archbishop landing, demanding also that the Countess of Flanders should stop his embarkation at Witsand, the common port of sailing for England. Geoffrey side-stepped this last obstacle by embarking at Boulogne, arriving at Dover in mid-September.

The constable of Dover was married to Longchamp's sister Richenda, and Richenda was in charge when Geoffrey landed. Her agents had orders to arrest the archbishop, but, disguising himself before landing, he eluded them and rode rapidly to a nearby priory, St. Martin's. Here he took sanctuary. It was said that the first words he heard on entering the church, where Mass was being celebrated, were St. Paul's: "He that troubleth you shall bear his judgement, whosoever he be." If so, they were to prove prophetic. For four days, the constable's men surrounded the priory. Then, losing patience, they violated the sanctuary, dragged the archbishop from the altar, still in his vestments, and marched him through the streets to the castle, where he was made captive.

News of the outrage, raising echoes of Becket's martyrdom, created a popular sensation and proved ruinous to Longchamp. Already widely detested, he was now opposed solidly by Church, state and people. Hugh of Lincoln, a much-respected bishop, excommunicated all concerned in the detention of Geoffrey. In Dover, London and elsewhere, the citizens called for justice. John demanded the immediate release of his brother. Shaken by the outcry against him, Longchamp complied, vainly protesting that his orders had been exceeded. But the country was in no mood to excuse him. Geoffrey, travelling first to Canterbury, and then to London, was greeted as a hero and escorted in solemn procession at St. Paul's. Meanwhile, a body of influential men had converged on John's castle at Marlborough, Wiltshire, to discuss action against Longchamp with the king's brother. Among them were the venerated Hugh of Lincoln, William Marshal with two fellow-members of the regency council, and the king's emissary, Walter of Coutances. These were not mere intriguers against lawful government, nor supporters of a usurping prince, as Longchamp maintained, but responsible men protesting against what they deemed to be irresponsible treatment. Coutances possessed the king's authority to supplant Longchamp if necessary.

From Marlborough, the party moved to Reading, on the Thames, some ten miles from Windsor, where Longchamp had established his headquarters in the castle. From Reading, writs were issued for a grand council meeting of bishops and barons to be held on October 5 on the bridge of Lodden, between Reading and Windsor. Geoffrey and Longchamp were summoned to attend. On the appointed day, a great host of prominent men gathered by the bridge, the rich caparison of their horses and the costumes of themselves and their retainers heightening the colour of the autumnal countryside. Angry shouts went up when it was announced that Longchamp had sent word that he was too ill to attend. The meeting went on without him. Geoffrey produced documents from the king authorising his return to England; Walter of Coutances produced his Messina instructions, after which it was moved and adopted that Longchamp should be deposed. Next day, the bishops excommunicated the chancellor, and he was ordered to appear at the bridge on the following morning without fail. It seems that he set out intending to do so, but, on hearing that an armed force was moving to cut off his retreat, turned tail and fled toward London.

On the road, he was challenged by a party of John's men. Drawing his sword and spurring his horse, the desperate chancellor (looking like a monkey in armour, as Gerald had it) hacked his way through the mêlée, leaving the leader of the interceptors mortally wounded. With John and the barons pounding the road behind him, the friendless Longchamp raced on to London, where, at a hastily convened meeting in the guildhall, he tried to convince the citizens that John was planning to seize the crown. The notion gained him so little support that he judged it prudent to lock himself in the Tower of London. Built by Gundulf, Bishop of Rochester, in the early days of Norman rule, this great fortress on the east side of the city was among the most formidable bastions in England. It covered an irregular hexagonal area, and was surrounded by a moat fed from the adjacent Thames. Within the moat, two lines of fortifications enclosed the mighty White Tower, or keep, which was flanked by four turrets. Here Longchamp was safe while he tarried.

Before long, his pursuers were clattering through the narrow streets of London. From his massive retreat, Longchamp heard the tolling of a bell, summoning the citizens to another meeting, this time at St. Paul's in the presence of Prince John. At this concourse, prelates, barons and burghers confirmed the deposition of the chancellor, proclaimed Walter of Coutances chief justiciar in his stead, recognised John as heir to the throne failing issue of Richard, and, according to one source, proposed to make the prince "chief governor of the whole kingdom," with the control of royal castles.

Lastly, John and his associates granted to the citizens of London the privileges of a commune, or municipality, a form of city government already well known on the Continent but new in England. As a commune, Londoners had the right to govern themselves through an elected mayor and aldermen with direct responsibility to the king, without the intermediate jurisdiction of any lord. It was a much valued gift, and the citizens gratefully swore their loyalty to John, who, in turn, led everyone present in an oath of fidelity to the king.

With all England against him, save a few of his own relatives and followers, Longchamp had no hope of being rescued from the Tower. Holding out was merely perpetuating his own misery. When a belated attempt to reach a private accommodation with John failed, he yielded the keys and formally surrendered the royal castles in his custody. On October 10, at a public meeting in a field near the Tower, Longchamp faced his enemies to make a spirited defence of his loyalty to Richard. Here he was on his strongest ground. Indeed, it was not disloyalty to the king which had brought about his downfall, but the disservice he had rendered through his tactless and auto-

Plate 1 A thirteenth-century map of England by Matthew Paris

Short-cross penny
London mint. Obverse

Short-cross penny
London mint. Reverse

Short-cross halfpenny
London mint. Obverse

Short-cross halfpenny
London mint. Reverse

Lord of Ireland halfpenny
Dublin mint. Obverse

Lord of Ireland halfpenny
Dublin mint. Reverse

John after accession penny
Dublin mint. Obverse

John after accession penny
Dublin mint. Reverse

John after accession halfpenny
Dublin mint. Obverse

John after accession halfpenny
Dublin mint. Reverse

Plate 2 A selection of contemporary coins

cratic methods. His reception was hostile, and next day, amidst unfriendly demonstrations, he made his way south to the coast.

Longchamp had been forbidden to leave the country until the castles had changed hands, but a few days later he was discovered trying to board a vessel at Dover disguised as a woman. A popular, if apocryphal story had it that his sex was detected by an impudently amorous fisherman. Gleefully avenging the earlier treatment of Geoffrey, the people of the town dragged the chancellor through the streets and threw him into prison. On October 29, John charitably ordered his release. Longchamp ignominiously left the country.

The relatively orderly manner in which the conflict between John and Longchamp had been conducted was an eloquent tribute to the administrative system and the respect for centralised justice which Henry II had bequeathed the nation. Under Henry, the ordinary freemen had become familiar with the king's executive officers, the representatives throughout the country of central government, and were continually reminded of a power in the land greater than the feudal magnate. That this unifying structure was sufficiently well established to survive in the king's protracted absence, was not the least important feature of Richard's reign. Without it, the struggle between Longchamp and his opponents must have resulted in the bloody anarchy which had bedeviled Stephen's reign. Instead, the issue was contended largely with at least overt respect for the law, and in compliance with orderly processes of government. In a situation which he might easily have exploited more radically, John acted in the main with restraint, associating himself with men of authority and, while not lacking initiative, binding himself by their advice. He had shown himself an innovator in the granting of the commune, and had proved popular with citizens and barons alike.

The next developments revealed John in a more questionable

light. He had, in the deposition of Longchamp, found his political feet. They seemed now to lead him down opportunist avenues. Shortly before Christmas, Philip Augustus of France returned from his crusade, leaving Richard in command of the Christian armies in the Holy Land. In the course of his travels, the English king had been persuaded by his mother to take a Spanish bride, Berengaria of Navarre, thus jilting Philip's sister Alice. The French king arrived home in no mood of Christianly brotherhood. After a fruitless attempt to get the seneschal of Normandy to hand over to him some of the border castles of the duchy, he invited John to France for a discussion, holding out the possibility of the prince marrying Alice and taking possession of Richard's continental dominions. John was already married, but it would not have been impossible to procure a divorce, and he was inclined at least to talk to the French king.

In February 1192, Eleanor, mistrustful of Philip's intentions, arrived back in England to protect Richard's interests. Finding John preparing to sail for Normandy, the energetic old lady immediately contacted Coutances and his councillors, and, between them, they forbade the prince to leave the country. As a deterrent, they threatened to seize his lands in his absence. The notion that John intended to fall in with Philip's plans was presumptuous, but the new chief justiciar and his colleagues already had reason for looking at John askance. Whether or not the St. Paul's concourse had granted John control of the royal castles is debatable. What is certain is that he had now taken matters into his own hands, persuading the constables of Wallingford, Berkshire and Windsor, in the same county, to make over their castles to him. In March, a disturbed council assembled in London to discuss the prince's action. Its members never got round to that business.

Having pursued his cause on the Continent to no great satisfaction, Longchamp had contacted John with the offer of a substantial sum of money if he would help him return to office in England. John, perhaps wishing to play him off against the now powerful Coutances, did not dissuade him. Longchamp landed at Dover, where he took refuge with his sister, on the day before the meeting in London, and the first business the council was faced with was his demand for a trial before the king's court. The councillors would have nothing to do with Longchamp, and wished to drive him from the country, but the king's mother spoke earnestly in favour of his appeal. Reluctant to act without either Eleanor or John on their side, the council members prudently dropped the matter of the castles and asked John for his help.

John, still smarting from the veto placed on his French trip, savoured the situation. Mischievously, he ignored successive invitations to meet the council. When finally he relented, he intimated frankly that he needed money—money which Longchamp had promised to pay him. Richard of Devizes, the Winchester monk, writing at that time, professed to know the very words that John used: "This chancellor cares nothing for the threats or favours of any or all of you. Within the next seven days he will pay me seven hundred pounds if I remain neutral. You see, I want money. A word to wise men is enough." The wise men took the hint. "It was agreed that they should give or lend him some money, but not of their own. They resorted to the treasury of the absent king."

At a time when power and alliances were openly auctioned, the deal was not so unusual. Richard had set a fine example in salesmanship. Eleanor, according to one contemporary, had accepted a bribe from Longchamp. The real price of John's assistance was not money so much as the council's independence. It had been forced to seek John's help, and accept it on John's terms. Before the meeting broke up, everyone present, including the queen mother, swore an oath of loyalty to John as the king's heir.

On April 3, 1192, Longchamp retreated dismally once more

to the Continent. For nine months England was quiet, John employed in the business of his estates, the council in running the country. Shortly before Christmas, word arrived that Richard was on his way home. His ship had been sighted at Brindisi, Italy. The next item of news astonished the nation. The King of England was imprisoned in a German castle, held against ransom by the Emperor Henry.

Chapter 4
THE DECADE OF THE LION'S HEART

Why should we expend labor extolling so great a man? He needs no superfluous commendation.

Itinerary of Richard I

Richard had left England in December 1189. By the following summer he had concluded arrangements for the governing of his continental dominions and was ready to set off on the journey East. At Tours in June he received the scrip and staff of a pilgrim, and at Vézelay, Burgundy, next month met Philip to finalize plans for the crusade. The massed tents of the two kings, pitched amidst cornfields and surmounted by gaudy pennons, stood out in the countryside like a multi-coloured city. Among the other effects of his household, Richard had brought with him a resplendent wardrobe, including a tunic of rose-hued samite, a mantle spangled with silver crescents and a cap of scarlet embroidered with gold. He rode the finest of Spanish stallions, superbly caparisoned, equipped with a gorgeous carved and inlaid saddle and a bridle set with precious metals. At Vézelay the kings pledged themselves to support each other at all times, and to divide equally the spoils of conquest—a reminder that there was more to crusading than purely spiritual endeavour.

From the harbours of England, Normandy, Brittany and Aquitaine, Richard had gathered a fleet probably in excess of a hundred vessels. Marine construction changed little during the twelfth century, and from the Bayeux tapestry, worked not earlier than 1150, some idea can be obtained of Richard's ships, long, sleek double-enders, some tarred a sombre black, others striped from stem to stern in vivid fair-ground colours. Though possessing sails, they could be rowed when the winds were not advantageous. Working mostly in oak, the shipwrights of the day had used the clinch method of overlapping planks on the hulls, fastening them on the overlap with metal rivets or bolts and either bolting or tying the planking to the ribs. The seams were caulked with a mixture of pitch and animal hair or wool. In most cases, a single mast was fashioned from a tree trunk, probably fir or pine, to be set amidships in a keel-block with an open-ended channel or fish-tail socket to control the slide of the mast as it was raised or lowered. The completed mast was stayed fore and aft and fitted with shrouds.

The large square sails were of linen or woollen cloth, probably woven in sections, stitched together and given brailing lines of some sort of skin. The most up-to-date of Richard's ships may have possessed fixed rudders, which came in towards the end of the century. The older ones had steering oars, normally secured to the starboard quarter by means of a pivot-chock. The steering oar could be raised in shallow water, or for beaching, and lowered at other times to provide the effect of a keel. A number of the larger vessels of the day had light castles fore and aft. According to Richard of Devizes, fourteen ships in the fleet were of exceptional size and strength. These, known as busses, carried "three rudders, thirteen anchors, thirty oars, two sails, and triple ropes of every sort. It [the first of the busses] had everything a ship needs in pairs, with the exception of the mast and boat. It had an efficient captain with fourteen picked sailors under his orders. The ship carried forty horses trained for battle and assorted arms for as many riders, together with forty footmen and fifteen sailors. It also carried a year's provisions for men and horses . . . The king's treasure, exceedingly great and of inestimable value, was divided among the ships so that if one portion was lost the rest might be safe." There seems to be some exaggeration in this picture. Certainly, the average ship would have carried far less.

Richard chartered his vessels for a year at a payment of two thirds of their reckoned value, and hired their crews at the rate of twopence a day for seamen, fourpence for steerers or captains. In view of the motley nature of the fleet, and the need to hold it together for a lengthy duration, a stern code of discipline was drawn up at the start.

"Anyone who kills a man on board shall be bound to the corpse and cast into the sea; if the killing is on land, the assailant shall be bound to the corpse and buried with it. Anyone convicted of wounding shall lose his hand; if he hits another with his hand without drawing blood he shall be immersed three times in the sea. Anyone using abusive or blasphemous language against another shall be fined an ounce of silver for each occasion. A convicted thief shall be shaved, tarred and feathered and cast ashore when the ship reaches land." Gambling was forbidden to the lower ranks on pain of flogging or keel-hauling.

In the summer of 1190, Richard set off by land to Lyons and thence down the Rhone Valley to the coast, ordering his fleet to meet him at Marseilles. Philip crossed the Alps to Genoa, where he had arranged his own shipping. At Marseilles, Richard discovered that his fleet had yet to arrive. In fact, it had put into Lisbon, where its personnel enjoyed themselves terrorizing the populace. Losing patience, the king hired local vessels for his personal retinue and started east along the Mediterranean coast, leaving orders for the main fleet to join him at Messina. From the outset, Richard was in his element, the swashbuckling, overbearing soldier, taking what he wanted where he found it. Travelling ashore in Italy, he provoked an angry incident with the local inhabitants by stealing a hawk from one of their number. At Messina, he and his crusaders were abhorred by the citizens.

Relations had quickly been strained by the unruly conduct of his followers, when Richard was confronted by an angry mob of townsfolk, who jeered at his nationality and asked if it were true that Englishmen had tails—a common jibe outside England. The infuriated king responded by donning his armour, summoning his army by trumpet and leading a general sack of the city. Everything of value in Messina was looted. The choicer women were shared among the crusaders, and Sicilian galleys in the harbour were burnt to prevent anyone escaping with his property. Richard compounded his unwanted action by meddling in Sicilian politics. Count Tancred of Lecce, a leader popular with the islanders, was contesting the crown of Sicily with the German emperor, Henry VI, who, in his aspiration to universal empire, claimed the island through his wife Constance. Richard not only recognised Tancred as King of Sicily, but agreed to engage his own nephew and heir presumptive, Arthur of Brittany, to Tancred's daughter. The compact gained him twenty thousand ounces of gold from Tancred—an advance on his daughter's dowry—and the enmity of the German emperor, a consequence Richard would regret later at some leisure.

It also led to the first of many wrangles with Philip, who claimed his share of the money by the agreement made at Vézelay. Relations between the crusading kings were further strained at this stage by Richard's proposed marriage with

Berengaria of Navarre, an alliance conceived to protect the southern border of Aquitaine. Philip was incensed by Richard's rejection of his obligations to Alice, and it was not until the English king agreed to pay the Frenchman ten thousand marks, and concede a number of changes in their continental territories, that the row was patched up and the crusaders resumed their travels. On April 10, 1191, Richard sailed from Messina, his original fleet now enlarged by some sixty Mediterranean vessels, the majority of which were oar-propelled galleys. On May 6, having been delayed by a gale which wrecked three of his busses, Richard reached Cyprus. If the Cypriots had heard of his behaviour in Sicily, they must have been extremely apprehensive.

In Cyprus, the ruler was Isaac Comnenus, a Greek related to Duke Leopold of Austria. Quickly taking offence at the high-handed manner of his uninvited visitor, Comnenus was sparing in hospitality. Richard wasted no time on diplomacy. Attacking and capturing Limasol, the chief town, he went on to ransack and plunder the island. When Comnenus eventually surrendered on the single and pathetic plea that he might not be placed in irons, Richard granted the request, then evaded his obligation by ordering that his prisoner should be placed in silver chains. On June 8, having married Berengaria in Cyprus—she was accompanying the crusade together with Richard's sister Joanna—Richard finally joined Philip and the other crusading armies before the walls of Acre, the main harbour and vital gateway to the Holy Land.

Acre had been captured by Saladin in 1187. For two years, Guy of Lusignan, King of Jerusalem, had tried in vain to recapture it. During that time, he had been joined by crusaders from all over Europe, but the Christian forces had lacked unity and strong leadership. They had also lacked adequate supply lines and were harassed by Saladin from outside the city. Their plight had been unenviable. At one period, they had come near to starvation. Disease was an ever present enemy. Here had perished Glanville, the former justiciar of England, the patriarch Heraclius, the counts of Flanders, Blois, Ponthieu and elsewhere, and barons and bishops by the dozen. The arrival of Philip had brought fresh heart to the Christians, but the French king had proved no more successful than the rest in his assaults on Acre. His interest was divided. He now demanded half of Cyprus from Richard. Richard retaliated by winning over many of Philip's soldiers with offers of higher pay.

Backed by the substantial reinforcements he brought with him, and his reputation as a military leader, Richard quickly took command of the siege operations. He decided against frontal assault in favour of an all-out artillery bombardment of the city. The two main forms of medieval artillery were those employing a catapult action depending on twisted cords for elasticity—a form known since ancient times—and, a more recent innovation, the sling-action machine incorporating a pivoted arm actuated by counterweights. Some of these were said to have weighed twenty thousand pounds or more. Both types of machine were used to project, among other things, stones, inflammable substances and (an early example of bacteriological warfare) the diseased carcasses of animals, or human corpses.

Richard kept up the bombardment without respite. Sometimes there would be a direct duel between Christian and Muslim machines. One projector employed by the crusaders, nicknamed "Bad Neighbour," was several times damaged by projectiles from an enemy weapon known as "Bad Kinsman." Another Christian machine was constantly attended by a priest, who prayed for its success and collected money for its maintenance. "The Count of Flanders," wrote an eyewitness, "had a splendid machine of large size which, after his death, was acquired by King Richard, together with a smaller one, equally efficient. These were perpetually trained on one of the gates used by the Turks until part of its ramifications collapsed. King Richard had constructed two others of excellent workmanship and material, which would strike at an incalculable distance . . . He also prepared others, one of which was of such violence and rapidity that its projectiles reached the heart of the city market-place. These engines were operated day and night, and it is common knowledge that a stone from one killed twelve men with its blow. The stone was afterwards carried to Saladin for inspection."

It took Richard just over a month successfully to conclude the siege which his allies had pursued for two years. To emphasise the personal nature of his victory, he refused to allow another crusading lord, Leopold of Austria, to raise his emblem in the city. The surrender of Acre led to one of the most appalling massacres of the crusades. Under the terms of truce, the Muslims undertook to release sixteen hundred Christian prisoners and pay twenty thousand pounds in gold to the victors. Richard took two thousand six hundred hostages against the payment, which was to be made in instalments. After many days of quibbling, during which envoys passed between the rival camps, Richard and Saladin failed to agree on the sequence in which the terms should be carried out. At this, both leaders slaughtered their captives in cold blood, Richard ordering that his should be beheaded in sight of Saladin's tents. Shortly after the fall of Acre, Philip, smouldering at Richard's assumption of overall leadership, departed the crusade on the excuse of ill health and went home to see what damage he could do the English king in his absence.

On August 22, Richard left Acre on the long march south to Jerusalem. It was a torturous undertaking. The heat was intense, lack of transport meant that supplies and equipment had to be man-handled, and repeated flank attacks by the Saracens forced the army to march in fighting formation. The further the crusaders progressed, the greater the number who dropped out from exhaustion, to die of exposure, disease or at the hands of Saladin's men. Horses collapsed, and knights were forced to tramp the scorching sands humping their armour. Wherever the land might have been expected to yield sustenance, the country had been devastated by the sultan. At Arsuf, between Acre and Jaffa, Saladin attacked in force. Hordes of Arabs, Turks, Soudanese and Bedouins encircled the Christians, urged on by the emirs and the sound of horns, drums and other martial accompaniment. At first, Richard, fearful of losing yet more of his dwindling army, tried to continue the march in defensive formation. His enemies made the most of their advantage. The sultan's horsemen, mounted on fiery Arab steeds, struck quickly at the extremities of Richard's ranks, then galloped away to reassemble and swoop again. Tall Soudanese, their black faces disfigured by ritual scars, raced forward barefoot, hurled their spears, then ducked out of range of the Christian bowmen. The rear guard of Richard's army was forced to march backwards to meet the assaults upon it.

Such provocations were too much for the crusading knights. Roaring invocations to the saints, they broke ranks and charged the swarming enemy. Richard, unable to restrain his men, spurred his horse to their head and led the attack. In the confusion which followed, both sides gained the upper hand in localised engagements, but losses among the lightly equipped Saracens were heavy and it was they who withdrew from the conflict. The crusaders resumed their march and entered Arsuf in safety.

As the Christian army advanced, Richard and Saladin were locked not only in physical conflict but in a remarkable diplomatic struggle. Amidst gifts and flowery phrases, methods of partitioning the Holy Land to their mutual satisfaction were proposed and counter-proposed until the English king, now doubtful of ever recovering Jerusalem with the forces at his disposal, put forward an unexpected offer. He would marry his sister Joanna to Saladin's brother Safadin if the sultan would hand over the Holy City. The idea appealed to Saladin. It did not, however, appeal to Joanna, who flatly refused to become the spouse of a Muslim. Richard then offered his niece Eleanor of Brittany, instead, but it was Joanna whom the sultan wanted, and negotiations ended in stalemate.

Richard continued his military campaign. Twice, he almost reached Jerusalem, but had to make tactical withdrawals. Once, he retired to Acre itself, to relieve that city, which was now under siege to Saladin. Finally, he won a brilliant victory at Jaffa, where, perhaps tutored in Harold's stand at Hastings, he formed a wall of shields to repulse the Saracen horsemen. By now, Richard, like so many of his followers, was debilitated by fever. For all the vast expense and endeavour, there seemed no prospect of recovering the Holy City. At the beginning of September 1192, a truce was reached with Saladin under which the Christians retained a portion of the coast, including Acre and Jaffa, and the right to make pilgrimages to Jerusalem. On October 9, Richard sailed from Acre on his homeward journey.

The trip remains something of a mystery. According to some chroniclers, Richard could not land at Marseilles, since the Count of Toulouse had been offended by the king's officers during his absence and might bar the roads to him. Why he did not sail on round Spain for Brittany, England or Normandy, is unexplained. Instead, seemingly after some now obscure misadventures, he landed at Friuli, at the head of the Adriatic. From here, rather than travelling west along the Po Valley toward France, as would seem reasonable, he headed northeast into Austria. It has been suggested that Richard was making for Hungary to call on the king of that country, Béla III, with whom he had political relations. If so, he was taking a remarkable risk in moving through Austria with an escort which seems to have been limited to seventeen men. Richard had bitterly offended Duke Leopold of Austria at Acre, and by his treatment of the duke's relative in Cyprus, and could expect a poor welcome on Leopold's territory. At last, having been chased from village to village by the duke's men, the English king was arrested near Vienna toward the end of December.

Leopold's neighbour and suzerain, Emperor Henry VI, heard the news with delight. Richard's alliance with Tancred of Sicily had aggravated an already sore situation for the emperor, who was surrounded by enemies associated with England. In February 1193, at Würtzburg, it was agreed that Henry should have custody of the prisoner, and that the emperor and the duke should share a ransom fixed at a hundred thousand marks (sixty-six thousand pounds). This figure was accepted by Richard, who thus committed his domains to another huge expense on account of his warlike exploits.

Accounts of John's reaction to his brother's imprisonment are not free from confusion, and it seems likely that his calculations were more complex than has generally been credited. It is impossible to say how much faith he placed in the emperor's intentions to release his brother, when and to whom. The arrest of Richard on his journey from the Holy Land was entirely contrary to the ethics of crusading, and little trust could be placed in those who condoned it.

The first person Henry informed of Richard's capture was Philip of France. Clearly, Philip was encouraged to hold hopes of being able to outbid Richard's adherents, to become himself the jailor and detain the King of England against the break-up of the Angevin dominions. If John anticipated Richard's eventual release only on condition of the loss of his French possessions, or if he expected a prolonged detention, perhaps of many years, then his actions appear in a different (if not necessarily better) light than if he believed that payment of the ransom would obtain an immediate release of the English king. At an early stage of the proceedings which follow, John asserted that his brother was dead. Whether this was a crude lie, or based on some misinformation, it is not impossible that he imagined that Richard would indeed be dead before his predicament could be resolved to the satisfaction of all sides.

The steps which John now took to usurp his brother's rights, or to secure an undivided Angevin empire, depending on the viewpoint, were very much in accord with the traditions of his family and their shifting alliances. The news of Richard's capture, "welcome above gold and topaze" to Philip, had quickly travelled from Paris to England. This time, nobody stopped John sailing for the Continent, where the seneschal and barons of Normandy asked him to meet them at Alençon and discuss the matter of the king's release. Roger of Howden, Yorkshire, a cleric and annalist educated under Hugh Puiset, Bishop of Durham, began recording his own observations from about this date (his annals for the previous two decades had been rewritten from another chronicler, Benedict of Peterborough). According to Roger, John told the Normans: "Receive me as your lord, swear fealty to me, and I will join you and defend you against the King of France. Refuse, and I will not come." The Normans did refuse. John then proceeded to Paris, where he appears to have done homage to Philip for the continental possessions, agreeing to marry Alice and cede the Norman Vexin. While John returned to England, Philip marched into Normandy for a brief trial of strength before withdrawing to plan an invasion of England. That these moves were concerted with John, though frequently implied, has not been established.

John arrived back in England with a body of mercenaries

to strengthen the garrisons of his castles at Wallingford and Windsor. Many continental mercenaries, culled from the desperadoes and adventurers of western Europe and described broadly as *routiers* or Brabançons, were promiscuous murderers and plunderers, loathed by all who encountered them. The Church had already forbidden their use, but the relative cheapness of their hire brought them increasingly to the front in European wars. John also recruited a number of Welshmen, and attempted to gain the support of the Scottish king, but William the Lion rejected his overtures. Having secured his castles, the prince travelled to London, demanding that Coutances and his colleagues of the council surrender their powers to him. Their position was difficult. Against the uncertain future of the king had to be weighed the positive pressures of Philip and John. One was threatening an invasion; without the support of the other, they might succumb to it. The temptation to give way before the man they had themselves recognised as Richard's successor must have been considerable.

Two factors strengthened their resolution to stand firm. One was Eleanor, now in her seventies, a woman of rich experience in foreign affairs and the intrigues of her family. Eleanor refused to be frightened either by Philip or her son John. The other was the mood of the country. If Richard had failed to return, the stories of his epic feats in the Holy Land had not. Acclamation of his Christianly virtues was as widespread in England as it was largely undeserved. When the queen mother, the justiciar and the council jointly called upon the nation to demonstrate its allegiance to the captive king, the response was immediate. Oaths of loyalty were renewed; Coutances, Geoffrey and Puiset raised forces to march on John's castles; knights and levies turned out in such force to guard the coasts of southern England that Philip's invasion fleet never landed.

Plate 3 The Battle at Gisors, from a fourteenth-century MS

Plate 4 Lismore, one of the Irish castles built by John to defend the Waterford area

Ironically enough, just when John looked very much like being worsted by the romantic shadow of his captive brother, he was saved by the arrival of a delegate from Richard himself. This was Hubert Walter, Bishop of Salisbury, whom the king had designated for the see of Canterbury. Walter was a lawyer and a man of the world, as ambitious, industrious and acquisitive as Longchamp, but more acceptable in England since he was more English. He had been born at Dereham, Norfolk, and brought up in the household of Glanville, the former justiciar. Returning from Palestine, Walter had travelled to Germany, where he had been allowed a meeting with Richard.

Walter's allegiance to Richard was unquestionable, but he advised a more conciliatory line with John than that which Coutances and his colleagues had embarked upon. Walter knew from a first-hand assessment of the situation in Germany that the prospect of Richard's release was both remote and uncertain. If a ransom could buy the king's freedom, then the co-operation of John, who controlled the revenues of a large part of the country, was indispensable. If the emperor did not intend to release his prisoner alive, then the loyal barons and bishops might be faced with crowning the man they were now attacking. At Walter's persuasion, the governing body made a truce with John, the terms of which were not unfavourable to the prince. Those of his castles not left in his hands were to be held by Eleanor on the understanding that if Richard were not released by a given time, they should be returned to their owner. John undertook to assist in the collecting of the ransom.

During the spring of 1193, relations between Henry and his captive improved significantly, probably on the basis of their mutual antipathy toward the King of France. Richard was allowed to hold court in Germany, to transact business and to receive his friends and subordinates there. Philip's chances of laying his hands on Richard, so far as they had ever existed, now faded. For Henry, the French king had served his purpose, enabling the emperor to raise the ransom asked to a massive one hundred and fifty thousand marks. Of this, Henry intended to keep one hundred and thirty thousand for himself, cutting Leopold's share to a mere twenty thousand. At the end of June, Richard agreed to the increased ransom. He had already sent messages to his dominions urging his subjects to contribute liberally, suggesting particularly the "borrowing" of Church treasures. It seemed that his release might be imminent. In a much-quoted passage from Roger of Howden, Philip was alleged to have warned John: "Look out for yourself, the devil is loosed!"

The message was premature. Despite exceptional measures, Richard's collectors had as yet raised an insufficient portion of the ransom to secure the king's release. The work continued ceaselessly. A general tax of all rents and chattels was levied on clergy and laity alike. Church plate was requisitioned, those orders which possessed none being obliged to pay in wool or other produce. Once more, offices were put up for sale at high prices, and fines were imposed on all possible excuses. In July, John, who had not exerted himself in the matter, was guaranteed in the holding of all his lands, castles and titles by Richard in return for "furnishing money for the king's ransom." At the same time, in an attempt to obviate further trouble from Philip, Richard ceded to the French king a large part of eastern Normandy and promised him a gratuity of twenty thousand marks, to be paid in instalments.

That these agreements were entered into in the weakest of spirits became clear in the general manoeuvring which preceded and surrounded Richard's release. In a pact of mutual protection between John and Philip, the former promised the latter large areas of Normandy and Touraine. By the end of the year, a sufficient advance now having been paid on the ransom, the emperor announced that he would free Richard in January. When the appointed day arrived, he postponed the event until February. He then showed Richard letters from France in which John and Philip offered him substantial sums of money for continuing to hold the King of England in captivity. So far as this was a ploy to increase the ransom even further, it did not work. By promises of liberal rewards from England, Richard induced the princes of Henry's court to insist that the emperor now keep his bargain. On February 4, 1194, a year and six weeks since he had been captured, Richard was delivered into the arms of his mother, who had travelled to Germany with Coutances to collect him. Already, he had spent the money of his subjects on all sides. His first act of freedom was to pledge even more of it to the leading princes of Germany and the Low Countries by way of securing their alliance against France.

After a leisurely voyage home, embarking at Antwerp with his favourite skipper, Alan Trenchemer, Richard landed at Sandwich, Kent, on March 7. It was more than four years since he had set foot in England. The following day, he paid devotion at the shrine of St. Thomas in Canterbury; then, advancing toward London accompanied by excited crowds, was met in Rochester by Hubert Walter. On March 16, he made a state entry of London. In a great procession of clerics, civic dignitaries, magnates and soldiers, the returning hero was escorted to thanksgiving at St. Paul's. The city was *en fête*. Londoners knew how to let their hair down on high days and holidays. Then schoolboys took fighting cocks to their tutors, and the hours were spent not in study but in watching the birds do battle. The city elders and wealthy citizens gathered in the open spaces on horseback to encourage their juniors at such sports as archery, wrestling, putting the stone, throwing the javelin and various ball games—"and it seems that their blood is aroused by watching the action and by contemplating the joys of untrammelled youth."

Young men of means held mimic contests on horseback with blunted lances, or jousted from boats on the Thames, endeavouring to knock each other into the water. All manner of animals, from boars and bulls to fighting bears were set against each other, or to "do combat to the death against hounds let loose on them." Nor was there a shortage of professional entertainers: actors, jugglers, musicians, acrobats (some of them women) and fools or jesters. One medieval cleric considered that this last category was doomed to hell's flames unless they left their profession. "Some contort their bodies in disgusting leaps and gestures, or expose themselves shamefully." Others "tell scandalous tales behind people's backs," or "attend public drinking sessions and places of low repute to sing songs which arouse men to wantonness." Kings, princes and lords held jesters in higher repute than did churchmen. Some court jesters, among them Rahere, who was employed by Henry I, grew rich; others went a shade too far with their mockery and were whipped or dismissed. Their costume normally included a form of monk's cowl adorned with bells or asses ears, and they carried a bauble, or short staff, with which to perform mock castigations.

While London celebrated, John watched events with mounting discomfort from Normandy. As soon as Richard's release had become imminent, he had sent a confidential clerk, Adam of St. Edmund's, to England with letters ordering that his castles there should be prepared for defence against the king. Five days after Richard's liberation, Adam chanced to meet Hubert Walter in London. Walter, perhaps suspicious of Adam's purpose, invited him to dinner. Food and wine loosened the tongue of the messenger, who was soon boasting of his master and his connections. With a nice sense of social etiquette, Walter allowed his guest to leave his table unmolested. Before

Adam could reach his lodgings, however, he was arrested and his letters examined.

Next day, the governing council unanimously decreed that John should be deprived of all his land in England, and that his castles should be seized, if necessary by force. Walter marched against Marlborough, old Bishop Puiset invested Tickhill, the earls of Huntingdon, Chester and Derby surrounded Nottingham. Elsewhere, other strongholds were brought under siege. Most yielded within a few days. At St. Michael's Mount, Cornwall, a monastery which John had fortified, the commander was said to have died of fright on hearing that Richard was at hand. The surrender of the last to hold out, Nottingham Castle, was taken on March 26 by the king himself, after he had hanged a number of John's men within sight of the defenders.

Before leaving Nottingham, Richard held a council meeting at which he asked for judgement against John, and against one of John's abettors, Hugh of Nonant, Bishop of Coventry. The council ordered them both to appear for trial within forty days, John to "forfeit all claims to the kingdom" if he failed to do so. Bishop Hugh later bought the king's pardon for two thousand marks and withdrew from public life. John ignored the council's order.

While the forty days slipped by with no sign from his brother, Richard subjected himself to a fresh coronation, seemingly to erase the humiliation of his captivity, and entertained his friend William the Lion of Scotland. But these were passing distractions. Money was Richard's enduring preoccupation. The balance of the ransom had yet to be raised, and the king was eager to mount an expedition in Normandy, where Philip was engaged in renewed depredations. Richard mobilised a third of the knights who owed him service, and required the remainder to pay a scutage of one pound on the knight's fee towards the balance of the ransom. This was only a start. Once again, the familiar practice of confiscating titles and reselling them was employed in England. Lords were turned from their offices without scruple. Gerard of Camville and Hugh Bardolph were displaced from the sheriffdoms of Lincolnshire and Yorkshire, and these offices put up for auction. Archbishop Geoffrey of York bought the latter for two thousand pounds. Bishop Godfrey Lucy was deprived of the sheriffdom of Hampshire.

The large sums of money men were prepared to pay for the office of sheriff suggested that, apart from the power and prestige the rank conferred, it was also a lucrative one. As the chief representative of the Crown in his shire, heading its fiscal, judicial, military and administrative business, the sheriff was in a choice position to enrich himself at the expense of the people within his jurisdiction. The range of abuses indulged by some sheriffs covered favouritism, victimization, embezzlement, extortion and other forms of corruption. One was charged with evading rates and taxes on his properties, another with pocketing unauthorised duties from ships in a local port, others with bribery, the unwarranted confiscation of goods and chattels, and so on. At times, the outcry against sheriffs was widespread, and the legend of Robin Hood, who may or may not have existed, is illustrative of the esteem accorded those who defied them. Both Henry I and Henry II had taken steps to rectify this matter, dismissing a number of the powerful local magnates who had once dominated the offices of sheriff and replacing them with professional administrators trained in Crown service and identified with central government. Nevertheless, abuses persisted, and Richard's sale of offices did nothing for the integrity of local government.

Among the most callous of Richard's money-raising measures was the dismissal of Bishop Puiset from his Northumberland holdings in order to resell them. No one had served the king more loyally in his absence than the aged bishop. The heroic Richard was continuing where Longchamp had left off. Longchamp himself, having been closely in touch with Richard during his imprisonment, was now reinstated in the office of chancellor, though little of the remaining years of his life was spent in England. Walter of Coutances also faded from the English scene at this time, to concern himself with affairs on the Continent. The government of the country was left to Hubert Walter. On May 12, two days after the expiry of the forty days' notice served on John, the king sailed for Normandy with a fleet of a hundred ships to resume the occupation which most befitted him—fighting. He would never return to his kingdom.

Somewhere in Normandy, probably at Lisieux (though the chronicles differ on the venue), John and Richard were reconciled through the intervention of their elderly mother. The biographer of William Marshal, who wrote more than a quarter of a century later, provided a colourful version of the meeting between the brothers. According to this source, Richard was staying with the archdeacon of Lisieux, John of Alençon, when he noticed that his host was uneasy. "What are you worried about?" demanded Richard. "You have seen my brother John, that's it, isn't it. Well, let him come to me without fear. A brother need not be afraid. If he has behaved foolishly, I will not reproach him."

The archdeacon, as the story had it, hurried to John and gave him the reassuring news: "Step forward boldly. You are lucky. The king is frank and merciful, more kindly disposed to you than you would have been to him." Apprehensively, John approached Richard, throwing himself at the king's feet. Richard pulled him up and kissed him. "Think no more of it, John. You are only a child who was left with evil counsellors. What can I give you for dinner?" Just then a salmon was brought in as a present for the king. "Cook it and serve it to my brother," said Richard.

The notion that John, a man of twenty-seven, should have

been forgiven as a mere child greatly appealed at a later date to his detractors, and to Richard's panegyrists. Whatever the truth, this king who had once allied himself to Philip in order to destroy his aged father was ill placed to strike moral attitudes. Brothers or not, it was no more than sound politics on the part of Richard that John should now be harnessed to the continuing struggle against the King of France. Events proved the wisdom of both parties in effecting a rapprochement.

John, once again "Lackland," for Richard had not reversed the decision of the council at Nottingham, set himself to earn the recovery of his titles in battle. Placed in command of a substantial portion of his brother's army, he began by making a lightning raid on Evreux, in eastern Normandy, which Philip's troops were holding, and captured the castle there. He then organised the defence of Normandy while Richard marched south through Touraine and into Aquitaine, routing or capturing Philip's men wherever he encountered them. So delighted was the German emperor at Philip's discomfort that, in 1195, he sent Richard a golden crown and remitted the balance of the ransom, seventeen thousand marks, as a contribution toward the English king's campaign expenses. The same year, Richard, in turn, expressed his pleasure at John's conduct by restoring to him the county of Mortain and the earldom of Gloucester together with an annual allowance of two thousand pounds. Roger of Howden had portrayed Richard, at the time of his captivity, dismissing John's military talent with contempt. The "slightest force" would deter him. If Richard ever held such a view, he seems to have reversed it.

In 1196, John captured the castle at Jumièges, and, the following spring, led a daring raid into Philip's territory as far as Beauvais, north of Paris. In this campaign he was accompanied by one Mercadier, the captain of a band of notorious Brabançon mercenaries whose ruthless cruelty, plundering and destruction were feared throughout the Continent. In the battle for Beauvais, John not only defeated the bishop of that place, Philip of Dreux, one of the most redoubtable warriors of his day, but captured the bishop and many of his knights. Richard was overjoyed. He had a private grudge against the bishop, who had been one of Philip's emissaries to the emperor during his captivity, and the knights would fetch a good ransom. While the rank and file of medieval armies were shown little mercy if they fell into the hands of the enemy, knights were normally preserved and sold back to their liege lords, who were commonly under contract to pay up in such circumstances. Richard needed all the money he could get. That year, Hubert Walter announced that he had provided the staggering sum of one million one hundred marks for the king's use in the past twenty-four months. It was becoming increasingly difficult to raise funds for the king's war.

The struggle between the rival monarchs, with its sieges, counter-sieges, truces and renewed forays, dragged on for another two years. Early in 1199, after a crushing victory for Richard and Mercadier at Gisors, where a bridge collapsed and hurled many French knights into the river, Philip made a desperate attempt to break up the two brothers by declaring that John had gone over to the French side. John sent two knights to Philip's court to defend his innocence by the trial of battle. When none of the French knights would take up the challenge, Richard was convinced that the story was a trick. On January 13, Richard and Philip met on the Seine, between Vernon and Les Andelys, where they agreed on the terms of a five-year truce. So distasteful was the meeting to them that Richard stood in a boat on the water, while Philip sat astride a horse on the riverbank.

Richard was now forty-one and growing corpulent, but still eager for battle so far as money permitted. In March, the opportunity arose both to exercise his sword arm and to profit by it. A ploughman near Limoges, in the Haut-Vienne, had unearthed a Gallo-Roman treasure hoard. This Richard claimed by right of being the overlord of the area. The local vassal was the Viscount of Limoges. He offered to share the treasure, but refused to part with all of it. Richard, accompanied by Mercadier, rode south to lay siege to the castle of Châlus, the stronghold of the obstinate viscount. The place was poorly garrisoned and in need of repair. Richard and Mercadier were inspecting it with some complacency, prior to launching an attack, when a bolt from a crossbow struck the king at the base of his neck. The wound festered. Ten days later, on April 6, 1199, Richard was dead.

The dying king bequeathed his entrails to rebellious Châlus, his heart to Rouen—a mark of gratitude for the fidelity of the Normans—and ordered that what remained should be buried at Fontevrault, at the feet of his father, concerning whom he had eventually developed a conscience. More important, and contrary to his earlier preference for his nephew Arthur, he named John as heir to all his dominions, and made everyone present swear to be true to him.

Chapter 5
KING JOHN

A great prince, but scarcely a happy one.

Barnwell annalist

By an ironic coincidence, John was staying with his rival for the succession, Arthur of Brittany, when Richard died. To the Bretons, well versed in the legend of the devil's brood, Arthur's guest was a diverting visitor, gay and charming when the occasion demanded, at once compelling and suspect. Compactly built, his lack of height caused him to strut to keep pace with taller men, the scabbard of his sword almost scraping the ground behind him. Above trim, Mephistophelean beard and moustaches, his bright eyes shone with a mocking humour which had eluded his earnest father and the pugnacious and boorish Richard. His courtiers were known for their wit and levity, qualities which dismayed the tonsured clerks who wrote of them, and who regarded John as the least God-fearing of a not particularly reverent family.

Surrounded by Bretons, John's position on the death of his brother was perilous. Though Arthur was only twelve years of age, and might have lacked the nerve to seize or dispose of his uncle, his mother Constance and her barons would not have missed the chance. Luckily for John, he heard the news of Richard's demise before it reached his hosts. Bidding them a hasty farewell, he rode rapidly for Anjou. The fact that he had been nominated heir by the late king was no guarantee that he would succeed to his brother's throne and possessions. Designation was only one of several keys to the medieval kingdom. Election played a part in king-making, and so did kinship with the royal house. In England, the Anglo-Saxon kings had traditionally been elected by the witan, or the king's councillors, at a witenagemot, or meeting of the so-called Wise Men. Where a candidate was weak, a number of these might appear as the junta which brought him to office; where he was strong, their approval was sought as little more than a formality. Now the barons had replaced the Wise Men.

Kinship had gained importance as a factor of succession. In the eleventh century, Harold could be elected King of England though lacking blood relationship with his predecessor, Edward. By John's day, however, kinship had become an essential ingredient, short of out-and-out conquest on the part of one candidate. At the same time, the establishing of precedence between two or more candidates of the same blood could lead to confusion. The customs in different parts of the Angevin empire were at variance. The author of a twelfth-century treatise on English law confessed himself uncertain whether a younger brother, or the son of a deceased older brother, had the better claim. On the whole, he opted for the nephew. But a contemporary authority on Norman customs had no doubt that in such circumstances the uncle rather than his nephew was the closer heir.

The biographer of William Marshal penned an example of the discussion in progress following Richard's death. Marshal and Archbishop Hubert Walter, two men highly respected by the late king, were at Vaudreuil, at the mouth of the Eure, at the time. News that the king had expired reached Marshal as he was going to bed. Dressing hurriedly, he hastened to the archbishop, who was staying at the nearby priory of Nôtre Dame du Pré. "We must lose no time in choosing a successor," said Marshal, according to his biographer.

"I think," said Walter, "that Arthur should be the king."

"In my opinion, that would be a bad choice," asserted Marshal. "Arthur is advised by traitors, and is haughty and filled with pride. Put him at our head, and he will cause us much harm, for he does not love our people . . . But consider John. Surely he is the nearest heir to his father and brother."

"Marshal, is this what you desire?"

"Yes, my lord, for it is proper. A son has a better right to his father's land than a grandson."

"So be it," said the archbishop. "But you will regret it."

Thus, as the writer saw it, Walter distrusted John, Marshal distrusted Arthur, and the matter was settled on a point of legality. The underlying assumption of the conversation was one of choice, the elective element. In fact, the argument against Arthur reposed not so much in the boy's character as in the background of hostility between Normans and Bretons, and in the history of Breton independence and defiance of the Angevin rulers. So far had this developed since his father's death, that Arthur had actually been educated at the court of the King of France, along with Philip's own son. Philip Augustus would have asked nothing better than that the Angevin empire should be placed in Arthur's immature hands. John now acted with the characteristic vigour of his house to prevent it.

Riding hard for Chinon, in Anjou, the repository of the Angevin treasury, he emulated his great-grandfather Henry I, whose first act on the death of William Rufus had been to gain command of the treasury at Winchester. John reached Chinon on April 14, three days after his brother's burial at Fontevrault, and was placed in possession of the treasury and castle by the seneschal of Anjou, Robert of Turnham, an English knight who had fought with Richard in the crusade. One chronicler asserted that the seneschal handed his trust to John on Eleanor's persuasion. Certainly, Eleanor was already active on her son's behalf, and it may have been she who had warned him to get out of Brittany. Support for John was mounting. Walter and Marshal had left for England to promote his interests there, and, through his mother, he could depend on Aquitaine. Thanks to Robert of Turnham, he had secured not only Chinon, but another royal stronghold in the region, Loches, southeast of Tours on the river Indre.

Then there were the men who had sworn loyalty to the prince at Châlus, among them William of Briouse, Thomas Bassett, Gerard of Furnival and Peter of Stoke. Their subsequent standing in John's favour leaves no doubt that they were as good as their word to the dying king. Indeed, one annalist claimed that William of Briouse, a particularly powerful baron, was second to none in his efforts to obtain John's succession.

At Chinon, John was joined by members of Richard's household who swore to uphold him as his brother's heir. He was also joined by perhaps the most venerated of English prelates at that time, Hugh of Avalon, Bishop of Lincoln, formerly a trusted adviser of Henry II. The bishop had been travelling to visit Richard when the king died, and had officiated at the funeral in the abbey at Fontevrault. At John's instigation, they now journeyed to Fontevrault together so that the prince might pay his respects at the tombs of his father and brother. The biographer of Bishop Hugh, at pains to establish the prelate as a sound moral influence on this youngest son of a family not renowned for its piety, depicted him regaling the prince with pontifical warnings. When John promised to support the nuns of Fontevrault with benefactions, it seems that the bishop interjected with a caution against falsehood. "Beware not to make promises unless you mean to keep them," said the prelate. "You know I detest lies."

When John brightly showed his companion an amulet hanging at his neck, declaring that it was a lucky charm handed down by his ancestors, Bishop Hugh was said to have admonished him for his superstition, advising him to trust "not in that stone, but in the corner stone of God." The bishop appears to have missed few chances to moralise. As they left the abbey at Fontevrault, Hugh pointed out a representation of the Last Supper sculpted above the porch. The bishop showed John a group depicting doomed monarchs sporting their regalia among the damned, warning him of the peril attending a king who shirked his responsibilities. John, who had taken it all in good humour, turned to another group, in which kings and angels approached the realm of Heaven. "My Lord Bishop," he said with a twinkle, "these are more appropriate. This is the example I intend to follow."

If John took religious dogma and ceremony lightly, he needed no persuasion to respond compassionately to the poor and the humble. Hugh's biographer does not deny that when ragged beggars and feeble old women accosted him on the road, the prince spared time to talk with them and acknowledge their greetings—behaviour by no means common among the domineering nobles of the era. For the bishop's sermons, on the other hand, his patience was limited. At Mass on Easter Sunday, when Hugh launched himself upon a lengthy peroration on the rewards and punishments of good and bad princes, John attempted three times to cut him short with messages that he wanted his dinner. Each time, the bishop's sermon became more pointed and fervent.

The awful retribution of God toward sinners was a theme

very dear to the clerics of John's day. Roger of Wendover, a monk and writer of St. Albans whose chronicles of John's reign were to form the foundation of much hostility among later historians toward the prince, incorporated in his history of England vivid examples of divine vengeance which few would today take seriously. One of his anecdotes told of a singularly unfortunate washerwoman who had rashly dared to ply her trade on the Sabbath.

> The vengeance of God was not lacking, for on the spot a type of small black pig suddenly adhered to her left breast and could not by any means be torn away. By continual sucking, the pig drew blood and, in a short time, had consumed almost all the bodily strength of the wretched woman.

In another story offered by Wendover as factual history, a peasant from the Essex village of Twinstead was guided on a tour of purgatory by St. Julian.

> The surface of the place crawled with a multitude of worms, monstrous in size and deformity, horrific beyond conception. Jaws gaping hideously, exhaling fire from their nostrils, they flayed the crowds of wretched beings with remorseless voracity. Devils, hurrying in all directions, raging like mad creatures, seized the wretched beings and cut them to pieces with their fiery prongs, tearing their flesh off to the bone, then hurled them into the fire, melted them like metals and restored them in the shape of burning flame . . . In a brief space of time, I saw them destroyed by a hundred or more different kinds of torture.

John and Hugh had spent Easter Sunday at Beaufort-en-Vallée, in Anjou. Next day, they parted company, John intending to take possession of Angers, his grandfather's capital. He was prevented from doing so by some alarming news. Angers, a mere fifteen miles from Beaufort, was in Arthur's hands. While John had been receiving the treasury at Chinon, and fraternising with the Bishop of Lincoln, Arthur and Constance had marched east with a Breton army, seized Angers without a fight, and rallied a host of barons from Anjou, Touraine and Maine to Arthur's flag. At the same time, Philip had marched west with his own army and was advancing on Maine and Anjou. On April 20, the Bretons and their allies entered Le Mans, where they were shortly joined by Philip. Between them, the converging armies had cut clean through the middle of the Angevin domains. In Le Mans, Arthur did homage to the French king for Anjou, Touraine and Maine.

Two days ago, John's progress toward command of his brother's empire had been unimpaired. Now the whole of Anjou, with the exception of the two castles held by the seneschal, was in the hands of Arthur's supporters, and much of the adjacent land. John was forced to flee to Normandy for safety.

Nothing could have appalled the Normans more than the prospect of being ruled by a Breton. The seneschal, William FitzRalph, an English knight of loyal service to the royal house, was for John. So was the Archbishop of Rouen, Walter of Coutances. The nobles stood squarely behind them. On April 25, in the cathedral church of Rouen, "by the election of the nobles and the acclamation of the citizens," John became Duke of Normandy. Having placed a crown of golden roses on the prince's head, Coutances girded him with the sword of justice and handed him a lance complete with the banner of Normandy. At this point, John, who seems not to have been overawed by the occasion, turned to exchange words with some friends nearby and let the lance slip to the floor. The incident, which outraged the monkish scribes who recorded it, was recalled as an omen of malevolent happenings.

For the moment, however, the new duke was on firmer

ground. With the strength of Normandy behind him, he marched purposefully south to make an example of Le Mans for having opened its gates to his enemies. Philip and Arthur had departed, and the garrison was no match for the Normans. John destroyed the castle, pulled down the city walls, seized the leading citizens and burned their houses. Meanwhile, Eleanor had engaged Mercadier and his mercenaries in her son's cause. Leaving Anjou, Maine and Touraine to their tender mercies, John retraced his steps to Normandy and prepared to leave for England. On May 25, he landed at Shoreham, Sussex, accompanied only by his personal suite, and rode promptly for London.

In England, the customary disturbances attendant upon the death of a monarch had broken out, though these were less political in nature than instances of opportunist plundering and the settling of local feuds. Arthur's cause found little support in the island, and the government moved firmly to put down civil disorders. After Hubert Walter had become Archbishop of Canterbury, the office of chief justiciar had passed to Geoffrey FitzPeter, sheriff of Staffordshire and Yorkshire, and a member of the ruling council during Richard's reign. FitzPeter had acted with alacrity on John's behalf, alerting the garrisons of the royal castles and employing bands of knights to police the more troublesome of the shires. Oaths of allegiance to John were exacted on all sides.

Upon Walter and Marshal returning to the country, they had joined FitzPeter in convening a grand council at Northampton, to which they took care to summon those lords from whom John might expect opposition. Among these were Ranulf of Chester, a powerful and greedy magnate who had contracted an ill-fated marriage with Constance of Brittany after Geoffrey's death (the two did not live together); Richard of Clare, Earl of Hertford, who was married to one of the Gloucester heiresses passed over when John married her sister;

King John

Roger of Lacy, who had hanged the two knights who had surrendered castles to John; and David, Earl of Huntingdon, and William, Earl of Derby, who had also acted with Longchamp against John. Together with others who possibly held personal grievances, these belonged to a wider class of acquisative barons whose influence had been much curtailed by the growth of strong central government during recent reigns, and whose purses had been depleted by Richard's persistent demands for money. They now took the opportunity to make their support for John conditional upon the assurance that their powers and privileges would not be further diminished by the new king. John's representatives promised them their full rights, whereupon they swore to be loyal to him.

John reached London on May 26, and was crowned in Westminster Abbey by Hubert Walter the next day. The abbey was hung with hundreds of yards of coloured cloth for the occasion. Seventeen prelates, ten earls and "many barons" were present. Twenty-one fat oxen were supplied for the banquet afterwards. Few other details have survived, the chroniclers dismissing the ceremony with a brevity which suggests that it did not differ remarkably from previous coronations. By the coronation oath, John and his predecessors defined their obligations to their subjects. The Kings of England promised to uphold the peace of the land, to govern mercifully and fairly, to renounce "evil customs" and to be guided by the laws of Edward the Confessor, which were generally held to have been beneficial to the nation.

Once crowned, however, a king's temptation to ignore any restraints was not lessened by the sweeping functional powers and the profound emotional potency of the medieval monarchy. The king was widely held to derive his authority from God, to be "Christ's deputy" among his people. As such, he was supreme not only among his lay subjects but among his Church officers, who held their appointments by his authority.

The theory of kingship held people in thrall. Genealogists traced the ancestry of kings back to Adam, or to the ancient heroes, and it was supposed that they could perform miracles of healing by their touch. In secular matters, the king's powers were all-embracing. He chose his own officers of state, and dismissed them at will; he decided his own policies at home and abroad; he declared his own wars, commanded his own armies and made his own terms of peace. "No man can make himself king," wrote the homilist Abbot Aelfric at the end of the tenth century, "but after he is consecrated he has authority over the people, and they cannot shake his yoke off their necks." Things had not changed so much by John's time. "The prince," declared the twelfth-century scholar John of Salisbury, "is controlled by the judgement of his mind alone."

John's first action on being crowned King of England was to reward the three men who had been instrumental in securing the throne for him. The same day as the coronation, he girded William Marshal with the sword of the earldom of Pembroke, and Geoffrey FitzPeter with that of Essex. For some time past, they had enjoyed the estates of these earldoms, but now the titles were formally confirmed. In good spirits, the two men waited on their new king during the coronation feast. The same day, Hubert Walter was appointed to the office of chancellor.

When the effects of the banquet had been slept off, John personally received the homage of the barons. How many presented themselves to the king is unknown, but it could have been quite a crowd. There were about two hundred and forty baronies in England, accounting for more than seven thousand knights' fees and one hundred and forty castles. At the time of Richard's death, John himself had been the most powerful baron in the country, with some three hundred knights' fees and three castles. Second in power was the acquisitive Earl Ranulf of Chester, with two hundred knights' fees. Then

King John

came two earls of more contented disposition, William of Arundel and Hamelin Plantagenet of Surrey, an illegitimate brother of Henry II, each with rather less than two hundred fees; and behind them, with upwards of one hundred and forty fees, Richard of Clare, Earl of Hertford; Roger Bigod, Earl of Norfolk; Robert of Beaumont, Earl of Leicester; and Constance, Countess of Richmond.

Among the English barons, John's accession had been remarkably free from dispute, but it had involved promises by his representatives that he would look into their claims and reconcile them. That it had been easier to make such promises than to honour them would soon become manifest. Richard's endless taxes had produced a flood of discontent, and the nobles looked to John for redress. Yet if he made financial concessions, his own revenue would suffer at a time when prices were rocketing. The hire of mercenary troops had increased two-fold since his father's day. His defence estimates called for more money, not less. On the other hand, if John placated his barons with castles and territories, he would undermine his own capacity to cope with possible rebellion. The younger brother had inherited a formidable problem from his senior.

The first demand of substance came not from England but Scotland. William the Lion had not been slow to exploit the possibilities of Richard's death. His price for transferring his allegiance to John, he now announced, was the border counties of Northumberland and Cumberland. John, still on the Continent when he heard the news, had bought time with a conciliatory message. If the Scottish king would keep the peace until he, John, arrived in England, he would "satisfy him in all his demands." That John had any intention of surrendering two counties to William is highly improbable, but it had been important to postpone the issue until he could negotiate from the strength of the English throne. Soon after the coronation, three envoys arrived from Scotland with a sharp ultimatum: hand over the border counties forthwith or William would "regain all to which he was entitled" by armed force. John replied diplomatically that if his "very dear" neighbour would come and meet him, "I will do whatever is right in relation to his requests." The Bishop of Durham was sent to Scotland to escort William into England, while John, after a brief pilgrimage to Canterbury, St. Albans (north of London) and St. Edmunds (East Anglia), travelled to the midlands to await his guest at Northampton.

William never arrived. Instead, he gave John forty days to meet his terms, or suffer the consequences. By now, John's patience had run out. Having secured England, his pressing need was to return to the Continent. Placing the defence of Cumberland and Northumberland in the hands of a new sheriff, his adherent William of Stuteville, the king headed south to embark for Normandy. Nothing came of William the Lion's bravado. Perhaps he had been bluffing; or perhaps, as Roger of Howden had it, he had been deterred by a sense of impending misfortune. "When William was preparing to invade England with an army, he went to the shrine of St. Margaret, the former queen of the Scots, at Dunfermline, and passed the night there. Whereupon, he was warned by a divine admonition not to invade England, and he dismissed his army."

On June 20, 1199, John sailed from Shoreham for Dieppe, at the mouth of the Béthune in eastern Normandy, "accompanied by a very big army from England." Almost immediately, there was a brief test of strength with Philip, who besieged a castle in this part of the duchy, only to be driven away by John's men. That the Normans had awaited John's return eagerly was evidenced by the fact that, a mere four days after his landing, they flocked on horse and foot to meet him at Rouen, offering their services against the French. But John was not ready for a major clash. Accordingly, he agreed to a truce with Philip until August 16, thus gaining some eight weeks in which to mature his plans. During John's stay in England, his mother had continued to harry Arthur, energetically attacking her grandson and his followers at Tours and elsewhere. Cunningly, the old lady had contacted Philip and bowed her wizened head to him in homage for the dukedom of Aquitaine. The French king could not dispute her right to the vast territory she had inherited so long ago from her father. What he did not know was that she had secretly agreed to abandon the practical sovereignty of Aquitaine in favour of her son John.

The close understanding between the aged Eleanor and her single surviving son at this time contrasted agreeably with the mutual hostilities of the family in bygone days. John used the weeks of the truce to cultivate other alliances. He entered into negotiations with the powerful counts of Flanders and Boulogne. On August 13, Baldwin IX of Flanders did homage to the English king. There was also contact betwen John and his nephew Otto, the son of his sister Matilda by the Duke of Saxony. Otto IV had succeeded to the crown of Germany on the death of the old emperor, Henry. He promised to send help against Philip. During the same period, John's half brother Geoffrey, Archbishop of York, arrived in Rouen from Rome. Business in Italy had caused him to miss the coronation. Now he was warmly received by his royal relative.

On August 18, the truce having expired, Philip and John met at the castle of Le Goulet, on the French border, where Philip asked his rival to ratify him in possession of the Vexin, which had been ceded by Richard, and to acknowledge his right to grant the Angevin counties to Arthur. Other demands, now obscure, were made by the French king, which, in the words of the historian of the conference, "the King of England would in no way grant, nor was it proper that he should do so." John's diplomatic endeavours had greatly strengthened his hand.

That same day, he signed an alliance with the Count of Boulogne, and received the homage of a number of French nobles who had been allies of Richard. Presumably, they anticipated an easier time under a king of England than under the king of France.

Philip was in disrepute all round. He had not put himself right with Rome following a disastrous marriage (his second) to a Danish princess named Ingeborg, with whom he had spent but a single night. After obtaining a divorce on very dubious grounds, he had subsequently married Agnes, daughter of the Duke of Meran. The Church was scandalised. "Philip's heart was hardened," wrote a contemporary. "He could be persuaded neither by threats nor kindness to get rid of his adulteress and take back his lawful wife." The ecclesiastical displeasure hanging over him was an acute embarrassment in his foreign dealings.

Now that the two kings had failed to reach agreement, warfare of the usual desultory nature broke out again. In September, Philip's arrogance led him into a further diplomatic blunder. That month, he captured Balun, in Maine, and razed the castle there. When the leader of Arthur's Breton army, William of Roches, protested at the destruction of a stronghold which, by Philip's own recognition, should belong to Arthur, the Frenchman retorted that he would do as he liked with his conquests. This "opened the eyes" of Arthur's commander, who immediately rode to John's camp, begged an interview with the king, and promised to persuade Arthur, Constance and all their barons to submit to him on condition that he, William of Roches, might advise on their future. John gave him *carte blanche* to arrange the terms of a peace with "my very dear nephew, Arthur . . . to our mutual honour and advantage." With considerable élan, John now engaged Philip near Vendôme, on the Loir, drove him north to Le Mans and, finally, clear out of Maine itself.

At Le Mans, John found Arthur and Constance waiting to make their peace. Here he also received the surrender of Chinon and the seneschalship of Anjou. If John bore any malice toward his nephew and Constance, he was commendably restrained in his behaviour, for he rode to Chinon next day, leaving them to their freedom. Despite this display of goodwill, Arthur appears to have nurtured the suspicion that his uncle intended to imprison him. As soon as the king had departed, Arthur, Constance and many of their followers fled southwest to Angers, which was then in possession of their own camp. Here Constance, despite her marriage to Ranulf of Chester, whom she detested, was wed anew to Guy of Thouars, a noble who hailed from across the Loire, south of Angers. John made no attempt to apprehend them. Instead, he rode to the family pantheon at Fontevrault to assist in the funeral of his sister Jane. Jane had married the King of Sicily, on his death becoming the wife of the Count of Toulouse. She was the nearest in age to John of Eleanor's children, and they must have seen a good deal of each other in their childhood.

Autumn brought a new truce. It was arranged by the pope's legate, Cardinal Peter of Padua, who was still in France after negotiating a peace between Philip and Richard earlier that year. Peter was anxious that this original truce should now be renewed. Since such an understanding implied papal recognition of John as his brother's heir, the English king was not reluctant to be pacified. Philip, for his part, could not afford to offend the pope further. At the end of October, therefore, it was agreed that hostilities should cease until the middle of the following January. The understanding was that there might then be a more lasting treaty.

John spent Christmas peacefully in Normandy, while in England the twelfth century gave way to the thirteenth on a festive note. Among the last orders John issued in 1199 was a measure to regulate the price of wine in his kingdom. John was a great wine drinker. When his court took to the road, fifteen wagons were needed to carry the barrels. But wine was too expensive for the majority of people in the island. It had to be imported, and the middlemen took a good profit. John ruled that red wine should not be sold above fourpence a gallon, and white wine not above sixpence. The law became effective in December, and the merchants promptly announced that it was ruining them. To help them, the maximum prices were raised by twopence a gallon. Even so, wine now became available to a new class of drinker, with the immediate result, according to Roger of Howden, that "the land was filled with drinking and drunkards."

This was nothing new in England, where heavy drinking and eating was a long-standing tradition among those who could afford it. The followers of Anglo-Saxon chiefs had spent the winter evenings drinking themselves into torpor or, not infrequently, into insult and violence. Their drink was a highly charged fermentation of honey and water called mead. "He who grapples with me and struggles against my strength," wrote a Saxon poet of the sugary mead, "inevitably seeks the earth with his back." From its earliest days, the Church had tried to discourage drunkenness, but without great success. An elaborate set of early Christian laws stipulated: "If priests become drunk through ignorance they must do penance on bread and water for seven days. If through negligence, fifteen days. If through wantonness, forty days; deacons and monks four weeks, subdeacons three, clerks two and laymen one week. He who encourages a man to get drunk through kindness must do penance twenty days. If for spite, he is to be adjudged as a homicide."

Though the Romans had introduced wine to England, the popular Anglo-Saxon drinks were mead and ale. The Normans reintroduced wine to the country. Hitherto, they had been noted for their frugality and temperance, but the English apparently changed all that. According to the contemporary historian William of Malmesbury, they taught their conquerors "to eat till they became surfeited and to drink till they were sick." Norman London tempted the visitor with an abundance of food and drink. Wrote William FitzStephen, a clerk in the service of Thomas Becket:

> On the riverside of London, where the wine flows from ships and cellars, there is a public cook-shop. Every day, depending on the season, one can find here roast, fried and boiled dishes, fish large and small; the tougher flesh for the poor, the more tender for the wealthy, including venison and birds big and little . . . No matter how many knights or foreigners arrive at the city, or are about to depart, at whatever hour of night or day, they can satisfy their particular appetites.

By John's time, the Church seems to have made little progress towards temperance. Indeed, many ecclesiastics had nothing to learn about eating and drinking from their flocks. Gerald of Wales was disgusted by the excesses he witnessed at the table of the prior of Canterbury.

> Sixteen or more of the most costly dishes were heaped on the table in order, or rather out of any order. Potherbs were scarcely touched. For one could see such a selection of fish, roast, boiled, stuffed and fried, so many dishes made with eggs and pepper by accomplished cooks, so many flavourings and condiments mixed with similar skill to titillate gluttony and stimulate appetite. Amidst such plenitude, one discerned an abundance of wine and strong drink, metheglin [a spiced or medicated liquor], claret, must, mead, mulberry juice and all that intoxicates—drink so choice that the good beer of England, made at its best in Kent, found no place among it. Beer among such drinks is as potherbs among such dishes. Such excess and

extravagance might one see both in food and wine that those who indulged themselves must have reached the point of revulsion. Even to look at it made one weary.

John and Philip entered the thirteenth century—that era of imaginative stirrings which was to produce Dante and Giotto, Innocent III and the consolidation and spread of Christianity, St. Louis and the great diffusion of French culture and Gothic art—in an appropriately constructive mood. The end of the truce period in mid-January coincided with the pronouncement of an interdict on the kingdom of France to punish Philip for his marital discrepancies. He had enough on his hands without a renewal of the old war, and John approached the second round of negotiations tactfully. At a conference between the two kings at the old trysting place near Les Andelys, there was a refreshing co-operation which clearly owed something to John's restraint in the face of his rival's embarrassment. As the foundation of a peaceful settlement, they agreed that Philip's only son, Louis, who was then thirteen, should marry John's niece, Blanche, the young daughter of his sister Eleanor by Alfonso VIII of Castile. John was to provide the bride with a dowry of such Norman castles as Philip had possessed at the time of Richard's death, the city and county of Evreux in eastern Normandy, and a sum of English money, variously stated at twenty or thirty thousand marks. He also undertook to end his alliance with Emperor Otto. Upon the fulfilment of these terms, Philip was to recognise John as heir to all Richard's possessions not ceded by the treaty.

On John's behalf, the remarkable queen mother, Eleanor, now set out to cross the Pyrenees, escorted by Mercadier, to fetch her granddaughter from Castile. At the same time, John, accompanied by Archbishop Geoffrey, sailed for England to raise the money for Blanche's dowry. After consultation with the justiciar, a scutage of two marks on the knight's fee was called for, and a tax of three shillings imposed on every hide of land, a hide being approximately one hundred and twenty acres, or as much land as might embrace one free family and its dependants. In March, John travelled to York, where he summoned William of Scotland to meet him, but William once again failed to turn up.

At the end of April, the king returned to Normandy and took possession of Blanche, whom Eleanor had successfully secured from her daughter and son-in-law. The trek to Spain and back had been a hard one. On the return trip, Eleanor lost the captain of her escort. "On the second day in Easter week, Mercadier, chief of the Brabançons, was slain in the city of Bordeaux by a knight in the service of Brandin [a rival mercenary captain]. After this, Queen Eleanor, being fatigued with old age and the length of the journey, retired to the abbey at Fontevrault, where she remained." On May 22, the treaty of Le Goulet was concluded. Blanche, a pretty child who was to grow into a beautiful woman and a faithful wife, was married to Louis by the Archbishop of Bordeaux. Philip invested John with the Angevin dominions, including Brittany, and Arthur was produced to do homage to his uncle for that duchy. The youth then returned to Paris in Philip's charge.

John now embarked on a triumphal tour of his continental territories, travelling south by way of Angers and Poitiers to Bordeaux. "He took a substantial army," declared Roger of Howden, "but nobody was found to oppose him." In England, men sneered at the concessions their king had made to Philip, and called him a "peace-lover." In fact, most of the territories conceded had been in Philip's hands already. These and the cash settlement in Blanche's dowry had been a small price to pay for the disposal of Arthur's claim, the end of a costly war and the undisputed title to an empire extending from the Tweed to the Pyrenees, from the mountains of Donegal to the peaks of

Auvergne. John could be proud of his diplomacy. In less than twelve months since his coronation at Westminster, he had won more from Philip than had Richard in the entire ten years of his reign.

Chapter 6
ISABELLE OF ANGOULÊME

Cry havoc, kings! back to the stained field.
Shakespeare, King John, *II.i*

For ten years, faceless, formless and forgotten in the chronicles, a ghostly figure had haunted John's history—the figure of Isabel of Gloucester, his wife. Desirable, one assumes, she was not, for in all John's travels and campaigns since the marriage at Marlborough, there was no indication that he was ever accompanied by his lawful bedmate. Nor, as events would bear out, was John by any means impervious to the pleasures of female companionship. Controversial, or even colourful, Isabel cannot have been, for there was no mention of her asserting herself in her own right. The coronation at Westminster was reported without a mention of her name, and her whereabouts before or after can only be guessed at. Perhaps she settled quietly and insignificantly at one of her husband's English seats, Marlborough or Lancaster, passing some of the time with her sisters and her powerful brother-in-law the Earl of Hertford.

At any rate, after ten years of marriage Isabel was childless, and John, having availed himself of her dowry and the earldom of Gloucester, set about freeing himself from his retiring wife. The task was not difficult. Isabel was John's cousin. In the terminology of matrimonial law, they were related in the third degree of consanguinity and could not be deemed properly married unless the pope gave them dispensation. At the time of the marriage, the primate of the day, Archbishop Baldwin, had forbidden them to cohabit, and had expressed his displeasure by laying an interdict on John's estates. This had been lifted by a papal legate then in England, presumably on the ground that John would press an appeal to the pope. Significantly, the prince had done no more about the matter. Already, he seems to have had doubts about the durability of the relationship. Consequently, on becoming King of England, John was in the flexible position of being married in due form, while retaining a useful legal let-out.

His motives in seeking to dismiss Isabel were not entirely, perhaps not even primarily, personal. After ten years, the fruitless marriage seemed unlikely to produce an heir to oppose the pretensions of Arthur, while the freedom to choose another wife from the eligible daughters of Europe conferred an obvious political advantage. Unlike Philip of France, whose indiscreet disposal of an unloved partner had brought upon him the wrath of an outraged Church, John moved in a thoroughly circumspect manner. No less than six bishops were consulted, three from Normandy and three from Aquitaine, the consensus being that the marriage was void, that John was a single man. Isabel did not protest at the decision. Perhaps she was glad to be free again. She was still a considerable heiress, and was to remarry twice.

Back in the marriage market, John turned his eyes south. Richard had wed a Spanish princess from the border kingdom of Navarre in order to have friends on his southernmost fron-

Isabelle of Angoulême

tier. Beyond Navarre, however, the hostility of Castile and Aragon towards their Navarrese neighbours proclaimed them the natural allies of Philip Augustus. By logical progress, John looked beyond Castile and Aragon for an alliance that would divert these kingdoms from their northerly interests. The solution seemed to be Portugal, whose king had a marriageable daughter. Early in 1200, perhaps by invitation, Portuguese envoys were at John's court with proposals which interested the king sufficiently for him to dispatch a return embassy to Lisbon. Their journey was wasted. By the time they arrived back to present their report, events had overtaken them. John's eye had settled elsewhere. He had already remarried.

From Bordeaux, John's tour of his continental fiefs following the peace with Philip, had taken him south to St. Sever, at the foot of the Pyrenees, then in a great anti-clockwise loop through Aquitaine, via Agenois and Périgord to Angoulême. In September 1199, Eleanor had formally transferred Aquitaine to John as her rightful heir, instructing her vassals to do him homage and receive him peacefully. John knew enough of the dominion, which his brother had ruled by the sword, and in which he had perished, to realise that the best guarantee of a peaceful welcome was the army he took with him. With the possible exception of Ireland, Aquitaine harboured the most unruly barons in the Angevin empire. Many were a law unto themselves in their own districts, and disorder and rebellion were their traditional way of life.

Of all the lords of Aquitaine, none was more awkwardly independent than Count Aymer of Angoulême, whose county, the Angoumois, lying at the very crossroads of the duchy, dominated its passages in almost every direction. So contemptuous was Aymer of the Dukes of Aquitaine that, ignoring his obligations to them, he performed homage directly to the King of France. Even Richard, who had defeated Aymer in battle, could not break the count's wayward spirit. At last

Richard had been driven to a more subtle strategy in dealing with the family of Angoulême.

To the north of Angoumois, in lower Poitou, dwelt another great fighting family, the Lusignans. For years, the Lusignans had pitted their warlike skills in rebellion against the Angevin rulers, slaying their representatives and threatening the counts of Poitou. But there was a bond of common interest between Richard and the Lusignans in their passion for crusading. Hugh the Brown of Lusignan, the present head of the family in Poitou, was a distinguished crusader, while two of his uncles had been crowned King of Jerusalem. During the third crusade, Richard and Hugh had struck up a friendship, and this the king had sustained on their return by extending favours to the family.

Among other things, he had held before Hugh the prospect of acquiring the rich lands of La Marche to the east of Angoumois and lower Poitou. La Marche was jealously coveted by Aymer of Angoulême, and by encouraging their rivalry for the territory, Richard had achieved a balance of power in the locality, which conveniently neutralised the broader troublemaking propensities of the two families. On Richard's death, the feud was disrupted. Exploiting the confusion which surrounded John's succession, Hugh had abducted Eleanor and extracted from her under duress the surrender of La Marche. With this issue settled, the two families had agreed to come together to their mutual advantage, and it had been decided that Aymer's daughter and heiress, Isabelle, a girl of about twelve, should be betrothed to Hugh the Brown. At the time that John led his triumphal cavalcade through Aquitaine, therefore, his satisfaction was somewhat undermined by the prospect of a marriage that would unite two notoriously rebellious families and establish a bloc of territories almost the size of Normandy to cut his continental dominions in half.

It was against this background that the King of England, hav-

Isabelle of Angoulême 103

ing completed his tour of southern Aquitaine, led his festive column north into Poitou and became, in the first week of July, the guest of Hugh of Lusignan at his ancestral castle between Poitiers and Niort. Here, in accordance with custom, the young Isabelle was living with the family of her prospective husband until she should be considered of marriageable age. John appears to have been captivated by the girl from the start. Her youthfulness did not dismay him; perhaps it aroused him. Clearly, the second Isabelle was everything the first Isabel was not, for in her it was said of him at a later date, "he believed he possessed everything he could desire." Suddenly, passion and policy fused in a bold plan.

The king had summoned Aymer to meet him at Hugh the Brown's castle, and now, under the roof of an unsuspecting host, John proposed to make Isabelle his own bride. At one stroke he would gain the loyalty of the house of Angoulême, secure the vital passages of Angoumois, break up the threatening alliance of Aymer and Hugh the Brown, and take himself a captivating child bride.

Portugal was forgotten. Aymer, in no hesitation about breaking his contract with Hugh to make his daughter Queen of England, snatched Isabelle from under the nose of her betrothed, carried her back to Angoulême, and there, on the twenty-third of the next month, married her to a king too impatient to submit to a formal engagement. John and Isabelle left Angoulême a few days after the wedding and proceeded north at a leisurely amble, calling at Fontevrault, where the little bride was presented to an ailing Eleanor. September was spent sightseeing in Normandy, doubtless a revelation to a girl who cannot ever have been so far from home before. Here, Isabelle saw the sea for the first time. At the beginning of October, the couple crossed to England.

On the eighth of that month, her young mind perhaps still reeling at the dramatic events which had befallen her, Isabelle of Angoulême was crowned Queen of England at Westminster by Hubert Walter. The sum of about thirty pounds seems to have been spent on her royal robes. Amidst the rugged, jostling barons in the abbey, she must have presented a frail and touching figure. John now set out to complete the grand tour of his dominions started on the Continent. His design was to familiarise himself with as much of his empire as possible. By the time he had added the systematic exploration of England to that already completed oversea, he would have attained a personal knowledge of his vast and varied realm unprecedented in the history of his royal predecessors.

Amidst the reddening leaves of autumn, the long convoy of creaking carts which comprised the bulk of the royal entourage coiled in a great sweep south to Guildford, west through Marlborough and Malmesbury, and north via Gloucester, up the Severn Valley to Bridgenorth. Having viewed the Welsh March, John turned east across Cannock Chase to the Trent Valley, which he followed to Nottingham, and on to Lincoln. A long-standing tradition forbade the English kings to enter Lincoln on pain of sudden death, but John waved aside the superstitious among his followers and passed through the city gate. He wanted to see everything. Visiting the new minster there, still under construction, he offered a golden chalice at the altar.

The occasion was indeed accompanied by a death, but not the death of the venturing king. The aged and venerated Bishop Hugh, who had regaled John with his solemn advice upon Richard's death, had returned from the Continent with quartan fever. At the time of Isabelle's coronation, John had gone to his sick-bed in London, confirming the bishop's will and comforting him with the promise that the wills of all prelates would be honoured in the future. Until then, it had been the royal custom to confiscate the property of prelates upon their death.

Hugh's demise coincided with John's stay at Lincoln, and the king showed his regard for the old bishop by helping to carry the coffin to its last resting place. The new minster had acquired its first wonder-working agency, an important acquisition for any cathedral, since the tombs of the venerated were held to possess healing properties, and those who visited them brought alms to the church box. The first miracle attributed to the remains of Hugh was the restoration to life of a Lincoln boy who had been dead for many hours.

Meanwhile, a further summons had been issued to William of Scotland to meet John at Lincoln. This time, William prudently put in an appearance, accompanied by an impressive and colourful retinue. Also present to meet the king in that city were Gruffyd ap Rhys of Wales, son of the great Rhys, and the Prince of Galloway. Lincoln had never seen such an assembly. The streets and hostels were filled to overflowing with bishops and barons from England, Scotland, Wales and Ireland, and their multifarious retinues. On November 22, John led William the Lion to a hill just outside the city, "where all could view them," and accepted the Scot's fealty "for life, limb and for earthly honour against all men," William pressing in return for the cession of Northumberland, Cumberland and Westmorland. John promised to think about it.

Before leaving Lincoln, the king was approached by twelve Cistercian abbots who complained that foresters were driving their cattle from the royal forests and pastures. The Cistercians, a stricter offshoot of the Benedictine order, were renowned for their austerity, "believed and asserted to be the surest way to heaven." According to William of Malmesbury, "they wear nothing made with furs or linen, nor finely spun raiment. They have two tunics with cowls, but wear nothing extra in winter . . . They sleep clothed and girded, use no light other than daylight, and at all times observe the strictest silence." The

Cistercians were substantial sheep farmers, and their industry and frugality had combined to make them prosperous. Richard had thought them worthy of his patronage and favours.

Earlier in John's reign, however, the Cistercians had incurred his displeasure by refusing to pay taxes without the authority of their general chapter. In a moment of anger, he had deprived them of the privilege of grazing their beasts on the royal lands. While he had quickly reversed this decision, it seems that his change of heart had not been understood by his foresters. So upset was he by the news the abbots brought him, that he now knelt at their feet and begged their forgiveness. Not only did he confirm them in their grazing rights, but he promised to build them an abbey. This he did later, at Beaulieu, Hampshire, endowing it with its own holding of land in the New Forest together with one hundred and thirty-two head of cattle and an annual gift of two hundred and fifty gallons of wine.

Travelling south through Northampton and Abingdon, John spent Christmas with Isabelle at Guildford, where "the king distributed many raiments of a festive nature to his knights." Britons had celebrated December 25 as a festival long before Christianity came to their country. The first certain identification of that date with the birth of Christ falls in the year 354, whereas Bede, the oldest of English historians, related that "the ancient peoples of the Angli began the year on December 25 when we now celebrate the birthday of the Lord; and the very night which is now so holy to us they called in their tongue *modranecht,* or mothers' night, probably because of the ceremonies they performed in an all-night vigil." In northern lands, mid-December was a crucial time for pagan sun-worshippers since it was then that the days were shortest and the sun at its weakest. They held feasts at the period later known as Christmas, building great fires to give the sun god strength and to bring him back to life. Medieval Christians still built fires

Isabelle of Angoulême

to celebrate their festival, a custom eventually fossilised in the shape of the yule log.

The depth of winter was not a time normally chosen for travelling by those who could avoid it, but John had yet to complete his inspection of the nation, and January saw him heading north again. Picking up his original trail at Lincoln, he made for the Northeast, crossing the Humber into the East Riding of Yorkshire, then proceeding via Beverley, Scarborough, Durham and Newcastle as far as the old Roman wall which had separated England from the Scots, before turning west along the Scottish March. This brought him to Carlisle, in Cumberland, where the wagons, litters and outriders of the perambulating court, windswept and weather-beaten, must have caused a sensation. The city had not been visited by a member of the English royal family since John's grandfather had called there in 1149. It was mid-March before the king and queen, braving the wolf-infested Pennines (wolves did not become extinct in Britain until the end of the fifteenth century), returned to the South, in time to spend Easter at Canterbury.

Easter (a name derived, according to Bede, from Eostre, the Anglo-Saxon goddess of spring) was the greatest of the medieval festivals. In France, the year was reckoned to start at Easter. Churches were decorated with the most splendid ornaments available, baptisms were plentiful, and acts of generosity, such as the releasing of prisoners, were performed by those in authority. It was also one of the three great feasts of the year, together with Christmas and Whitsuntide, when the English kings traditionally wore their crowns, exhibiting themselves in all their magnificence and dignity to impress their subjects. Henry II had allowed the custom to lapse, but John revived it, he and Isabelle wearing their crowns during Mass at Canterbury Cathedral before proceeding to a lavish banquet as guests of the archbishop, Hubert Walter.

The brief but busy interlude marked by the royal tours of England and the Continent revealed interesting facets of John's character. His desire to see how his subjects lived and what was going on in the various corners of his empire, was characteristic of him. His humility in redressing the wrong done the Cistercians, though not lacking self-interest, showed him willing to acknowledge mistakes and to repent the fiery side of his nature, while in placing his shoulder to Hugh of Lincoln's coffin he displayed a very human attachment to a well-meaning companion. The inclinations to stand by old friends and to tolerate those who upset him for their honesty of purpose were not the least of his attributes. He also acknowledged the value of tradition in reviving the crown-wearing. For Isabelle, it must have been a promising, if hectic, introduction to her husband and his kingdom.

For several months, the Lusignans nursed their injury quietly, perhaps expecting John to compensate them in some way for the loss of Isabelle. When compensation was not forthcoming, they began to plot the revenge of the insult. This John must have expected. Indeed, the breakdown of the alliance between the families of Lusignan and Angoulême, the renewal of the old rivalry between them, was among the most predictable results of his marriage. It proved, however, a dangerous policy, for the house of Lusignan had many ramifications—including the county of Eu in Normandy, which was held by Hugh's brother Ralph—and the trouble threatened to be more widespread than John had anticipated. In order to contain it, he struck the first blow, commanding his seneschal in Normandy, Guarine of Clapion, to seize the Count of Eu's castle at Driencourt. The king also called upon the men of La Marche to pay homage directly to him instead of to Hugh the Brown. When the enraged Lusignans threw off their allegiance and called on Philip of France to help them, Eleanor, Aymer and

Isabelle of Angoulême

others urged John to come over in person before things got out of hand.

On May 1, John issued writs to those in England who owed him military service to be ready at Portsmouth on the thirteenth for an expedition to the Continent. The barons demurred. Assembling at Leicester, a body of them sent a message to the king informing him that they would not attend at Portsmouth unless "he gave them their rights." The same phrase had cropped up at the time of John's accession and, since John had not deprived them of any rights, it seems likely that the term was used to denote those feudal privileges of the baronage which had been curtailed by the centralisation of law and administration under the Angevin monarchs. In other words, the barons wanted some measure of regression to the days when each had made his own justice, exercising absolute and irresponsible control of his territory.

If they had anticipated in John a weak ruler from whom such privileges might be wrung, there was already some reason to feel disappointment. The king's progress through the kingdom, clearly demonstrating his intention of stamping his authority on the provinces, had been viewed with apprehension by the local lords. There was also a growing reluctance among the barons, who became more English with each generation, to identify with the king's continental interests, and consequently to follow him abroad in foreign wars. At least, this was perhaps felt to be a good time to bring pressure to bear on John for concessions, and there may even had been some sympathy in England for the Lusignans, who, in protesting their grievances, were setting an example many an English baron would like to have felt strong enough to emulate.

John's reply was swift and unequivocal. He threatened to take the castles of those who failed to obey him, making an example of one William of Albini, who narrowly averted the seizure of his stronghold by giving his son as hostage for his future behaviour. The barons, unprepared for such positive action, promptly stopped demanding their "rights" and hastened to Portsmouth. If the episode can be taken as a preliminary round in the struggle between John and his magnates, the king clearly won it without undue effort. At Portsmouth, he coolly dismissed the majority of his half-hearted nobles from the feudal force, retaining instead the money they had brought with them for their expenses. With the money, he could hire continental mercenaries. He did, however, send a force of two hundred knights to Normandy ahead of him to defend the borders of the duchy under the capable command of William Marshal and Roger of Lacy. Shortly afterwards, John and Isabelle crossed the Channel.

Philip Augustus cannot have been unaware of the advantage to be gained by him in exploiting the Lusignan dispute. But he held his hand for the moment. John's show of strength in Aquitaine and his other territories following the treaty of Le Goulet had been impressive, and the French king could not yet know to what extent loyalty to his rival had eroded. He therefore received the appeal from the Lusignans cautiously. When John arrived in Normandy, Philip urged them to cease their rebellious activities in Poitou, while he rode to Les Andelys for a conference with the English king. The details are unknown, but that John was persuaded of the goodwill of Philip is attested by the fact that the former, accompanied by his queen and court, almost immediately paid a state visit to Paris, a rare gesture by an Angevin monarch. Here, Philip entertained them lavishly, even moving out of the royal palace so that they could move into it. In convivial spirit, the kings agreed that John should allow his rebellious vassals to submit their grievances against him at a legal trial.

John did not rush to implement the undertaking. Philip's eagerness to please him was reassuring, especially since the last thing he could afford was another protracted war. Moving down to Chinon, where he was close enough to the Lusignans to make them feel uneasy, he let them simmer in their anxiety while he spent the summer amusing Isabelle and settling some continental business. Richard's widow, Berengaria, came to him and asked that he should settle her estate. He gave her, in accord with the terms of her marriage, the city of Bayeux, two castles in Anjou and an income of one thousand marks. Constance of Brittany died, seemingly reconciled to John in the end, and he supervised the execution of her will. At last, he turned to the Lusignans. Richard would have visited them with fire and sword. John's methods were less drastic. He had agreed to put the dispute to legal trial, and this he did—though not as Philip had intended. John arraigned the Lusignans for treason, and invited them to prove their innocence by judicial duel.

The judicial duel, or trial by combat, was a perfectly lawful procedure. The assumption behind it was simple: God would bless the just cause with victory. In the words of a thirteenth-century text, "If the defendant can defend himself until the stars appear in the sky . . . it is our will that judgement shall pass for the defendant." It was an age in which the law, though hedged with complex formalities, left a great deal in the final throw to divine justice. Litigation, very much a question of one man's word against another, commonly involved "witnesses" testifying to the trustworthiness of the word rather than giving objective evidence. Thus the defendant who could bring a required number of compurgators, or "oath-helpers," to swear that his oath of innocence was pure, won his case and might go free. If he could not, or if the case was such that the plaintiff's oath had priority, matters were often resolved by the ordeal.

At least three types of medieval ordeal are recorded: the so-called ordeals by iron and by hot and cold water. In the ordeal by iron, the accused was required to carry a glowing iron for nine feet; in the ordeal by hot water, to plunge his hand and arm into boiling water and pick up a stone. These proceedings were carried out in church, the hand then being bound and left for three days. If it had not festered in this time, the man was cleared. The third ordeal, also supervised by the clergy, was less sporting in its chances. After a three-day fast, the accused was stripped and thrown, with his thumbs and toes tied together, into cold water. At the same time, the priest adjured the water, in the name of the Father, Son and Holy Ghost, "that thou do not in any manner receive this man if he be guilty by act, consent or knowledge of what he is accused, but make him swim upon thee so there may be no counterfeiting." If he floated he was guilty; if he sank, he was innocent.

In the trial by combat, the well-to-do were commonly represented by their champions, and in John's case he had employed a group of notoriously lethal duellists to uphold his challenge. Understandably loath to stretch the resources of their Deity too far, the Lusignans spurned the challenge and appealed once more to Philip Augustus. The early months of 1202 passed in a battle of sophistry between the two kings, each testing the resolve of the other while endeavouring to present himself in a correct light. When Philip pressed for a fair trial for the Lusignans, John agreed, fixed a date, but finally refused to guarantee the defendants safe conduct to the meeting place. Their predictable failure to appear was interpreted by the English king as the rejection of a genuine offer. When Philip demanded three of John's castles as security for the honouring of his promise, John complained bitterly that his rival was abusing the treaty between them, and called upon Hubert Walter to witness his own humility and moderation.

Philip next summoned John to Paris to answer for his failure of justice. The English king responded with a nice technicality: as Duke of Normandy he was excused by ancient law from attending the French court anywhere but on the land of the duchy. With equal aplomb, Philip replied that the summons

Isabelle of Angoulême

was addressed not to the Duke of Normandy, but to the Count of Anjou and Maine, in which capacity John was bound to come before him. Thus the wrangle continued through bluff and counter-bluff. Neither king was entirely sure of his ground, but John was playing the more dangerous game, and perhaps playing it a trifle complacently. For while his desire for peace was founded on the need to consolidate what he already held, and to nurse his depleted financial resources, Philip's reluctance to declare war resulted merely from a temporary uncertainty. His ultimate aim had not changed. Sooner or later, he intended to smash the Angevin hold on France.

On April 28, John failed to meet the deadline set for his appearance before the French court. In his absence, the French barons judged him an insubordinate vassal of their sovereign and pronounced his forfeiture of the lands he and his ancestors had held of the King of France. Philip then knighted Arthur of Brittany, declaring him the master of all the fiefs inherited by John, except Normandy. Normandy, the vital doorstep to the Continent from England, Philip meant to keep to himself. Meanwhile, French forces had already been active on the Norman frontier, destroying a castle at Boutavant, near Les Andelys, and capturing a number of other border towns. On both sides, knights and barons reached for their armour. The armoured knight of the thirteenth century was a formidable spectacle. The familiar conical helmet of the Normans had largely gone out of fashion, replaced by the flat-topped barrel helm, the shape of an inverted saucepan. The aperture cut in front to give vision was of many forms, from slits to a sort of porthole. Some took the shape of crosses, while in more complex helmets there were adjustable visors. The barrel helm gave its wearer a frighteningly robotlike appearance, but, oddly, was considerably less practical in a protective sense than the conical helmet. Whereas the latter presented a glancing surface to sword or axe blows, the flat top of the barrel helm was vulnerable. Moreover, a blow on the side could render the wearer unconscious.

The rest of the knight's armour was at a stage of development between the simple hauberk, or mail coat, of the Normans, and the fully plated armour of a later date. While the Norman coat of mail had commonly stopped short at the knees, the mail of the thirteenth century completely embraced the wearer, legs, feet, arms and hands being covered. Small pieces of plate were beginning to appear, particularly at knees and elbows. On top of the suit of mail, the thirteenth-century man-at-arms wore a loose sleeveless smock, girded about the waist by his sword belt, and he carried a heart-shaped shield emblazoned with the device of his house. This might be repeated on the flag or pennon affixed to his lance. Horses were not armoured, but wore wide striped breast-straps, and were sometimes caparisoned in rich materials.

John was poorly prepared for a renewal of the war with France. Since the commencement of the peace of Le Goulet, he had neglected his contact with Otto of Germany; his ally Baldwin of Flanders had become more interested in crusading than fighting the French; the Count of Boulogne now identified his cause with Philip. There was also the ever present problem of money. Writing to the Cistercian abbots, whom he had asked for a loan, John pleaded the treachery of his enemy: "It is common knowledge, as you must know, how the King of France unjustifiably assaults us, seeking by any means in his power to take from us our inheritance, in breach of the peace made between us and sealed by oaths and documents." On July 8, having captured the covering stronghold of Gournay, near the border, Philip advanced with braying trumpets and lofted pennons into eastern Normandy as far as Radepont, some ten miles from Rouen. John placed the defences of Rouen in order, spent the best part of a week organising the mercenaries his recruiting officers had raised in Flanders and elsewhere, then sallied forth to drive the French from the vicinity.

Philip Augustus, now thirty-seven, bald and prematurely aged by twenty-two years at the taxing helm of France, was no dashing general. Such was his concern for the safety of his person that he would ride only the quietest of horses. Faced by John at Radepont, he chose characteristically to retire and renew the pressure elsewhere. In this, he was persistent, hammering doggedly at the eastern defences of the duchy while Arthur, an eager fifteen, led two hundred knights boldly through the Loire Valley to stir things up in the South.

For one whose basically peaceful disposition had earned from the English barons the disparaging sobriquet "Softsword," John had so far proved a remarkably capable commander. At this stage, his strategic instinct did not fail him. Detailing part of his force to harry eastern Brittany, thus diverting many Bretons who might otherwise have marched to join Arthur, he left the Norman garrisons to hold off Philip and rode south with the rest of his army to protect the vulnerable heartland of his empire. He was in time to effect one of the most dramatic rescues in medieval history.

At Tours, Arthur was joined by Hugh the Brown, Geoffrey of Lusignan and other rebels. Hearing that Eleanor of Aquitaine, despite her eighty years and her ill health, had left Fontevrault and was scurrying south for Poitiers to secure her son's interests there, Arthur resolved to capture his grandmother. On July 30, John was approaching Le Mans when he was informed that his mother was in acute danger. Arthur and the rebels had given chase to her, and her seizure was imminent. The king waited to hear no more. Accompanied by the most mobile section of his army, he spurred his horse in pursuit of the pursuers. Eleanor and her handful of retainers had taken refuge in the castle of Mirebeau, between Thouars and Poitiers, and more than eighty miles from Le Mans. The gates had scarcely closed behind them when the rebels swept into the town and assaulted the castle walls. "There was not strength in the garrison to resist them." On July 31, the old lady looked out from the keep to see her grandson's knights in the inner enclosure of the stronghold. There was only the door of the tower, "and a few soldiers," between her and capture.

With their quarry at their mercy, Arthur and his men settled within the castle for the night, content to leave the storming of the keep for the morning. Meanwhile, "travelling by day and night," John reached Mirebeau in a speed which amazed the French chroniclers, routed his enemies in the town and found an unguarded way into the castle. The rebels within the stronghold were breakfasting on pigeon pie when John's knights burst in upon them with drawn swords and took them with hardly any resistance. "We captured," John wrote to England exultantly, "our nephew Arthur, Geoffrey of Lusignan, Hugh the Brown, Andrew of Chauvigni, the viscount of Châtellerault, Raymond Thouars, Savary of Mauléon, Hugh Baugé and all our other enemies there. There were more than two hundred knights, and not one escaped. Praise God for our victory."

It was a brilliant stroke. John had led his force from Le Mans to Mirebeau, seized the town, reconnoitred the castle and set up his dawn attack in less than twenty-four hours. In one swoop, he had rendered the rebellion against him leaderless. In Normandy, John's captains on the eastern front were elated. Philip was besieging Arques, on the north coast. William Marshal sent a monk across the lines to the French army to inform Ralph of Lusignan, Count of Eu, that his brothers had been captured. "He will be pleased with your tidings," William told the monk merrily. Ralph heard the news tight-lipped turned red in the face and retired to his tent. Philip was shaken. Forgetting Arques, he headed south with his army for Tours presumably with the idea of challenging John for the prisoners

But when John approached, the French king retreated, venting his frustration by burning and plundering the country.

John returned in triumph to Normandy, carrying his captives, securely fettered, in farm carts. Arthur and Geoffrey of Lusignan were placed under close guard at Falaise, the birthplace of William the Conqueror. Others were incarcerated elsewhere in Normandy and England, many being placed in Corfe Castle, Dorset. By autumn, their strongholds were in John's hands, and the English king roamed Maine and Anjou unopposed. The year's end saw Philip smouldering in Paris, his bid to sweep his rival from the Continent seemingly doomed to disaster. The King and Queen of England passed Christmas sweetly at Caen, on the coastal plain of Normandy, "dining sumptuously and lying in bed till dinner-time."

Part 2
POPE AND EMPIRE

Chapter 7
THE DISAPPEARANCE OF THE YOUNG DUKE

There is no sure foundation set on blood;
No certain life achiev'd by other's death.
Shakespeare, King John, *IV.ii*

Since history was first recorded, reputations have been raised on whims and ruined by prejudice. Both Richard and John were widely disliked in their own day, by the barons who resented their power, and by churchmen who found them short in piety and patronage. Yet posterity was to regard Richard as the personification of gallantry, chivalry and Christian virtue, the most heroic of English kings, while reviling John as the most evil of tyrants. When Richard was killed at Châlus, a contemporary observed that "avarice, crime, unbounded lust, unscrupulous pride and blind desire have reigned for twice five years; all these an archer lay prostrate by the skilful handling of his weapon." Within a few years, however, it was being accepted that "With him were buried the pride and honour of the chivalry of the West." The foundation of Richard's glowing posthumous career was established by an anonymous panegyrist who accompanied him to the Holy Land and portrayed him as a hero of classic proportions in a work entitled *The Journey of the Crusaders*. Later writers, concerned with promoting the "good fight," upheld Richard the Lion-Hearted as an exemplary figure.

John was less fortunate. At about the turn of the century, a particularly rich seam of historical writing, which had projected Henry II and Richard in a relatively comprehensive light, ran out. William of Newburgh, an Augustinian monk in the West Riding of Yorkshire, who wrote with some sense and sound judgement, died in 1198. Roger of Howden, also writing in Yorkshire, died in 1201. Ralph of Diceto, the French scholar and writer who became Dean of St. Paul's, died in 1202 or 1203. Gerald of Wales lived on, but devoted the last part of his life to writing memoirs of bygone days. From this point, future generations would receive the continuing story of John's life from the scrappy chronicles of cloistered monks prejudiced and embittered by the struggle between Church and state which commenced in earnest in the first decade of the thirteenth century. Isolated in their monastic cells, they knew little of the king save as a disembodied and reputedly hostile force. They did not even record what he looked like.

But there was one man who claimed to know it all. Roger of Wendover, the St. Albans monk, could quote John at the most intimate moments of his reign, knew precisely why this and that happened and had a fund of grisly anecdotes about this king who dared to take issue with the clergy. That Wendover did not pen his account of John's reign until a decade after the king's death, that he laced it with the most improbable and demonstrably inaccurate detail, and that his avowed purpose was didactic rather than historical, did not deter his readers, who lapped it up. What *The Journey of the Crusaders* did for Richard, Wendover's *Flowers of History,* with its travels through purgatory and its cautionary tales of divine wrath, did for John in inverted measure.

Wendover's *Flowers* were brought to full bloom by his successor at St. Albans, Matthew Paris, who performed what the literary world of a later age would describe as a rewrite job. Equal to Wendover in imagination, and surpassing him as a stylist, the fiercely pro-baronial Paris piled picturesque distortion upon distortion to produce a libel of John so hypnotic that it was to bemuse biographers of the maligned king centuries afterwards. From the pen of Matthew Paris flowed the traditional portrait of King John: "a tyrant rather than a king, a destroyer rather than a governor, an oppressor of his own people . . . an insatiable extorter of money, an invader and wrecker of the possessions of his subjects . . . envious of his nobles and relations, violator of their daughters and sisters, wavering and distrustful of the Christian faith." Nor did Paris spare Isabelle, "an incestuous, evil, adulterous woman . . . the king ordered her paramours to be seized and strangled by a rope on her bed."

What one historian has called "the terrible verdict" of Wendover and Paris is at its most potent when the facts of John's life are most puzzling. Then it can be tempting to explain events by traducing his character. The remarkable happenings of 1203, both astonishing and mysterious, have commonly been held to underline the king's blameworthiness.

The triumph of Mirebeau, the last great victory of an English king on French soil until the reign of Edward III, would seem to have left John in an excellent position to secure his holdings on the Continent. If anyone had proclaimed at the time that Normandy, hitherto the most trustworthy of the English king's French fiefs, would virtually be lost to him within twelve months, such a person would have become a figure of derision. Yet, amazingly, this came to pass. Wendover offered a simple explanation. John, as he saw it, was suddenly overcome by "sorcery or witchcraft," so infatuated by his young wife that nothing mattered to him save lying in her arms, passing the days in "incorrigible idleness."

According to Wendover, when messengers came to the king with news that Philip was on the march again, capturing castles and leading away their commanders "ignominiously tied to the tails of their horses," John replied: "Let him get on with it. Whatever he now seizes I will in due course recover." In this portrait, John appears complacent to the point of dementia. "In the midst of all his losses and shame, he remained cheerfully unconcerned, as if he had lost nothing."

A French historian, Charles Petit-Dutaillis, took Wendover's explanation a step further by suggesting that John was a cyclothymic, one given to alternating bouts of inertia and violent activity. None of this fits the known facts, which show this tough, sturdy, energetic little man to have been as restless and continually active as his father. Administrative records reveal him constantly on the move about his territories, seldom spending more than a day or so in one place. More particularly, they indicate that 1203 was no exception. Throughout the year, John was busy attending diligently to the affairs of his domains, both in England and on the Continent.

Another traditional explanation for the surprising reversal of fortune after Mirebeau is that John alienated his adherents by the cruelty with which he treated his prisoners. Cruelty was one of the norms of the age, but there is no evidence that John, at this stage, was excessively brutal—no more so, for instance, than Philip. On the contrary, part of his trouble stemmed from the fact that he quickly released the captured Lusignans, accepting their protestations and oaths of future loyalty. Among others of the king's officers, William Marshal considered such conciliation dangerous, holding that it could only renew the rebellion in the South. Marshal was right. As soon as they were

The Disappearance of the Young Duke

free, the Lusignans broke their pledge and began intriguing against John.

The prisoners at Corfe, in England, were less lucky. Twenty-two out of twenty-five were starved to death, a tragedy often cited as evidence of John's harshness. Yet the thirteenth-century Annals of Margam, penned by an anonymous hand in Glamorganshire, Wales, maintained that the prisoners had seized the keep in an attempt to break out of Corfe Castle and preferred to starve to death rather than surrender their position. If this is correct, John can scarcely be blamed for what happened. At least one of the Corfe prisoners, Savary of Mauléon, seems to have borne no grudge against the king, for he turned up later in the loyal service of his captor.

Perhaps more damaging to John's image at the time was the puzzling disappearance of Arthur of Brittany, and the consequent rumour that implicated John in his murder. It is an episode surrounded by doubts and speculation which loomed sensationally in its own age, which caught the imagination in due course of Shakespeare, and which has remained unsolved to our own day. It is worth noting at the outset that even Wendover, not usually slow to indict John, had reservations. "Throughout France and the continent in general," he wrote, "an opinion about the death of Arthur gained credence in which, apparently, John was suspected by all of having slain him with his own hand; for which reason many turned their affections from the king." The chronicler was content to report the rumour without offering opinion. Matthew Paris went no further. He was uncertain what had happened, and hoped that John was not culpable.

What Wendover did claim to know about was an interview between John and Arthur prior to the latter's disappearance.

After a while, King John came to Falaise castle and commanded that his nephew should be brought before him. When Arthur appeared, the king spoke to him with kindness, promising him many honours if he would break from the King of France and pledge loyalty to his lord and uncle. But Arthur unwisely replied with indignation and threats, demanding that the king should surrender to him the kingdom of England and all the territories Richard had held at the time of his death. With an oath, Arthur asserted that all these possessions belonged to him by hereditary right, and that unless they were quickly restored to him, John would not enjoy much peace. The king was upset by these words, and ordered that Arthur should be removed to Rouen and detained under close guard in the new tower there. Shortly afterwards, the said Arthur disappeared.

The first assertion of known date that the sixteen-year-old Arthur was murdered was contained in a document issued by Philip of France in 1216. Philip went on to claim that John had been condemned by the supreme court of France to forfeit all his dominions as the murderer of his nephew. This supposed trial and condemnation was almost certainly an invention, trumped up to justify the French invasion of England in the year the accusation was published. At about the same time, Philip's chaplain, William the Breton, embroidered his master's allegation in a poem which included a description of the alleged murder.

In this, John and Arthur supposedly ventured on the Seine one night, alone together in a boat. Suddenly, the king ran his sword through Arthur's body, rowed three miles with the corpse, then consigned it to the river. It is a strange picture. Its only merit seems to be that, since John was the sole surviving witness, only John could deny it.

A less ludicrous, if equally colourful story was offered by Ralph of Coggeshall, abbot and writer of the Cistercian monastery at that place. According to Ralph, John's advisers urged him to have his nephew blinded and castrated by way of rendering him harmless as a rival. When the appointed execu-

The Disappearance of the Young Duke

tioners of this deed arrived at Falaise Castle, the officer in charge, Hubert of Burgh, refused to allow them to proceed with their gruesome task, deeming it stupid and barbarous. Instead, he announced that Arthur was dead, hoping that the Bretons would lose heart if they believed themselves without a leader. But the Bretons, as Ralph had it, were the more enraged against John, thinking their duke had been murdered. When Hubert realised his mistake and protested that Arthur was still alive, no one would believe him.

The weakness of Ralph's story was pointed out by the writer himself, for the proposed outrage against Arthur would indeed have been stupid and barbarous, and John was neither. To have cast a wretchedly maimed Arthur upon the world as a living incitement to the hatred of John's enemies, and the discomfort of his friends, could have served no sensible purpose. It would have been better to kill Arthur outright. Yet why should John harm his prisoner at all? The man with the greatest interest in Arthur's death was not John but Philip. Philip had never acknowledged Arthur as heir to Normandy, the territory vital to maintaining the unity of the Angevin empire, and was clearly interested in the young duke merely as a tool to bring the rest of the continental fiefs under his own influence. What could suit Philip better than that John should murder Arthur? It would lend moral fervour to the cause of the French king, now a righteous avenger, and enable him to claim the direct homage of the barons of the French fiefs.

Indeed, by the first part of 1203 Philip was already manoeuvring in anticipation of Arthur's permanent effacement from politics. In March he received the liege homage of one Maurice of Craon "for the term of Arthur's imprisonment," and on the understanding that should Arthur break faith with Philip, or die, Maurice would remain Philip's man. The French king also granted castles on the same terms. Meanwhile, he made no attempt to secure Arthur's release.

There were therefore considerable disincentives to restrain John from killing or drastically maiming his nephew, though, since Arthur was a traitor to his liege lord, such punishments would not have been held illegal. When Philip later tried to make an issue of the matter with Pope Innocent III, that dignitary maintained that Arthur deserved little sympathy. The fact remains that by any strategic reckoning John's interests were best served by keeping Arthur alive and intact, ideally persuading him to declare himself John's man, but, failing that, preserving him in suspended animation. This was the policy John adopted towards Arthur's sister Eleanor, another of the king's captives, and his closest hereditary rival upon her brother's death. John kept her a prisoner for the rest of her life, but he treated her handsomely, granting her money, rich clothes and splendid saddles and reins for her horses.

There was one early story connected with Arthur's disappearance which avoided the incongruities of those outlined so far. The Annals of Margam related that at Rouen on the Thursday before Easter, April 1203, John, "being drunk after dinner, and possessed by the devil," killed his nephew with his own hand, tied a heavy stone to the body and flung it into the Seine. The body, brought up by a fisherman's net, was identified, but, "for fear of the tyrant," was buried secretly in the church of Nôtre Dame des Prés, near Rouen. The notion that John acted irrationally in a fit of Angevin rage, perhaps provoked by a vain attempt to persuade Arthur to renounce his pretensions, is not altogether implausible. Becket's murder had resulted from a similarly destructive impulse on the part of Henry II, and John had been observed in a paroxysm of murderous fury when crossed by his old enemy Longchamp.

This tale dispenses with the premeditation implied in the boat anecdote. A further element at first sight sustains its credibility. One of the earliest barons to declare for John upon Richard's death was William of Briouse, who had then been at

Châlus. Briouse, a staunch supporter and companion of John in his subsequent campaigns on the Continent, was better placed than most to account for Arthur's disappearance—and the Briouse family were patrons of the Cistercians of Margam. On closer inspection, however, the evidence is less impressive. The surviving manuscript from Margam dealing with the early years of John's reign was not compiled until 1221 at the earliest, and well before that the Briouse family had fallen from John's favour and had reason to regard the king with enmity. Information attributed to this source, therefore, is liable to the charge of being tainted with malice.

When all is considered, the possibility that Arthur died in sickness, or in an accident while attempting to escape, as John's friends asserted, seems at least as likely as any of the ingenious explanations contributed by those with cause to malign him. This being the case, it might well have seemed politic to John to keep quiet about Arthur's fate and leave Philip and the Bretons mystified. According to one source, Philip admitted he had no idea whether the Duke of Brittany was alive or dead in October, while another source asserted that the French king was still ignorant of the truth six months later.

Meanwhile, the triumph of Mirebeau was being undermined by factors altogether more tangible than Wendover's theory of "sorcery" and the speculation over Arthur's fate. There was, it seems true, an element of complacency in John's behaviour after Mirebeau, and while he was by no means so rash as to squander his advantage in pursuit of idle pleasure, he did make a serious mistake in dispensing with the services of a valuable ally. When William of Roches had given up his command of the Breton army to join John during the struggle for succession in 1199, he had made his switch conditional upon John making him a party to the future of Arthur and Constance. Since then, he had upheld John's interests in the strategically important lands of the Loire as seneschal of Anjou and Touraine. Once more, at Mirebeau, where he had played a leading role, William of Roches had extended his assistance to the English king on the understanding that in the event of Arthur being captured, he, William, should have a say in the disposal of the young duke. This time, however, John had felt strong enough to ignore his seneschal when Arthur was in his hands, and the youth had been removed from the influence of his former captain.

The result of this was that William of Roches deserted, formed a league of Breton barons, seized Angers, and, together with a number of sympathisers from Anjou and Maine, threatened John's lines to the south. Among William's allies was Amery, Viscount of Thouars (not to be confused with Aymer of Angoulême, who had by now died). The viscount held land on the south bank of the Loire. When the Lusignans were released to join the dissidents, John's hold on the central belt of his continental territories began to look very dubious.

In January 1203, John heard that Isabelle, who was staying at Chinon, close to Thouars, was endangered by the rebels. The treachery and unrest surrounding the Loire lands was vividly illustrated by the fact that the king himself felt it imprudent to go further south than Le Mans. Instead, he sent a posse of mercenaries to rescue the queen. The biographer of William Marshal told of John's anxiety for Isabelle's safety. When she rode into Le Mans escorted by the leader of the posse, Peter of Préaux, "The King was extremely pleased with Peter." Cautiously, the royal party headed back towards Normandy by devious roads and bridle paths, uncertain whom it could or could not trust.

Towards the end of April, Philip linked forces with the rebels of the Loire, attacking and taking Saumur, between Chinon and Angers. He could now turn south for Aquitaine in the comforting knowledge that a deep screen of rebel lands protected his rear from John in Normandy. For a while, he encouraged the Poitevin dissidents by joining them in attacks on castles in Aquitaine, then, having stoked the rebel fires of the South, marched north again to resume his interrupted assault on the eastern frontier of Normandy. By now, the flames of southerly rebellion had swept north as far as Alençon, within the very bounds of Normandy itself. John had dined with the Count of Alençon during the sortie to rescue Isabelle. Soon afterward, that lord had declared for Philip. Incredibly enough, within a few months of Mirebeau, John was cornered in a Normandy surrounded to the landward by his enemies.

But this was not, in itself, a novel situation. In the original fight for his inheritance, he had stood on the firm soil of the duchy and defied Philip to the east, the Bretons to the west and a largely hostile barony in Maine, Anjou and Touraine. On that occasion he had drawn strength from the loyalty and resolution of the Normans, issuing forth from the bounds of the duchy to confound and subjugate his enemies.

For a century and a half, Normandy had stood by the kings of England. Many of its barons and bishops held estates in both countries, its towns and merchants were tied to their cross-Channel counterparts by mutual interests, its warriors were accustomed to fighting shoulder to shoulder with Englishmen. Normandy was conditioned to repelling its enemies. Its barons were resourceful. Reinforcements could pour in unhindered from England. Its marches were protected by a chain of formidable castles, the most recent of which, Château Gaillard, towering over the Seine Valley at Les Andelys, was considered the last word in defensive construction.

What *was* novel, and profoundly disconcerting to the English king, was the dawning realisation that he could no longer trust the Norman barons. Seven centuries later, this *volte-face* in Norman sentiments emerges with puzzling abruptness. But its roots must have been widespread and advanced in development before it finally burst into daylight.

Since their earliest days, the Dukes of Normandy had combined defiance of the Kings of France with an interest in England, a land already settled by their ancestors the Norsemen. The first Duke of Normandy was a Scandinavian emigrant named Rollo, who had died about 931. If, as seems probable, Rollo was one and the same as Hrolf the Ganger, a character famed in Norse saga for his huge size, it would appear that his southerly orientation had come about after banishment from Norway for plundering his own people. Dudon, the father of Norman historians, described Rollo operating against England from the Hebrides before, perhaps finding the opposition there too strong, sailing for France in search of somewhere to settle. William of Jumièges, the eleventh-century writer, and Robert Wace, the twelfth-century Jersey poet-historian, developed this story, telling how the prowling dragon boats, tempted by the wide gap of the Seine estuary, had eventually come to the promised land.

The first substantial Viking invasions of France had begun in the middle of the ninth century, and when Rollo eventually landed at Jumièges, some fifteen miles short of Rouen, he had been able to supplement his forces with Danes and Norwegians who had preceded him. The Rouennais, terrorised too often in the past by Vikings to be unaware of the grim consequences of an unsuccessful action against them, had offered to accept Rollo's forces into the city provided he guaranteed the safety of persons and property. For the next sixteen years, he had held sway as virtual ruler not only of Rouen but of most of the province, raiding and ravaging beyond its boundaries until his gigantic frame, reputedly too heavy to travel by horse, had become synonymous with dismay and panic throughout France

The first French king to have had the misfortune to encounter a Duke of Normandy had been Charles the Simple. In an effort to halt the murder and violation, he had offered Rollo his daughter in marriage and "all the maritime district between the river Eure and Mont St. Michel" if the pirate chief would adopt the Christian faith and do homage to the Crown.

Rollo, surfeited with battle, bored perhaps with the restless life of a freebooter, appears to have accepted respectability on the king's terms. He was to prove as energetic a legislator as he had a warrior. Having rewarded his followers-at-arms with land (scrupulously measured, tradition has it, by rod and line, thus supposedly initiating the rectilinear pattern of much of pastoral Normandy), he had set out to maintain an iron discipline in his dukedom. The predatory nature of the Norsemen, accustomed since they could remember to live by pillage, had called for the most vigorous and ruthless suppression of crime, and Rollo had been quick to provide it. Having set the pattern of treating from strength with the King of France, and of hammering his tempestuous subjects, he had had little time to renew his interest in England.

It had been left to his grandson, Richard the Fearless, third Duke of Normandy, to lay the foundations of the English connection. His daughter Emma had become the wife of two English kings in succession, Ethelred and Canute, and the mother of a third, Edward the Confessor. From now on, Norman eyes had been cast with increasing ambition to the north. Richard's son Robert the Magnificent, so called for his flamboyant taste and ostentatious manners, had been cast in the classic medieval mould of brutality and piety. The first act of his reign had been to build the abbey of Cerisy, near St.-Lô, and the last, when he was still not twenty-five, to go on a pilgrimage to Jerusalem, riding part of the way on a gold-shod mule. Between whiles he had found time for a successful attack on the widow of the King of France, and to launch an invasion of England. This expedition, mounted at Fécamp, had failed when unfavourable winds drove the Norman fleet to the Channel Islands.

It had devolved upon his son William to conquer England, still maintaining the traditional Norman defiance of the French monarch. While William and his descendants had occupied the throne of England, it could be said to the esteem of the Normans that their duke ruled the island kingdom. With the eventual elevation of the house of Anjou, however, came a subtle but crucial change. Now it seemed rather that the King of England ruled the Norman barons. The duke was no longer a fellow-countryman; not quite an Englishman, perhaps, but certainly a "foreigner." Meanwhile, a more profound metamorphosis was taking place. Over the generations which had followed Rollo, the Scandinavian strain had been absorbing the culture of the land it had settled on, becoming increasingly French in character. At the same time, Paris had been emerging as the cultural hub of France—by the thirteenth century, the leader of cultural and social fashions in western Europe, attracting more and more Frenchmen to its limelight.

To some extent, the mood in Normandy ran parallel to the growing insularity in England, the mounting disinclination among English barons to identify their interests with the Continent. If Englishmen were becoming increasingly reluctant to jeopardise their lives and sacrifice their resources for the Duke of Normandy, there were Normans who had begun to ponder the wisdom of making sacrifices for the King of England. Richard had burdened them with huge financial exactions; already, their adherence to John had twice surrounded their borders with hostile armies. When the King of France fell out with the King of England, it was not England he attacked but Normandy. The illogicality of an alliance which destined them to live in enmity with their immediate neighbour for the sake

The Disappearance of the Young Duke

of one whose principal throne was oversea, was stirring in Norman minds.

This growth of discontent among the Norman barons was fraught with greater peril for John than the chronic rebellions to the south, because its development was submerged, concealed beneath the custom of many reigns, and its aim was more radical. The turbulent barons of the South fought for personal, short-term gains. The smouldering discontent of the Normans was working toward a sweeping realignment of loyalties. The new threat to their borders set the duchy aflame. Not the least of Norman grievances was the behaviour of the mercenaries John assembled on their lands for his campaigns. These rough professional brawlers had little respect for person or property, and one band in particular, led by a Provençal captain known as Lupescar, The Wolf, aroused the deep animosity of its hosts toward its employer. Lupescar, said Marshal's biographer, treated the peaceful Normans more brutally than other commanders were accustomed to treating their enemies.

John's mounting distrust of the Norman barons was evidenced in his restless movements about the duchy as the year proceeded, repeatedly changing his plans for fear of betrayal. While Conches, Vaudreuil and other places in eastern Normandy fell, or were handed to Philip by their commanders, John prowled warily in the neighbourhood of Rouen, not knowing whom to trust, afraid to commit himself. John had always preferred peace to warfare; now it was not merely a matter of preference but of necessity. He sent William Marshal to Conches to inform Philip of his willingness to negotiate, but Philip was not interested. Philip had waited too long for this moment to be robbed of it by diplomacy. Marshal's biographer reported the French king in a sardonic mood.

"In France of old, traitors were burned at the stake, quartered or torn apart by horses," complained Marshal. "How do you account for the fact that they are now welcome as lords and masters in your realm?"

"It's all in the way of business," riposted Philip. "Traitors are like torches—one uses them, then drops them down the privy."

At last, the dominant trumps were in Philip's hands. He had even patched up his quarrel with the pope. Perhaps this was as well for him, since John had already complained to Rome of Philip's aggression, requesting Innocent to intervene in the cause of peace. Philip responded by dispatching his own messengers to the pope, rehearsed in his version of the conflict. In May, Innocent informed the two kings that he was sending commissioners to arbitrate between them. "While you are battling with each other, churches are destroyed, the wealthy are impoverished, the poor are oppressed. The religious are compelled to beg at times when they used to be praying. Nowhere is safe, nor is either sex. Women who have dedicated their virginity to the Creator are sacrificed to the lust of the plunderers."

For some reason now unknown, the pope's commissioners spent the whole of the summer reaching Philip. When he finally met them in August, he told them bluntly that "his rights over a fief and vassal were not subject to the decisions of the Apostolic See." The same month, John made two attempts to recapture Norman castles held by Philip's men, but he did not persist and was unsuccessful. The treachery all around seems to have robbed him not only of the initiative but of his nerve. Because he could not trust the barons, he was reduced to the company of mercenary captains and retainers in his personal service. The Duke of Normandy had become little more than an alien in a hostile land. The only castles he could depend upon were those held by English commanders, and they were like islands in a sea of uncertainty. "He could bring no relief to the besieged," wrote Ralph of

Coggeshall, "because he travelled in constant fear of his subjects' treachery."

At the end of August, Philip massed his army, his engineers and his siege machines for the reduction of Château Gaillard, the pride of Richard the Lion-Hearted, who had built the massive fortress in the closing years of his life as a symbol of Angevin power and defiance of France. Embodying the latest refinements in castle construction gleaned by the crusaders from the Saracens and Byzantines, Château Gaillard perched atop a precipitous limestone crag overlooking the town of Les Andelys and a great loop in the Seine upstream of Rouen. To prevent the French sailing downstream from the direction of Paris, a stockade had been placed across the river upstream of the castle, while a bridge connected the stronghold with the opposite bank.

Philip could have by-passed Château Gaillard in his advance and struck directly at Rouen, but there were obvious disadvantages in leaving so formidable a stronghold in his rear while it was in enemy hands. Moreover, as a psychological stroke, nothing could be more devastating to John's supporters than the capture of this symbolic stronghold. If Château Gaillard could not repulse Philip, could anything?

The castle was commanded by an Englishman, Roger of Lacy, who, while not the greatest of John's friends, was a resolute and energetic officer, and could be relied upon not lightly to surrender his trust. His first action, on learning that the French were advancing on the far side of the river, was to destroy the bridge. Philip responded by hacking a gap in the stockade, floating pontoons downstream, and constructing a new bridge just below Les Andelys, thus denying river communication between the castle and Rouen. Meanwhile, Lacy had gained the time to put his defences in battle order and to inform John of Philip's attack. With so vital a challenge before him, John showed himself once more a tactician of imagination and vigour. His plan, laid at Rouen, was a night operation of combined land and water forces. William Marshal and Lupescar, with a strong force of mounted men-at-arms and footmen, were to advance up the riverbank under cover of darkness and fall upon the French camp before dawn.

At the same time, a fleet of some seventy boats, mustered from their moorings at Rouen, was to proceed upstream under the command of the veteran naval captain Alan Trenchemer, laden with food, armaments and a further force of mercenaries. By smashing the pontoon bridge, they would cut the besieging army in half; then, while some of the waterborne troops joined the attack on Philip's camp, others would carry the supplies to the castle. At best, the siege would be raised and the French army driven off; at worst, Château Gaillard would be re-stocked.

As it happened, there was a critical flaw in the timing. Marshal and Lupescar took the French by surprise and gained an initial advantage. But the assistance they had expected from the waterborne element did not materialise. The bridge remained in the hands of the besiegers, who, quickly regrouping, beat off the land attack. The oarsmen in the heavily laden boats had been unable to keep pace in the swiftly running current. By the time they arrived at the appointed landing-place, Marshal and Lupescar were retiring in disorder, and the amphibious force faced the full weight of Philip's army. It was repulsed with heavy losses. "The river was red with blood."

As Marshal saw it, the failure to relieve Château Gaillard marked the end of John's usefulness in Normandy. Dismally, he advised the king to leave the field of hostilities. "Sire, you have not friends enough to challenge your enemies." John was indignant. "Let the timid flee," he retorted. "I shall remain for another year, and if I then depart it will only be when you yourself go." Many of the English nobles who had

The Disappearance of the Young Duke

been in Normandy had already left the duchy, ostensibly to tend their estates in England, and with unconvincing promises to return later. John had not tried to detain them.

Even at this time of peril and stress, John could accept the human frailty of his friends and followers, and was not scornful of their limitations. When Robert FitzWalter and Saer of Quincy, two men who had enjoyed his special favours, had surrendered Vaudreuil Castle to Philip without a fight, contempt for their action had spread to England, where derisive ballads recalled the episode. Even Philip had been disgusted by the lack of resistance at Vaudreuil. Yet John had declared that FitzWalter and Quincy were not to be blamed, and continued to regard them with generosity. To Roger of Lacy, he wrote thanking the commander of Château Gaillard for his faithful service, asking him to do "as much as lies in your power," but telling him that if he could hold out no longer he was to act at the discretion of the king's representatives. It was plainly not John's desire that lives should be sacrificed needlessly on his behalf.

In September, John switched his attention to the opposite side of Normandy, attacking Fougéres and Dol, just across the frontier with Brittany. Both places were burned and sacked by John's mercenaries, and the relics of a local saint, Samson, were looted from Dol Cathedral. The king may have hoped to supplement his diminishing forces in western Normandy, anticipating that the barons there would be less susceptible to Philip's blandishments than those in the east. Or he may have hoped to lure the French king from Château Gaillard, as the victory of Mirebeau had drawn him from the siege of Arques. Either way, he was unsuccessful. Lacy had now been forced to eject all but his combatants from his stronghold, and a pathetic crowd of some four hundred camp-followers and refugees huddled outside the walls of Château Gaillard. When they tried to approach the French lines, they were driven off by arrows. When they turned back to the gates of the castle, they found them barred and bolted against them.

As the winter wore on, these wretched creatures died by the dozen of starvation and exposure in the barren no-man's-land between defenders and besiegers, the survivors reduced to chewing roots, grass and leaves for sustenance. At last, urged by belated compassion, or perhaps by fear of disease, Philip ordered that those still alive should be rescued. They numbered no more than two hundred, and for many their first meal was the seal on their misery. They had not the strength to digest it. Few of them recovered.

Despairingly, John spent October and November roaming the duchy in a vain attempt to drum up support against Philip. He had long since been reduced to appointing mercenary captains as the administrators of his territories, to the increased resentment of the natives, and he was now forced to dismantle castles for the lack of trustworthy men to defend them. It was to be the last resort of the last Duke of Normandy from England. Marshal's chronicler described John's final and anguished days on the Continent.

> The King stopped for a short time in Rouen, declaring his intention to go to England to seek the aid and counsel of his barons there, and asserting that he would return shortly. But many, seeing that he took the Queen with him, feared that he would be away for too long. His preparations were brief, since he had already sent his baggage in advance. From Rouen, he travelled to Bonneville, sleeping in the village rather than the castle as a precaution against treason, for he had been warned that many of his barons had sworn to betray him to the King of France.
> Of this, he affected to be ignorant, but he stayed away from them just the same. He instructed Marshal, and other trusties, to be up before daybreak. They were, but the King had already departed without wishing them farewell while they thought him to be still asleep. By the time this was known, he was seven leagues

away. He headed for Bayeux, via Caen, covering twenty leagues that day—leagues of the Bessin, which are longer than French leagues. From Bayeux, he went to Baffleur, where a crowd of his adherents wished him goodbye. It was obvious they could not expect him back quickly.

John sailed for England from Barfleur on December 5. He did not come back quickly. He did not come back at all.

Chapter 8
GOOD-BYE NORMANDY; COME BACK POITOU

Know you, that if you return to our fealty and service, we will reject all ill-will and pardon you entirely.

King John to the barons of Poitou

"Abstract liberty, like other mere abstractions, is not to be found," wrote the eighteenth-century English statesman and political writer Edmund Burke. "Liberty inheres in some sensible object; and every nation has formed to itself some favourite point which, by way of eminence, becomes the criterion of its happiness. It happened that the great contests for freedom in this country were from the earliest times chiefly upon the question of taxing." Taxation certainly contributed to the unpopularity of the Angevin kings of England. Englishmen resented their money being spent abroad. They did not happily turn out their pockets, for instance, to enable the king to subdue his vassals in the South of France. It was John's misfortune to come to the throne at a time when his people were still smarting from the unprecedented exactions of his predecessor, and with no option but to find new revenues to continue the policies forced upon him.

Richard had taken over a healthy exchequer from his father, only, by dint of ambitious foreign travels and misadventures, to leave a country deep in the red. At John's accession, tax arrears had still been owing from the time of Richard's crusading. The necessity of raising further money to pay for wars originating from before his own reign compelled him to increase taxation, and, in consequence, his own unpopularity among the tax-paying classes. His first action on returning, shorn of resources, from Normandy at the end of 1203, was to amass a fresh fund with which to finance a counter-offensive on the Continent. Above all, he needed money with which to recruit new mercenary forces.

Wendover described the exactions which John now demanded of the barons, and others, with a word applied by more or less incensed Englishmen down the ages to taxation—"robbery." To start, there was a further levy on chattels. "He took from them a seventh of all their moveable goods, not abstaining from grasping the property of conventual or parochial churches, employing Hubert, Archbishop of Canterbury, as the agent of this robbery of Church property, and Geoffrey FitzPeter, Justiciar of England, in respect of the laity. They spared no one in the execution of their duty." The distasteful nature of the procedure is evident in the euphemisms used by medieval collectors for taxes, which were commonly referred to as "aids," "gifts" or "tributes."

John sought "aids" from the Irish Church, from the Gascons, even from the Channel Islands. A tallage (the arbitrary taxation of tenants of the king's lands, including the royal boroughs) was taken from the towns, and port merchandise was taxed at a fifteenth of its value. On January 2, within a month of his return to England, the king convened a council at Oxford and imposed a scutage of two and a half marks on the knight's fee—the highest amount ever demanded in shield money.

As the revenues began to come in, albeit slowly, John regained some confidence. He had spent Christmas at Guildford, as the guest of Hubert Walter, banishing the nightmare of Norman treachery around blazing log fires and laden tables. Château Gaillard still defied Philip. Rouen was prepared for a French attack, its larders stocked, its walls strong, manned by citizens who had prospered under the Angevins. Should Philip break through on the Seine, there were three more rivers to cross, the Risle, the Touques and the Orne, before the whole of Normandy fell to him. The Touques in particular, dividing eastern and western Normandy, was notable for strongholds which had yet to declare for French rule. It was all a question of time. If John could raise the money to marshal a crushing army of mercenaries before Philip could complete the subjugation of the duchy, the Norman barons might yet be forced to acknowledge the English king.

As January and February passed, with Château Gaillard still holding out, John became positively sanguine. Supplies were beginning to flow across the Channel from England to the loyalists in Normandy. On March 6, the king went so far as to arrange for his hounds and falcons to be shipped to the duchy, to provide him with hunting when he reopened his campaign there. Perhaps he was tempting fate, for that very day the main prop of his resurgent optimism was shattered. Château Gaillard fell.

Towards the end of February, realising that time was working for the English king, Philip had given up hoping to starve the garrison and had set about carrying the stronghold by assault. The first part of his plan had been to occupy a triangular-shaped outer-work of the castle as a base from which to tackle the main bastion: an outer wall with towers, and an inner wall and keep. Trundling a covered gallery of wood up the slopes to the triangular compound, the French had been able to fill in part of its ditch, screened by their mantle from the arrows of the defenders. At the same time, they had undermined the largest of the towers in this outer-work, bringing a large section of the wall down in rubble. Scuttling over the filled ditch and through the hole in the wall, they had taken possession of the outer-work, forcing the defenders to retire across a drawbridge to the main bastion. By a stroke of luck, the French had now discovered a window in the outer wall of this structure, giving into a small chapel. By wriggling through the window and assembling within the chapel, an intrepid band of attackers had been able to burst into the outer compound of the castle, lower the drawbridge, and admit their comrades-in-arms. Lacy's men had been forced back within the inner ward and keep of the fortress. When an entrance had been battered in this by Philip's siege engines, the defenders were beaten.' Amidst the clatter and cussing of hand-to-hand battle, they had been overwhelmed by superior numbers. The hundred and fifty-odd who survived were taken prisoner.

The assault of Château Gaillard dismayed Philip's enemies. If the French could burst into the mighty fortress at Les Andelys, they could do the same at Rouen. Events in Normandy seemed to be moving too fast to suit John's plans. At a meeting of the king's council in London, it was decided to try once more to negotiate. This decision was prompted by the presence in England of a member of the pope's peace-seeking commission, the Abbot of Casamario. Philip had already rejected the intercession of the legates, and there seemed little reason to suppose that he would have changed his mind at this point. But at least he would have to listen to a delegation headed by the pope's representative, and such a mission might delay his offensive.

The delegation was a strong one. With the abbot went Hubert Walter, William Marshal, Robert, Earl of Leicester and the bishops of Norwich and Ely. Their brief was to sound Philip and discuss possible terms for an armistice. Predictably, the French king was interested in little short of the complete surrender of the French fiefs. Blandly, he demanded the return of Arthur, if Arthur was still alive. Failing this, he stipulated the handing over of Arthur's sister, Eleanor, and the surrender to him, as her guardian, of the entire continental aspect of the Angevin empire. Such conditions were not worth discussing. But Philip had one proposition which interested at least two of the English envoys.

Any of John's subjects, he said, who came to the French court within twelve months and a day to do homage to him for Norman holdings would be granted confirmation of their tenure. Marshal and the Earl of Leicester both possessed estates in Normandy. After some discussion, they agreed to pay Philip five hundred marks apiece on condition that he did not touch their Norman lands. If, at the end of twelve months and a day, John had not recaptured the duchy, they would do homage, they promised, for those lands to the French king. This intriguing example of medieval pragmatism seems not to have upset John at the time. "I know you are loyal to me," he told them, "and that your hearts cannot be turned from me."

There is no reason to believe that either Marshal or Leicester regarded the bargain as a betrayal of their English lord. Indeed, William Marshal was looked upon by his contemporaries as the epitome of honour and chivalry. As the Middle Ages had progressed, chivalry, the attempt to realise social ideals through established forms and customs sanctioned by the Church, had become recognised as a desirable mode of life by an increasing body of the noble and freeborn. The crusade had done much to promote it. Like knighthood, the chivalric character was not inherited as was nobility. Though containing little enough of an intellectual nature, it was a learning and a discipline, a vocation with defined aspirations and rules to be acquired by training—in a sense, a knighthood within a knighthood.

Broadly speaking, the ideals of chivalry were those later accepted as the ideals of a "gentleman." In the terms of chivalric reference, the knight summarised his obligations to God, his lord and his lady. Of course, they were superimposed upon, and did not eradicate, the more primitive aspects of medieval conduct. Such chivalric attributes as reverence for superiors, courtesy toward women, formal observance of the word of honour, and disregard of personal advantage except in military glory, combined incongruously with savage ferocity, cruelty, deceitful cunning and lack of military discipline. "Chivalry," one historian has written, "taught the world the duty of noble service willingly rendered. It upheld courage and enterprise in obedience to rule, it consecrated military prowess in the service of the Church, glorified the virtues of liberality, good faith, unselfishness and courtesy. Against these may be set the vices of pride, love of bloodshed, contempt of inferiors and loose manners. Chivalry was an imperfect discipline, one fit for the times."

If chivalry sanctioned the violence of its era, it was at least a regulation of evils and an advance toward civilised conduct. With it came an increasing gentleness and a general amelioration of manners. The education of the knight proceeded in two stages—that of the page, ranging roughly from the seventh to the fourteenth year, and that of the squire, which continued to early manhood. All ranks of chivalry customarily placed their offspring with the households of their feudal superiors, where they were trained through household or court service. The page commenced his apprenticeship with simple duties about the castle, waiting in particular on the ladies. Later, he served at the table, a duty he continued to perform as a squire, when he took on a wider range of services to his lord, not only at home but abroad and on the field of battle. The knight had always learned in boyhood to ride, to hunt and to bear arms. As a *chivalrous* knight, he learned also the rudiments of kindliness, gentility and charm; the accomplishments, perhaps, of the minstrel and poet, and the formalities of courtesy and good manners.

Special importance was attached to the various forms and obligations of the plighted word. For instance, he must know that the noble who did homage to a lord for his fiefs owed knights' service for those fiefs to his lord when he went to war. He must know that the noble who held fiefs of two lords was obliged to render knights' service to each according to his separate contracts if those lords made war on each other. If, however, a vassal took an oath of fealty to his lord, that is, he became in the fullest sense the man of that lord, then his obligation was to follow that lord in person when he went to war. These nice distinctions were to cause trouble between John and the chivalrous Marshal later.

Meanwhile, within a month of the fall of Château Gaillard, John received the depressing news that his mother had at last died. Eleanor was eighty-two, a remarkable age for her day, and had been the wife of two kings and the mother of two more. By any reckoning, she was an outstanding example of medieval womanhood. She had fought tirelessly to control the barons of her great duchy of Aquitaine; she had been crusading to the Holy Land; she had fought for her sons against their father; she had shrugged off twelve years of imprisonment as if a mere episode in her life; she had travelled to Germany to fetch Richard from captivity, to Navarre to procure a daughter-in-law and to Castile to escort her granddaughter to Normandy. As queen, mother, politician, warrior and diplomat, she had followed, and sometimes determined the story of the Angevin empire from its inception to the eve of its destruction. She died on April 1 and was buried

Good-bye Normandy; Come Back Poitou

at Fontevrault beside the husband she had come to hate, and the son she had loved with fierce devotion.

In the closing years of her life, Eleanor had become a symbol of strength to John. The old lady had been ready to endanger her life for him, while the victory of Mirebeau had stemmed from his affectionate regard for her. She had lived to see the fall of Château Gaillard, but was spared the final convulsions of John's cause in Normandy. Philip handled the dissection of the duchy with masterly precision. Ignoring Rouen, the most likely stronghold to delay him, thus facilitating John's chances of a come-back, the French king swung southwest into the hills of southern Normandy. By-passing the rivers Risle and Touques at their sources, he took Argentan at the headwaters of the Orne and veered north onto the plains of Calvados, charging boldly toward Falaise and Caen.

The stroke was as shrewd as it was unexpected, a ranging left hook at the western portion of the duchy, disorientating its already confused defenders and threatening the very shores upon which John hoped to land. Falaise was held by Lupescar and his mercenaries. They made a nominal resistance, then joined the French king. Caen surrendered without a fight, after which Philip detailed forces to take Bayeux, Coutances and the Cherbourg peninsula. Everywhere, barons and burghers did homage to the exultant monarch.

To those Normans who had not yet succumbed to the threats and blandishments of the French king, further resistance seemed pointless. While Philip had been appropriating the Northwest, the Bretons had crossed the border to the south of him, completed the conquest of western Normandy and joined him at Caen. There remained Rouen, the last major stronghold loyal to John. Early summer saw the French army bearing its banners and lances confidently toward that city by way of Lisieux. Convinced by now that John could not save them, the Rouennais wavered in their will to resist. What good were strong walls and battlements if they merely prolonged a siege which would ruin the trade, the very life-blood of the city? Without access to Rouen, its commercial contacts would take their trade elsewhere—to Caen, perhaps, which had capitulated hastily and resumed normal business.

On June 1, the military commander of Rouen, Peter of Préaux, made terms with Philip which safeguarded the interests of the citizens while enabling Peter to seek advice from the English king. It was agreed that the city would surrender if not succoured by John within thirty days. Meanwhile, its people should remain unmolested. Messengers were immediately sent to England. John was honest about his impotence. They should not look to him for assistance, he told them. He was in no position to help. Nor did he expect of them blood and heroics. They should, he is said to have urged, "do whatsoever seemed in their best interests." They decided to admit Philip before the expiration of the truce. On June 24, he entered the city. With the exception of the Channel Islands, the duchy had passed from the Angevin empire.

According to Wendover, John lost Normandy beneath the quilts of the marriage bed, "finding all kinds of delights in his queen," indolently luxuriating while his castles collapsed like playing cards. John certainly enjoyed luxury. Unlike his father, he dressed himself and his household splendiferously, accumulated a vast collection of jewelry and ornamentation, and entertained lavishly. For one banquet alone, he ordered twenty oxen, one hundred pigs, the same number of sheep, fifteen hundred chickens and five thousand eggs. And that was a fairly routine occasion. But that the king was indolent made nonsense. In the months following his return from Normandy, he set himself untiringly to catch up on his business in England. Had Wendover consulted the administrative records, he would have found John on an endless commutation between city and city, town and town; now down in Devon, now up in Yorkshire,

Good-bye Normandy; Come Back Poitou

now circumambulating the midlands in a roundabout of activity that is giddy-making to contemplate. Few kings threw themselves so personally and unremittingly into the task of ruling as did King John.

Among his primary concerns was the maintenance of law and order, the administration of justice. While he was on the Continent, many English lawsuits were postponed until his return, so that he could hear them personally. Back in England, he sat at pleas with judges all over the country. His thoroughness, fairness and compassion commended him to judges and judged alike; men clamoured to air their complaints, and to be tried, in the king's presence. For this privilege, the wealthy might pay as much as a hundred pounds; but John was not contemptuous of the poor, and would lend his attention to the most mundane of cases for as little as half a mark.

Thanks largely to John's interest in judicial matters, and particularly to his emphasis on the relevancy of evidence, the gradual evolution from oath compurgators to material witnesses, and to competent juries, made noteworthy progress during his reign. He also took a close interest in the financial business of the exchequer, supervising the audit of sheriffs' accounts and authorising changes in their liabilities. Toward the end of 1204, he undertook a reform of the currency, issuing coins of improved design and weight.

At the time of John's accession, there had been no new coinage since the days of his father, and many of the silver pennies in circulation had been mutilated by clipping, or paring at the edges, a practice much in vogue among profit-scratching Englishmen. John made it an offence to possess clipped coins after January 13, 1205. Those who did so were liable to be arrested and have their chattels confiscated. The new coins, issued later in that month, had rims to make clipping more difficult. Anyone found with clipped pennies of the new coinage was to be thrown into prison at the king's mercy. Old pennies were still acceptable after the new issue provided they conformed to a minimum weight. Demand for the new coins by foreign merchants and others enabled the English exchanges to make remarkable profits. In the year 1201–2, the profits from the exchanges and mints of England had been one hundred and sixty-six pounds. In 1205–6, profits from the mint and exchange of London alone were seven hundred and ten pounds.

Another of John's innovations, this directly attendant upon the loss of Normandy and its Channel ports, was the creation of a standing fleet, a full-time royal Navy. The earliest English Navy on record appears to have dated from about 896, when King Alfred, harassed by Vikings, had decided to tackle the invaders at sea. In the words of the Anglo-Saxon Chronicle, he had "ordered the building of warships to meet the Danish vessels . . . they [the ships he built] were faster, more stable and had more freeboard than the others. They were built neither after the Frisian nor the Danish design, but to that which seemed to him the most serviceable." For some time in the ensuing period, mercenaries had played an important part in the island's naval defences, regular patrols guarding the coastal waters during the summer months. By 1050, however, Edward the Confessor had paid off most of the professional crews in an effort to reduce the strain on his exchequer, and Harold had inherited little in the way of a standing sea force.

What Harold inherited was a special arrangement with a number of towns in the South, later known as the Cinque Ports, whereby he could raise a fleet when he needed it. In return for naval service, these ports—namely Sandwich, Dover, Hastings, Romney and Hythe—were granted various privileges, including exemption from tolls for their burghers, the profits of justice in their courts and exemption from military obligations on land. This arrangement was supplemented by a general territorial duty throughout the country to provide sea-warriors and ships when required, much on the lines of the feudal army recruiting system. The navy available from the Cinque Ports and elsewhere suffered from the weakness that it was a reservist force liable only to limited periods of service. For most of the year, its members were catching herrings, trading wool or otherwise occupied earning a livelihood.

When the Channel ports were in friendly hands, this arrangement had been adequate. English kings who required large fleets for their travels, as had Richard for his crusade, hired, purchased or requisitioned merchant vessels, disposing of them accordingly when they had served their purpose. But such methods of raising fleets were time-consuming, inadequate in an emergency. And with Philip now hovering threateningly across the Channel, the need for a strong and ready Navy was urgent. John confirmed the individual charters of the Cinq Ports, and set about forming a full-time naval establishment, which, in 1205, comprised some fifty royal galleys stationed in fifteen harbours, the bulk in the South of England. There was also the king's own vessel, exceptionally fast and sizeable, normally berthed at Southampton and captained by Alan Trenchemer.

In the tense months following the loss of Normandy, it looked very much as if the fleet would be needed to defend England against Philip. He had long since predicted an invasion of the island. Now, free to indulge his prophesy, he had found allies in the Duke of Brabant and the Count of Boulogne, both of whom claimed English estates in the right of their wives. Renaud of Boulogne and Henry of Brabant were married to granddaughters of King Stephen of England, and these ladies considered themselves to have been cheated of their rightful English inheritance by Henry II. Philip was most sympathetic. Let Renaud and Henry descend upon John with their armies, he purred, and he would join them within a week or so. Anxiously, John ordered his officers on the south and east coasts to prevent all shipping departures, and all sailing in their waters, without his permission. He was suspicious of all movements in the Channel.

William Marshal and Robert, Earl of Leicester, were not the only nobles with lands in both England and Normandy. There were many. When Philip had decreed that the Norman estates of barons who were in England would be confiscated unless these lords came over to him by a certain date, John had replied with a corresponding order in respect of English estates held by barons in Normandy. Henceforward, magnates with a footing on both sides of the Channel would have to decide whether to become Englishmen or Normans. And John could not be sure how some of his barons would react. The disastrous desertion of the Normans had sapped what confidence he had in his English vassals. He was close to few of the great baronial families, whose members, on the whole, were not drawn to the royal court. Of the rare exceptions, William of Briouse was perhaps a fair example—the ambitious scion of a lesser baronial house, moved by self-interest rather than affection. The one intimate friend John appears to have had among the greater English barons at this time was his half brother William, Earl of Salisbury, a natural son of Henry II. John trusted Salisbury on a number of missions, military and political, and liked to drink and play cards with him.

True, the chief officers of the state were loyal to the king, but they were professional administrators rather than aristocrats, and lacked the pedigree which bonded the blue-blooded classes. The justiciar, Geoffrey FitzPeter, had emerged from the lower ranks as a protégé of Ranulf Glanville, had used his influence at court to marry a minor heiress and had risen through long and trusty service with the Plantagenet kings. Hubert Walter, chancellor and primate, had risen in much the same fashion. He had started his career as a clerk with

Glanville, hoisting himself by political astuteness, stimulated by a robust appetite for wealth, power and luxury. William Marshal, who had served three kings faithfully, especially as a soldier, had set out in life as a landless knight, gaining preferment by military prowess.

Marshal was respected by the barons as a man of courage and chivalric correctitude, but, in the main, there was a marked social distinction between the barony and the king's officers. Since the accession of Henry II, the great landed families of England had carefully been excluded from posts of administrative power and influence. Their funds had been taxed, their privileges eroded, their pride outraged by a succession of low-born officials—upstarts, as they saw it—acting in the name of the Angevin monarchs. So far in John's reign, their dissatisfaction, though imprecisely recorded in the chronicles, had rumbled in ominous demands for the restoration of their "rights," for a return to "the good old days" of the past. Now, at the beginning of 1205, their underlying discontent did little to encourage John in his struggle with Philip.

In mid-January, the king summoned the bishops and barons to a council in London, where he took steps to prepare against the twin dangers of invasion and baronial treachery. An oath of fealty was demanded of all present, and afterwards expected of every Englishman above the age of twelve. "For the general defence of the realm, and for the preservation of peace, it was decreed that a commune should be established throughout the kingdom, and that all men, great or humble, should swear to uphold it." The feudal levy, or nation in arms, was raised and led by the earls and barons. By organising the country as a huge commune, John proposed a method of raising an army independently of the feudal lords. His ordinance provided for a national levy to be mustered when appropriate by his own law officers, the chief constables of the shires, and subordinate constables for every hundred (subdivision of a shire), city and township.

Each year of John's reign had witnessed the granting of charters to cities and larger towns. London had been declared a commune by John before he came to the throne. Norwich, Nottingham, Gloucester, Shrewsbury, Ipswich and Lincoln were to follow. By calling directly upon the burghers to defend the country, the king was effectively asking them to defend their new liberties. If the baron raised doubts in the king's mind, it seems that the ordinary freemen could be relied upon. Indeed, they were eager to support John.

Mutual distrust between John and the barons became evident at a further council in Oxford at the end of March. It had been a bitterly cold winter. Rivers had frozen, the ground had withstood the ploughman, food fetched exorbitant prices. Frost lingered in the hearts of the magnates. Before they would render John their oaths of obedience, they compelled him to swear once more "to uphold the rights of the kingdom untrammelled"—by which they clearly meant their own rights.

Preparations against invasion proceeded with urgency. Castles were provisioned and strengthened, especially near the coast; new ships were commissioned, old ones repaired; supplies of all kinds, from farrier's nails to sides of bacon, were assembled at depots. On Palm Sunday, John issued a writ mobilising one knight from every ten in the country, the remaining nine to pay the costs of the enlisted man. At Whitsuntide, the full host of the land was ordered to muster, and the fleet was gathered at Portsmouth. It was an awe-inspiring turnout. People of the day could not remember when so large an army, or so many ships, had been assembled at one time. An estimated five thousand pounds or more, something like a quarter of the year's revenue, had been spent on armaments alone. On the last day of May, John took residence at Porchester, close by his armada.

In all this, one factor was ultimately missing—any sign of a hostile landing in England. At some stage during John's preparations, the strategic pattern had altered. Instead of invading the island kingdom, Philip had turned south, directing his offensive against the possessions John still held in Poitou and Touraine. The provisions made to defend the shores of England could therefore be switched to the recovery of John's lost dominions. Precisely when his soldiers and sailors became aware of their new role is uncertain. It probably suited John that the realisation should dawn gradually. At all events, the discovery that they were now intended for an offensive rather than a defensive operation seems not to have dismayed the rank and file of his forces. Emboldened by their numbers, and the inspiring dimensions of the waiting fleet, they were "ready and willing to follow the king oversea."

But the barons were not. If John had anticipated their reluctance, perhaps relying on the loyalty of the general levy to induce them to co-operate, what he had not anticipated was that two men whose support he had not questioned, William Marshal and Hubert Walter, would side with the barons at the critical moment. It seems that Marshal had visited the Continent before Easter and done homage to Philip for his Norman lands in accord with their earlier compact. John had originally acquiesced in this procedure. But Marshal had gone a step further. He had pledged Philip "liege-homage on this side of the water"—an unusual formula creating a double personality, Philip's man on French soil and John's man in England. With his customarily inflexible adherence to the codes of honour, Marshal now maintained that he was ineligible to bear arms against Philip on the Continent.

John lost his Angevin temper. Rounding on the barons who were present, he demanded that they should pronounce Marshal's attitude treasonable. They "looked at each other and drew back" in silence. "By God!" spluttered the king, "not one of my barons is with me. The matter looks ugly!" And he stormed off to dinner.

There the episode rested until June 9, when every ship had been armed and provisioned, and its complement of troops allocated. At this stage, Walter and Marshal tackled John together. Ralph of Coggeshall, who noted that "they used every possible means of dissuading him from sailing," summarised the interview as follows:

> They pointed out the great harm that could come from an adventure abroad, urging the perils of placing himself among so many enemies without a secure base on the continent, and explaining that the French king, with the resources of so many territories, could field a force far outnumbering the English army. There was also the danger of exposing himself to the treachery of the Poitevins, ever fickle and scheming against their masters, and the likelihood that the Count of Boulogne and his allies would hasten to invade England when they learned that its army and its leaders were absent. Thus, while trying to regain his lost lands, the king might very well lose those which he still held. Furthermore, he had no heir to take over government should anything happen to him on the continent. When he remained unconvinced by these and other arguments, they knelt before him, grasped his knees to stop him leaving, and declared that if he took no heed of them they would detain him forcibly rather than that the kingdom should be reduced to confusion by his absence.

How far John would have succeeded with a full-scale cross-Channel onslaught can only be guessed at. It could be argued that now, if ever, was the time for such a gamble. But the king dared not ignore the combined weight of his magnates and his ministers. The realisation that he had been thwarted left him disconsolate. "Weeping and crying," he demanded to know what alternative they recommended. They suggested that a select force of knights should be dispatched to assist those who

Good-bye Normandy; Come Back Poitou

remained true to John in Poitou and the South of France. The rest of the army and the fleet should be dismantled. In a fit of desperation, the king flounced aboard his own ship and sailed off in solitary protest. Perhaps he hoped to shame the barons into following. Perhaps he needed solitude in which to compose himself. At any rate, he went no further than the Isle of Wight. Three days later, he disembarked at Studland, west of Portsmouth, and put an end to the expedition.

His soldiers and sailors were vociferous in their indignation. Abuse was directed not at the king, but at those whose "detestable advice" had aborted the enterprise. Doubtless, the resentment of the rank and file sprang to some extent from the expense and inconvenience they had been put to by the call-up. But there seems to have been genuine disappointment at the abandonment of the project. While the barons were gratified, ordinary men watched glumly as the mightiest armada that could be remembered in England was dispersed. In its stead, a detachment of knights under the Earl of Salisbury set sail for La Rochelle, halfway round the Bay of Biscay, to strengthen the garrison then under siege there.

If John had abandoned the expedition of 1205, he had not abandoned hope of recovering his French fiefs. In the spring and summer of the year of his costly flop, Loches and Chinon, two strongholds which had bravely held out against Philip in Touraine, had been captured. John helped to meet the ransoms of their commanders, Gerard of Athée and Hubert of Burgh, and called them to England. He needed such trusty men. Philip now possessed direct control of Normandy, Maine, Anjou and Touraine, while his allies controlled Brittany, La Marche and most of Poitou. In Poitou, two important strongholds defied Philip's forces: the port of La Rochelle, "fair city of the waters," whose formidable defences had recently been strengthened; and Niort, which covered La Rochelle to the east. Niort was commanded by John's old prisoner, Savary of Mauléon. At all costs, John had to prevent his enemies overrunning Aquitaine and completing the conquest of his continental dominions.

So far, he had provided the Archbishop of Bordeaux with twenty-eight thousand precious marks to hire mercenaries in Gascony, while taking steps to secure the commodious harbour and landing facilities at La Rochelle. It was now clear that any fresh English offensive must be mounted in the South, availing itself of the loyal support there, rather than in the North, where no aid could be expected. During the winter 1205–6, John resumed his travels through England, again journeying as far north as Yorkshire and Cumberland. The chroniclers had little to tell of the king in the months which followed the 1205 muster, but he must have reached some compromise with the barons he visited, for it transpired that many, especially among those of northern England, would be ready to follow him next summer on a more limited offensive. Probably, they saw the new project as a safer bet than its ill-fated forerunner. Perhaps the prospect of sailing to the support of their compatriots at La Rochelle appealed to their chivalric notions. Or maybe they no longer had support among the king's officers.

Hubert Walter had died at Teynham, Kent, shortly after opposing the 1205 expedition. Marshal may well have found an offensive in the South less conflicting with his conscience than one in Normandy. Without the alliance of such men, the barony must have been more amenable to John's plans.

The second expedition, more modest than the first but still impressive, sailed from England at the beginning of June 1206, and arrived at La Rochelle on the seventh. It was greeted enthusiastically by the barons of Aquitaine. Philip had now become the main threat to their freedom; the King of England a more remote, consequently more tolerable, overlord. They rallied to John's banner in heartening numbers. But the king was not provoked to rash action by their fervour. Eschewing a direct challenge to the French king, he planned to chop his way north in a series of surprise raids on enemy strongholds in Poitou and the Loire lands, undermining the confidence of Philip's allies.

Six days after landing on the Continent, John rode east to Niort to congratulate and encourage its garrison, after which he scouted the country toward Poitiers as far as St.-Maixent. Before turning north, it was necessary to ensure that his rear was free of rebels. Accordingly, in July, he moved his base south to Bourg-sur-Mer, a small port near Bordeaux at the mouth of the Garonne. Rather more than a hundred miles up-river, a force of hostile barons had established itself in the castle of Montauban, a massive fortress which, according to legend, Charlemagne had once besieged for seven years without success. Following the Garonne, John arrived at the walls of the castle, which he proceeded to pummel with siege engines. On the fifteenth day, a breach was opened, the English soldiers scrambled in and overwhelmed the garrison in a ferocious sword and axe duel. Apart from a haul of eminent prisoners, the profit in horses, weapons and other spoils was munificent.

Back at Niort in August, the English king struck hard across Poitou to Montmorillon on its eastern border, then clean back across Poitou to Clisson, to the northwest. John had not lost his talent for raiding. By now, at least one of the more powerful Poitevin barons, Amery of Thouars, brother of Guy of Thouars, had considered it prudent to desert Philip and join the English. With a strong ally in northern Poitou, John turned daringly north into Anjou, crossing the Loire south of Angers. This was a sufficiently memorable achievement to gain a colourful mention in the annals of the province. "When the king arrived at the Loire," wrote the scribe of a local abbey, "there were no boats available . . . appealing to God for help, he made the sign of the cross above the water, then forded the river with all his host, a marvellous thing to recount, and one never before heard of in our time." Fighting his way into Angers, John spent a week there, holding court in the old capital of his forebears.

Before turning back to Poitou, he flung a further rude gesture in Philip's face by striking at Le Lude, almost as far north as the border of Maine. By now, the French king was seriously disquieted. Mobilising his army, the lord of Paris strutted south. But, impressed by the stabbing thrusts of his rival, and John's renewed authority in Poitou, he stopped circumspectly short at the southern border of Anjou. There was now an impasse. At this stage, the continental empire of the Angevins was roughly halved between the two monarchs, Philip holding the North, John the South. Philip was still concerned with the consolidation of Normandy; John was not yet the full master of Poitou. Philip was loath to expose his army to the fickle barons of the South; John was reluctant to chance his luck against Philip's host. The result was a truce, proclaimed in October to last for two years. By its terms, both parties pledged to maintain the status quo, to allow normal trade between their dominions, and to abide, in case of dispute, by the decision of a court of arbitration comprising two barons from either side.

For the moment, John could be satisfied. He had secured the South, won back much of Poitou and, perhaps more gratifying, reduced the cock-a-hoop Philip to a truce which confirmed the gains of the English. He could return to England and hold his head high among his barons. So much had been achieved with relatively limited resources. All being well, he had two years in which to raise the revenue and enthusiasm for a supreme effort to recover the rest of his territories. Prior to re-embarking at La Rochelle, John had Queen Isabelle recognised as countess of her homeland, Angoulême. He arrived at Portsmouth on December 12.

Chapter 9
JOHN AND THE POPE

Every king before me conferred archbishoprics, bishoprics, and abbeys.

King John to Pope Innocent III

One charge that could not be levelled at the medieval Church was that it was aloof from, or out of touch with the laity. It was richly, and often racily, involved with temporal life at all levels. Among its higher echelons, such archbishops as Lanfranc, Anselm and Hubert Walter had stood at the very helm of the nation, remembered at least as much for their secular as for their spiritual offices. Bishops were great temporal lords in their own right. They sat on the king's council with barons, they officiated as judges, and many made names for themselves as warriors. Anglo-Saxon history recalled Hereford's battling bishop, Leofgar, who had strapped on a sword and led his priests to war against the Welsh. The Norman warrior prelate Odo, Bishop of Bayeux, having qualms about wielding a sword or lance, had charged into action at Hastings laying about him fiercely with a cudgel.

At a humbler level, the parish priests shared the penury, and commonly the ignorance, of the peasants among whom they lived, and to whose ranks they frequently belonged by birth. "The hovels of the parish clergy," wrote Gerald of Wales, "are full of hectoring mistresses, squeaky cradles, new-born infants and bawling brats." In some cases, churchmen not only shared the ribald taste of their parishioners, but celebrated it in their churches and cathedrals. In Paris, and elsewhere in thirteenth-century France, the Feast of Fools was a popular occasion. "The priests and clerks elected a pope, an archbishop or a bishop, conducted them with much pomp to the church, and entered dancing, masked and dressed in women's clothes, or impersonating animals or merry-Andrews. Here, they sung infamous songs, played dice, converted the altar into a buffet where they refreshed themselves during the celebration of the holy mysteries, burned their old sandals instead of incense, and leaped from seat to seat striking indecent postures."

Another festival, the Feast of Asses, was celebrated at Beauvais. "They chose the prettiest maiden in town, mounted her on a richly harnessed ass, and placed an infant in her arms. Attended by the bishop and clergy, she was led from the cathedral to the porch of St. Stephen's, into the sanctuary and placed near the altar. The Mass began. Whatever the choir sung was followed by the delightful refrain, *Hee-haw, hee-haw!* Half in French, half in Latin, they extolled the fine qualities of the animal, exhorting him to make a devout genuflexion." The ceremony concluded with a priest singing three times, "Hee-haw, hee-haw, hee-haw," and the congregation answering likewise "to imitate the braying of that solemn animal."

Monasteries, and even nunneries, were infamous in some quarters for the loose morals of their inmates. "Women and girls were by no means secure when they passed by abbeys," wrote one historian. But it was their interest in education that involved monks more seriously in secular activities. During

John and the Pope

Anglo-Saxon times, the monasteries virtually monopolised education. It was not until the eleventh century that there was academic schooling on a notable scale outside the monasteries, and not until the thirteenth that monks were replaced in any numbers as teachers, even in secular academies. Throughout this period, almost every monastery had an interest in learning, and all education was either in the monasteries or under the direction of monks.

As the administration of kingdoms and vast estates became more sophisticated, kings and lords needed educated men—men who could read, write, translate and keep accounts—around them. They found them in the Church. Thus churchmen came to occupy more and more official posts in a secular capacity. The word "clerk" in the English language came to be synonymous with both a churchman and a book-keeper.

For ambitious youngsters of humble families, the Church was a door of opportunity leading to the courts and offices of great men. For their employers, clergymen fulfilled a dual requirement by being both educated and cheap to hire. At the bottom of the administrative ladder, the clerk could be rewarded by the grant of a parish church, from which he could cream the revenues, leaving a curate to do the work. At the top of the ladder, the favoured officials of the king could be found bishoprics—even, perhaps, an archbishopric. Opportunities in the royal administration were manifold. The exchequer, the chancery and the law courts were full of officials in Holy Orders. It happened increasingly, therefore, that bright young men aspiring to high office in the civil service, took Holy Orders as a first step to a primarily secular career.

Hubert Walter was a good example of this process at its most successful. Both as justiciar and chancellor, he had proved a brilliant administrator. He had rescued the country from a potentially disastrous situation during Richard's crusade, he had controlled the administration during the French wars, he had helped to maintain law and order at the time of John's accession, and he had initiated many bureaucratic reforms, including the enrolment of chancery documents, the charter, patent and close rolls. He was an outstanding civil servant. Yet as Archbishop of Canterbury he had left much to be desired. His interest was almost entirely secular. So much so that the monks of Canterbury had actually protested to the pope that the archbishop was neglecting the Church.

Not surprisingly, the growth of temporal activities and ethics within the Church had provoked a reaction among those with a more profound view of the religious role on earth. While the royal clerks were attaining the top rungs of administration, happily receiving bishoprics among their perquisites, a reforming movement was gathering momentum through Europe aimed at disengaging the clergy from lay society and re-establishing its spiritual purpose. About the middle of the eleventh century, the Apostolic See had broken free from the patronage of the German emperors, to be reorientated by a succession of high churchmen toward an ideal superseding the rule of kings and princes—the ideal of a universal rule of righteousness based on a common conception of human history and spiritual destiny.

During the eleventh and twelfth centuries, the theory was advanced by Rome of the indisputable superiority of the papacy over all temporal monarchs, not only because kings received unction from churchmen, but because "royal power borrows the splendour of its dignity from pontifical authority, as the moon borrows its light from the sun and is therefore inferior to it." This argument was hardly congenial to monarchs who regarded themselves as the direct link between God and their subjects, nor were the well-organised bastions of individual monarchies likely to fall before the hopeful generalisations of this or that pope. It was not until the end of the twelfth century, when Innocent III succeeded to the papal throne, that

John and the Pope

such kings as John and Philip began to feel the pressure, and pontifical theocracy came close to reality.

Innocent had been thirty-eight when he became pope in 1198, a clean-shaven man possessing, if one can trust the stylised portraiture of the time, a small mouth, deep chin and reflective demeanour. As Lothario of Segni, he had studied theology in Paris and law in Bologna, becoming a cardinal in 1191 under his uncle, Pope Clement III. He was destined to be a great pope. Practical in outlook, he was a shrewd lawyer and politician with a clear, analytical mind exactly suited to giving legal shape to the pontifical doctrine, to harnessing theory to a workable formula. Innocent saw his role as universal ruler on two planes: 1) spiritual, the head of the universal Church, all churches being answerable to the primacy of Rome; 2) temporal, as supreme governor of the world, asserting authority through intermediary kings and princes whose political actions were answerable to Christian judgement. Ideally, the individual monarchs would become vassals of the pope by doing homage to him within the feudal framework, and to some extent this aim would be realised.

By establishing the appointment of papal legates to various countries on a permanent basis, Innocent further promoted the mechanics of centralisation, enabling him to keep abreast of world affairs. At the same time, to counter the abuses of hedonism and sybaritism within the Church, he encouraged the monks to emerge from their retreats and set an example of evangelical poverty and celibacy.

At the beginning of the thirteenth century, therefore, two conflicting forces were at work within the pattern of Church life. On the one hand, clerics were serving lay masters in secular capacities on a scale never before exceeded, and being repaid with ecclesiastical preferment. On the other hand, the clergy was being made increasingly aware of its separate status in the kingdom, and its privilege to look to Rome as the source of authority. It was among John's misfortunes to be caught at the turbulent crossing of the currents.

According to Matthew Paris, John was overjoyed by the death of Hubert Walter, exclaiming gleefully: "Now, for the first time, am I truly King of England." It is most unlikely that John said anything of the sort, and even more unlikely that, had he done so, Paris would have known about it, for no earlier chronicle mentions the incident. Paris pinned this piece of dramatic invention on the role Walter had played in frustrating John's plan to invade France in 1205. But it was not in John's nature to bear a grudge, and no one knew better than the king how much he owed to his minister. Moreover, the complications involved in the election of a new Archbishop of Canterbury were generally tricky. The prospect was more likely to have occasioned a royal headache than royal exultation.

Canonically, the electors of the archbishop were the monks of Christ Church Priory, Canterbury, many of the episcopal sees in England being monastic in origin. The monks of Christ Church formed the chapter of the cathedral, their conventual church, and claimed the right of choosing in the same man their abbot and the archbishop. But the bishops of the dioceses in the archbishop's province, the southern half of England, could not be content with such an arrangement. Not unreasonably, they protested their right to a say in the choice of their metropolitan. Further to complicate the issue, the king had an obvious interest in the election. The archbishopric was the highest reward he could offer a churchman in his service. Its holder became not only a great landowner and temporal baron, but also a leading figure in the king's councils. Ideally, the monks, the bishops and the king might agree on the same man. More often, there was friction, and the king's will prevailed. The chroniclers made no bones about the practicalities. They wrote of kings "giving" bishoprics and archbishoprics to their favour-

John and the Pope

ites as a matter of course. And, indeed, it was traditional. Nevertheless, the matter was one of delicacy, and had to be handled with tact.

When Walter had been buried, John spent six days at Canterbury, "talking graciously and at length" with the monks of Christ Church. He also conferred with the bishops, making the Bishop-elect of Winchester, Peter of Roches, a present of some of Walter's trappings. The outcome was a postponement of the election for six months, until the end of November, during which time John sent messengers to the pope seeking approval of his nominee for the archbishopric. The name he put forward was John Gray, Bishop of Norwich, the king's secretary and a close friend. Gray, a native of Norfolk, was an erudite man, a trained administrator and a relaxed and genial companion. John claimed in this likeable and efficient civil servant a worthy successor to Walter, a fellow East Anglian.

But the monks and the bishops had also sent envoys to Rome, pressing separately their respective claims in the matter. When the monks of Canterbury heard that the king's agents were lobbying the pope for Gray's promotion, a number of the younger and more impulsive members of the chapter resolved to outwit him. Meeting secretly by night, they elected their subprior, one Reginald, as abbot and archbishop, vesting him at the altar and placing him on the primate's throne. They then sent him to Rome with a further delegation to reinforce the claims they had already put forward. Before he left, Reginald was placed on oath to say nothing of the election save as an emergency measure to turn the scales against John or the bishops.

Reginald's friends seem to have underestimated the heady effects of his election on the subprior. As soon as he reached Rome, perhaps even before he got there, Reginald openly styled himself Archbishop-elect of Canterbury, revealed confidential letters from the monks confirming his election, and begged the pope for his blessing. Innocent, keenly interested in episcopal elections, noted developments and announced that he would conduct a full investigation into the position at Canterbury. When word of the secret election got back to England, there was uproar. The monks hastily repudiated their indiscreet subprior. Both monks and bishops sped new emissaries on the road to Rome. A furious John descended on Canterbury.

Faced with the full Angevin wrath of the monarch, the monks of Christ Church persisted in the lie that no election had been held, pleading that they be allowed to demonstrate their innocence by choosing an archbishop in John's presence. Sweetening his temper, John agreed, suggesting that the combined interests of king, Church and country could not be better served than by the election of John Gray. That this would also be in the interests of the monks themselves, was a point clearly taken. On December 11, having renounced their appeals to Rome, the chapter unanimously elected Gray, investing him with the temporalities of the see. A loan of five hundred marks was granted to defray his expenses. It remained for the pope to confirm the new primate.

Things, however, were not to be so simple. Around Christmas, 1205, John sent a deputation including, among others, six of the Canterbury monks, to Rome to announce the election of Gray and to seek the pope's blessing. The deputation was provided liberally with money to win the favours of the papal court. But the bishops had not been consulted, and their representatives in Rome lodged strong complaints against the monks of Christ Church. Innocent was surrounded by conflicting delegations. Reginald and his companions denounced the second election as invalid; John's agents maintained there had been no election save that of Gray; the bishops' delegation attacked both elections, protesting that the original claim of the bishops for a voice in the matter was still pending. To add to the babble, further monks arrived in Rome from Canterbury, apparently with plenipotentiary authority.

Calmly, in his own good time, Innocent delivered his findings. Dismissing the claim of the bishops, he declared that the right of electing the metropolitan belonged to the Canterbury monks, and to none else. Reginald's election was invalid, he asserted, because it had been conducted irregularly. Only a section of the chapter had been involved, and it had excluded in particular the older and more experienced monks. The election of John Gray was likewise pronounced void. It had taken place, Innocent pointed out, before Reginald's election had been annulled. Thus the see was still vacant. At this stage, it might have been expected that the pope would direct the holding of a fresh election in England. But Innocent had other plans. Faced with a God-sent chance to establish a man of his own choosing at Canterbury, he did not ignore it. To the surprise of all parties, he instructed the delegates of the cathedral chapter to hold an election there and then at the papal court.

In the confusion of the moment, Innocent played his hand expertly. When some of the monks pleaded that the royal assent, and the concurrence of their fellows at home, would be needed, they were assured that this was not so, and that they were fully empowered to hold an election at the Apostolic See. Then, with the partisans of Reginald and Gray uncompromisingly deadlocked, Innocent smoothly suggested a solution. Why did they not forget their disputes and elect a candidate unassociated with either side? He proposed an Englishman then present at the consistory, Stephen Langton, Cardinal of St. Chrystogonus. Langton had been born in Lincolnshire rather less than fifty years earlier, and had made a name for himself as a lecturer in theology at the University of Paris. Innocent commended his scholarship, virtue and diplomacy, and declared that the cardinal would be an asset both to the Church of England and the king's council. It was hardly necessary for him to point out that Langton shared his views on Church reform.

A long way from England, awed by the shadow of St. Peter's rock, the monks succumbed to the will of the pope and the cardinals. It seems that only one of their number, Elias of Brantfield, abstained from voting. The remainder—"muttering and reluctantly," as Wendover had it—accepted Innocent's bidding and elected Stephen Langton. John's agents in Rome refused to sanction the proceedings with the royal assent, but the pope was unimpressed. In a letter to John, received a few weeks after the king's return from La Rochelle, Innocent informed him of the election and demanded his approval. The result was explosive. That the pope had acted, as he believed, in the best interests of Christendom, was of little moment at the English court. The kings of England had long regarded themselves as "Christ's deputies" among their subjects; the Archbishops of Canterbury as their highest lieutenants. The news that the appointment of a primate of England had been settled in a foreign capital, as if John had not existed, left the king dumbfounded.

Once again, astonishment gave way to anger. As John saw it, he had been tricked. And those who had made it possible, first by the clandestine election of Reginald, and then by reneging on their support for Gray, were the monks of Canterbury. The king had had enough of them. Furiously, he ordered their expulsion from the country, later installing monks of St. Augustine's on their property. Sixty-seven of the monks from Christ Church emigrated to the Continent, while the revenues from their lands, and the lands of the archbishop, were diverted to the royal purse. Fulk Cantelu, one of John's household knights, was placed in charge of the cathedral properties.

In a scathing reply to the pope, John accused him of a blatant attempt to deprive the crown of its just rights and privileges, expressed incredulity that Innocent thought so little of the

John and the Pope

friendship of the King of England, and claimed that the only thing he, John, knew about Langton was that the man had lived in France for many years and was the friend of Philip Augustus, England's bitterest enemy. This was partially true and partially incredible. Langton had spent little of his mature life in England and had, indeed, become friendly with Philip while living and teaching in Paris. On the other hand, Langton's fame was widespread. He was known for his revision of the Bible, which he had divided into chapters for speedier reference. He had written the famous hymn *Veni, sancte spiritus*. And his lectures on religious and moral issues had aroused interest far beyond the confines of Paris. His insistence that the obedience of subject to sovereign was conditional, and that there was no absolute right against the right of the Church, was probably all too familiar to the English king.

In any case, John thundered, he had no need of Langton's learning. England possessed ecclesiastics aplenty, skilled in the widest range of scholarly subjects. He did not have to beg the assistance of strangers. In short, Langton was quite unacceptable. John Gray, Bishop of Norwich, was the man the king intended to promote to the archbishopric. Gray he knew, and Gray he trusted. If the pope ignored his wishes, he would sever all connections between England and Rome, and Rome would be the poorer by the wealth that customarily flowed there from England in gifts and tributes.

Innocent's reply was icily meticulous. He had discovered that John had sent messages of congratulation to Langton at the latter's elevation to the office of cardinal. It was curious, observed the pope, that the King of England professed not to know the man to whom he had written, and who enjoyed such widespread fame for his attributes and accomplishments. Langton, he reminded the king, was a doctor of the University of Paris in both arts and theology, and a prebendary not only of Notre Dame in Paris, but also of St. Peter's in York. John should not think that because his approval had been sought for the election at Rome, that his approval was necessary. He, Innocent, had complete authority over the Church of Canterbury. The canonical procedures had been invoked, and nothing would swerve him from his purpose. "We defer to you more than we ought," wrote the pope. "You heed us less than you should." John had best render honour where honour was due, "and thus earn the goodwill of God and the Pope," before he found himself "in difficulties which might not easily be overcome."

A lesser monarch than John might also have jibbed at such coercion. It was not merely his prestige which was at stake, but a principle which cut to the very core of relationships between king and Church. Philip Augustus had defied the pope for four years in the dubious cause of a bigamous marriage. John could hardly have been expected to submit meekly to Rome with so much precedent on his side, and when no less than his authority to rule his own subjects was in peril. Metaphorically hitching his sword belt, he prepared to take on Innocent III, as well as the King of France, in the struggle to defend his inheritance.

At the beginning of 1207, new measures to equip himself for the hot war with France brought a further chill to the cold war between John and the Roman Church. At a grand council at Westminster on January 8, a demand was made for a tax on the moveable property of both the clergy and the laity. Patently, the rising cost of administration, and the heavy financial demands of warfare abroad, could no longer be covered adequately by the system of feudal dues. Trade was healthy, and the standard of living was improving. But agricultural productivity was lagging, and the cost of living was rising, too. In this inflationary situation, a form of taxing related to individual wealth was more realistic than the time-honoured systems. A levy on chattels had already proved successful in meeting earlier emergencies, and, linked with a tax on regular revenues, was to become standard procedure in days ahead.

But now the clergy opposed it, and, at a further council at Oxford in February, John agreed that the tax (a thirteenth, or twelve pence in the mark, on rents and moveables) should apply to the laity only. His half brother Geoffrey, Archbishop of York, immediately claimed exemption for laymen holding lands of the Church. This John refused. Whereupon Geoffrey, protesting vigorously, retired to France, where he was to die in 1212, having taken no further part in the affairs of England. Meanwhile, the temporalities of York, like those of Canterbury, passed into the king's hands. The Church of England faced the fateful days ahead with its highest offices unoccupied in North and South.

When Innocent realised that John had no intention of capitulating unconditionally, he went ahead and consecrated Langton at Viterbo in July. This he followed with a succession of directives to the bishops and barons of England, instructing them in the action they should take against the sovereign. Three prelates, Mauger, Bishop of Worcester, Eustace, Bishop of Ely, and William, Bishop of London, were detailed to seek audience with the king and, if he could not be converted by reason, to threaten him with an interdict. This interdict was to apply to Wales as well as England. Bishops of both countries, warned the pope, should be prepared to fight for the "liberty of the Church" regardless of self-interest. The barons should join them in prosecuting God's cause. Finally, amends should be demanded for Geoffrey.

Wendover constructed a colourfully partisan account of John's meeting with the three bishops. While the bishops "entreated him humbly and tearfully" to receive Langton and recall the monks of Canterbury, "the king became nearly mad with rage, blaspheming against the pope and his cardinals, swearing by

God's teeth that if they, or any other priests, presumed to lay his dominions under interdict, he would dispatch all prelates and other ordained persons of England to the pope, and confiscate their property." Any envoys of the pope who were found in England would receive worse treatment. He would send them back to Rome "with their eyes plucked out and their noses split." According to Wendover, John dismissed the bishops with the tender advice that, if they wished to keep their own bodies intact, they would do well to remove themselves from his sight.

In fact, John was neither so unreasonable, nor half so reckless. When the first flush of his anger had subsided, his thoughts seem to have turned toward compromise. Despite his persisting resentment of the pope's methods, one learns from the king's own communication with the bishops that he was prepared to satisfy Innocent's requirements concerning the Church of Canterbury so far as "might be decent . . . saving for himself and his heirs his right, his dignity and his liberties." In other words, the pope might have his way this time, but it was not to be established as a precedent. It was a concession calculated to preserve honour on both sides, but it did not satisfy the pope's men. In February 1208, far from wreaking vengeance on envoys from oversea, John offered safe-conduct to Langton's brother Simon, to come to England and negotiate. Talks took place in Winchester that March, but Simon Langton would have nothing to do with the reservation of royal rights, insisting on unconditional submission. "When we spoke to him of retaining our dignity," John wrote balefully, "he told us that he could not concern himself with that unless we threw ourselves wholly upon his mercy."

At last, on Passion Sunday, March 23, the threatened interdict was proclaimed in England and Wales, to take effect on the Monday. The precise implications of the phenomenon are not known. Probably, they varied from place to place, for the

John and the Pope

sentence was scarcely a common one and the niceness of its regulations, insofar as ordered regulations existed, appears to have baffled not a few of the clergy. Broadly speaking, the interdict was a withdrawal of the Church's services from the public. Innocent's instructions to the Bishops of Worcester, Ely and London had been to announce the general imposition of a punishment "permitting no clerical office except the baptism of infants and the confession of the dying." Church doors were closed; sermons were preached only on Sundays, and then draughtily among the slabs of the churchyard; Christian burial was suspended, bodies being disposed of in bogs, woods and ditches. Marriages and the churching of women took place, it seems, in church porches.

For the devout, life without Mass, without the singing of service and the reading of prayers, must have been a profoundly upsetting experience. Those who believed that a grave in consecrated ground was the first step to heaven, and that prayers after death were essential to salvation, undoubtedly lived among dark and potent fears. Here lay the weakness of the interdict, which, like all forms of indiscriminate retribution, caused the greatest suffering to those blameless in the eyes of its perpetrators. Theoretically, such suffering was held to deprive the offender of general sympathy. England's earthy and independent sons balked at such a devious and mean role.

Few Englishmen could see the justice of the pope's case. Those who knew Gray regarded him as a worthy choice for the archbishopric, whereas Langton was an unknown quantity. That the King of England's chief counsellor could be elected in Rome, and forced on him against his wish by papal decree, seemed to ordinary men a disgraceful procedure. Furthermore, who, if not the king himself, could feel safe from papal intrusion? What offices in the land would be secure to Englishmen if the pope could fill them with outsiders? Far from robbing John of sympathy, the immediate effect of the interdict was to rally the nation behind him. "The entire laity, the majority of clergymen, and many monks were on the king's side," wrote the Margam annalist. The Cistercians, and doubtless others, "rang their bells, voiced their chants and celebrated the divine offices," in open defiance of the interdict. The pope rebuked them sharply, but the general reaction in England probably worried him, for after a while he relaxed the terms of the sentence somewhat.

John prepared his response to the interdict thoroughly; his administration functioned smoothly. Several days before the pronouncement of the interdict, royal officers were standing by throughout the kingdom with orders to confiscate the property of all ecclesiastics "who are unwilling to celebrate the divine office." If the pope could deprive the king's subjects of their religious functions, the king could deprive the pope's subjects of the possessions they held by right of supervising such functions. The moment the churches closed their doors, the king's officers moved about their business. Having fulfilled the pope's orders, the three bishops appointed to act for him promptly fled the country—like fearful boys, as one historian has put it, who "set fire to their squibs and make fast away from them." Their flight was not followed, as has sometimes been asserted, by a general exodus of English prelates. John Gray, Bishop of Norwich, Peter of Roches, Bishop of Winchester, and, among others, the Bishops of Rochester, Salisbury, Bath, Durham and Coventry, remained in the country. A number of sees was already vacant, and this number was increased when the Bishops of Durham and Coventry died within a few months.

Having demonstrated his capacity to act as sweepingly as his adversary, John set about his real purpose of separating those who unreservedly supported the pope from those who accepted the custom of the country. Within days of the publication of the interdict, negotiations were in hand with individual Church authorities which led to the majority o churches and monasteries resuming the management of their estates, and even expanding them, in much the normal manner. In some cases, the proportion of revenue payable to the crown was increased, and in other instances churchmen had to bail out their property. According to one chronicler, the payment of a fine enabled most rectors to recover their possessions. But there seems to have been little extortion of a drastic nature at this stage. The royal revenue from Church sources was not grossly inflated during 1208 and 1209.

The majority of Englishmen supported the king's measures. Some, it appears, expressed their feelings in no uncertain manner, for shortly after the commencement of the interdict John responsibly pronounced that anyone molesting, or even insulting, a monk or priest should be hanged from the nearest oak tree. He did, however, allow some amusement at the expense of the more worldly clerics by ordering that their mistresses should be detained by the sheriffs' officers and held to ransom. One contemporary, Abbot John Ford, considered that the most scandalous feature of the whole interdict was the readiness with which priests handed over their money to recover their concubines.

During 1208 and 1209, John made further, and unfruitful, gestures of compromise. He sent the Abbot of Beaulieu to Rome to announce that he was willing to reinstate the Canterbury monks, to place the temporalities of the see in the pope's hands, and to meet Langton, though not as a friend or familiar. Innocent countered that complete restitution must be made for all Church property confiscated since the pronouncement of the interdict. This was unacceptable to John. He did, however, offer safe-conducts to the three bishops, and to Stephen Langton himself, to come to England. The bishops came, with instructions from the pope that if his terms were not fulfilled within three months of January 1209 they were to promulgate and enforce a sentence of personal excommunication on the

English king. When the time was up, the bishops circumspectly left England, leaving those who remained to publish the excommunication.

But the bishops still in England refused to do such a thing. Toward the end of summer, John offered the exiled bishops partial restitution, and, in October, allowed them to return to the kingdom accompanied by Stephen Langton. Justiciar Geoffrey FitzPeter, and the Bishop of Winchester, met them and parleyed. When the visitors still insisted on the entire fulfilment of the pope's terms, they were courteously led back to their ships.

How genuine was John in seeking an accommodation with the pope? It was hard to say, and the chroniclers were hushed on the subject. Certainly, he had moved further toward Innocent's position than Innocent had moved toward his, but the interdict had failed to rouse the country against the king, and he was far from bargaining in abject weakness. The prospect of excommunication posed a more direct threat. Anyone who associated with an excommunicated king would be in danger of himself being excommunicated, and, that autumn, John acknowledged his apprehension by calling for a general renewal of homage from his English and Welsh subjects. In November, the excommunication was published—not in England, but from France—and by Christmas it was known throughout the kingdom that the dread anathema had been attached to the English king. It seems to have made little difference to the seasonal festivities at Windsor, which were well attended by the nobility. The Bishops of Winchester and Norwich showed contempt for the sentence, and few of the royal clerks were moved to relinquish their offices.

A proportion of the English clergy did leave the country, including the Bishops of Rochester, Lincoln, Salisbury and Bath, together with some lesser clergymen. John seized their estates and impounded their revenues. Excommunication provoked a more drastic retribution against the churches than had the interdict. Property belonging to the Archbishop of Canterbury was sold on behalf of the Crown, and a castle belonging to the Bishop of London was destroyed. The king's revenue from ecclesiastical sources rose steeply following the imposition of the personal stigma. In the second year of the interdict the exchequer had received some four hundred pounds from such sources; in the first year of the excommunication, the figure was nine times greater. In 1211, it rose to twenty-four thousand pounds. And this did not include large amounts extorted from the Cistercians and others, though, remarkably, Cistercian abbots remained in attendance at the royal court.

Ironically, the pope's endeavours to humble John relieved the king of his most pressing embarrassment to this date—lack of money. For several years, thanks largely to the wealth he appropriated from the pope's supporters in England, John was to be free of financial worries. Not only could he contemplate raising fresh armies without imposing new taxes, he could dispense with much taxation altogether. This was a considerable boon to the barons, who, far from exploiting the king's struggle with Rome to push their own ambitions, stood solidly beside their unrepentant monarch. Innocent inveighed sharply on their failure to help the Church. On the other hand, the monastic writers, shocked by the diversion of Church revenues and capital to the king's purse, not to mention the general ignominy of the interdict, formulated from this period the notion of John as an irreligious tyrant which was to survive down the ages.

The image of John as a blaspheming despoiler of churches, who scoffed at priests and, according to one indignant scribe, Adam of Eynsham, never communicated in his adult life, was hardly sustained by the records. One of John's first acts upon Richard's death had been to visit the tombs of his father and brother at Fontevrault. He had followed his coronation with a pilgrimage to the shrines of three English saints. He had fallen on his knees to ask the forgiveness of the Cistercian abbots who had complained to him of the behaviour of his forest officials, and he had built for them Beaulieu Abbey. He had visited Bishop Hugh of Lincoln on his deathbed, and had put his shoulder to the coffin at the funeral. He had made countless benefactions to religious establishments (and actually increased these during the interdict), frequently spent money on chalices, altar cloths and other church trappings, and was an earnest reader of the Bible and books on theology. Like his father, he tended to be impatient of protracted religious ceremonial, but in such practical aspects of Christianity as charity, tolerance, forgiveness and the preference of peace above warfare, he compared very favourably with the rulers of his own age.

John bore no animosity in principle against the Church or the papacy. His concern was to preserve what he saw as his sovereign rights. It was his immediate misfortune to have clashed with a pope so purposeful as Innocent—and, in the longer term, perhaps to have failed to endow those monasteries which were to produce hostile chronicles.

Chapter 10
SERFS, CELTS AND SPECTRES

> Gives not the hawthorn bush a sweeter shade
> To shepherds, looking on their silly sheep,
> Than doth a rich embroider'd canopy
> To kings that fear their subjects' treachery?
> *Shakespeare,* King Henry VI, *Part 3, II.v*

The first child born to John and Isabelle arrived on October 1, 1207, in the eighth year of their marriage. Since by all accounts the match had been a warm one, even an affair of passion, and the couple had been much together, the delay in conception seems to have resulted from some physiological vagary of Isabelle's rather than lack of effort on John's part. The infant, a boy, was delivered at Winchester, and christened Henry after his grandfather. His appearance, if belated, was not untimely. The delay had allowed Isabelle, now about twenty, to reach maturity before entering motherhood, while the birth of an heir at a particularly vulnerable period of John's reign bolstered his position and confidence. Entering his forties, grey-haired, stout and energetic, John had already fathered a number of illegitimate children. Five are known (a modest offspring compared with the twenty-odd of Henry I) all born before the marriage to Isabelle of Angoulême. But of the king's alleged misdemeanours with the wives and daughters of his barons, none is substantiated. Among his recorded mistresses, only one, the widow Hawise, Countess of Aumale, is known to have been of any rank.

Nevertheless, his detractors portrayed the king in middle age as a lascivious, sadistic and money-grubbing ogre. Wendover told how a cleric in the king's service, Geoffrey, Archdeacon of Norwich, quit his post rather than remain in the employ of an excommunicated monarch. "When this came to the knowledge of the king, he was greatly angered and sent the knight William Talbot, with some soldiers, to seize the archdeacon. They bound him in chains and threw him into prison." At John's command, so the tale went, "a cope of lead" was made for the cleric, and placed upon his shoulders. Deprived of food and crushed beneath the leaden weight, the prisoner supposedly died in agony. Though cited by many later historians as an example of John's cruelty, the story is deflated by the fact that, far from "departing to the Lord" in 1209, as the author had it, Archdeacon Geoffrey was appointed Bishop of Ely in 1225.

Equally memorable, though hardly more credible, is another Wendover anecdote relating to a certain Jew of Bristol who had his teeth knocked out one at a time, on John's orders, until he agreed to hand over ten thousand marks. The Jew supposedly capitulated after losing the seventh tooth. There is no vestige of evidence for this yarn. The Jews were under royal protection, and the king was by law the heir to all of them. When a Jew died, he took over not only his money and possessions, but also his credit notes. There was little need for lesser forms of extortion.

But the classic calumny came from Matthew Paris. Paris

Serfs, Celts and Spectres

would have had his readers believe that John responded to the pope's displeasure by offering to place himself and his kingdom under the protection of the Sultan of North Africa, and personally to renounce Christianity in favour of the Muslim faith. As usual, Paris embroidered his story with imaginative detail, naming the king's ambassadors and quoting their private talks with the emir. To point the moral, one of the royal messengers in Matthew's anecdote was a clergyman who felt constrained to tell his Muslim host the awful truth about the English king. "When the sultan heard this, he not only despised John, he abhorred him."

From less colourful, but more reliable sources, John emerges at this period as considerate of the proletariat, a friend of traders both English and foreign, and the patron of much constructive work. To the personnel of his roving court, from the lords of his immediate entourage to the scroungers and harlots in their wake, he was generous to a fault. The monkish scribes complained that he pampered and spoilt his followers with extravagant dispensations of largesse. When the price of corn was high due to poor crops, the king ordered his sheriffs to provide cheap loaves for the impoverished. John gained the gratitude of traders by relieving them of many of the discouraging exactions imposed at seaports, and he had the dockyard at Portsmouth improved. "We order you to construct a good strong wall round our dock at Portsmouth without delay," he wrote his officials there, "so that, when winter comes, we may avoid damage to our vessels and their appurtenances." He also urged forward the building of London Bridge, which was completed in 1209 with a chapel at its middle under which was buried Peter of Colechurch, who had supervised much of the construction.

On the west coast of England, John founded a much-needed port of trade and access to Ireland. Into the tidal waters of the Mersey, north of the Welsh border, poured a small stream, which formed a pool at its mouth. Probably as a corruption of the Norse *Hlithar-pollr,* or Pool of the Slopes, the place had come to be known as Liverpool. Henry II had given the manor and village there to a favoured falconer, Warine, but John, noting the fine harbourage potential of Liverpool, took it back from the Warine family in exchange for other lands. At the end of August 1207, he issued letters patent giving Liverpool the status of a free borough, and invited his subjects to settle there with guaranteed protection and trading rights.

The town was planned on the old Roman pattern, with the main streets in the form of a cross, and lesser streets joining them at right angles. A hundred and sixty-eight houses were built to be let at a shilling a year, and each tenant was provided with an allotment of two acres on which to grow food or keep animals. John ordered that a market should be held in the town every Saturday, and a fair once a year, in November. Though Liverpool developed slowly during John's reign, by the end of the thirteenth century it had seen considerable use as a shipping link with Ireland and points on the Welsh coast.

Like all medieval kings, John loved hunting the countryside. One learns that he "haunted woods and streams and greatly delighted in the pleasure of them." Hunting was the regular diversion of the feudal aristocracy, a wild, exhilarating, savage version of the sport which exists today, by comparison, as an emasculated relic. Hunting accidents were plentiful. Danger was part of the stimulant; blood lust orgiastically consummated at the kill. For the nobility, this was the nearest pursuit, in peaceful times, to the practice of war, and the hunting field fulfilled a rough and ready role as a training ground for military leaders. Such men kept their eye in, also, with the bow and arrow, shooting at game from horseback, or on foot when it was driven toward them from cover. Hawking was another popular diversion, but nothing satisfied the temper of the age quite so thoroughly as the thrill of the chase. English kings hunted the length and breadth of the kingdom as their courts moved from shire to shire, and they took hounds and hawks oversea with them when they visited the Continent.

A complexity of local arrangements facilitated royal hunting. One manor might owe the king a supply of hare hounds, another would provide larger dogs for stag hunting, while the rent of a third might include a good sporting bird or some horses. An army of officials gained employment from the royal sport, from the huntsmen and kennelmen who tended the animals, to the foresters and verderers who upheld the laws of the hunting grounds. Among the commonest complaints against the kings of the Norman and Angevin dynasties was the harshness of their forest laws. The ordinary folk of the forest might graze their cattle and pigs in the woods on payment of a small fee, but they were not allowed to lop or fell trees, to carry bows and arrows or to keep dogs, unless these had certain claws removed to hinder their running.

Manorial lords, and other favoured tenants, were sometimes granted the right of free-warren, that is, the privilege of hunting such smaller animals as foxes, hares and wild-cats on their own holdings. The hunting of the larger animals, deer and wild boar, was the exclusive prerogative of the king and his guests, and poaching could be punished by death, mutilation, imprisonment or heavy fines.

These laws applied not only to the royal estates, but to vast areas of wooded country giving cover to the larger game, whether the land belonged to the king, his barons or the Church. The area covered by forest law had expanded remorselessly under the Norman kings—whose punishment of offenders had been barbarous—to reach its apogee in the reign of Henry II. By this time, almost a third of the entire kingdom had been maintained as a game preserve. John diminished this area, selling his rights in a number of forests, including those of

Devon and Cornwall, and mitigating the forest laws. He also initiated a drive against the wolves which lurked in the woods to harass sheep farmers, offering the princely sum of five shillings for a wolf's head.

It is very easy in the elaborate moves of kings, knights and bishops which dominated the medieval chessboard, to forget the long-suffering pawns: the multitude of illiterate, hard-labouring peasants who formed the mass of the populace. All the barons and bishops of England put together numbered no more than a few hundred in a total population of something like two million. While the lords bargained and warred for power, acquisition and privilege, ordinary people were grateful for little more than subsistence. In the towns, through the election of mayors and aldermen, through merchant guilds and by the rudimentary expression of fears and anger in mob action, commoners were beginning to find a collective voice. But town dwellers, while increasing in numbers, were still a relatively insignificant proportion of the national mass. The great majority lived a rustic life, tied by their obligations and toils to the small corner of the countryside in which they had been born and brought up.

To most inhabitants of medieval England, the shire was more important than the province, the village incomparably more important than either. Their England was the village street, its thatched huts and farm buildings, the timbered hall of the lord of the manor, a small stone church, and the immediate tracks and enveloping land. Between village and village, and thence to the shire towns, ran a tracery of unsurfaced lanes trodden flat by generations seeking the safest and easiest way about their business. Many such tracks, following the courses of diminished streams or erstwhile river beds, still ran with water in winter. Here and there, a great Roman road cut straight and true across this minor network. Along it moved the wagons of merchants, the officers and ambassadors

Serfs, Celts and Spectres

of the powerful, and, occasionally, the royal court. Unbending from their spine-warping labours, the peasants gazed upon their sovereign as upon some earthly god. When that god was strong, there was peace in the country. When the god was weak, and the barons were on the rampage, the humble cringed at the very sound of hoofbeats.

The Normans had found an acutely class-conscious populace in England, divided, roughly speaking, into three major categories: an upper class of thegns, an intermediate class known most commonly as ceorls, and a lower and less numerous order of slaves. Since this structure had played an important part in the evolution of John's English subjects, it is worth looking at rather more closely. The slave of Anglo-Saxon times had been a chattel, to be sold like an animal or a plough. Some slaves were prisoners of war, some were descendants of those ancient Britons the Romans and Saxons had encountered in their invasions, others the offspring of freemen forced by poverty to sell their kin into slavery.

Though contrary to the law, the export of slaves had persisted into the eleventh century. "We know full well of such miserable deeds as a father selling his son at a price, or a son his mother, or one brother another, into the power of foreigners," wrote the Anglo-Saxon Archbishop Wulfstan, who had preached with fervour against slavery. Sometimes slaves were redeemed, perhaps by ransom, perhaps by the goodwill of their owners, or the concern of the Church. Others tried to run away—a desperate venture, since runaway slaves might be stoned to death.

The ceorl was a freeman, at his most successful a farmer with one or more hides of his own land, a hide varying from about forty to a hundred and twenty acres depending on its situation in the kingdom. For a tenant farmer, the rent of a hide was heavy. In one part of Hampshire, for instance, it had involved an annual payment in money, ale, wheat, barley, wood and fencing, plus part-time work on behalf of the landlord every week of the year except three. In the locality of rivers, the landlord might demand his rent in rods, yarn, labour on the weirs, and one out of every two fish his tenant caught. The most favoured of the tenant class, sometimes called the *geneat,* paid rent for his land and gave services when needed as horseman, bodyguard, hunt assistant and so on. Then there was a lower order, the *gebur,* who, in return for a small holding and initial stock, might pay an annual rent in money, corn and hens, plus, in some places, a lamb, "or twopence," at Easter. On top of this, he was required to do a regular stint of ploughing and harvesting for his lord, and probably to help care for his lord's hounds and to carry his lord's seed. On the death of the *gebur,* an event often hastened by overwork and, among other prevalent hazards, osteo-arthritis and whooping cough, his land reverted to the estate.

At the bottom of the land-holding scale came the so-called *cotsetla,* or cottage dweller. A general oddbody on call for all types of heavy duties, the *cotsetla* might labour the whole of August for his lord, and perhaps a day a week for the rest of the year, in return for as little as an unproductive five acres from which to scratch his own living. In a bad year, the *cotsetla* was frequently faced with starving or selling himself, or his family, into slavery.

Just as the kin of an impoverished ceorl might sink into slavery, so it had been possible for a prosperous ceorl to rise to the upper class, that is, become a thegn. According to one late-Saxon document, he was worthy of up-grading if he possessed, among other status symbols, five hides of his own land, a church, a kitchen, a bell-house and a gate to his estate. As a thegn, he carried altogether more prestige. Like the knight who succeeded him, the thegn was the mainstay of the army, by tradition the king's man. Whether he was a magnate with a score or more estates in various counties, or little better off than a well-to-do ceorl farming his own land, his class distinction was a matter of the same pride.

With the growth of centralised administration which followed the Norman conquest, this complex class structure, in all its variations, was necessarily simplified by the bureaucrats. The development of common law in the twelfth century placed the main distinction between those who qualified for the protection of the courts, and the rest—that is, between the free and the servile peasants. While the multi-hued nature of class consciousness survived civil service methodology, the administrators strove to reduce the population in law to two categories: on one hand the freeman, on the other the villein, or serf. As a broad generalisation, it might be said that the freeman paid money rent to the lord of the manor, while the serf paid for his holding by regular work on the lord's demesne, or home farm.

The serf of John's day was not a slave in the Anglo-Saxon sense. The original slaves had been emancipated by the Normans, and had joined the ranks of the lesser ceorls, the cottage dwellers. Nevertheless, the conditions of the serf's tenancy were not far removed from slavery. His lord could tax him, sell him, evict him at will, fine him if his daughter married, force him to use his mill and oven on the lord's behalf, and take his best cow when the miserable fellow died. The serf was not allowed to carry weapons in his own defence. His gnarled hands were for the fork and plough in unremitting labour, toiling for a meagre livelihood from his holding when not working long hours on the demesne of his landlord. Not only was he obliged to accept his lord's tasks without argument, he was forced to do them at a moment's bidding—"nor shall he know in the evening what he shall do on the morrow."

The records of an estate at Guiting, Gloucestershire, toward the end of the twelfth century, set out a detailed account of the work demanded from the villein tenant in return for his virgate of land, perhaps about thirty acres. During the slack period, from early winter until haymaking, one man's work was owed the landlord for two days each week, then four days a week until the hay was cut and carried. From the end of haymaking to August 1, if haymaking was completed by this date, the due became again two days' work a week. From the beginning of August "until the corn is carried," each virgate owed two men's work on Mondays and Wednesdays, and one man's work on Tuesdays and Thursdays. This meant that twice a week two members of the villein's family had to labour for the landlord. From the end of the corn harvest until the onset of next winter, one man's work was owed for four days of each week. On top of this, each virgate owed the ploughing, harrowing and sowing of an acre and three quarters, the threshing of seed corn and "the carrying of loads to Gloucester or wherever the master wishes." Serfs must also plough two acres of pasture, "make a load of malt for Christmas and another for Easter, and collect a load of wood for drying the malt. At the master's will, the said workers must also move the sheepfold twice a year, and spend two days washing and shearing sheep."

By John's reign, the change from a real to a money economy was in progress throughout much of the country, and villein services were not infrequently commuted for cash payments. Theoretically, this did not give a serf his freedom. Landlords could, and did when circumstances warranted, reimpose labour services on such tenants. Real freedom could, however, be bought from a consenting landlord, or gained by joining holy orders. It could also be acquired by the serf who could escape to a town and remain unreclaimed for a year and a day. New and underpopulated towns, among them Liverpool, encouraged escaped serfs to come their way. Confusion over

Serfs, Celts and Spectres 193

who was, or who was not free, was commonplace—heightened by marriages between free and bonded families, with the resultant problem of classifying the offspring. Everywhere, men aspiring to escape the dispiriting shackles of serfdom looked to the king, through the royal courts, to release them from the claims of the landlords. The courts were packed with peasants pleading their free status. John was not without compassion for such men.

During his dispute with Rome, John had not forgotten his old enemy Philip, and the conflict with France continued on a diplomatic level. In 1207, John's nephew Otto of Germany, engaged in a bitter civil war which had raged since 1198, arrived in England to seek help from his uncle. Since the treaty of Le Goulet, John had not afforded Otto much assistance, but now he gave his nephew a cordial welcome. The streets of London were decorated for the occasion, and the citizens turned out to greet Otto in their best clothes. The meeting between uncle and nephew marked the reawakening of the Anglo-German alliance and the re-enlistment of the Low Countries in a common cause against Philip. John sent Otto home with six thousand marks, and began to subsidise the princes of the Low Countries. Otto returned the compliment, presenting John with a splendid crown, a sceptre, a golden rod and other expensive gifts.

A year later, John received the heartening news that Otto's rival, Philip of Swabia, had been murdered, and that Otto was undisputed emperor of a once more united Germany. In the spring of 1209, Otto's powerful brother Henry, the count palatine, came to England. John secured his alliance by granting him a pension of a thousand marks a year, and undertook to educate his young son at the English court. Before long, the bond between John and Otto was strengthened by the latter's excommunication for his open determination to unite southern Italy and Sicily to the empire, a policy to which Innocent was implacably opposed. Innocent now joined cause with Philip of France to provoke a revolt against Otto in Germany. The rival camps were becoming increasingly well defined.

One of the most outstanding men to swing to John's side was Renaud of Dammartin, Count of Boulogne. Shrewd and cultured, a dilettante whose talents embraced politics, the arts and the battlefield with like familiarity, Renaud was among the greatest vassals of Philip Augustus. As well as the county of Boulogne, he held the Norman fiefs of Mortain (John's old county), Domfront and Aumale. It said much for the apparent prospects of the Anglo-German alliance that Renaud should have defied Philip to lend his organising gifts to the coalition of the Low Countries. When Philip retaliated by driving Renaud from France and seizing his possessions, the count applied himself wholeheartedly to the overthrow of the French king. Thanks to his considerable powers of persuasion, Theobald, Count of Bar, on the borders of Lorraine, and Ferrand, Count of Flanders, joined the alliance. In the spring of 1212, Renaud arrived in England, where he did homage and swore fealty to the English king. John was jubilant. "Our friends may rejoice," he exulted, "our enemies be confounded!"

Renaud was rewarded with land in England and a generous pension. Meanwhile, John had been industriously engaged in yet another sphere of strategic importance—the traditionally unruly frontiers of his realm in Wales, Scotland and Ireland. Before he could give his full attention to a new continental offensive, he needed to be sure that these rugged extremities of his kingdom were suitably respectful of his authority. Earlier kings had made sporadic forays in this direction, but had achieved little in the way of comprehensive security. The barons and princes of the Celtic fringe had been a constant menace in the rear of English monarchs engaged on the Continent, while their territories provided shelter for disaffected English lords.

In the three years 1209, 1210 and 1211, John executed a brilliant series of preventive campaigns in these areas, aimed at guaranteeing the defence of his kingdom in the event of a major offensive against France. The year 1209 saw the no uncertain humbling of William the Lion of Scotland, now a bearded veteran in his late sixties. Henry II had forced him, while captive, to acknowledge the overlordship of the English Crown, but Richard had abandoned this advantage in his scramble for crusading money. John had been pestered by the Scot from the moment of his accession. On several occasions, William had snubbed invitations to meet John, while his demands for Northumberland, Cumberland and Westmorland had been persistent, occasionally threatening.

John had suffered him patiently for ten years. In the first half of 1209, the English king charged the ageing Lion with harbouring a number of clerics who had fled north in connection with the interdict, and he demanded security for William's behaviour in the shape of three Scottish castles. When William snarled defiance, John marched a strong army to Norham, Northumberland, on the doorstep of Scotland, and arrayed it in battle order. So businesslike was his bearing that William hurriedly sued for peace. By the end of summer, John had the assurances he needed. William's son did homage to him "for the aforementioned castles and other lands"; William agreed to buy the "goodwill" of the English king for fifteen thousand marks, to be paid in instalments; the Scot gave hostages against his undertaking, and he placed his two legitimate daughters, Margaret and Isabella, in John's hands as a token of his future conduct.

According to the chronicler Gervase of Canterbury, one of William's daughters was to be married to a son of John. A second son, Richard, had been born to the king and queen in

January, but since the older of the two princes, Henry, was not yet two, while the younger of the Scottish princesses was already in her teens, it seems likely that a natural son of the king was intended. John treated the young ladies indulgently, dressing them, as Scottish history has it, "like fairies, the princesses in dark green, their damsels in light green," and presenting them each with "a hundred pounds of figs." The exercise had been triumphant and bloodless. William had escaped physical chastisement, but he had been frightened. No more was heard of his claim to the English border counties.

John next turned his attention to Ireland. Twenty-five years had elapsed since his first visit to that country, and the greater part of the generation he had then encountered had died out. Their sons, however, were scarcely less turbulent. The descendants of the invading barons had gradually driven the native princes west, squabbling and fighting among themselves for the lands and spoils. Not only was their independence offensive to the Crown, but their stomping grounds had proved particularly attractive to English barons out of favour at John's court. In Ireland they could defy the king with impugnity. John of Courcy, the conqueror of Ulster, who had become governor of the Irish March on the departure of John's original expedition, was still alive. But he had been succeeded in 1191 by a succession of governors (or justiciars, as they were designated during John's reign) mainly notable for the scant respect they received from the barons of the country.

In 1200, John had appointed his cousin Meiler FitzHenry, a son of Henry I by the Welsh princess Nesta, as justiciar to Ireland. FitzHenry's authority was challenged by Courcy, and when Courcy was driven from Ulster by Hugh of Lacy, son and namesake of that Lacy who had met his end at the edge of an Irish battleaxe, John created Hugh Earl of Ulster. The Lacy family was already the most powerful in Ireland Hugh and his brother Walter were lords of Ulster and Meath

Plate 5 Two strategic Northumberland strongholds during John's reign, (*above*) Bamborough and (*below*) Alnwick

Plate 6 Seal of Richard I (*above left*) obverse, (*above right*) reverse. Seal of John (*below left*) obverse, (*below right*) reverse

respectively. They now joined forces against FitzHenry and, in 1208, forced the justiciar out of the country. John sent the Bishop of Norwich to take his place, but Gray was not an outstanding soldier, and John decided to lead an expedition to Ireland in person to subdue the Lacys, and others, and bring the country under a strong administration.

With the money which had come his way from the Church, John was in a position to equip a formidable armada, and in June 1210 he landed at Crook, near Waterford, quickly advancing via Kilkenny and Naas to Dublin. Here he received the homage of some twenty or more Irish chiefs, including the King of Connaught, Cathal O'Connor, and the Prince of North Munster, Donough O'Brien. Marching swiftly in a wide arc through Trim and Kells to Carlingford, beneath the Mourne Mountains on the east coast, John pursued the startled Lacys and their allies north, seizing or destroying their castles. From Carlingford, the king pressed on to Downpatrick, and thence to Carrickfergus on the northeasterly point of the island, where his enemies at last stood to face him. It was little more than a gesture. The Lacys and their friends had no chance. They had been hit too hard and too suddenly. With the reduction of Carrickfergus, they fled to Scotland and, eventually, to France.

Retracing his steps to Dublin, John joined Gray in reorganising the administration of Ireland on English lines. The barons were obliged to swear observance of the laws of England, counties were mapped out, sheriffs and other officials were appointed. The local currency was overhauled to bring it in line with that of England, new coins being minted with the image of an Irish harp. Finally, John Gray was confirmed as justiciar, and the king re-embarked for England. He landed at Fishguard, Pembrokeshire, before the end of August. In less than three months, he had brought the barons of Ireland to their knees, driven out the worst of the offenders, and established order and peace in a country which had not known either in many years. If any malodour had lingered from John's youthful excursion in Ireland, it must have been expelled once and for all by this expedition. It had been a model operation.

The problem of Wales was an old and thorny one. Passionate and individualistic, Welsh princes had made trouble for a long succession of English kings, Saxon, Norman and Angevin. Few had dared tackle the resilient and mobile Welsh warrior amidst the hills and valleys which were his native haunts, and from which he sallied periodically to strike fear in the towns and hamlets of the English border counties. Henry II had achieved a measure of peace by befriending the formidable Rhys ap Gruffyd, but Richard had offended him, and Rhys had spent the last years of his life as an enemy of the English crown. John was well informed on Welsh politics, having for ten years held the position of a border baron as Earl of Gloucester and lord of Glamorgan. He had observed Welshmen both as enemies and as mercenaries in his own pay, and respected their fighting qualities. The essential weakness of the Welsh lay in the mutual animosities of their princes, and John's policy had been to balance one against another, to prevent an overall independent leader emerging, and to forestall dangerous alliances between the Welsh and the English marcher barons.

John's accession had closely followed a fierce struggle in South Wales between three rival claimants for the throne of the great Rhys—his sons Gruffyd and Maelgwyn, and one Gwenwynwyn, son of Owen Cyveiliog, Prince of Powys. By the end of 1198, Gruffyd had triumphed, but had not long to relish his victory. In 1200 he died, and Gwenwynwyn momentarily held sway in the South. In the North, a greater power than Gruffyd, Gwenwynwyn, or any other southern chieftain, had risen in the person of the warrior prince Llywelyn ap Iorwerth, celebrated in bardic verse as a giant among Welshmen. When Llywelyn proceeded to reduce most of South Wales to subservience, John had either to plan his overthrow or win him as an ally. For a while, the English king tried friendship. In 1206, a marriage took place between the Welsh prince and Joan, a natural daughter of King John. Gwenwynwyn was detained in an English prison. In 1209, many Welsh chieftains travelled to England to do homage to John. It seemed that diplomacy had paid off. But Llywelyn was no puppet, and, with most of Wales dependent on him, was soon looking for fresh victories. An English frontier fort at Dyganwy, on the Conway, was demolished by his followers, and Llywelyn descended savagely upon the northern border lands of the Earl of Chester.

Determined now to humble his son-in-law, John joined forces with Gwenwynwyn, Maelgwyn and his brother Rhys, and, in the spring of 1211, led an expedition into North Wales. Llywelyn withdrew into the mountainous fastnesses of Snowdon and left the inhospitable terrain to fight his battle for him. It did so effectively. With his supplies expended, his men demoralised by hunger and the rigours of searching a hostile land for an invisible enemy, John turned back to prepare a larger and better-equipped offensive. By July, he was ready. This time, he made no mistake. Penetrating as far as Bangor, an important base for Llywelyn at the foot of the Snowdon range, John destroyed the town, captured its rebel bishop, Robert of Shrewsbury, and compelled his son-in-law to sue for peace. Llywelyn sent his wife to her father to obtain the best terms possible. Then, under guarantee of safe-conduct, the Welshman came in person to make his submission. John asserted his supremacy over Wales, deprived Llywelyn of some of his territories, exacted a heavy fine in cattle, and took twenty-eight hostages against his son-in-law's future behaviour. The Celtic trilogy had ended in absolute royal success.

No one could doubt the generalship, resourcefulness and resolution of a sovereign who could force the submission of his most unruly frontiers in three successive victories, at the same time defying the pope and manoeuvring to outwit the King of France. The simultaneous deference to the Crown of the whole of Briton and Ireland struck John's contemporaries as an astonishing achievement. "There was no one in Ireland, Scotland or Wales," wrote one, "who did not obey his nod, a circumstance unknown among all his predecessors."

Paradoxically, John's grip on fortune had never seemed stronger than in that period of crises when the loss of Normandy was followed by the interdict and excommunication. To some extent, the loss of Normandy, centring the activities and resources of men of hitherto divided interests on England, was a gain to that kingdom. Fortuitously, the interdict had provided a new source of finance for the government. John had money; he had the backing of the people, even the barons, in his measures against the Church; he had secured the nation against its more rebellious extremities; and he had reactivated the continental coalition against Philip. On the face of it, his power was approaching its zenith. Fate's arrows had been diverted with remarkable dexterity.

Inwardly, however, they had lodged in a raw spot. John had grown up in an atmosphere fraught with distrust. As a child, he had learned to suspect the loyalty of a baronage still seething with resentment at the curbs imposed upon it by his father, and he had watched his very brothers turn their swords on the monarch. John was not alone among medieval princes in harbouring a disposition toward suspicion, but he had experienced an uncommon measure of betrayal, even by the standards of his own day, and the treason of the Norman barons had raised his fears to a level very close to paranoia. This self-destructive element in his deeper make-up was exacerbated by the personal affronts of the interdict and his excommunication. While others saw the king as omnipotent—"No one in the land could resist his will in anything," wrote Gervase of Canterbury—John increasingly acted as one alone among powerful enemies bent on his destruction. It was not an illogical outcome of the trend toward absolute monarchic government. But, for John, it was a disastrous one.

As the power of the Crown had spread and strengthened in the twelfth and thirteenth centuries, the role of the feudal baron, the erstwhile warrior chief and palatine, had become rather that of the landed aristocrat. With the recession of his own power in relation to the mounting influence of the sovereign, the baron had buried old feuds with his neighbours and acknowledged common interests through family marriages and alliances. The result was an aristocracy of increasingly like-minded families who, while no longer a match for the king as individuals, possessed a formidable potential as a pressure group. With the crown's authority established, and anarchy a fading memory, the time was ripe for a royal move toward gaining the goodwill of the nation's aristocrats. Such a move would seem to have been particularly apposite at the time of the interdict, when the king direly needed the support of the barons, and when the barons, in fact, defied the pope with him. It was eloquent of the blinding force of suspicion that a man so perceptive and calculating as John should have ignored the opportunity, choosing to keep his barons in order by severity rather than affection.

From a compassionate point of view, there is much to be said for a prince who was generous to the weak and humble, while leaning hard on the powerful and privileged. But, from a political viewpoint, such a posture was untenable. The people were powerless, and his own officers were falling victim to his distrust. No ruler can stand for long without an influential phalanx, and John was no exception. Had he been as indulgent to the baronage as he was to the proletariat, he might from this point have forged ahead to greater personal triumph. As it was, unbalanced by the fear of treachery, he bore down on the barons until their burden was intolerable, and the ranks of the faithful dwindled accordingly. Not even his closest lieutenants escaped his consuming suspicion. Among the most remarkable manifestations of this complex was the persecution of William Marshal and William of Briouse, men he had personally rewarded for their services, both in promoting his accession and standing by him through subsequent contingencies.

It is hard to discover any reason for John's bitter vendetta against the upright, and now ageing Marshal, save a seemingly unreasonable fear of the power he had himself conferred upon him. Marshal had upset the king by his opposition to the expedition of 1205, and by the somewhat unusual accommodation he had reached with Philip in relation to his Norman lands. Marshal, however, had then sworn his unswerving loyalty to the English king, and it was not in John's normal nature to bear a grudge. Nevertheless, from now on Marshal and his friend Briouse, fellow landowners in Wales and Ireland, became the victims of royal animosity. Briouse was dismissed from the office of bailiff of Glamorgan, and Marshal was relieved of the sheriffdom of Gloucester and custodianship of Cardigan and the Forest of Dean. Two mercenary captains, Gerard of Athée and Fawkes of Bréauté, were appointed to replace them. John also approved the raiding of their Irish lands—Marshal was lord of Leinster; Briouse, lord of Limerick —by FitzHenry, the Irish justiciar, in 1206.

Marshal bore the humiliation and deprivations with characteristic correctitude. Without complaint, he surrendered castles and hostages, including his own children, as tokens of his loyalty, and, at one point, offered to put his honour to the test of judicial combat. Nobody took up the challenge. When

John eventually discontinued his harassment of the old nobleman, Marshal forgave him and returned to the king's side.

For Briouse and his family, the episode ended tragically. That Briouse had grand aspirations was unquestionable. He had been among the first to assert John's right to the throne upon Richard's death, and he appears to have regarded himself as something of a king-maker. John had rewarded him liberally with lands and honours, and Briouse had pledged large sums of money for the privilege of extending his holdings. His pretensions, it seems, exceeded his discretion, for by 1207 his dues to the Crown were five years in arrear.

Briouse was pushed forward by a singularly forceful wife, Matilda. Dynamic and masterful, Matilda was regarded with awe on the family's Welsh estate. The peasants joked that she had built a castle in a single day, carrying the stones in her apron, and that she had dislodged a boulder nine feet long from her shoe and hurled it into a churchyard three miles away. It was Matilda's proud boast that she owned twelve thousand dairy cattle, and such an abundance of cheeses that a hundred besieged knights could live on them for a month and have enough left over to sling against their enemies. Wendover believed that John's displeasure was fanned to fury by Matilda's arrogance. John had demanded hostages of Briouse against the settlement of his debts. According to the chronicler, when the king's agents called for the hostages, "Matilda, with the cheek of a woman, took the reply out of her husband's mouth, announcing: 'I will not deliver my sons to your lord, King John, because he despicably murdered his nephew, Arthur, whom he should have treated with honour.' Her husband rebuked her, saying: 'You have spoken foolishly against the king, for if I have given offence to him I am ready to make good without the need for hostages, according to the ruling of his court and barons, if he will fix a time and place.' When the messengers told the king what they had heard, he was furious."

If this incident were true, it would seem that William Marshal must have known of it. Yet Marshal's biographer confessed himself mystified as to the cause of John's behaviour toward his patron's friend. On John's own evidence, his concern, in the first place, was simply to recover the money owed him by Briouse. The same excuse could have been used to get at many of his barons. Financial indebtedness to the Crown was widespread in John's time. It arose from many factors, not least the poor estate management practiced by medieval landowners, and the ambition and cupidity of the barons. Huge estates were maintained largely as pleasure grounds for the sport of the nobility. Though they provided a certain amount of game and timber, such areas were absurdly unproductive. The majority of barons had an annual income of less than two hundred pounds, and this is an inflationary situation. Certainly, they could live a lordly life on the free labour and kind provided by their tenants, but when cash was demanded they were frequently hard-pressed.

The desire of the barons to increase their power and revenues created a steady demand for new fiefs, Crown offices and heiresses. These the king might be pleased to acknowledge, but at a price the baron could meet only on an instalment basis.

John was not reluctant to gain a hold on his barons by allowing them to burden themselves with debts to him. He had asked Briouse a thousand pounds apiece for the heiresses the baron wished his sons to marry, and had fixed the going price for his first wife, Isabel of Gloucester, at a gigantic twenty thousand marks. Through death duties, which the king could fix arbitrarily, and various fines, he could increase the financial burdens of a family. He could also force a baron to buy his "goodwill" after some misdemeanour, however slight or technical. For the most part, the king was content to let these debts ride. It meant that he could ruin, or seriously embarrass, a baron who stepped out of line, by foreclosure, confiscating his land and his chattels.

Briouse, who lacked Marshal's dignity and forebearance, reacted violently to John's efforts to reduce his power and influence. Having handed over castles on his Welsh estates as security for five thousand marks he had promised for the lordship of Limerick, Briouse, perhaps prompted by Matilda, thought better of the action. According to John, in a statement attested by the Justiciar of England and twelve others of high rank, the wayward baron and his sons not only attempted to recover the pledged castles by force, but consoled themselves in failure by attacking and burning Leominster, on the Welsh March. At this, the king proclaimed him a traitor and ordered Gerard of Athée, who had moved into Briouse country with a force of law officers backed by infantry, to enlist the baron's vassals in the king's service.

During the summer of 1208, Briouse defied Athée and neglected a summons to appear at the royal court. But he was no longer safe on his Welsh lands, and, in the autumn, fled to Ireland with his family to seek the protection of his son-in-law Walter Lacy. In the spring of 1210, alarmed by John's preparations for the Irish expedition, Briouse returned to Wales and, as John had it, offered forty thousand marks to clear his debts and regain his castles. "We told him," the king wrote, "that we knew very well this was beyond his power, if not beyond the power of his wife; and we proposed that he should go to Ireland with us to settle the matter. He chose rather to remain in Wales and make harm for us." As John's forces swept up the east coast of Ireland that summer, Matilda and her family had fled before them, eventually embarking, like the Lacys, for Scotland. Here, she was detained by a Scots lord, Duncan of Carrick, and turned over to the English king. Among those captured with her were her eldest son, his wife and their two children.

On returning to England, John allowed Briouse to confer with the captive Matilda. According to John, they now offered fifty thousand marks for freedom and release from financial obligations. But Briouse, turned loose to raise the money, promptly decamped to France. Matilda, taxed by John's lawyers, was obliged to admit that the most she could raise was four thousand marks, some jewelry and fifteen ounces of gold. The official version of the affair ended with the outlawing of Briouse. It was left to the chroniclers to record Matilda's unhappy destiny. They did so with a unanimity and conviction altogether more impressive than their gossipy speculation over Arthur's death. The tale differed only in minor detail from chronicle to chronicle. Matilda and her eldest son were locked in prison (by some accounts at Windsor, others at Corfe) and deliberately neglected until they starved to death. Their bodies were eventually discovered huddled together against a wall. In her anguish, the woman had gnawed at her son's flesh.

There seems no reason to disbelieve John's responsibility for this atrocity. It tallied with the pathological fear of treachery which had gripped him since the loss of Normandy, and was consistent in method with a squeamish mind. Few medieval princes shrank from the sight of murder. From William the Conqueror, who chopped off the limbs of his captives and hurled them at his enemies, to Richard, who had ordered the decapitation of hundreds of hostages at a time, John's predecessors had thought nothing of putting prisoners to the axe or the sword. John had shown no relish for such barbarity. It is only at this advanced stage of his life that he can be identified positively with an act of gross inhumanity—and this he had contrived remotely and ashamedly beneath the cloak of negligence. Briouse died at Corbeil, France, soon afterward, and was buried by an earnest sympathiser, Stephen Langton.

Matilda's daughter-in-law and her children were released unharmed. If John regretted the tragic product of his distrust, he could not have guessed its tremendous impact on the days ahead.

Chapter 11
THE POPE'S MAN

Rejoice with me; for I have found my sheep which was lost.
St. Luke 15:6

The destruction of the house of Briouse was perhaps the cardinal blunder of John's reign. The family had powerful connections. Such relatives as the Earls of Hereford and Hertford, Henry of Bohun and Richard of Clare, must have been severely shocked and affronted by the murder of Matilda and her son. Among the barons in general, the episode grimly demonstrated the changing temper of the sovereign. His capacity to ruin those who displeased him had long been implicit. Now his readiness to do so was manifest. A king who trusted no one, it was said, could be trusted by no one. And if further proof were needed of John's increasingly nervy and intolerant reaction to those who crossed him, it was to be found in a spate of harsh penalties in the months ahead.

Early in 1212, William of Scotland sought John's aid in dealing with a Celtic pretender, Cuthred MacWilliam, who was threatening the Lion's throne. The English king sent a force of mercenaries to capture MacWilliam, and had him hanged out of hand. When Llywelyn of Wales broke the terms of the treaty signed by him, John ordered the execution of the twenty-eight Welsh hostages. Even a cranky prophet who predicted the king's downfall was put to death. It was not that such sentences were startling in themselves. An armed rebel like MacWilliam invited the death penalty, while the distasteful but commonplace system of hostage-holding would have been pointless without the ultimate threat. It was the changing mood of John himself that was ominous. The king who had pardoned, even found excuses for, traitors and enemies—the king who had preferred to treat rather than to slaughter, to fine rather than execute—now seemed ready, under stress, to revert to the brutal style of so many of his predecessors. His barons, taking note, were nowise the merrier.

In the summer of 1212, John's gaze turned once more to the shores of France. An official inquiry was carried out to discover the precise military services due from the royal tenants-in-chief throughout the kingdom. On June 15, writs were sent to thirty-nine English towns ordering them to provide armed contingents "ready to cross the sea with the king when he should require it." Again, supplies were requisitioned and assembled at Portsmouth. By the end of summer, however, these plans had been rudely checked. In Wales, Llywelyn, provoked by what he called "the many insults of the king's men," and by Philip Augustus, whose agents urged him to break his pledge with John, had formed an alliance with his old Welsh rivals, and was bent on reducing the English frontier posts and beheading their garrisons.

In July, an exasperated John abruptly postponed his continental expedition and diverted his forces for a massive attack on Wales. His army, assembled at Nottingham in the second week of September, was an impressive one. According to a contemporary, "no man of our day remembers such an array or such numbers." Nor was the muster entirely of combatants. Instructions had been issued for the recruitment of an extraordinary engineering force comprising more than two thousand trenching specialists and carpenters, and six thousand labourers equipped for felling and trimming trees. John intended to trust nobody this time. Paths would be cleared and fortresses razed as he advanced. Once and for all, he determined, the Welsh were to be brought under English rule.

Again, his plans miscarried, this time in circumstances of sinister portent. Rumours of a most alarming nature had reached Nottingham. Not all the barons who had mustered at John's summons, it was reported, had come to kill Welshmen. There was a conspiracy afoot, so the warnings went, to get rid of John and "choose another king in his place." Wendover presented the scene melodramatically. John had sat down to dinner after the hanging of the Welsh hostages, the scribe asserted, when two messengers burst in upon him. One was from his daughter Joan, Llywelyn's wife; the other from the King of Scots. Both messengers bore letters whose contents, they advised John, were of the greatest urgency and importance. When the letters were opened, their contents proved virtually identical. The barons, cried Joan and William in foreboding harmony, were preparing to eliminate the king under cover of war with Wales, either by slaying him themselves in the thick of the battle, or by turning him over to the enemy.

There was more to the rumours than that. In various forms, it was whispered that the treasury at Gloucester had been looted, that the young Prince Richard had been murdered, and his mother raped. These tales were not true. But John treated the warnings of treachery among the armed barons surrounding him at Nottingham very seriously. So seriously, indeed, that he called off the expedition even more abruptly than he had aborted the expedition to the Continent. "We cannot go to Wales at the moment," he wrote his barons cryptically, "because certain affairs call us back." That his fears were not entirely unfounded was suggested by the sudden and unexplained withdrawal from the army at this time of two barons, Robert FitzWalter and Eustace of Vesci, who fled respectively to France and Scotland. FitzWalter was the man John had exerted himself to exonerate after the spineless surrender of Vaudreuil. Vesci was married to an illegitimate daughter of William of Scotland, and had been employed extensively by John on missions to the Scottish king.

Later generations, bent on John's denigration, excused the defection of these men by weaving exotic fictions round their womenfolk. According to one legend, FitzWalter's beautiful daughter Matilda had been put to death by the king for rejecting his dishonourable advances. He had contrived to feed her a poisoned egg—a story as fantastic as another which confused this virtuous damsel with Maid Marion, the mistress of Robin Hood. Seventy years or so after Vesci's desertion, a monk of Furness Abbey, Lancashire, wrote of a scheme by John to lure the baron's wife into bed with him during her husband's absence. Vesci, learning of the king's design, hired "a vile prostitute" to take his wife's place. Bedding with the harlot by dark of night, John remained ignorant of the switch worked on him until Vesci maliciously informed him that he had slept with a common whore. This diverting fable had a pedigree many centuries in length by John's day. The Furness author may have borrowed it from the Byzantine historian Procopius.

Though no concrete evidence was produced to back the rumours of conspiracy, it seems clear that from this time the widespread and long-fomenting discontent of the barons had given rise to notions of concerted action among their more disgruntled members. A note of alarm transcended the distrust which now motivated John's precautions. FitzWalter and Vesci were outlawed, their lands seized and two castles belonging to the former, Bennington in Hertfordshire, and Baynard's Castle, to the southwest of St. Paul's in London, were destroyed. In the North, where Vesci was influential, and where the barons were inclined by tradition to independence, John made a tour of strength. Throughout the country, he demanded hostages and castles as security. In some cases, he wanted both.

"We have your son as hostage for your loyalty," the king wrote David, Earl of Huntingdon. "We command you now to deliver the castle of Fotheringay to our faithful servants." Not even the "faithful servants" escaped his mistrustful scrutiny. His administration was closely screened for subversives, and his mercenary captains were obliged to give hostages. Assassination had become a real fear in John's mind. The queen and her children were closely watched, and the king went about his affairs armed, and accompanied by an armed bodyguard.

At the same time, he showed solicitude for those who lacked the power to harm him. Contemporary writers affirmed that he was "gracious to widows," anxious for domestic peace, and that he discouraged his officials from harassing pilgrims, merchants and other travellers. In the light of John's concern for harmonious public relations with the masses, his advisers became more than a little apprehensive about the activities of an eccentric Yorkshire rustic, Peter of Wakefield, who had been regaling the North with the prophesy that John's reign was coming to an early end.

Peter, an emaciated and seemingly deranged vagabond who lived on bread and water, was held to be something of a prophet among the simple country folk who knew him. His fanatical insistence that the king would have ceased to reign by next Ascension Day gained wide currency. Peter could not say whether John would abdicate, die or be deposed. "All I know," he exclaimed, as the writer Walter of Coventry had it, "is that a vision has revealed to me that the king shall not rule

Plate 7 Jerusalem is shown in part in Matthew Paris's *Itinerary to the Holy Land*

Plate 8 Beaulieu Abbey was built for the Cistercian order by John, who endowed it with a holding of land in the New Forest

Chinon, the repository of the Angevin treasury, where Henry II died

The Pope's Man

more than fourteen years, at the end of which time he will be replaced by someone more pleasing to God."

John laughed at the prophesy, but some of his officers, uneasy about the alarmist effects of the story, had Peter seized and detained as a vagrant. His arrest merely added importance to his utterings, which now swept the country. Enchanted by his own powers, Peter declared that if he should be proved false in his preaching, the authorities might dispose of him as they wished. England, in those days of 1212, held its breath. "The land," as one chronicler reported, "kept silence." The tension was affecting. Rumour abounded. The baronage smouldered. The superstitious awaited the outcome of Peter's prophesy. The devout pointed grimly to the papal anathema. John might surround himself with hirelings and hostages, but an excommunicated king, they averred, was a doomed man.

In the sudden reversal of royal fortune which had followed the tragedy of the Briouse family, John looked a desperately friendless king. He badly needed the support—at least moral, if not physical—of some popular and influential figure in his kingdom. It came, at the crucial moment, from Ireland, in the form of an unequivocal affirmation of loyalty by his old and ill-used lieutenant William Marshal. After suffering John's abuses for some six years, the stoic Marshal now gathered twenty-eight Irish barons about him, and, in conjunction with John Gray, Justiciar of Ireland, persuaded them to renew their oaths of fealty to the king. In a manifesto addressed to "all faithful Christians," the Irish magnates, with Marshal and Meiler FitzHenry at their head, expressed their readiness "to live or die with the king," and their "grief and astonishment" that the pope should expect them to do otherwise. Marshal advised John to settle his differences with Innocent, and offered to come over and assist in negotiations if necessary.

The immediate result of this demonstration of loyalty was to steady the hands of the English barons, particularly those connected with the house of Briouse, and to enable John to recover from his loss of confidence. The king was effusively grateful. He sent his heart-felt thanks to William Marshal as the spokesman of the Irish barons, "and as the instigator of this matter, to whom we are indebted for the disposition and devotion of all the rest." He would be sending, he said, letters of thanks to everyone. Though he appreciated the earl's offer to assist in negotiations with the pope, he felt that Marshal would be more useful in Ireland, helping Gray to govern that country. He would, however, welcome any suggestions from the Irish barons as to how he might end the dispute with the Church without prejudice to his own rights and liberties. Concluding on a chatty note, John informed Marshal that his son, held as hostage at court, "needs a horse and some new clothing. If you wish, we will provide these for him, and place him in the care of any of your knights who might be with us."

Marshal's advice that John should make peace with the pope was sensible. In France, Philip Augustus, delighted by tales of treason and unrest among the English barons, was again contemplating the conquest of England, intent upon raising his eldest son, Louis, to the island throne. This threat, so closely following the projected English attack on France, underlined the instability of John's position. One moment he had been dominating the home frontiers and preparing to hammer Philip; the next, he was dismissing his army in fear for his very life, while the French king made plans to invade England. The see-saw of initiative lurched disconcertingly. In Germany, the fortunes of Otto had slumped again. At the pope's instigation, King Frederick of Sicily had been elected emperor in Otto's stead, and Frederic and Philip of France had sworn friendship. For John, one more power in the enemy camp was one too many.

He needed a reduction, not an increase, in his problems, and the most effective single step to easing them at home and

The Pope's Man

abroad would be to regain the goodwill of Innocent. He could no longer afford to have the Church against him. By the end of 1212, John had decided to swallow pride and principle, and pay the price demanded for the pope's friendship.

Negotiations with the papacy had dragged on fruitlessly for four and a half years, during which the pope had not budged from his original demands, nor had John been moved by the interdict and excommunication. In consultation with his cardinals and bishops, Innocent was preparing to use his ultimate weapon, a decree that John should be deposed from his throne, when an English embassy headed by the Abbot of Beaulieu arrived in Rome with instructions to accept the pope's terms. By now, Stephen Langton had actually left Rome for France with documents announcing the deposition and requesting Philip of France to help enforce it. This was not a step the pope can have relished. The balance of power between England and Paris worked in Rome's favour. The prospect of Philip ruling an empire combining France and England raised Innocent's misgivings. Accordingly, on the abbot's arrival, he sent urgently after Langton, who was overtaken before the decree could be published. At the same time, it was necessary to ensure that John was serious. In February 1213, the pope wrote John demanding that he ratify the terms agreed with the Abbot of Beaulieu, failing which the deposition would have to go ahead. The deadline set by Rome for the ratification was June 1.

At the beginning of April, in council at Soissons, northeast of Paris, Philip announced his intention to invade England. The possibility of projecting his offensive as a holy war against a ruler outcast by Rome and surrounded by barons absolved from their oaths of allegiance, was a heady stimulant to the French king. His army was summoned to assemble at Rouen on the first Sunday after Easter, April 21, and ships and victuals were gathered on a huge scale.

John responded vigorously to the French threat. Unnerved by problems of mood and shadowy discontent, he was often at his best when faced with physical crises. This is not inconsistent with an imaginative temperament, whose worst fears may be self-manufactured rather than of independent origin. He now ordered all English ships to stand by at their home ports, while a fleet of the largest vessels was called to Portsmouth, "well manned with brave and proficient sailors." Everyone who owed military service was summoned to the South. Five hundred knights came over from Ireland. Even landless men, who did not possess weapons, were called upon to arm themselves as best they could and report for the king's pay.

In order to feed this swarming host, sheriffs were commanded to close down the markets in their areas and dispatch traders and provisions to the military assembly points. They were also ordered to bring nominal rolls of the servicemen within their boundaries so that the king might know who had avoided the call-up. Those who did so were threatened with "perpetual servitude." So impressive was the turn-out that many of the more poorly armed men were dismissed. Despite all logistical precautions, there simply was insufficient food to feed everyone.

The select body which remained was inspected by the king on Barham Down, near Canterbury. It was still a mighty army, and the chroniclers regarded it as equal in numbers to any which could be brought against it. There were doubts, however, about the resolution of the barons. On the whole, it seems likely that they attended in good faith. A call to defend their own country was very different from a summons to serve oversea, and there is no indication that the mutinous attitude of 1205 prevailed; nor, for that matter, were the rumours of the Nottingham muster repeated.

This time, William Marshal was firmly behind the king. This was reassuring for many of the barons, who, after all, had no reason to suppose that a regime presided over by Philip and Louis would be more agreeable than that of King John. In any case, John had sufficient faith in his Navy to anticipate the destruction of a substantial part of Philip's armada before it reached England. Indeed, before it ever sailed, he deployed elements of his fleet against Fécamp, Dieppe and other mustering points on the French coast. Finally, having established strong detachments of his army at possible landing places in the South, John stationed himself at Ewell, near Dover, and waited for Philip to do his worst.

He was still waiting when his envoys to Rome returned with a papal legate, the subdeacon Pandulf. John wasted no time in talk or ceremonial. On May 13, he met Pandulf at Dover and immediately accepted the pope's terms. He agreed to receive Stephen Langton as archbishop, to reinstate the exiled clergy and to recompense the Church in full for its losses. A group of powerful nobles, including the Count of Boulogne and the Earls of Salisbury, Warren and Derby, stood as guarantors for the king's word. That same day, the proceedings were published in letters patent, and excited messengers carried the news through Kent to the rest of the country. King and pope were reconciled. Soon, the church bells would ring again, church doors would be opened, baptisms and marriages would be celebrated under God's roof, and the dead could be buried once more with propriety. For many, the tidings brought joy and profound relief. Life in England was complete again.

But the threat of invasion had not vanished. If Philip could no longer pose as the pope's champion, he had no intention of abandoning his long-contemplated plans to add England to his empire. Pandulf had seen something of his preparations as he had passed through France. The French king had flaunted his power before the legate, boasting the strength of his forces and the readiness of the English barons to defect to him. When

Pandulf told John and his advisers what he had seen in France, the prediction of Peter of Wakefield ceased to seem funny. With Ascension Day less than a fortnight distant, the king called an emergency conference with Marshal, Gray and Geoffrey FitzPeter, at which a dramatic measure was debated and carried.

On May 15, two days after the meeting at Dover, Pandulf was summoned to Ewell, where a remarkable document was drawn up. Attested by John, the Justiciars of England and Ireland, seven earls, including Marshal, and many of the most powerful barons, the Charter of Ewell "granted and freely surrendered" to God and to Pope Innocent, and his Catholic successors, the entire realms of England and Ireland, reserving for the king and his heirs "his rights, liberties and regalities," to receive them back as a feudatory of God and the Roman Church. In Pandulf's presence, John swore fealty to the pope and pledged his successors to do likewise, undertaking to provide a tribute of a thousand marks a year to the Holy See. John of the Devil's Brood, the bane of Rome and the whipping boy of the monkish scribes, had pronounced himself the vassal of Pope Innocent.

Some controversy surrounds this startling, but not unprecedented gesture. Innocent already had Aragon, Portugal, Sweden, Denmark and Sicily as his vassals. According to Wendover, the pope had demanded that England should join them. The more credible, and generally accepted view, however, is that the vassalage was John's idea, supported by his advisers and senior barons. Walter of Coventry stated that John "added it on his own initiative" to the agreement already completed at Dover. Though at first sight, the adding of servitude to surrender seemed somewhat ignominious, it was not long before it proved a very shrewd stratagem. The real capitulation had been at Dover. The pope's terms regarding Langton and the exiled clerics involved heavy expenses and some political sacrifice. The oath of fealty, on the other hand, cost little and gained much. "The sovereignty in your hands," Innocent assured John, "is now stronger and more august than before, for your kingdom has become sacerdotal and the sacerdocy has acquired a regal character." Whatever John might make of that, the immediate profit he had salvaged from surrender by becoming the pope's man was Innocent's protection.

"By this act, John served both himself and his people with prudence," wrote a contemporary. "For when he once put himself under Apostolic protection, and attached his lands to the patrimony of St. Peter, no ruler in the Roman world dared invade or attack him, since Pope Innocent was held in awe by everyone." By an adroit twist, John had extracted more than a little satisfaction from his losses. He had acquired the support of the Church and its devotees; he had deprived the rebels among his barons of papal sanction; and, by the simple expedient of doffing his crown and replacing it, he had banished the superstitious expectations spread by Peter of Wakefield. Ascension Day, May 23, held no fears for the English king. He had a royal pavilion raised on the Kentish Downs, and issued a general invitation to his subjects to spend a day of festivities with him. "And a truly joyful day it was," burbled one chronicler, "the monarch making merry with his bishops and nobles." Only the poor, eccentric Peter had cause to rue it. On May 28, he was dragged from prison, tied at a horse's tail and drawn to Wareham, Dorset, where, before a derisive crowd, he was hanged.

The most dramatic result of John's stratagem was the collapse of the projected French invasion. Pandulf, crossing to France, informed Philip that England was now a papal fief and that any hostile act toward it would incur the pope's gravest displeasure. The French king was furious. He had spent, he said, thousands of pounds, and endless time, on his preparations to attack John, and did not mean to be thwarted at this stage. But, on second thoughts, discretion prevailed. Instead of invading England, Philip turned his wrath on his feudatory, Ferrand of Flanders, who, true to his agreement with Renaud of Boulogne, had stubbornly refused to join forces with the French against John. Ordering his fleet to sail to the Swine estuary, the northern seaway to Flanders, Philip crossed the border to the south with his army and laid siege to Ghent. Ferrand appealed frantically to England for help.

The English fleet, and much of John's army was still on stand-by. In consultation at Ewell with Ferrand's messengers and his own advisers, John decided to send five hundred ships to the Swine with some seven hundred knights and a strong force of mercenaries, the whole commanded by his half brother William of Salisbury. On May 30, entering the Swine after battling against perverse winds, the English were astonished by the scene which confronted them. Close by the town of Damme, then an affluent commercial centre and the port for Bruges, the anchorage and beaches were encrusted with French ships, their gunwales kissing with the lap of the water, their masts too numerous to be counted. Philip's chaplain, who accompanied the French fleet, estimated its strength at an amazing seventeen hundred vessels, many laden with provisions, weapons and the baggage of French barons. This was the mighty armada which would have disgorged on the shores of England had it not been for John's timely tribute to Pope Innocent.

To add wonder to wonders, reconnaissance revealed that the French ships were practically unguarded. The troops had gone ashore to loot Damme, to ravage the surrounding district, or to join Philip in the siege of Ghent. Salisbury sailed straight into the great shoal of wallowing Frenchmen, cutting three hundred ships adrift and burning more than a hundred after seizing their contents. "It seemed that the very sea was on fire," observed Marshal's biographer. Smoke was still rising from the beach

The Pope's Man

next day, when Ferrand came to greet the English and confirm his alliance with King John. Disembarking his men, Salisbury now mounted a land attack on Damme. The move was not successful. Philip, drawn from Ghent by news of the English raid, intercepted his enemies with an army of overwhelming numbers, and Salisbury was forced to seek the safety of his vessels.

Nevertheless, the operation as a whole had been a sparkling triumph. John's Navy returned safely from its first major victory, its decks piled with prizes. "Never came such riches to England since King Arthur," boasted one thirteenth-century writer. Philip, fearing another raid before he could extricate his stricken transports from the Swine, set fire to many of the vessels rather than leave them to the enemy. There was no longer the means of invading England had he wanted to.

On July 20, beneath an azure sky, John and his courtiers, resplendent in silks and satins, and mounted on brightly caparisoned destriers (chargers) and palfreys (lighter horses), rode to the crest of Morn Hill outside Winchester. Below them, sheltering in the misty cradle of the chalk downs, lay the grey-walled repository of so much English history. The Romans had founded Winchester, their Venta Belgarum, as a garrison town —their first on English soil. Looking down from the neighbouring heights, John and his companions could see that the main street was still as straight as a spear shaft, while its subsidiary lanes intersected it with military precision. Here, amidst such thoroughfares as Fleshmongers', Shoemakers' and Shieldmakers' streets, the farmers of Sussex came to trade their wools, corns and cheeses for cloths, leather goods and other city wares.

From the gates issued Roman roads of characteristic directness to Silchester, Cirencester, Porchester, Salisbury, Southampton and elsewhere. Through those gates, in their time, had passed the great figures of Wessex, to the vast wooded earldom of Harold of England and his family.

Here, Cerdic's Saxons had created their centre after splashing ashore in the sixth century. Here Coenwalch, son of Cynegils, had built a temple to the honour of St. Peter and St. Paul. Here, at the beginning of the ninth century, the West Saxons had defeated the Mercians and gained tribute from the Northumbrians. And from here Egbert had pronounced the kingdom of Wessex supreme in all England, making Winchester properly the national capital. It was from Winchester that Alfred the Great, the Dane-fighter, had waged his lifelong struggle to save the very foundations of English culture from obliteration; and it was under Alfred that the city had first achieved widespread fame as a centre of intellectual life.

In the half-century prior to the birth of Harold Godwinson, Winchester had been at the heart of the revival of art and learning that had accompanied the new monasticism of Archbishop Dunstan and his strong man, Bishop Athelwold. Athelwold had erected a fine minster in Winchester. It stood square-built in two stories, four large bells in the lower, and a single bell in the upper, roofed in red tile and surmounted by pinnacles, balls of burnished gold and a huge golden weathercock which pivoted and glowed in the sun.

Now, within the gaze of the golden weathercock, on St. Margaret's Day, 1213, John watched a column of mitred ecclesiastics and their followers approaching over the Sussex Downs. At their head was Stephen Langton, at last uncontested Archbishop of Canterbury, and with him the lately exiled Bishops of London, Ely, Hereford, Bath and Lincoln. John had already put in motion arrangements for their return, issuing orders for the restitution of temporalities earlier that month. The scene of conciliation at Winchester seems to have been a touching one. It was reported that the plump and somewhat flamboyant little monarch knelt at the feet of the austere and scholarly Langton, exclaiming: "Welcome, father! Welcome!" The archbishop, unable to embrace a man who was still technically excommunicated, blew John a kiss. "The prelates and the rest, when they beheld this, could not refrain from weeping." Drying their eyes, the members of both parties proceeded to Athelwold's minster, where John swore on the Gospels to love and uphold the Church, to make full restitution of property appropriated during the interdict, to restore the good laws of his predecessors, especially those of Edward the Confessor, and to judge all men by the just deliberations of his court.

Apart from the clause concerning restitution, this was virtually a confirmation of the coronation oath. It was not without significance at the time, however, for the repeated demand of the barons for their "rights" was very much involved with legal justice. While John, like his father before him, was devoted to the authority of his courts—and, indeed, had done more than most to promote it—the pressures of governing vast and troublesome dominions were such that the Angevin kings had almost inevitably strayed outside the law themselves, ruling at the crunch by decree and arbitrary judgement. It was this duplicity of practice, binding the barons to the law in their own conduct, while the sovereign too frequently denied them recourse to it against his actions, that created much ill feeling and truculence. At a later date, the barons would formally define the king's coronation oath "to render to all men their just rights," as a guarantee against arrest or molestation, save by judgement of a court of peers within the framework of English law. For now, they were content to hear John repeat the traditional formula at Winchester, once within the minster and once from the church porch.

When this was over, Langton formally absolved the king from excommunication, bestowed upon him the kiss of peace, and led him back into the minster to celebrate Mass. John showed no desire, in the days ahead, to dodge his obligations to the pope. Not only did he arrange restitution for the clergy, he even promised safe-conduct and reinstatement in their lands for Eustace of Vesci and Robert FitzWalter, the barons who had fled England for no such good reason as the churchmen. The problem of indemnity for the exiled bishops was more difficult. On the day after his absolution, John detailed his sheriffs to send representatives to St. Albans, in August, to sit on an investigative committee "to ascertain the truth concerning damages due to the several bishops."

Meanwhile, eager to hit Philip while his fleet was depleted and his attention on Flanders, John had called for an expedition to Poitou, only to meet with what were becoming familiar arguments from the barons, especially those of the North. The conditions of their tenure, they claimed, did not bind them to follow the king oversea; beside which, "they were exhausted and impoverished by campaigns within the kingdom." His knights also made representations to him that funds had run out during the period of standing to arms against invasion, and that they could not possibly follow him further unless he paid their expenses. Mustering his mercenaries, the king headed not for France but for the North of England, to deal with the barons who had disobeyed his summons.

John set out from Winchester. Langton, who heard of the king's mission in London, made haste to intercept him. They met at Northampton, where the archbishop warned John that any action against the barons that was not the outcome of proper legal judgement would be a gross violation of his recent oath.

Almost before he had had time to unpack in England, Stephen Langton had intervened in the most sensitive area of domestic politics. It is hard to imagine which emotion was uppermost in John's breast, shock or outrage. The notion

The Pope's Man

that evasion of military service, the open disobedience of a royal command, was a matter for the courts rather than swift and exemplary retribution at the sword point, might technically be correct. But when it came to reality, few medieval kings were inclined to debate points of law with mutinous subordinates and military deserters. John tartly informed the archbishop that questions of lay jurisdiction were outside his province, and pushed on to Nottingham in a foul temper. Langton followed him, threatening to excommunicate every one of the king's party if John persisted in his intentions. The expedition continued, but its royal leader, compromising belatedly, contented himself with a non-violent show of strength—his second warning to the northern barons in a short time.

At the end of September, John returned to London to meet a new papal legate assigned to England for the specific purpose of supervising the restoration of that kingdom to the Communion of the Church. From the attitude of this legate, Cardinal Nicholas of Tusculum, it soon became evident that Innocent's pleasure at acquiring his new vassal was to express itself in terms of considerable advantage to the English king. From the first, Nicholas did all he could to smooth John's path through this tricky period, and to convey that in the pope the king had found a genuine ally. Altogether, there were six vacant sees and thirteen vacant abbeys to be filled in the kingdom. John ordered that elections should be held in his presence, implying that, as of former custom, the chapters were to elect candidates designated by the king. The bishops immediately protested, claiming for the churches their canonical right to free election, subject only to royal assent.

This was the selfsame argument which had led to John's clash with Rome in the first place. To the surprise and agitation of Langton and the bishops, the pope's legate was now on the king's side. Innocent himself ruled that the vacancies should be filled with men "faithful to the king, supporters and advisers of benefit to the realm, appointed with regal concurrence by canonical election or postulation." Pointedly ambiguous, this statement clearly left the way open for Nicholas to act in John's favour, and the legate showed no reluctance to do so.

By a stroke of irony which Langton, for one, cannot have relished, men who had unashamedly remained in the king's service through the years of the interdict were raised, with the approval of Nicholas, to some of the choice posts. The bishoprics of Worcester and Lichfield, and later the archbishopric of York, went to men who had suffered little for Rome in the dark days. John Gray, the king's friend and Langton's former rival for the primacy, was forced on the chapter of Durham, despite the fact that it had already elected a bishop of its own choice in one Richard Poor, Dean of Salisbury. Such coercion differed from John's original attempt to force Gray into Canterbury only to the extent that, this time, it succeeded. John's homage to Innocent continued to pay dividends. Within a few months of arriving in England, Langton was complaining to the pope about various appointments devised by John and sanctioned by Nicholas.

Innocent was not impressed. In the King of England he had won his most glittering vassal, and it suited him to demonstrate the advantages such a concordat might hold for other secular princes. His generosity was displayed not only in the matter of clerical appointments, but in his consistent support for John, from this time forward, against the English barons. Nicholas, instructed to end "all conspiracies and factions" against John, had persuaded the northern magnates to renew their allegiance. Future outbreaks of baronial protest were to be condemned from Rome as the work of the devil. Even in the matter of indemnifying the Church for its losses, the pope veered to John's side.

The interdict could not be raised formally until damages had been settled, and, at a council at London on September 30, the king offered the bishops a total of one hundred thousand marks. Nicholas urged the acceptance of this offer, but the bishops deemed it a poor recompense to "those who had had their castles destroyed, their houses levelled and their woods chopped down." The dialogue continued through the rest of the year without agreement. Finally, it was determined to leave the decision to the pope. Innocent pronounced John's offer of one hundred thousand marks ample, and Nicholas helpfully arranged for payment by instalments—forty thousand marks before the lifting of the interdict, twelve thousand a year afterward. Even these terms were relaxed at a later date. When the interdict was actually abolished, in July 1214, the king had handed over less than thirty thousand marks.

The pope was proving a most benevolent overlord. For a nominal premium, John had gained a uniquely comforting insurance.

Chapter 12
THE GRAND DESIGN

Boast not thyself of to-morrow, for thou knowest not what a day may bring forth.

Proverbs 27:1

John was not so foolish as to push his luck too far against Stephen Langton. In their scuffle at Northampton, the archbishop had revealed an obdurate spirit, and the legate Nicholas would not always be standing behind the throne. When the cardinal was gone, John and Langton would have to live together. More important in the immediate future, the king's plans for carrying the war against Philip back to the Continent made it imperative that the primate he left in England should be co-operative. Before leaving for France, John wrote to Langton waiving the royal claim to be present at the election of clerics. Instead, he delegated the power of assent in such matters to those, including the archbishop, who would have charge of the realm in his absence. "Be assured," the king told Langton soothingly, "that there is no controversy between us."

The Grand Design

Other domestic affairs required action before John could leave the country. In October 1213, the veteran justiciar Geoffrey FitzPeter died. For fourteen years, the stolidly reliable FitzPeter had placed his legal and financial expertise, and his baronial connections, at the disposal first of Richard, and then of his brother. According to Matthew Paris, John laughed at the news of FitzPeter's death. "When he arrives in hell," smirked the king, as presented by Paris, "he will doubtless be greeted by Hubert Walter." No reaction on John's part seems more improbable than levity. FitzPeter had been among the few men John could entirely trust, and the king's plans to go oversea raised the problem of appointing a new and dependable justiciar within a few months.

He chose Peter of Roches, a hard-headed Poitevin adventurer who had been made Bishop of Winchester for his faithful services to John in the past. The bishop—"A man of rock," as he was punningly described by Roger Bacon, the philosopher of a later generation—was tough and capable, undaunted by his triple role as clergyman, soldier and statesman. John placed much trust in him. The English barons, on the other hand, having learned to co-exist with FitzPeter, resented Roches as an upstart and a foreigner. His ruthless efficiency on John's behalf would do nothing to diminish their discontent.

To conciliate FitzPeter's eldest son, Geoffrey of Mandeville, the king arranged his marriage to Isabel of Gloucester, the greatest heiress in the kingdom and John's first wife. There remained to be settled the Welsh problem and the government of Ireland. Langton's first political act on John's behalf was to persuade the princes of Wales to restrain their belligerence. In Ireland, John Gray had resigned the justiciarship to go to Rome as John's ambassador. The Archbishop of Dublin was appointed to take his place.

Toward the end of 1213, John called a great council at Oxford, probably to discuss the preparations for his expedition to France in the new year. Nothing is known of the meeting itself, if it ever took place. But the summonses are interesting on two counts. In the first place, the barons were ordered to attend without their arms: a clear indication that the fears which had caused John to call off the Welsh expedition were still alive. In the second place, the king summoned to the meeting not only the barons and knights, but "four prudent men" from each shire, to be detailed by the sheriffs. This is the earliest known occasion on which ordinary freemen of the shires, as opposed to tenants-in-chivalry, were called to a council of the realm.

The projected Oxford gathering has been described as "the first representative assembly" in the records of English government. That is stretching it too far. Apart from the fact that the assembly itself is not on record, as nominees of the sheriffs the freemen could not qualify as representatives in the true sense. Nevertheless, it can be claimed for John that he was probably the first English statesman to summon yeomen, the humblest of free subjects, to a national council, and it is not insignificant that, when he eventually sailed for France, his army comprised many men of the poorer classes, and few barons.

At last, John was drawing near to the day when the formidable system of continental alliances he had been fostering so patiently with lavish subsidies and secret negotiations was ready to strike the definitive blow at France. Among its more important leaders were Otto of Germany, the Counts of Holland, Boulogne and Flanders, and the Dukes of Lorraine and Brabant. No ally, large or small, was spared the king's blandishments. To the Duke of Limburg, John wrote fulsomely: "Come and see me . . . it will give me rare pleasure to meet and talk with you." To Guy, Count of Auvergne, he proclaimed: "We cannot and we shall not fail you." Even Amery of Thouars,

The Grand Design

a fickle friend at best, was assured of John's support. "I am sending you," the king promised, "an unbelievably large force."

It is eloquent of the complexity of Rome's foreign relationships at this time that the pope's latest and brightest vassal should have been allied with the excommunicated Otto in a projected assault on Innocent's own ally of the imperial struggle, Philip. To heighten the paradox, the pope had initiated a ruthless crusade against the anti-sacerdotal Albigenses, or Catharist heretics, in the far South of France, a policy which brought John's new protector into savage conflict with the English king's allies Peter II of Aragon and Raymond VI of Toulouse. In September 1213, the Albigensian Crusade reached a climax at the battle of Muret, when Peter was killed and Raymond stripped of most of his possessions. To the horror of Cardinal Nicholas, who denounced him as a heretic, Raymond turned up in England to beg the king's aid. Though now a liability rather than an asset, even the unfortunate Raymond found John generous. According to Ralph of Coggeshall, he went away with ten thousand marks.

The strategy resolved upon by John and his allies was a simultaneous attack on France from two sides. The coalition forces of the Low Countries would strike in the northeast while John, marching up through Poitou, would reclaim his lost dominions and squeeze Philip from the southwest. In accord with the first part of this plan, William of Salisbury returned to Flanders with a force of mercenaries to organise the Flemish knights retained in John's service. His immediate task was to distract Philip by harassing the French in that country, and to help cement the alliance by distributing further subsidies among its members. At the beginning of February 1214, John embarked at Portsmouth, leaving England to "the protection of God and the Holy Roman Church." Peter of Roches had instructions to act in consultation with Langton during the king's absence, and the two men could depend for advice and assistance on the trusty William Marshal. Marshal sent his knights with John, but still declined to break his pledge to Philip by campaigning personally on French soil.

Details of the composition and strength of John's expedition are lacking, but it seems that the baronage was poorly represented. The Earl of Chester, husband of the late Constance of Brittany, was present. So was the Earl of Derby, who had regained the king's pleasure. For the rest, the chroniclers characterised the force as "a great multitude of low-born soldiers," mercenaries and ordinary freemen. Apparently John had abandoned his attempts to muster the barons for foreign service. Together with "incalculable riches in silver, gold and gemstones," the king took with him the queen, his son Richard, and his niece Eleanor, the sister of Arthur of Brittany. The inclusion of Eleanor and the Earl of Chester in John's party suggests a design to replace the regime Philip had established in Brittany. After a short stop at Yarmouth, in the Isle of Wight, the English armada spread sail for La Rochelle—and the restitution of the Angevin empire.

John landed at La Rochelle on February 15. The port, which enjoyed profitable trading connections with England, had remained loyal, and many of the barons of Aquitaine met the king with affirmations of allegiance. His first concern, before turning north, was to establish a front from La Rochelle east to La Marche, and to ensure the favourable disposition of the lands to the south of it, that is, those territories of Aquitaine which would be in his rear when he marched against Philip. During the second half of February, and the opening days of March, he secured the strongholds covering La Rochelle, including Mervent and Milécu close to the seaport, the abbey of La Grâce-Dieu on the border of Saintonge, and Niort, to the east of his landing place, on the Sèvre River.

The Grand Design

On March 8, John sent home a communique, addressed to the "good men" of the larger cities of England, outlining his early progress in glowing terms:

"Know you that we and the loyal followers who came with us to Poitou are safe and well, and that, by God's grace, we have already taken steps to confuse our enemies and bring joy and satisfaction to our friends. On the Sunday before Mid-Lent we besieged the castle of Milécu, which had been armed against us, and on the following Tuesday we captured it." He had, he declared, taken command of many castles.

Having consolidated his position around La Rochelle, John now struck east across his front, following the river Charente to Angoulême, through Aix in the Limousin, and into La Marche. Stopping a day or two in the more important places, he received the homage of barons and appointed seneschals and other officers. From La Marche, he retraced his steps to Angoulême and the Charente, passing through Limoges. In April, he plunged deep into the country behind this east–west line to satisfy himself that his rear was not in danger. Passing through Périgord, he went as far south as La Réole, on the plain of the Garonne, southeast of Bordeaux.

Philip's biographer, William the Breton, mocking John for avoiding combat with the French king, who was lurking uneasily on the Poitevin border, explained the English king's march south as a cowardly retreat. At the same time, the French writer admitted that Philip was bemused by his rival, a general whose tactics were as deceptive as "the way of a serpent, a ship at sea, or a feather in the wind." Philip did not commit himself by moving further south, nor was John goaded to a premature clash by the proximity of the French army. It was no part of John's plan to defeat Philip in battle only to find anarchy and rebellion in the French fiefs. Instead, it was his intention to consolidate his gains as he pressed forward, establishing reliable government in his wake. Among considerable lords who had already pledged themselves to his cause were the Count of Périgord and the Viscount of Limoges.

"I have done homage to you in the past," the latter wrote apologetically to Philip, "but my traditional master, King John, has brought such a powerful force into my fief that I can neither resist him nor await help from you. I have been to meet him and have done homage. I tell you this that you will no longer depend on me."

By now, the situation in Flanders was alarming the French king. Emblazoning a grim warning on the countryside of Poitou, where he left crops and villages charred and smouldering, Philip detailed his son Louis to keep watch on John while he, Philip, hustled back toward his northeastern frontier. John had one more item of business to conduct before he could himself head north into enemy territory. In Poitou, the house of Lusignan had remained bitterly hostile to John ever since he had snatched Isabelle of Angoulême from under the nose of Hugh—now Hugh IX, Count of La Marche. Hugh and his two brothers, Ralph of Eu and Geoffrey of Lusignan, constituted a formidable alliance, which John had hoped to win over by diplomacy. As a token of reconciliation, the king proposed to offer his first legitimate daughter, Joan, still an infant, in marriage to Hugh's heir, whose name was also Hugh. A temporary truce had enabled John to pass freely through Lusignan lands in his initial procession to La Marche. But the truce expired without agreement, and, in May, John set out to subdue the brothers by force, directing his efforts chiefly against Geoffrey, the most recalcitrant member of the family.

In a detailed letter home to his government, John described the steps he took to gain the fealty of the Lusignans:

> On the Friday before Pentecost [May 16] we deployed our army against a castle of Geoffrey's at Mervant. It was reputed to be impregnable. Yet on Whitsun Eve [May 17] we took it by assault

in an action lasting from dawn to one o'clock. On Whitsunday we besieged another of Geoffrey's castles, at Vouvant, in which he had taken refuge with two of his sons. For three days, we hammered it continuously with stone-throwers. It was close to falling, when the Count of La Marche arrived and persuaded Geoffrey to surrender himself, his sons, his castle and all in it.

Close by the castles of Mervent and Vouvant, northeast of La Rochelle, Geoffrey had a third castle, Montcontour. While John was at Vouvant, Prince Louis, fearing the defection of the Lusignans, laid siege to Montcontour. At the same time, Philip, seemingly intent on subverting a reconciliation between John and the Lusignans, appears to have offered a son of his own in marriage to the baby Joan. On the face of it, this seems an improbable gesture, but it was written plainly in John's letter:

> On hearing that Louis was besieging Montcontour, we set out to engage him [Louis retired on John's approach]. On Trinity Sunday [May 25] we were at Parthenay [east of Montcontour] when the Counts of La Marche and Eu, together with Geoffrey of Lusignan, did homage and fealty to us. Having already discussed the marriage of our daughter Joan and the son of the Count of La Marche, we now granted this to him, although the King of France requested her for his own son. This request was a trick. We recalled how our niece was given to Louis, and the outcome of that. May God make this marriage more profitable than that other one! Now, thank God, we are ready to attack our chief enemy, the King of France, beyond Poitou. We inform you that you may rejoice at our success.

The letter was written at Parthenay, where an impressive assembly of Poitevin barons gathered to witness the betrothal of John's daughter to Hugh's son. As it happened, these nestlings were destined not to marry. But, for the moment, their engagement served John's purpose. He had enlarged his army by much of the chivalry of Poitou. Free at last of the systematic and tedious operations involved in securing the South, the king could shake his spurs, flourish his sword arm and swing north in the jinking, dust-raising pattern of swift raids and deceptive changes of direction in which he excelled. During the first half of June, it must have seemed to Louis—a capable soldier but bewildered by John's tactics—that he was guarding his father's lands against a will-o'-the-wisp.

Leaving Parthenay, John rode east toward Poitiers, coming within a few miles of the city before revealing the movement as a feint. Describing a wide U-turn to the north, he struck diagonally across the lower part of Anjou, heading for Ancenis, where the border of Brittany met the Loire. To the peasants of Anjou, busy in the hay-scented pastures of John's ancestors, the long train of armed knights and footmen winding between the Main et Loire and the Vendée must have been a rousing sight—the stumpy king and his lieutenants, finely mounted, in the van, the royal banner of triple leopards streaming overhead, the vivid aprons and tunics of cavalry and infantry coalescing in rainbow-speckled coils in the summer haze.

On June 12, having thoroughly alarmed Philip's adherents in Brittany, John moved up the Loire toward Angers. Then, while the French scouts drew their conclusions and sped the news to their masters, he suddenly reversed direction, racing back down-river, past Ancenis, to descend on the Breton seaport of Nantes. The dismayed garrison, hastening to defend a bridge between John and the city, was swept aside by the English and their Poitevin allies. Together with the port itself, John captured twenty French knights, including Philip's cousin Robert of Dreux, the brother of Peter, Count of Brittany by favour of the French king.

If John intended to establish Eleanor of Brittany at the head

The Grand Design

of a regime to rival that of Peter, there is no indication that he took steps to do so at this stage. His main interest in Nantes was doubtless as an additional port and base to La Rochelle, one closer to the action as his campaign shifted from Poitou to Anjou and Brittany. By bearing well to the west in his northerly advance, John was stretching communications between Louis and Philip to the utmost, at the same time confusing them with dummy marches and sudden changes of target. Until Salisbury and his allies were ready to strike from Flanders, this was sound policy. It culminated, around the middle of June, in the unopposed entry of the English king to Angers, the original seat of his forefathers.

At this emotional and satisfying point in his campaign, John ill-advisedly altered his tactics. Philip's seneschal of Anjou, William of Roches, a former partisan of John's who had gone over to the French king, had barricaded himself in a fortress at Roche-aux-Moines, a few miles from Angers. So far, John had ignored isolated enemy fortresses, teasing Louis by stopping nowhere more than a day or two. Now he led his entire army to Roche-aux-Moines and sat down in front of it for a fortnight. Perhaps he considered the seneschal a prize of extraordinary importance. Perhaps the capture of Nantes and Angers had made him complacent. Certainly, he was not lacking in confidence, for he issued orders from his siege camp that the queen and his children Joan and Richard should be brought to him, together with his treasure and fresh horses. Whatever his motives, the result was that for the first time since John had broken north from Poitou, Louis was able to pin him down and challenge him.

The news that Louis was advancing on Roche-aux-Moines from Chinon, did not perturb the English king. According to a French chronicler, Louis commanded twelve hundred men-at-arms, two thousand light horse and seven thousand foot soldiers. The size of John's force is unknown, but his scouts returned from a perusal of the French army to assure him that the English and Poitevins had a comforting superiority in numbers. John decided to stand and do battle. To the French prince's personal challenge, he responded loftily: "Come, and you will find us ready to fight. The sooner you come, the sooner will you regret it." But it was not Louis who regretted his audacity.

The English knights and yeomen, together with John's mercenaries, were preparing to take the field when the Poitevin barons, led by the accomplished turncoat Amery of Thouars, gave notice that they were not prepared for a pitched battle. Amery, professing to doubt John's intention to confront Louis, flung a few face-saving insults at the English king and galloped off with his retainers. The barons of Poitou mounted and followed him.

For any general, such desertions in the face of the enemy would have been daunting. For John, haunted since the Norman betrayals by the spectre of treachery, the signs were disastrous. Imagining traitors everywhere, he abandoned siege engines, tents and baggage, scrambled to cross the Loire, and rode the best part of twenty miles south before halting. Tears of rage and disappointment, it was said, mingled with the dust on his flushed face. By July 9, a week after the flight from Roche-aux-Moines, the king was back where he started, at La Rochelle—with the difference that his equipment was lost, and Poitevin aid had been written off. Against this, Louis had not attempted to follow him, and the English army was largely intact, if demoralised. There was nothing for it but to dissemble the importance of the set-back, plead for reinforcements from England, and hope to be reorganised in time to synchronise with the Flanders offensive.

In the second week of July, John sent an SOS to "all his faithful men in England," thinly disguised with a note of spurious confidence. "Know that we are safe and sound," he

The Grand Design

wrote, "and that, thanks to God, prosperity and joy abound with us." Expressing his thanks to those who had already helped in the furtherance of the expedition, he entreated the many barons who had yet failed to do so "to join us immediately, with due concern for our honour and the reclamation of our territory." Those who did so, he promised, would earn his perpetual gratitude. "And if any of you," he added, "has cause to fear our displeasure, the surest way to set things right is by answering this summons."

But the grand design to crush France between two fronts was crumbling. While John had been ready in Anjou to co-ordinate with the expected offensive in the northeast, Salisbury had been killing time and very few enemies in Flanders, waiting for his allies to stop feuding and bickering, and for the imperial leader, Otto, to turn up. By the time Otto's dragon and eagle insignia had belatedly joined the banners of the Rhineland princes, John was back in La Rochelle, cursing the Poitevin barons. If the original strategy were to be implemented, Salisbury and his allies would now have to delay their offensive until John had been reinforced and could strike again.

It would have been difficult under the most favourable circumstances to hold the coalition forces together for very long. And the circumstances were deteriorating with rapidity. The delay imposed by Otto's late arrival, and other problems, had allowed Philip Augustus time in which to muster and organise his feudal host, and to arm the citizens of his communes. Beside which, John's retreat to La Rochelle, easing the pressure in the South, had allowed the French king to switch a substantial portion of his son's army, including some four hundred knights, to the northern front.

Philip had mustered his army at Péronne, on the Somme between Paris and Flanders. By July 23, he felt strong enough to carry the fight to his enemies. Advancing through Cambrai and Douai, the French king marched into Flanders, intent on turning the flank of the allied force. In the event, he overshot the target. Otto and his comrades-in-arms were at Valenciennes, near the border, preparing to march on Paris, when they learned that the French army was at Tournai, in their rear. On the morning of July 27, a Sunday, Philip, realising he had advanced too far, retraced his steps to the village of Bouvines, where a bridge crossed the river Marque. He had crossed the bridge two days earlier, noting the spot as a good resting place, with shade for his men and water for their horses. The surrounding country, an open, gently undulating plateau, offered good manoeuvring ground for his cavalry, and obviated the danger of surprise attack.

It was a broiling summer day. The sun was at its zenith, and Philip had thrown himself in the dappled shadow of an oak tree to relax, when his scouts returned to the encampment on lathered mounts. The coalition army was approaching, they reported, its banners flying, knights armoured and helmeted. Philip called his captains around him. Before the sun set, the clear waters of the Marque would be tinted red, and the otherwise undistinguished hamlet of Bouvines assured a place in history.

Pitched battles, as has been seen, were neither common nor popular among the medieval aristocracy. Though warfare was a constant theme in the literature and art of the period, hostilities among Christians were frequently less deadly, less socially disruptive, than might appear superficially. The two most usual forms of warfare, raids and sieges, did not involve a high degree of peril for the nobility. Raids, aimed at destroying crops, ravaging villages and terrorising the peasantry, more often resulted in reprisals in kind than in physical confrontations of chivalry. Sieges might end in withdrawal, negotiation or the surrender of the besieged, who were customarily ransomed. For the most part, it was more profitable to capture knights than to kill them. Today, it seems odd that princes engaged in wholesale hostilities against each other were able to correspond politely, even amicably, at the same time, emerging from long conflicts with little apparent ill feeling. To the medieval mind, it did not seem incongruous, for the military activities of the upper classes were governed by codes and rituals which effectively minimised hurt to their own kind.

Pitched battles, however, stood outside this pattern. Leaders who resorted to open combat abandoned the rule book. Hand-to-hand engagement could hardly be ritualised, and honour demanded that the nobility bore the brunt of the fighting. Accordingly, in both camps that morning of July 27, there had been some reluctance to join issue with the enemy, some talk of postponing the conflict. Many of Philip's knights were in favour of crossing the bridge at Bouvines and pushing back toward Paris. Indeed, part of the French army had already crossed the river, and Philip had to recall it. Later, he destroyed the bridge to discourage withdrawal.

At a conference of coalition leaders, influential voices were raised against a general engagement. The King of France, it was said, should be allowed to continue his "retreat," a morale-sapping exercise which, hopefully, could lead to French desertions. Prominently opposed to this argument was Hugh of Boves, a mercenary captain. Hugh reminded the noble amateurs around him that John had not stinted his subsidies and grants to them, claiming that they owed him a battle. Having armed and assembled, Hugh challenged them, only cowards would refrain from marching forward. Affrontedly, the allied knights reached for their hardwear.

Battle-clad, the chivalry of Europe assumed a bizarre anonymity. Chain-mail shrouded limbs and torsos on both sides. Metal helms, some pointed like the beaks of great tin birds, some flat and apertured to resemble grimacing robots, rendered the aristocracy spookily faceless. Glimpsed amidst the swirling dust pounded from dry soil by their chargers, the leading men of the opposing forces could be identified only by the symbols on shields and aprons, or by the banners lofted beside them. Sweating and apprehensive within their armoured shells, the lords of a hundred lands jogged and creaked to the field of truth.

To the forefront of John's captains and allies rode Otto of Germany, Ferrand of Flanders, William of Holland, Renaud of Boulogne, Henry of Brabant (Otto's father-in-law), Duke Theobald of Lorraine, Count Philip of Namur, Hugh of Boves and William, Earl of Salisbury. Philip could boast few feudatories of such grandeur. Apart from the lesser nobility of Normandy, Picardy and the Ile-de-France, he was supported by the Duke of Burgundy and the representatives of the Count of Champagne, the count himself being too young, at thirteen, to fight. On the other hand, the French army was strong in warrior prelates, men who commanded devout and often sanguinary followers. Representing the Church Militant were the Archbishop of Rheims, the Bishops of Léon and Beauvais, and the Bishop-elect of Senlis.

As well as its hard core of men-at-arms, each side had a larger force of light horse, its riders either partially mailed or leather-clad, and a swarm of foot soldiers: axemen, bowmen, swordsmen and others. The German infantry was armed with two weapons which aroused special comment from the French historiographers—the halbert, or long-shafted battleaxe fitted with a hook to drag cavalrymen off their horses; and a "sword-dagger," possibly a version of the old Saxon short sword, or *seax*.

Estimates of the number of men involved at Bouvines are unreliable. English writers of the time claimed that the allies were heavily outnumbered, a ratio of four to one being mentioned. French writers asserted that the contrary was the case,

The Grand Design

one putting the strengths at eighty thousand allied troops, twenty-five thousand French. This is incredible. Indeed, it seems most unlikely that either side would have taken the field with a marked inferiority of numbers. More reliable sources suggest that the armies were roughly equal on a quantitative basis, at least in the crucial mounted arms. There is some agreement among medieval and later historians for placing the number of men-at-arms involved at between a thousand and fifteen hundred a side, and the light horse at around four thousand a side. There would have been several times as many foot soldiers as mounted men, and it seems probable that the allies, whose ranks included a particularly strong infantry contingent from Germany, outnumbered the French in this department. Even on conservative calculations, the armies were impressive. Numerically alone, Bouvines was one of the greatest battles to have erupted from Anglo-French rivalry.

Before the engagement, Philip offered a brief prayer in the village church, encouraging his followers with the thought that, since Otto was excommunicated, they were about to fight for a holy cause. God, he said, would bless them. The French army was drawn up with its back to the Marque, and to the sun, its wings on rising ground, its centre in a shallow hollow. Here, under the royal banner of golden fleurs-de-lys on an azure ground, the king took his own stand, surrounded by a bodyguard of French chivalry, supported by picked cavalry from France and Normandy. To his front, though late arriving since they had to be called from some distance, were the levies of various communes. The left wing was commanded by Philip's brother, Robert, Count of Dreux, supported by, among others, the fighting Bishop of Beauvais. The right wing was commanded by an equally redoubtable churchman, Brother Guérin, Bishop-elect of Senlis.

Facing them across the open plateau, squinting into the sun, which sparkled on arms and housings, the forces of the coalition were drawn up in three similar divisions. At the centre, Otto was guarded by a corps of hand-picked German knights. Above them, on a tall pole set on wheels, flew the standard of the eagle and dragon. To their front, massed in deep formation, was the Germany infantry. The left wing of the allies, facing the French right, was led by Ferrand of Flanders, whose force was notably strong in light horse. To Otto's right were Salisbury and Renaud of Boulogne, with their knights and mercenaries.

Having arrayed themselves in some semblance of order, the protagonists swiftly abandoned any pre-ordained strategy. Tactically crude, a free-for-all rumpus in which acts of individual prowess were more significant than directed manoeuvres, Bouvines proved characteristic of medieval pitched battles in defying lucid reconstruction. To the customary swirl of confused mêlées, unco-ordinated objectives and mercurial changes of fortune, had to be added a cloud of blinding dust which must have precluded any overall attempt to read the drift of the conflict. The fighting was initiated from the French right by a cluster of Guérin's knights. Their successful sally against Ferrand and his compatriots on the allied left presaged a series of hit-and-run assaults against the Flemish wing.

These lightning attacks, climaxed by a determined charge of French men-at-arms under the Duke of Burgundy, seriously unsettled the Flemings, who seem never to have made a real impression on the battle. Meanwhile, Renaud, whose military talent was to prove perhaps the outstanding feature of a violent but generally unimaginative tussle, had cut obliquely across the fronts of the opposing armies in an attempt to reach and overthrow Philip. Ferrand attempted to follow suit from his own wing, but both men were forced back to their stations by counters from the French left and right. Still, Philip was not safe. With his flanks otherwise engaged, he now became the target of a general advance by Otto and his infantry. Preceded

The Grand Design

by their battle cries, and the gleaming heads of levelled halberts, the German footmen plunged into the dusty hollow at the French centre in a solid phalanx, bearing remorselessly upon the levies of the communes. Overcome by the weight of the onslaught, the ranks of French infantry parted, leaving the king exposed.

A desperate and vital struggle now raged within the shadow of the French banner as the citizens of Philip's militia rallied and, joined by the household knights and other French men-at-arms, fought to halt and throw back the imperial infantry. So close to the King of France flowed the waves of the German tide at one stage, that Philip was actually hooked by a halbert and dragged from his charger. He was rescued by his standard-bearer, Galon of Montigny, and screened by his bodyguard until he could remount.

The tumultuous clash of metal, interspersed with the angry and agonised shouts of men and the cries of wounded horses, continued through afternoon to evening. The sun was lowering behind the village of Bouvines, when Ferrand of Flanders was unseated, severely wounded and captured. Repeatedly battered by charges from Guérin's wing, as well as harried by the forces of Champagne, the Flemish contingent had been under continuous pressure from the beginning. Now, with its leader gone, it broke and fled the field. At last, reinforced by that part of his right which had not pursued Ferrand's men, Philip was able to command the central issue. It was Otto's turn to live dangerously. With his infantry falling back on all sides, he found himself the focus of a savage mounted scrimmage between his household knights and a determined posse of French and Norman chivalry which had slashed its way through the battle toward him.

In places, the crush was so tight that it was difficult to wield a sword. The leader of the French knights, William of Barres, actually wrestled with Otto on horseback, twice getting a neck-hold on the German before being thrown off. Another Frenchman grabbed Otto's bridal rein and attempted to lead him off. Finally, the emperor's horse, stabbed through the eye, reared up and unseated its rider. As Otto sprawled on the ground, the demented animal galloped wildly through the mêlée before abruptly dropping dead.

By now, the German infantry phalanx was dispersed. The imperial household was holding its ground, but reinforcements from the French left threatened to surround it. Otto had had enough. Remounted on the charger of one of his followers, he departed the scene of the struggle, speeding with the Duke of Brabant to Valenciennes. Soon after, the German standard was torn down, and the encircled remnant of the emperor's bodyguard surrendered. On the allied right, Renaud of Boulogne was still fighting. Having failed in his initial attack on Philip, he had more than retrieved his military reputation as the battle progressed. Marshalling his tough *routiers* in a defensive horseshoe formation, he had led numerous and dashing cavalry sallies against the French, retiring meantimes to reorganise within the walls of his protective screen. Repelling wave after wave of French cavalry, Renaud's ring of *routiers* was to fight to the very end.

Nearby, Salisbury and Hugh of Boves had held their ground capably. It is noteworthy that, as well as confirming Renaud's reputation, Bouvines amply justified the value of John's mercenaries, for almost all the allied infantry still standing were hired men. The battle now entered its last phase. In a despairing bid to rescue the day, Salisbury wheeled his division and attempted to sweep diagonally across the field to the front of Renaud's position. For a moment he seemed to have succeeded. The French fell back before the thrusting English mercenaries. But the move exposed their rear, and the Bishop of Beauvais, perceiving his opportunity to wreak havoc, grasped it with unholy alacrity. Swinging his adherents behind the

English, he penetrated their formation, reducing the charge to confusion. According to William the Breton, the rugged prelate personally smashed Salisbury to the ground with the cudgel he considered less offensive to his vocation than a sword or lance.

The French episcopate served Philip handsomely at Bouvines. Soon after the Bishop of Beauvais captured Salisbury, the Bishop-elect of Senlis made Renaud his prisoner. The count's mounted contingent had been reduced to six weary knights. Ignoring their pleas to escape while there was still time, he fought on until his horse was felled and he was trapped beneath the animal. His ring of mercenaries, now surrounded by the whole French army, was butchered to the last man. It was getting on for eight o'clock in the evening, and the sun was setting, when the clash of arms subsided and Philip could take stock.

Perhaps wisely, he decided against pursuing his enemies. His men were tired; the allies, dispersed and defeated, but not destroyed. Encounters with them in the dark might prove dangerous. Instead, he satisfied himself counting and securing his prisoners. Among them were a hundred and thirty-one "men of importance" and five counts. It is hard to attribute the French success to any one circumstance. Historians have ventured the opinion that the confused and personal nature of the fighting favoured the French aristocracy, enthusiastic exponents of the tournament. It may also be that in an age when the tendency of soldiers to retire from battle at whim was one of the hazards of generalship, Philip gained a distinct advantage by having the river behind him. Again, it was in the nature of things that a national army defending its own boundary should have had more unity and purpose than a broad-based coalition fighting away from home. At all events, the French were too exultant to theorise. For the rest, it was too late.

Philip returned in triumphal procession to Paris, parading his prisoners before his overjoyed subjects. The students of the capital led the celebrations. "For seven nights," declared William the Breton, "they never stopped singing and dancing." A number of prisoners, including Salisbury, were released by negotiation, but Philip refused to part with Renaud or Ferrand. The former eventually died in chains; the latter was confined in a tower of the Louvre for thirteen years. John, at La Rochelle, was disconsolate. The desertion of the Poitevin barons had been bad enough. Now the great coalition upon which he had lavished years of diplomacy and a fortune in subsidies had disintegrated at a single blow. "Since I became reconciled with God and the Church," he moaned, "nothing has gone right for me."

The French victory was doubly decisive. When the dust settled at Bouvines, John's hopes of recovering his continental dominions were shattered, and Otto's imperial aspirations lay in tatters. By contrast, the French monarchy, its moment of peril behind it, was established beyond dispute. The destiny of France was securely in the hands of Philip Augustus. Toward the end of summer, prompted by Pope Innocent, John and Philip agreed on an armistice to last until Easter 1220. By its terms, both kings retained the lands they now occupied. John sailed from La Rochelle with a heavy heart. So much effort, so much expense, so many hopes—all for nothing. He never returned to France.

It was autumn when he landed in England. The situation awaiting him was scarcely brighter than the one he had just left.

Part 3
THE BARONS

Chapter 13
REBELLION

None can love freedom heartily, but good men; the rest love not freedom but licence.

Milton, Tenure of Kings and Magistrates

The Spanish writer Gracián, in his philosophical allegory *El Criticón,* has an anecdote about a Polish monarch who disappeared on a hunting trip and was found later by his courtiers working as a porter in a market. When they ventured to express their dismay that so great a lord should demean himself in humble labour, he told them: "Upon my honour, gentlemen, the load I have quitted is far heavier than the one you see me carry here. The weightiest load of the market is but a straw compared to that under which I toiled as a monarch. In four nights here I have slept more than I did in all the rest of my reign. I have begun to live; to be a king of myself. Elect whom you choose to rule you. For my part, being now so well suited, it would be madness to return to court."

From the ardour with which so many medieval kings not only fought for power, but, having gained it, defended it, one must conclude that they subscribed to no such philosophy. Whatever motive one may attribute to their zest for regality, it cannot be said that they opted for an easy life. The traditional portrait of John as an indolent tyrant passing his time in sinful pleasure, ignores the inescapable pressures and stresses of government. The market porter was not born who envied John the problems bequeathed to him. Nor could it be said that he had shirked responsibility. No English monarch had gone to more trouble to familiarise himself with his realm and its troubles than the present king. The real tragedy was that the harder he struggled to maintain and improve the system handed down to him, the nearer he drew to disaster.

In Philip Augustus, John had inherited a rival dedicated to the destruction of the Angevin empire at a time when all logic—geographical, cultural and political—pointed to the separation of France and England. At home, he had inherited an equally malignant problem in the discontent of the barons. They had seen the government of the counties pass from the hereditary lords to the king's sheriffs. They had watched the royal tribunal increasingly impinge on their own courts. They had witnessed the elevation of foreigners and professional administrators to the king's ministries instead of their own kind. In a multitude of ways, they had felt the curtailment of their powers and the increasing authority of the Crown, and their resentment mounted against John. Yet John had not inaugurated such policies. They had been pursued, more or less consistently, by his predecessors.

John had not gone to France with an easy mind about the situation in England. He had known that plots were hatching in his absence, and twice during the continental campaign had sent special emissaries back home with guidance for Justiciar Roches, and secret instructions to other royal officials. While the justiciar's loyalty was not in doubt, his tact was questionable. Among those he had contrived to upset that summer of

1214 were the Earls of Oxford and Devon, influential lords whose support the king valued. John could not afford to alienate such men. Rather, he had sought to increase the royal party by granting baronies to people he trusted. At the same time, he had complained to the pope of specific dissidents, and warned the legate Nicholas of conspiracies.

When John returned to England in October, he found many of the barons in open defiance. Had he triumphed in France, they might have shown more respect. As it was, they faced a king who had been worsted first by the Church, and now by Philip Augustus, and it must have seemed that the turn of the English baronage was imminent. The lastest grievance was a demand John had issued from Poitou in May for payment of a scutage by those who had failed to join the expedition. After the flight from Roche-aux-Moines, John had written of his willingness to overlook the wrongs of all who hastened to La Rochelle. Many barons, particularly in the North and East of England, had refused either to pay the scutage or accept the invitation. They could hardly escape some blame for the failure in France, and now, confronted by their injured king, they met his temper with arrogance.

When John pressed for payment of the scutage, the defaulters replied that they were exempt from military service in foreign campaigns, thus under no obligation to make recompense in lieu of such service. This argument, now popular, was not supported by any valid precedent. John could produce in its rebuttal a long history of knight-service in wars outside England, or, alternatively, its commutation by payment. "It has always been so," he insisted, "in our own reign, in our brother's and our father's before him." Moreover, he could point out, the commutation of military service by scutage was a matter for royal deliberation, not an automatic right of the tenant. Indeed, by refusing service, a baron violated the contract by which he held his lands, and was liable to forfeit such lands to the Crown. By demanding scutage rather than forfeiture, John was hardly being immoderate.

Precedent, the barons might have argued, was not inseparable from justice. They lived in an age of change, and what we now know as feudalism was as susceptible to mutation as all things. But the rebellious barons were not visionaries; they were not even revolutionaries. Their leaders were rough and overbearing men who, while seeking to evade established obligations, brayed tediously for old rights and privileges. Instead of looking to the future, these contumelious die-hards cast their eyes upon an imagined past, beyond the days of the Angevins, when lords were free from irksome restrictions, and blessed, they supposed, by undemanding sovereigns. One, in particular, caught their fancy. A century and a half after the Norman conquest, they harped back enviously to that very Anglo-Saxon society their forebears had succeeded, extolling the laws of King Edward the Confessor.

From the legend handed down of him, the barons pictured Edward as the ideal king. He had come to the throne in 1042, and reigned no less than twenty-three years. At the time of his accession, the painful and predatory Viking migration had run its course, while the danger from Normandy was not yet explicit. By a generous share of good luck, especially in the timing of foreign events, and by a tolerant attitude toward his earls, Edward had become as memorable for passivity as for his longevity. His was a period to grace the dreams of posterity; the lull before the Norman storm. Thanks to a devoutly fulsome biographer, succeeding generations came to regard Edward as pious, chaste and benevolent. That he might equally have been weak and impotent, was no part of thirteenth-century thinking. John's barons peered at the odd Edwardian coins which had come down to them and saw a face of sage-like inscrutability which passed for wisdom. Had not the Confessor acquired the trappings of saintliness in his own life? Had not the Saxon chronicler described him as "A king of excellent virtues, pure, benign and noble"?

No one could deny that the forbearing and unaggressive Edward had been a rarity among medieval monarchs. Unfortunately for the rebel barons of John's day, while they talked a lot about reviving the "good laws" of the Confessor, no one knew precisely what these laws were. When John demolished their excuses for not paying scutage by pointing to the customs of his father's and brother's reigns, the malcontents shifted their ground from Saxon to Norman times, clamouring for what they held to be the better customs of Henry I. They now produced a so-called charter of liberties, allegedly incorporating the laws of King Edward, which had been promised to the English by Henry in 1100, when he was seeking support for his seizure of the island throne. This charter was, in fact, quite distinct from Henry's "customs," for, once established, he had blatantly ignored its terms. Nor did it contain anything about scutage. It did, however, promise a number of concessions in areas which had aggravated baronial discontent.

Among other things, the charter of Henry I conceded that knights who held their land by service should be free "from all amercements and special obligations" in order that they might provide themselves properly with horses and arms in preparation for military duties, "and the defence of the kingdom." On the death of any baron holding land from the king, the charter provided that his heir should not be forced to redeem the land by virtual purchase ("as was the custom") but should pay no more than a just and lawful relief. Royal control over the marriage of heiresses and other women of noble birth was to be relaxed. Property would no longer be demanded from a baron in return for royal permission for the marriage of his daughter, sister, or other female relative; "nor will I forbid his giving her in marriage, unless he seeks to give her to one of my enemies."

The charter was much concerned with heiresses, wards and widows. Profit was not to be made by milking the property of heiresses given in marriage by the right of wardship, nor of widows, who should retain their dowries as a marriage portion. Neither wards nor widows should be given, as was not unknown, to husbands without their consent. "And I enjoin on my barons to act in the same way toward the sons and daughters and wives of their dependents." A common complaint was that the Crown seized the property of freemen upon their death to cover their debts, and did not always restore what was due to executors or next-of-kin. The charter upheld the wills of Henry's subjects and declared that, when a man died intestate, "his wife, children, parents or legitimate dependents shall distribute his money as seems best to them."

Above all, the charter was intended to please the Church. The foremost of Henry's promises confirmed the freedom of this institution, "so that I will not sell it, nor farm it out, nor will I, on the death of any archbishop, bishop or abbat, take anything from the domain of the Church, or its people, until his successor is established." Wendover reported a belief, plausible enough in view of the archbishop's constitutional convictions, that it was Stephen Langton who had first drawn the attention of the barons to the charter of Henry I. It had happened, it was said, back in the August of 1213, shortly after the primate had absolved John from excommunication. Langton had been conducting a service, attended by many ecclesiastics and barons, in St. Paul's. "According to report," wrote Wendover, "the archbishop called some of the nobles aside and talked to them privately:

> "Did you hear," he said, "how, when I absolved the king at Winchester, I made him swear that he would do away with unjust laws, and revive good laws, such as those of King Edward, causing them to be observed throughout the kingdom? Well, a

charter of Henry I, King of England, has just been found, by which you may, if you wish, recall your long-lost rights and your former condition." And handing them a document, he ordered that it should be read aloud to them . . . When the paper had been read, and its implications understood by the barons, they were much pleased with it, swearing that when the opportunity arose they would stand up for their rights—if need be, die for them. The archbishop promised to assist them to the best of his ability. On this note of agreement, the conference broke up.

Wendover offered the story as no more than a rumour, and some of its detail is dubious. The idea that the charter had "just been found" is colourful; it cannot have been new to students of English law. Nevertheless, by the period of John's return from Poitou, the rebel barons had indeed been inspired to modify their tactics. In 1212, the talk had been of dethronement, even of murder. Now the malcontents had adopted the more respectable cover of a charter.

Wendover's chronicle returns to the story toward the end of 1214. Probably about the time of the feast of St. Edmund, November 20, "the earls and barons of England" met at Bury St. Edmunds, the resting place of a martyred king whose shrine, and its sheltering abbey, were as much visited by pilgrims as any in England. Wendover asserted that the lords arrived at Bury St. Edmunds in the guise of religious devotees, then met secretly to discuss rebellion and the charter. "And all of them gathered in the abbey church and, beginning with the greatest, swore before the high altar that if the king refused to grant them their liberties they would take arms against him, and withdraw their allegiance, until he should seal a charter granting the things they wanted. They also agreed that, after Christmas, they would go to the king in a body and demand that he confirm the said liberties, meanwhile providing themselves with arms and horses."

A more dependable writer, the Barnwell annalist, corroborated the appearance of Henry I's charter after John's return from France, adding that the king postponed deliberation on it until the new year. As agreed, the rebel barons presented themselves before John after Christmas—at a conference in London at Epiphany, January 6, 1215. It seems they were armed and businesslike. When John put them off again until Easter, they raised strong objections, fearing the steps he might take in the interval. After some discussion, the delay was agreed, the malcontents being assured safe-conduct and a further hearing on the guarantees of a number of leading magnates and clerics, including Stephen Langton, William Marshal and Eustace, Bishop of Ely.

On January 15, with an eye to the support of the clerics, John confirmed the promises he had given Langton on the matter of church elections. Renouncing all precedent, he declared that the choice of prelates should be the right of none but their fellow ecclesiastics from now on. Though he reserved to himself and his heirs the custody and revenues of vacant sees, he pledged that he would not delay elections. The correct procedure, he explained, was that his permission should be obtained to hold an election, and his assent sought afterward. If permission were refused or delayed, the electors were authorised to proceed without it. If assent were refused, the sovereign would be obliged to produce a legitimate reason for refusing it.

Meantime, both John and the rebels lobbied the pope, as "overlord of England," to support their own sides in the dispute. John sent a confidential agent, Walter Mauclerk, to Rome. Eustace of Vesci approached Innocent on behalf of the dissidents. The northern baron had a glib tongue. The king, he said, was determined to stifle the complaints and liberties of the barons. He begged the pope to help them, intimating unashamedly that they had "boldly opposed the king on behalf of the Church" during the interdict, and that they had been instrumental in obtaining John's vassalage for the pope. Innocent's memory was not so short as to allow him to fall for that. Having listened to Mauclerk's account of baronial plots, and the refusal to pay scutage, he came down loyally on the side of his royal servant.

True, he advised somewhat vaguely that John should deal gently with the barons, heeding their demands insofar as these were just. But it was the barons and bishops of England who were to receive his most severe admonitions. The terms he addressed to them were unequivocal. Threatening to excommunicate all who ignored him, Innocent forbade any conspiracy or rebellion against the king, warning Langton and the English clergy of their duty to prevent such subversions.

The popular notion that the disputes of late 1214 and early 1215 involved a simple rift between John, on the one hand, and the barons on the other, originated in Wendover. His account of the conspiracy, with its secret meetings and the dramatic discovery of the charter, was by no means less memorable for being oversimplified. He made no attempt to qualify the opposition. He never spoke of a group or section of the baronage. It was, as he all-embracingly imagined it, "the earls and barons of England" who met at Bury St. Edmunds—a united front against a common enemy. This distortion was avoided by the main body of annalists. These, with remarkable unanimity, distinguished between the baronage as a whole, and the insurgents, by referring to the latter as Northerners. Ralph of Coggeshall wrote of the *Northanhumbrenses;* the Annals of Southwark alluded to the *barones norrenses*. As the Barnwell chronicler observed of what was itself an oversimplification (though nearer the truth than Wendover), the rebels were generally termed Northerners "since the majority had come from northern parts."

The North of England, remote from the central government and little visited by the kings of the past, had preserved a tradition of independence which reacted unkindly to John's systematic efforts to impress his personal authority on the whole of the kingdom. Ill feeling toward the king had been festering here for many years. Close links existed between the northern barons and the King of Scotland. William the Lion had given two of his illegitimate daughters in marriage to the Northumbrian barons Eustace of Vesci, who held the stronghold of Alnwick, and Robert of Ros, who held the castle of Wark. Other English barons were connected by ties of blood to the Scottish king.

There had been, accordingly, some sympathy for William in his dispute with John over Northumberland and Cumberland, and some correspondence with William's natural ally, the King of France. In 1209, the year of John's expedition against Scotland, a young Northerner, John Lacy, had sent word to Philip that he, with his friends and allies, was plotting a rising against the English king. John Lacy was the eldest son of Roger of Lacy, Constable of Chester, appointed some years earlier as sheriff of Cumberland and Yorkshire. The king appears to have had second thoughts about Roger's suitability. In the second half of 1209, he had deprived him of his offices in the vital northern shires, and replaced him with men of more trusty stock.

The complete success of the royal expedition against Scotland had damped the northern conspiracy, such as it was, of 1209. But discontent was not banished. It seems to have survived with particular vigour among the younger, more hot-headed braves of the region, among them John FitzRobert, son of Robert FitzRoger, sheriff of Northumberland, and William Marshal, Junior, who was under FitzRoger's custody. These young men were to join John Lacy as prominent figures of the impending rebellion. In 1211, Roger Lacy had died, and the king kept his heir waiting two years for possession of his inheritance. Even then, it was offered only on the stiff terms of a payment of seven thousand marks, a written guarantee of loyalty and the retention of two of the estate's castles in royal hands. The king appears to have been highly suspicious of John Lacy's activities.

None of the northern dissidents were barons of the top class. Eustace of Vesci, the chief activist among them, was a second-ranker, for all his notoriety. The heavyweights of the movement came from outside its northern concentration, chiefly from the East Country and the region around London. Robert FitzWalter, the man who would assume command, was lord of Dunmow, Essex, and Barnard's Castle, London—"one of the most powerful barons of England," with rich trading interests. He was certainly not among the most reputable. A conspicuous hector and braggart, FitzWalter had first fallen out with the king over the Abbey of St. Albans, an establishment in which the lord of Dunmow took a characteristically aggressive interest.

A long-running feud between the baron and the Abbot of St. Albans had been sparked by a quarrel over the ownership of a wood. Thereafter, FitzWalter appears to have picked every occasion he could to bully the abbot. He had disputed the latter's rights in a priory of St. Albans; he had complained of the number of monks in the priory; he had objected to the appointment of a prior by the abbot; and, according to the abbey chronicler, had forged a charter proclaiming himself patron of the priory. However that might be, Robert FitzWalter plainly had surpassed himself in what followed, for he had fallen on the priory at the head of an armed band and plundered its property. John, incensed by the outrage, had sent troops to restore order.

Another story, possibly apocryphal, but no less in character, told how a son-in-law of FitzWalter's once killed the servant of a Crown officer in a brawl over lodgings. When John threatened to hang the offender for murder, FitzWalter had thundered: "Hang my son-in-law! By God's body you will not! You will see two thousand laced helms in your land before you hang him!" The unrepentant baron had turned up for the trial, which was postponed, in full mail, surrounded by armed knights.

Neither the bullying FitzWalter, nor the glib Eustace of Vesci, inspire much sympathy. The former, with Saer of Quincy, another insurgent, had been responsible for the cowardly betrayal of Vaudreuil to Philip in 1203, while, in 1212, FitzWalter and Vesci had fled the country at the discovery of the plot to do away with John. In this context, as frustrated murderers, they appear perhaps in a truer light than in their later guises as advocates of a bill of rights.

Since their return to England under the pope's peace, FitzWalter and Vesci had been treated by John with a leniency few traitors can have expected of their intended victims. Not only had he returned their lands to them, he had agreed to pay them damages for the confiscation. On July 21, 1213, Vesci had received an advance of one hundred pounds, while his fellow conspirator had received one hundred marks. Many of the rebels, like their leaders, had an eye on the main chance; many more had personal grievances. Some, such as William Mowbray, who had spent several years in Vienna as a hostage for King Richard, felt that justice had failed them. Mowbray had offered John two thousand marks for satisfaction in a lawsuit concerning his barony. The king, with a fine disregard for the ethics of bribery, had allowed Mowbray to lose the case, while still demanding the money.

The huge debts they owed the king drove some barons to the rebel camp. Nicholas Stuteville, for example, had been obliged to pledge ten thousand marks to the exchequer for his inheritance. Geoffrey of Mandeville had pledged twice as much for Isabel of Gloucester. It may have delighted him to gain possession by marriage of most of that broad shire, but the reckoning had followed with a vengeance. The revenue from the territory proved quite inadequate to meet the terms of repayment. He did not even repay the first instalment. Quincy had been among those barons hard pressed by the Crown for settlement. Others had been provoked by having to pay fines to restore themselves to the king's favour, or to bail themselves from arrest after petty offences.

Among general grievances, the importation of foreign mercenaries, and the persecution of the Briouse family, were outstanding. John had always relied heavily on mercenary troops in his campaigns. After the loss of Normandy, they were increasingly based in England, where offices were found for their captains. To what extent their role embraced internal security is uncertain, but they were not liked, and their presence contributed to the ground-swell of discontent.

The Briouse affair had done perhaps more than anything to arouse resentment and fear among the barons, and Giles of Briouse, Bishop of Hereford, was prominent among relatives and friends of the victims who joined the insurgents. Family allegiances in a closely interrelated aristocracy extended the ranks of the malcontents. FitzWalter himself brought with him a family group including Henry of Bohun, Earl of Hereford, Robert of Vere, Earl of Oxford, and Geoffrey of Mandeville, as well as neighbours from two powerful houses, Roger Bigod, Earl of Norfolk, and Richard of Clare, Earl of Hertford.

Territorially, the rebels were clustered most densely in Northumberland, Yorkshire, Lancaster, Lincolnshire, Essex and East Anglia. The majority of the greater barons in these regions were against John, and their lesser neighbours tended, no doubt circumspectly, to support them. Surviving records and chronicles suggest that some forty-odd barons were attached to the rebel cause in the early months of 1215, of whom about half can be identified with the northern shires—if these are taken to include Lincolnshire. A dozen more held the bulk of their lands in the eastern shires—Norfolk, Suffolk, Essex, Middlesex and Kent—while the rest were dispersed, with some emphasis on Gloucestershire and Herefordshire (where the Briouses had connections) and elsewhere in the West.

The number of barons whose loyalty to the king is ascertainable at this time of crisis was about equal to that of the dissidents. But in power and integrity they were more impressive. At their head, William Marshal and Ranulf, Earl of Chester, were among the greatest figures in the land, respected lords and redoubtable warriors. Marshal had a squadron of Irish knights behind him, while Chester, with his fellow-loyalists William Ferrers, Earl of Derby, and Earl Henry of Warwick, carried a vast section of the Midlands for the king. Both Marshal and Chester were the more dependable for having been tempered in the fires of John's displeasure, which they had survived without cracking. The Earls of Arundel, Warren and Salisbury were, at the outset of rebellion, formidable deterrents against revolt in Sussex, Surrey and Wiltshire, while Earl William of Devon, supported by such Cornish and Devonian barons as Robert Courtenay, Henry of Pomeroy, Henry FitzCount and Robert of Cardinan, was a bastion of loyalty in the southwest.

The greater part of the English baronage was unaligned, seemingly anxious to stay out of trouble. Of a total of one hundred and ninety-seven baronies in the country, only thirty-nine can be identified as rebel-held, and about the same number established as positively loyal in attitude. Something like a hundred and nineteen, therefore, were either neutral or hesitant. Lesser freeholders played a very small part in the rebellion. The overriding duty of the English mesne tenant was fidelity to the Crown. He was under no obligation to follow his lord in revolt, and seems to have had little inclination to do so. The

Rebellion

number implicated in rebellion at the beginning of 1215 has been estimated by an expert on the feudal structure at less than five hundred. While the total of freeholders in the country is unknown, this must have represented an almost negligible fraction. When it is further realised that the great mass of the people, the serfs or ordinary peasants, were excluded from the argument, the traditional notion that the country was up in arms against tyranny is manifestly fanciful. Not only was the revolt largely baronial—at the onset of the crisis it involved little more than a fifth of the baronage.

A king quicker to take arms than John might have crushed the rebels at this stage. He had the generalship of Marshal, Chester and Salisbury at his calling, plus mercenary captains and campaign-hardened troops. There must have been hawks in his party who advocated the swift, pre-emptive strike. Had the rebel leaders come into the open under their true colours, demanding the emasculation of the monarchy and a return to the "good old days" of baronial irresponsibility, John might well have resorted promptly to armed force. But FitzWalter and Vesci had learned a hard lesson. Their direct appeal to murder and treason in 1212 had ended in wild flight. This time, they advanced warily behind a screen of moderation, flourishing a charter.

No baron could help but sympathise with the charter of Henry I, and so long as the rebels restricted themselves to promoting it John could not chastise them without risking the alienation of the neutrals. The nightmares of Norman and Poitevin treachery haunted him. He curbed his anger and resolved to meet the crisis with diplomacy.

The choice of Stephen Langton as one of the king's sureties for the truce until Easter, had been a shrewd move on John's part. It might have been tempting to reject the primate as a partisan of the rebels, the inspiration for the more sophisticated tactics which had entered with the charter. Langton had made no secret of what he saw as the king's obligations, and it can hardly have been possible to avoid connecting him with the resurrection of Henry I's assurances. Yet it was equally impossible to identify the archbishop with the cruder currents of regression which swirled beneath the rebel cause. In fact, Langton's role in the rebellion is a singularly hazy and obscure one. The pope was to indict him for failing to enforce the papal censures on the rebels. On the other hand, he appears to have acted as a moderating agent in the dialogue, and to have worked for the avoidance of civil war. Much as John may have resented the primate's intrusion in lay matters, clearly the king did not underrate his importance, especially as an influence on moderate opinion. He treated the archbishop with calculated respect and confidence, exploiting his standing with the barons to cool the situation.

Conversely, the rebels sought to increase the temperature. By provoking John to some rash stroke of anger, they might rally the all-important neutrals to their own ranks. Accordingly, where the king was conciliatory, his foes were provocative; where he was flexible, they were implacable. The game was a tense one, and the disaster-fraught opening months of 1215 saw John manoeuvring with all the subtlety he could muster. Among his first moves after the meeting at Epiphany was a call for an oath of liege homage from his barons, a renewal of allegiance which would have bound them, as one chronicler put it, to "stand by him against all men." When his opponents jibbed, declaring such an oath "contrary to the charter," John discreetly withdrew the demand, "considering the time inopportune for bringing disorder to his people."

That the charter said nothing at all on the subject, was a matter, it seems, of no consequence. What was not in the charter, the rebels had decided, was against it. On February 19, the king granted a safe-conduct to "the northern barons" to enable them to travel peaceably to Oxford for a conference

Rebellion 267

with the primate, his bishops and William Marshal. Perhaps as a result of this, or another meeting, John made a further conciliatory gesture.

At about the time he had sent Walter Mauclerk to the pope, John had summoned to his assistance a band of continental knights under the experienced Savary of Mauléon, soldier, poet and politician, one of the greater and more trustworthy nobles of Poitou. This was one method of reinforcing the king's military strength without offending native sensibilities by importing more mercenary captains. Mauléon might not be loved as a foreigner, but it had to be admitted that he was the social equal and fellow vassal of the rebels. He had landed in Ireland in the first part of February, awaiting instructions while royal agents moved through the English shires "to explain," as John put it, "our business." Other Poitevin detachments followed. Soon after the date appointed for the meeting between the royal commissioners and the northern dissidents, the king agreed to dismiss part of his reinforcements. A contingent of Poitevins was informed that its services were no longer needed, and that it could return to France.

This attempt on John's part to de-fuse the tension, was accompanied by his master-stroke. Since the truce between John and Philip, the pope had been eager for the English king to take the cross as a crusader. In March, the country learned that its sovereign had done so. There is no evidence that John had any intention of travelling to the Holy Land. His motive seems to have been simply the countering of rebel tactics. If his opponents could hide behind a charter, he could invoke the protection afforded a crusader—that is, the condemnation and prosecution by the Church against all who dispossessed or molested him between the taking of the vow and his return from the crusade. The stratagem was well timed. In April, John's position was further bolstered by the arrival in England of the pope's letters condemning baronial conspiracies, reproving

Langton and the bishops for having failed to check the malcontents, and urging the settlement of the dispute by fair and lawful means.

While John was undoubtedly ready to negotiate, the rebels were far from desiring a détente. All their actions suggested a reluctance to parley; a determination to dictate terms rather than discuss them. The rift between the rebels and Rome was not diminished by Innocent's insistence that John's demand for a scutage in respect of his late campaign was a just one. In the week of Easter, April 19–26, determinedly trouble-bent, the insurgents assembled in arms at Stamford, Lincolnshire. It was said that the gathering, the first overt act of rebellion, numbered forty barons and two thousand knights, together with lesser retainers. From Stamford, the rebel force moved threateningly south to Northampton, and then to Brackley, Northamptonshire.

John reacted calmly. Instead of taking steps to disperse the insurgents, he commissioned Archbishop Langton and William Marshal to meet them and discover in precise terms what the malcontents wanted. Their demands are not on record, but the presentation of them was audacious. If the king failed to concede at once, said the rebels, "they would compel him to do so by force." John, then in Wiltshire, described the claims against him as "utterly unreasonable." Why, he inquired sharply, did the dissidents not ask for his kingdom, and be done with it?

On May 3, having failed to gain John's surrender, the rebellious lords formally renounced their homage and fealty, confirming Robert FitzWalter as their leader. With striking irrelevance, FitzWalter assumed the title of "Marshal of the Army of God and the Holy Church." The insurgents now marched grandly back to Northampton and called for the submission of the royal castle there. Since the sheriff of

Northamptonshire, Henry Braybrook, held rebel sympathies, FitzWalter probably expected a quick triumph.

He was disappointed. John had taken the precaution of placing the fortress under the command of a mercenary captain, Geoffrey of Martigny, a relative of Gerard of Athée, and the garrison stood firm. After a futile siege of two weeks, during which FitzWalter's standard-bearer was transfixed through the head by an arrow, the "Marshal of the Army of God" abandoned the project and led his henchmen in search of less ambitious spoils. At Bedford, a fellow-traveller, William of Beauchamp, commanded a second-rate fortress. He admitted the rebels. It was an achievement of sorts, but a poor consolation for the snub at Northampton.

On May 9 and 10, pursuing his policy of moderation, John issued proposals that the whole dispute should be settled by a committee of arbitration comprising four barons of his own choice, and four appointed by the rebels, the proceedings to be under the auspices of Pope Innocent. As sureties for his acceptance of the findings, the king offered the Earl of Warren and a number of bishops. He also announced a significant preliminary concession: "We will neither seize nor dispossess the barons against us, or their men, nor proceed against them by force of arms, except by the law of our realm, or by the judgement of their peers in our court." On the face of it, this was a fair proposal; certainly one designed to woo moderate opinion.

Soon afterward, John granted safe-conducts to individual rebels who wished to discuss problems with him, or make their peace. Among those who responded were Simon Pattishall, a nobleman once employed to collect hostages for the king, and Henry Braybrook, the sheriff the insurgents had appealed to in Northampton. By mid-May, the insurgent leaders had rattled their swords loudly to rather slender avail.

John had refused to rise to provocation. He had remained calm and kept the path to negotiation open. Already, one or two rebels had eyed it wistfully. It looked as though diplomacy might have the beating of the militants.

Chapter 14
A KIND OF PEACE

And they hoped that England would enjoy peace and liberty, not only by protection of the Roman Church . . . but also through the mortification of the king, who they hoped was happily disposed toward peace and gentleness.

Matthew Paris

The old city had seen many assaults and incursions. In the earliest recorded mention of London, Tacitus told how the British warrior queen Boudicca had massacred the community while the legions of Suetonius were away in the northwest. Already, by A.D. 61, London had been full of merchants and their wares, and the Romans had eventually built a wall to protect it. Bede, the first writer to tag London the "metropolis," the mart of many travellers by land and sea, harked back to the stubborn paganism of its inhabitants. Early in the seventh century, Seberht, King of the East Saxons, whose chief town was London, had built a church in honour of St. Paul on the highest ground in the city. But, after his death, heathen worship once more held sway.

Only after several subsequent missionary efforts had ended in frustration, had Christianity finally been established in London. By the beginning of the ninth century, a contemporary reference could describe this resilient, marsh-bounded commune as "the illustrious place and royal city." London had prestige, importance and very much a mind of her own. Later that century, the "illustrious place" had become a rallying point against the depredations of the Danes. In 886, Alfred the Great made good the Danish damage and, according to his friend and biographer Asser, initiated extensive repairs to the city walls, which had since held firm against all assault.

As the Viking raids diminished, and the vessels plying the Thames to London were filled not with warriors but the goods of Europe and eastern lands, the old city had burst her ancient walls, throwing out suburbs of neatly placed dwellings. In John's time, they stretched from the city-centre to the Palace of Westminster, and many houses of stone had replaced the old timber buildings. London was pre-eminent among English cities in size, complexity and riches—"the queen of the kingdom." Its commercial importance lay in its inland situation on a tidal river, allowing goods to be carried to the heart of the southeast without the delays and expense of road transport. The stone bridge, put under construction in 1176, was nearing completion. This, the most ambitious link to date between the city, on the north bank, and Southwark, on the south, was to facilitate the flow of even more merchandise to and from London and the shires between the Thames and the south coast.

Merchant captains, sailing upstream from the estuary, first glimpsed London across the marshes which flanked both banks of the Thames. The city straddled two mounds of high ground divided by the little valley of a northern tributary, the Wall Brook. On the west boundary was another tributary, the Fleet, or Hole Bourne; on the north, moorland, and on the east,

A Kind of Peace

immediate to their approach, the fens commemorated presently in Fenchurch. Continuing upstream from the delta of the River Lea (then a tidal estuary swamping the Isle of Dogs) and drawing abreast of the flats of Bermondsey, the arriving seafarer saw London against a background of tree-crowned heights, now the urban districts of Highgate and Hampstead. Ahead, beyond the bridge, the Thames swung left to be joined by yet another tributary, the Ty Bourne, its estuary filling what later became St. James's Park, and isolating the Isle of Thorney.

London wall, falling into some disrepair at this time, ran north from Blackfriars, its southwest corner, along the rim of high ground above the Fleet to Newgate, from which a road roughly corresponding to the later line of Holborn and Oxford Street linked with the great northwest artery of Watling Street in the present vicinity of Marble Arch. From Newgate, the wall took a northeasterly direction to Aldersgate, inclined north again to a point slightly west of Cripplegate, then stretched east to Bishopsgate, which, with Newgate, comprised the chief land gates of the city. Two roads forked from Bishopsgate. One ran north toward Lincoln and York; the other, east across Lea and into Essex.

From Bishopsgate, the wall curved southeast in a shallow arc through Aldergate to meet the Thames again at the Tower of London. On the river side, there were port entrances at Dowgate, on the mouth of Wall Brook, and, away to the east, beyond the bridge, at Billingsgate. Within the walls, the city, like others of its time, was still relatively open. Small brooks coursed over green allotments, or ran beside huddled cottages, obliging washerwomen, thirsty goats and poultry with their waters. There was no shortage of space for the carnivals, horse-races, blood sports and other diversions, which made London a rare centre of pleasure.

From early times, the city had had its own courts. For

administrative purposes, it was divided into wards, each with a ward-moot, or assembly, presided over by an alderman. Civil cases were settled at a meeting called a husting, while a great folk-moot, summoned thrice a year by the bell of St. Paul's, was held for proclaiming and maintaining public law. When John had granted the commune of 1191, the mayor and aldermen had become the accepted governing body of London.

With its bustling, cosmopolitan ports, its streets alive with character, avarice and wit, London was the place in which to get rich, or fall into the hands of money-lenders, quickly. William of Malmesbury wrote of wharves "crammed with the goods of merchants from every country, particularly Germany." Merchandise from the East—gold and silver work, spices, precious stones, splendid cloths and coats of mail—reached London via the traders of Cologne, who held a leading position among the many foreign merchants in London. Henry II had given them special protection; Richard and John, motivated by political as well as economic considerations, had confirmed and extended their privileges.

Trade associations, or gilds, were well established in the city. With their periodic banquets, their arrangements of mutual benefit, their concern with training apprentices, and so on, they dated back to Anglo-Saxon times. The London of Edward the Confessor had had a "knights' gild." The goldsmiths were well organised in the city. The bakers were operating a gild early in the reign of Henry II. Their custom of distributing alms to the needy helped the gilds to achieve popularity. But one such organisation had become far from popular. The weavers of London had obtained royal sanction for their gild in the reign of Henry I. Partly due to the foreigners in their ranks, and the unusual power attained by their association, the weavers had aroused the hostility of their fellow-citizens. In 1202, "at the petition of the mayor and citizens," John had agreed to suppress the London gild of weavers on the understanding that the civic authorities compensated him for losing the revenue he drew from the gild. This the citizens had failed to do, and the gild had continued in the face of mounting opposition.

Among other factors, the favours accorded the weavers and foreign merchants by the Angevin monarchs were to militate against John in London. Meanwhile, the merchants of that populous and wealthy conurbation had followed the operations of the king and the rebel barons with more than peripheral interest. The news which reached them day by day of the tussle did not, at first, augur well for the insurgents. Behind his restrained and diplomatic front, John had systematically prepared his alternative argument—the mailed fist. As the rebels mustered their forces, the king's agents had been recruiting reinforcements oversea, and placing the royal castles of England in a state of military readiness.

John's fortresses, among them Wallingford, Berkhampstead, Oxford, Winchester, Marlborough, Exeter, Bristol, Gloucester, Bridgenorth, Newcastle, Chester, Norwich, Orford and the Tower of London, studded the country in formidable profusion. The loyal lords from the southern frontiers of Wales were assembled at Gloucester, then ordered to Cirencester, in the Cotswolds, whence they could be deployed east toward London, south toward Winchester or west toward Exeter. Savary of Mauléon and his Poitevins were brought into the same area, providing, altogether, a very serviceable royal army.

Before receiving the rebel demands from Stamford, John had sent his justiciar, Peter of Roches, to supervise his interests in the North. A number of king's men in the region, including Brian of Lisle, Gilbert FitzRenfrew, Robert of Vieuxpont and Philip of Ulecotes, were commanded to place themselves at the justiciar's disposal. At a word from their sovereign, Roches and his followers were ready to fall upon the lands of the absent northern rebels. To observers in London, and elsewhere, it must have seemed, around mid-April, that the king was preparing to crush the dissident barons the moment they gave him an adequate pretext. Yet the first act of aggression, the siege of Northampton, came and passed, and still the king failed to commit himself.

As May proceeded, the nation watched tensely while John continued to nibble round the problem of insurrection without taking a real bite. Report after report told of the deployment of royal forces, but never the decisive move: *May 5.* William Marshal, Earl of Pembroke, together with the Earls of Salisbury and Warren, were assigned to parade through the country in a show of loyalist strength, while John summoned reinforcements from Flanders. *May 8.* The king announced that a contingent of horse and foot were coming over under Gerard of Graveline. *May 10.* John followed his proposals for arbitration by offering Geoffrey of Mandeville and Giles of Briouse appeal to the king's court against the fiscal obligations which had placed them so heavily in debt to the crown. *May 11.* The rebels having ignored John's proposals, the king dispatched two of his captains, William of Harcourt and Fawkes of Bréauté, to check the defences of his castles. He also wrote the Bishop of Winchester about the re-posting of the Poitevins:

"We command you to send a trusty confidential agent, armed with your letters, to make over the castle at Winchester to our faithful Savary of Mauléon, who is to hold it with our Poitevins."

May 12. In his first direct move against the rebels, John ordered the seizure of their lands and chattels by his sheriffs *May 13.* Two loyalists, John of Erley and Henry of Pomeroy were appointed joint sheriffs of Devonshire to suppress a reported rising in the southwest. *May 14.* Special instructions were issued for the confiscation of the estates of Robert Fitz-Walter, Robert of Vere, Henry of Bohun, Giles of Briouse William of Mandeville, William of Huntingfield, Henry Bray brook and Simon Pattishall. *May 15.* The arrest was ordered of the son of Roger of Cressi, half brother of John FitzRobert, both serving in the rebel ranks. John warned his agents not to disturb Roger of Cressi's wife. *May 16.* Earl William of Salisbury was appointed to act as his half brother's representative in London, the most vital centre in the country, together with William of Cornhill, Bishop of Coventry and member of an influential London merchant family.

Both John and the rebels appreciated the importance of support in England's growing cities. The insurgents had wooed their inhabitants with promises of charters comparable to that of London. The king had wooed the citizens of London itself by confirming the commune he had granted in the days of Longchamp, and bestowing upon them the additional privilege of electing their mayor annually. It seems, however, that the king had underestimated the discontent of the city in such matters as the Jews, the weavers and foreign traders. Robert FitzWalter was well placed to exploit the grievances of the citizens. Apart from holding Barnard's Castle, his merchant interests assured him the ear of London's businessmen. The well-to-do among them saw the rebel leader as an ally—"the poor were too intimidated to protest."

The posting of Salisbury to London on May 16 suggests a response to reports, or rumours, that support for the rebels was mounting in the city. The response was belated. Having garrisoned Bedford, the insurgent army was already marching at top speed toward the great city which was to become the capital of England. FitzWalter's force beat Salisbury's mission to its destination, penetrating the conurbation on May 17, a Sunday, when many of the people were attending Mass. Slamming the gates behind them, the rebel barons quickly took command of the city, aided by the dissident merchants. A royal garrison in the Tower of London refused to surrender, but it was too small to venture outside the bastion.

Joined by an opportunist city mob, the insurgents sacked the homes of the king's partisans, destroyed the dwellings of the London Jews and used the rubble to patch up the city walls, which were manned against the possibility of a royal attack.

The occupation of London marked a new phase in rebel fortunes. After the fiasco of Northampton, and the relative insignificance of Bedford, this was a coup of major importance, especially for its psychological affect on the nation. By seizing the premier city of the kingdom, the insurgents had suddenly acquired what they had hitherto plainly lacked: a symbol of prestige, a token of unquestionable achievement. It threw into some doubt John's policy of non-violent counterpoise. Until May 17, the king could have smashed the rebel forces in the field whenever he wished. Against a small and for the most part inexperienced army, he could have thrown an overwhelming number of rugged foreign mercenaries and campaign-seasoned home troops. He possessed the only war-proven generals in the country.

It was not, therefore, fear of FitzWalter and his henchmen which had restrained John. His mind was tuned to a wider strategy. He wished to impress the pope with his forebearance and rectitude, and, above all, to avoid any action which might arouse sympathy for his foes among the great body of uncommitted barons in England, whose power could undoubtedly swing the issue either way.

While the triumph in London had saved the rebellion from a distinctly sickly infancy, it was far from being a winning blow. Militarily, the insurgents were less vulnerable behind the walls of London than in open country. Logistically, the resources of the city might enable them to defy a besieging army for some time. Spiritually, the success was uplifting. When that much had been said, the fact remained that whereas the rebels were cooped up in their stronghold, John controlled practically the rest of the kingdom and could do as he liked with their unprotected lands. The proclamation they now issued to the country from London reflected plenty of Fitz-Walter's bluster, but hopefully skirted the hard facts.

Every nobleman who wished to retain his goods and property, announced the rebels, should immediately forsake the king and join the fight for "peace and liberty." John, they declared with perverse logic, was in a state of revolt against his barons. Those who failed to oppose him would be punished. The insurgents would "carry their banners and arms against them as public enemies, sparing no effort to overthrow their castles, burn their dwellings, ruin their orchards and parks, and despoil their fishponds."

John contented himself with a sharp dig at the mutinous Londoners. These citizens, he proclaimed in a letter to "all his bailiffs and faithful subjects," had "fraudulently and seditiously" broken the terms of their allegiance. "We therefore command you, whenever they, their agents or their goods pass through your territories, to treat them as our enemies, heaping them with shame and misfortune."

The effect of these pronouncements, and the developments which had preceded them, was to expose the sympathies of some wavering elements of the baronage. John Lacy and William of Albini, Count of Aumale, already rebels at heart, were among others who came into the open. According to one annalist, those who rode to London to join the insurgents were predominantly of a younger generation allured by the prospect of military glory—the sons of fathers who, for the most part, kept faith with the king. This, if true, would seem to have deepened the pattern already established, in which experience and political sagacity reposed, on the whole, with the Crown.

Few of the rebels could claim noteworthy records of public responsibility of service, though many were powerful and prominent in their regions. Saer of Quincy had been one of the king's secondary justiciars for a period, and Eustace of Vesci had taken part in the negotiations that led to William the Lion's act of homage to John in 1200. But Quincy's career had been blotted by rebellion against Henry II in 1173, by his part in the surrender of Vaudreuil, and by frequent plunges into debt to the Jews. He had been a baron of small substance until 1204, when he had come into a substantial portion of the Earl of Leicester's vast estates through his marriage to one of that lord's two daughters, Margaret. Vesci had revealed where his true interests lay between John and the Scottish king when he fled to Scotland after the abortive murder plot of 1212.

Two of the grandest lords among the dissidents, Richard, Earl of Clare, and Roger Bigod, Earl of Norfolk, were members of old Norman families distinguished rather for their self-preservation than their public duties. Bigod's father had been noted for his treachery and violence under Stephen and Henry II, and, while Roger had seen service under Richard and John, he had dropped so far from favour as to be imprisoned in 1213. William Mowbray, nephew of the Earl of Clare, had been among those who had garrisoned their castles and prepared for civil war at the time of John's succession.

Among the rebels closely associated with the North, Richard Percy had extended his considerable holdings by snatching his mother's lands when she had died in 1196, while Robert of Ros, like his leader Robert FitzWalter, owed part of his wealth to special trading privileges granted by the king he now repaid with betrayal. Many of the insurgents had held regional offices, including Ros, as sheriff of Cumberland, and William Mallett (whose distant ancestor had fought alongside William the Conqueror), as sheriff of Dorset and Somerset. Some, like Mallett and William of Beauchamp, Lord of Bedford, had even taken part in the ill-fated expedition to Poitou.

A Kind of Peace

Others were sons of famed statesmen or soldiers. William Marshal the younger seems to have fallen below the high standard of fidelity set by his father. John Lacy was not destined for the heroism of his own parent, the defender of Château Gaillard. They were a mixed lot, yet all had one thing in common. The rebellion was their single outstanding gesture in national politics. None bore a burden of any real significance in the government of England, before the rising or after.

Meanwhile, both parties were busy soliciting allies outside the country. The Scots and Welsh were tempted with the promise of rewards if the insurgents gained power. William the Lion had now been succeeded by his son Alexander. The prospect of acquiring Carlisle and Cumberland, probably put to him by the smooth-tongued Eustace of Vesci, won Alexander for the dissidents. Llywelyn of Wales, approached by both factions, asserted his predisposition to fight against English authority, and renewed his raiding activities on the border. Philip Augustus was only too pleased to help the rebels—though discreetly, with one eye on the pope. Philip did not supply troops, but he did provide funds and ordnance. The latter was especially welcome to the dissidents, for, until now, the king's forces had enjoyed a monopoly of military engines. Philip also guaranteed to prevent any of his subjects enlisting with John against the "champions of English liberties."

This did not stop a strong contingent of Flemish knights, under an experienced leader, Robert of Bethune, joining the English king soon after the rebels took London. John was at Freemantle, a royal hunting lodge overlooking the woodlands of Wiltshire. He gave the men of Flanders, some of the best soldiers in Europe, a rousing reception, and put them almost immediately into action. The new sheriffs in Devon had been hard-pressed to contain the rising there, and it was reported that a force of insurgents was laying siege to Exeter. John attached the Flemings to the command of Earl William of Salisbury, who was ordered to restore law in the West Country.

The march to Devon took Salisbury and his allies across the northern point of Dorset, where, at Sherborne, it was learned that Exeter had fallen. According to local intelligence, the West Country rebels, far more numerous than the men with Salisbury, were preparing an ambush in which the royal troops would be massacred. To the indignation of the Flemings, who appear to have regarded it as a slight to their prowess, the king's half brother decided to withdraw to Winchester. Salisbury was a brave soldier, proven at Bouvines, but he was not a rash one. At Winchester, he sought John's advice in the light of the new situation. It was to proceed, as before, to Devon.

At Sherborne again, the people were no more optimistic. On the contrary, they reported that the numbers of the enemy were now even greater. But this time, as the contemporary Flemish chronicler of the event had it, the Flemings insisted on marching bravely forward. According to this probably over-enthusiastic scribe, the rebels at Exeter outnumbered the royal forces by ten to one, yet still fled the city on hearing of the approach of Salisbury's task force.

While still deporting himself with restraint, John continued the systematic build-up and deployment of his forces on a contingency basis. The second expedition to Exeter had departed Winchester May 24. The same day, the king issued instructions that all troops arriving from oversea to join his service should report to his chamberlain, Hubert of Burgh, for their orders. On May 25, part of his armed strength was directed toward London from Winchester, holding in the vicinity of Odiham and Farnham. The king also asked Langton if he might garrison troops in the archbishop's castle at Rochester. Langton acceded. From this Kentish stronghold, a force might advance on London by land or river, or intercept the flight of any rebels from the metropolis to France.

On May 29, John wrote to the pope complaining that the attitude of the rebel barons had made it impossible for him to leave the country and go crusading. Despite dire provocation, he said, it was his desire to conduct his affairs mildly and with humility, as befitted one who had taken the cross. Recounting the efforts he had made to maintain peace among his barons, he recalled that he had offered to abolish "evil customs," that he had promised the rebels the full justice of his court, and that he was willing to abide by the decision of the pope in every matter. Apart from the dubious question of the crusade, the main facts outlined in the letter were valid ones. The rebels could have had a full hearing and discussion of their grievances under the arbitration proposals of May 9. They had ignored the opportunity, trusting the sword before peaceful mediation.

Doubtless, the rebels questioned the impartiality of Innocent, and doubtless they pleaded the ingenuity of the king. But, equally, there was no joy for many of their number in a compromise based on specific grievances. Their revolt was a deeper eruption of the fundamental power struggle between king and baronage, its aim the resurgence of baronial potency and the humiliation of the sovereign. For some, answering the battle cries of predatory ancestors, the excuse to ride roughshod where they pleased, settling feuds with neighbours and flouting king's officers, was enough. Such men regarded the authority of the Crown and the rebel leadership with like disdain. When, at the end of May, a temporary truce was agreed between these two parties, rebel groups in the East, the Midlands and the West Country ignored it. John could not sit on his hands for much longer.

In an urgent dispatch to his oversea recruiting centres, he

now intimated that all troops intent on joining him should sail immediately. On Whitsun Eve, June 6, he ordered the mercenary captain Fawkes of Bréauté to reinforce Salisbury with four hundred professional warriors from Wales. Apart from the barons in London, where the Tower was still under siege, insurgents were in the field in Devon, Northampton and Lincoln. At Northampton, they had killed several members of the royal garrison. At Lincoln, in Whitsun week, they actually seized the city. In parts of the country, the administrative and judicial systems were in disorder. The work of the exchequer and some sheriffs' courts were disorganised by rebellious activities.

The situation was a classic preliminary for civil war: a government threatened by open insurrection; a breakdown of law and order in some areas, tending toward anarchy; a substantial moderate faction in full sympathy with neither side, yet increasingly drawn into involvement as the conflict flared and attitudes hardened.

So far, a major clash had been averted by John's determined diplomacy. By June, war seemed inevitable unless a third party could take the initiative. It did. At the crucial moment, Stephen Langton emerged from the neutral corner, backed by an impressive array of moderate bishops and barons. As John's emissary, Langton had been in touch with the rebel leaders since the outset of the rising, but he was no more the king's man than a man of the insurgents—or, for that matter, a man of the pope. Whatever else Langton was, he was staunchly independent. At one point, John had asked the archbishop to excommunicate the hostile barons. Though the request was supported by Pandulf, who had replaced Nicholas as the papal legate in England, and by the Bishop of Exeter, Langton had refused it. On the other hand, he had carefully reminded the rebels not to take his favour for granted by making his castle at Rochester available to the king's troops.

A Kind of Peace

Neither side could afford to make a foe of the primate, and he exploited his singular station adroitly.

Langton's aims, so far as they can be made out, involved the frustration of a clear-cut victory for either side, sovereign or rebels. Desiring neither an all-powerful monarch, nor an all-powerful baronage, the archbishop seems to have aimed at a nicely balanced situation in which the English Church could gain strength and operate to maximum advantage. This he strove to achieve by an agreement rectifying the more general grievances of the barons, while recalling the rebels to the obligations of their allegiance. John had already shown his willingness to negotiate. The insurgents, their catalytic purpose served in Langton's sight, would have little option but to co-operate if the full weight of moderate opinion turned against them. Already, they went in some awe of the primate, who had drawn to his support a group of highly influential noblemen and clerics, among them royalists of long standing whose advice the king respected.

This party, vital to the settlement which lay ahead, included two archbishops, seven other prelates, and four earls. Among them were William Marshal; Hubert of Burgh, a leading administrator, destined to become Justiciar of England; Hugh Neville, a former sheriff of Cumberland; and, together with others closely associated with John's government, the barons Alan and Thomas Bassett. Unlike most of the rebels, the powers of this faction were not men of merely regional influence, but lords experienced in the defence, the moral influence and running of the whole country, priests and politicians much occupied with the duties of kingship. Both the loyalists, and the bulk of hitherto unaligned barons—who might be said, by and large, to have desired some measure of reform without violence—could be expected to support them in backing Langton's initiative for a code of conduct agreeable to king, Church and baronage.

The detailed evolution of the code arrived at is not ascertainable, but four documents are evident in its development: the Charter of Liberties of Henry I, the so-called Unknown Charter of Liberties, the Articles of the Barons, and, ultimately, Magna Carta, or the Great Charter. The history of the Unknown Charter is elusive. It was not so much a charter as a series of notes intended as a draft for certain concessions to be granted the barons by King John. Somehow, the surviving document found its way to France, where it was appended to a copy of Henry I's charter, preceded by the observation: "This is the charter of Henry I by means of which the barons sought their liberties, and King John concedes the following . . ."

Unlike Henry's charter, it dealt with the problem of foreign service, urgent upon John's return from Poitou. None of the king's men, it provided, should serve outside England, "except in Normandy and Brittany." Scutage, it asserted, should be limited to one mark of silver on the knight's fee, unless a counsel of the barons of the realm considered the situation warranted an increase.

The Articles of the Barons, which originated at an uncertain date during their dispute with the sovereign, diverged in some features from the Unknown Charter in John's favour. It contained no reference to foreign service, or to its alleviation. While the Unknown Charter stated, for instance, that, on the death of a royal vassal, his goods should be apportioned according to his will, the Articles of the Barons provided that any debts owed the Crown should be paid first. Again, while the Unknown Charter called for the deforesting of all forests created by the Angevins, the Articles of the Barons mentioned only those areas afforested by John. Perhaps most remarkably, the first and pace-setting clause of the Unknown Charter—"King John concedes that he will not take a man without judgement, nor accept anything for justice, nor do in-

A Kind of Peace

justice"—was tucked well down the list of Articles of the Barons, and relegated even further in Magna Carta.

Exactly where the Unknown Charter fitted into the dealings between John and his barons is uncertain, but its concern with foreign service and scutage seems to place it around the time of the last expedition to Poitou. The Articles of the Barons were laid before the king in June 1215. By the beginning of that month, Langton and his party were pressing hard for an agreement. The archbishop flew to and fro between John and the rebels like a shuttlecock, judging the temper and exerting his pressure on both sides. On May 31, the king moved to Windsor, on the Thames above London, to facilitate negotiations with the insurgents in that city. Staines, on the river between Windsor and London, was picked as a meeting point, and on Whit Monday, June 8, John issued a safe-conduct for envoys travelling between Staines and rebel headquarters.

On June 10, the king rode to Staines in person and watched his seal affixed to the Articles of the Barons—a token that he accepted the document in principle. It was not a completed contract. While some of its clauses were presented in detail, others were entered merely as headings, alterations appearing in the form of appended notes. If John seems to have settled somewhat incautiously for these vague forms, their final content doubtless had been thrashed out orally. Moreover, the king was backed, in theory, by a reassuring let-out. Since his opponents had not only flouted the instructions of the pope, the overlord of England, but had violated the sanctity of the crusader, he could properly ask Innocent to revoke any concessions extracted from him in the name of peace, and deal with the rebels later.

Several days now elapsed while various clauses were altered or amplified. It was significant that while the barons' articles had commenced with a reference to a layman's grievance, the final draft, Magna Carta, began with a declaration of the liberties of the English Church. The bill for Langton's time and effort could not have been more prominent. On Monday, June 15, the opposing parties, together with spectators and referees, met amidst the buttercups of a riverside meadow near Staines known as Runnymede. The royal and rebel tents were pitched at a seemly distance from each other, and FitzWalter's followers, one is told, came "thoroughly well-armed." Perhaps they were fearful that their leaders might be tricked and arrested.

Already, the insurgents had seen their aims diverted and diluted by Langton and the moderates; their bid to cast off the bearing-rein of royal authority reduced to a wordy legal formula few of them entirely understood. What they did understand—what they grasped as firmly as they clutched the hilts of their long swords—was that this scribbler's remedy was so far from destroying the king's power as to be recommended to him by his own advisers. Nominally, Magna Carta was a list of articles "which the Barons demanded and the Lord King conceded." But the authorship of those articles was never that of FitzWalter's henchmen. Nothing known about the rebel leaders, or their actions before and after Magna Carta, remotely suggests that this was the sort of settlement they had hoped for, nor had it been that they commanded the legal skills and administrative mentality to create it.

The men who wrought the Great Charter from the turmoil of spring 1215, in an attempt to unite king and baronage in a settlement acceptable to the entire upper class of the country, were not to be found in the rebel ranks at Runnymede, but ranged beside John in the royal tents. Here, handsomely robed and adorned for the occasion, discussing final adjustments in the clauses of the charter with clerks from the chancery, or speculating on their implications for the kingdom, were statesmen, diplomats, administrators and Church leaders whose thoughts embraced the latest ideas in government.

Surrounding the dapper, bejewelled monarch, whose expanding waistline and greying beard betrayed his forty-eight full years, were Langton, Marshal, Burgh and Salisbury; the legate Pandulf, with the Archbishop of Dublin and the Bishops of London, Winchester, Lincoln, Bath, Worcester, Coventry and Rochester; the Earls of Warren and Arundel, together with Amery, Master of the English Knights Templars (a military order for the protection of pilgrims to the Holy Land), Alan, Lord of Galloway, and, among other noted barons, the FitzHerbert brothers, Peter and Matthew, Robert Ropsley, Philip of Albini and John Marshal, nephew of the Earl of Pembroke.

According to Matthew Paris, John chatted brightly and familiarly with everyone at Runnymede, smiling amiably and expressing himself well satisfied with the proceedings. Privately, however, so Paris had it, the king "sighed deeply, conceiving the greatest indignation, and gave mouth to sorrow and complaints. 'Why did my mother, unhappy and shameless woman, give birth to me?' he pondered. 'Why was I nursed on her knee and nourished at her breast? Would that I had been slain rather than allowed to grow to manhood!' He then began gnashing his teeth, scowling, and gnawing sticks and limbs of trees, which he demolished with extraordinary gestures, revealing the grief, or rather the rage, he felt."

How Paris achieved this graphic, but uncorroborated insight so long after the event is unexplained. It is easier to believe that the king conducted himself with aplomb at Runnymede, in what must have been something of a festive setting. The weather was fine, the trappings of a royal occasion would have added vivid colour to the river scene, lords from many parts of the country could meet and exchange news while their servants relaxed among the grazing horses. That Monday, Magna Carta was formally accepted, but it was not until June 19 that the final details were inserted and copies were ready.

The charter was then sealed, and the rebels were obliged to renew their oaths of allegiance to the sovereign.

At Runnymede, John and the barons pledged themselves alike to observe the provisions of the charter "in good faith, without any deception." The king immediately ordered his captains and sheriffs to desist from hostilities, instructed that the charter should be read in public places, and called for the appointment of twelve knights in each county to inquire into "evil customs," particularly those appertaining to the forest. A clause in the charter requiring the restoration of lands, castles and franchises to those unjustly disseised, was promptly observed, and, on June 23, Hugh of Boves was commanded to re-embark the foreign troops who had reached Dover.

Nevertheless, the authors of Magna Carta appreciated that neither John nor the rebel barons were wholeheartedly sold on the settlement, and a method of securing the further observance of its terms was set up. In this, twenty-five barons, a good proportion of them rebels, were to be responsible for holding the king to the bargain. They were authorised to demand assistance from "the whole community of the nation" if necessary. If the king, or any Crown officer, dishonoured the provisions of the charter, the misdemeanour was to be reported to four members of the twenty-five, and these four were to petition for redress from the king. If the fault were not rectified within forty days, the committee of twenty-five was to summon sufficient assistance to force the king to comply—by any means, short of injuring his person or family. To check the abuses invited by this scheme, it seems that a further committee of thirty-eight, well weighted with king's men, was appointed to watch the activities of the twenty-five.

For a short while, John appears to have done his best to keep the contract. Those of his mercenaries still in England were withdrawn from situations of confrontation and ordered to make good any damage they might have inflicted since the

A Kind of Peace

peace was signed. The rebel barons were granted his permission to stay in London, at least until August, and the Tower was placed in Langton's keeping. The unpopular Peter of Roches was removed from the office of justiciar and replaced by Hubert of Burgh. A number of officious sheriffs was sacked, their jobs given to men more agreeable to the barons. And court hearings were set in progress to judge the cases of those who claimed to have been deprived arbitrarily of lands, properties and privileges by the Angevin monarchs.

But the truce was a fragile one, and the Great Charter—so solemnly invoked in later centuries—a short-lived wonder in its own day. The chroniclers of the age dealt with Runnymede sparingly. Walter of Coventry dismissed the pact between John and his barons in a few sketchy phrases: "At length, after much deliberation, they made friends, the king conceding their wishes and confirming this by his charter. When the kiss of concord had been exchanged, and homage and fidelity renewed, they ate and drank together."

Ralph of Coggeshall was even more cryptic: "Through the intervention of the Archbishop of Canterbury, with his bishops and some barons," he wrote, "a kind of peace was made."

Chapter 15
MAGNA CARTA

It is enough for me if the knights applaud—I care not a fig for the rest of the house.

Horace, Satires, *X:76*

Magna Carta is perhaps the best known and most misunderstood document in English history. Popular mythology has provided it with a radical complexion, and many still regard it, as it has been variously regarded since John's day, as a guarantee of the freedom of the subject from the tyranny of kings, a bill of reforms, a charter of liberty, a declaration of the rights of the people, a cornerstone of democracy. In it, or in the revised and truncated version which appeared within a few years of John's death, have been detected the origins of many high-flown statements of principle and political theories. It was taken by legal minds of the seventeenth century to support trial by jury and the axiom of no taxation without representation, and was held by the first of John's twentieth-century biographers to embody "the conception of a contract between king and people which should secure equal rights to every class and every individual of the nation."

Such notions distort a reality at once more mundane, more worldly, and, in some ways, more intriguing. Far from securing "equal rights to every class and individual," Magna Carta was largely concerned with the relationship between the king and his tenants-in-chief, the barons. Since the barons could wield no power without their knights, lesser nobles circumspectly were drawn in, but the barons were scarcely fervent to promote the rights of their own tenants, and still less to win freedom for the serfs, the bulk of the populace, for whom Magna Carta meant virtually nothing. The majority of the provisions in the charter were directed toward clarifying and confirming the rights and privileges of the upper classes in terms which can rarely be called truly radical. In its affirmation of the feudal contract between king and baronage, and the limitations it placed on royal power in this context, Magna Carta was reactionary in principle, harking back to the laws and customs of Henry I, and even earlier.

Its less reactionary provisions—in the main, those dealing with the administration of justice—tended to accept existing law, especially as established by Henry II and his legal advisers. Reform, in the sense of innovation, was singularly lacking in the document.

Sweeping theories of equity and freedom were not, then, favoured by the authors of the charter. Instead, they applied themselves strictly to practicalities, ploughing doggedly through a profusion of feudal laws and technicalities in search of balm for baronial grievances and protection against the arbitrary power of a determined ruler. Written in the immaculate hand and pedantic Latin of the clerks of the chancery, the Great Charter erupted without pause or paragraph in a stream of provisions so numerous that later historians, intent on introducing some method of reference, enumerated more than sixty independent clauses. Some were modest, some extravagant; some expedient, others impractical; some fair and reasonable, some unfair and revengeful.

To generalise on the contents of Magna Carta is perilous. Almost any broad assertion draws a countervailing argument —an indication, perhaps, that the charter was born of compromise and a plurality of interests. Behind it lay many minds and motives, and not even the popular belief that it derived basically from John's misgovernment is correct. Fundamentally, Magna Carta was not so much a reaction to John's reign as a commentary—commendatory it may be noted, as well as reproachful—on half a century of purposeful Angevin government. So far as the barons had found that government oppressive, they could accuse John of few novelties. The seeds of discontent, especially of financial dissatisfaction, had been sown before the death of his brother. It had been left to John to reap the harvest of odium. Magna Carta, as it happened, solved nothing.

The king's part in the creation of the charter had been negative; the rebels had scant respect for the document. Legally, the whole painstaking operation was to be nullified within a few weeks of Runnymede. Nevertheless, the Great Charter, often reactionary and always contemptuous of the masses, stood in a sense for something better than its contents. For all its limitations, it was the most comprehensive code of law issued in England since the Conquest, and it arose not from the initiative of the ruler, but of his subjects, albeit the privileged. Its essential implication, that government was not above the law, was salutary.

Properly, an analysis of Magna Carta lies elsewhere than in the story of the life of King John. But for its insights to the customs and disputes which exercised the upper strata of Eng-

Magna Carta

lish society at this time, the charter is too compelling to be dismissed without some further inspection.

Magna Carta commenced with a grand regal flourish:

> John, by the grace of God, King of England, Lord of Ireland, Duke of Normandy and Aquitaine, and Count of Anjou, to the archbishops, bishops, abbots, earls, barons, justices, sheriffs, reeves, ministers, and to all bailiffs and faithful subjects—greeting. Be it known that we, by divine intuition and for the salvation of our soul, and the souls of our heirs and ancestors, and for the honour of God, and the exaltation of the Holy Church, and the amendment of our kingdom, by advice of our venerable fathers, Stephen, Archbishop of Canterbury, primate of all England and cardinal of the Holy Roman Church; Henry, Archbishop of Dublin; the bishops William of London; Peter of Winchester; Jocelin of Bath and Glastonbury; Hugh of Lincoln; Walter of Worcester; William of Coventry; Benedict of Rochester; and Master Pandulf, sub-deacon and Counsellor; Brother Eymeric, Master of the Temple in England; and the noble William Marshal, Earl of Pembroke; William, Earl of Salisbury; William, Earl of Warren; William, Earl of Arundel; Alan of Galloway, Constable of Scotland; Warin FitzGerald; Peter FitzHerbert; Hubert of Burgh, Seneschal of Poitou; Hugh of Neville; Matthew FitzHerbert; Thomas Bassett; Alan Bassett; Philip of Aubigny; Robert of Ropsley; John Marshal; John FitzHugh, and others our liegemen, have in the first place granted to God, and, by this our present charter, confirmed on behalf of Ourselves and Our heirs forever . . .

There followed the first provision—that "the English Church shall be free, its rights undiminished, its liberties unimpaired." As the charter observed, John had already conceded the right of free canonical election, and this was now confirmed. But the full liberty of the Church could be taken to mean more than the freedom of elections. It could be understood to involve the surrender of the principle that Henry II had fought for in the Constitutions of Clarendon, and which Becket had so stubbornly opposed: the subjection of the clergy to lay jurisdiction. If this were so, the Church would be free to ignore state taxation, and its clerics to claim immunity from the king's courts (though a later clause in the charter seems to refute this). Such a view would represent a renewed impulse in ecclesiastic pretensions, and mark the high stakes for which Langton was playing.

Another clause, closely involving the English Church, allowed anyone, with the exception of outlaws, prisoners and the king's enemies, freely to leave the country and to return without jeopardy. With Normandy gone and much of France under Philip's influence, there was little reason for the barons of England to go abroad. The clergy, on the other hand, constantly appealing or protesting to the pope, had every reason to travel the road to Rome. Under the Constitutions of Clarendon, all clerics, from village priests to archbishops, had been forbidden to leave the country without royal permission. The effect of the travel clause in the charter, therefore, was to repeal the earlier provision and grant churchmen the freedom to embark for Rome without risk of prohibition.

Well to the fore in the charter were a number of matters intimately involving the affairs of baronial families, and upon which most noble houses had some cause to feel aggrieved or apprehensive. The laws of wardship and marriage, dating back to Norman days, were particularly upsetting. It must be remembered that a man, at this time, did not inherit his father's estates automatically. On the death of a baron, his lands returned to the sovereign of whom he had held them. The heir obtained the grant of the lands from the king only by doing homage, swearing fealty and paying a sum of money, a relief. Often, an heir was obliged to bargain for his inheritance, the relief becoming a form of extortion.

This was bad enough, but the law of wardship could make it worse. Wardship gave the king the entire disposition of the person and property of an infant heir, with no obligation to do more than provide his ward with suitable maintenance. A king's officer was put in to run the estates until the heir came of age, the Crown took the revenues, and the lands might be utterly run-down, or "wasted" to provide a quick profit. Meanwhile, their heir had no income from which to pay the relief when the time came. Magna Carta asserted that the property of an heir in wardship was not to be "wasted" by the guardian; that it was to be handed over, in due course, well stocked; and that heirs who had been in wardship were to receive their inheritances without payment of relief.

Heiresses were also protected. Marriage, in the customary legal sense of the term, entitled the king to sell the hand of an heiress, even a widow or an aged woman, for the best price he could get. The charter provided that such females should be married "without disparagement"—that is, not beneath their social rank—and that their relatives should be consulted. Widows should not be forced to remarry. As a safeguard against a widow marrying her lord's enemy, however, she was obliged to give security not to remarry without her lord's consent. A widow, said the charter, should have her marriage portion (the land bestowed upon her by her father at the time of her marriage) and her inheritance at once on her husband's death, and should pay nothing for it, or for her dower (the widow's share of one third of her husband's lands). This should be assigned to her within forty days, during which time she had the right to remain in the house of her deceased husband.

These were neither particularly bold, nor entirely new provisions, in the face of iniquities which were not challenged in principle. But they did represent some comfort to those worried by problems of inheritance. To many more, the activities of bailiffs and money-lenders constituted the overwhelming medieval nightmare, and the question of debts and their payment was high on Magna Carta. In a state where insolvency was rife among the upper class, the collection of debts was a serious administrative business. Some preliminary maxims were stated in the charter. In the first place, a debtor's lands or rents were not to be seized when his chattels were sufficient to pay the debt. In the second place, a debtor's sureties should not be forced to meet the debt while the debtor was able to pay it. Furthermore, should the sureties be obliged to meet the debt, they should possess the debtor's lands and rents until the payment had been made up to them.

These basic provisions were so unexceptional as to suggest, by their inclusion, that the wholesale confiscation of estates in settlement of relatively small debts was not an unusual malpractice. The charter then tackled the matter in more detail. On the death of a man owing money to the Jews, it stated, no interest was to be paid on the debt while the heir was under age and the income from his inheritance going to the guardian. Because the charging of interest on loans was forbidden its followers by the Church, the Jews enjoyed a monopoly of money-lending at this time. Their affairs were supervised by the Crown, which inherited a portion of the estates of deceased Jews, and consequently often came to possess the bonds they had amassed. For this reason, the charter included the proviso that the king should also take only the principal of a debt inherited by a minor. It is interesting that nothing was said about the seemingly extortionate rates of interest charged on loans—normally between 50 and 75 per cent a year. Such figures illustrate the wide demand for money at this period—a phenomenon of which the king was as much a victim as his subjects.

When a man died in debt to the Jews, said Magna Carta, his wife and children were to be provided for, and the services due to his feudal lord paid, before anything went to the moneylender. On the other hand, should a man die in debt to the Crown, the debt was to be the first charge on his estate, and the residue left to the executors. To prevent the excessive confiscation of the dead man's property by unscrupulous Crown agents, it was determined that the sheriff or bailiff involved must produce a written summons establishing the amount of the debt, and list and collect chattels to the value of the debt in the presence of law-abiding witnesses.

After this, the remainder of the property (or the entire estate if no debt was owed) was to be at the disposal of the executors of the will, reserving reasonable shares for the widow and children of the deceased. Such shares were customarily fixed at a third for the widow, and a third for the children, leaving the remaining third for disposal under the terms of the will. These provisions, of course, applied only to personal property. All land belonged, fundamentally, to the king, and the laws concerning the succession to holdings of land were immutable.

To die intestate in John's day was to leave one's property vulnerable to confiscation. Wills were generally made in the presence of the priest who attended the deathbed, and lack of a testament implied a loss of Christian standing, especially since men of rank were expected to bequeath part of their wealth to the Church. In this situation, it was not unknown for the overlord of the deceased to step in and appropriate all the property. To stop this injustice, the charter provided that the chattels of a man who died intestate should be apportioned, after debts had been settled, by his kin and friends under the supervision of the Church.

Remarkably, no attempt was made in Magna Carta to resolve the vexed question of liability to oversea service. The ruling on this contained in the Unknown Charter was dropped, unaccountably, before the Great Charter was drawn up. There was, however, a significant reference to scutage and aids, those special taxes to meet exceptional circumstances. No scutage or aid was to be imposed other than in consultation with the common council of the kingdom, ruled the charter, except on three traditional occasions: 1) if the king were captured and had to be ransomed; 2) when his eldest son was knighted; and 3) when his eldest daughter was married for the first time. The aid, in these cases, was to be a fair one. The charter described how the common council—that is, the feudal council of tenants-in-chief—was to be assembled on such occasions. The archbishops, bishops, abbots, earls and "greater barons" were to be summoned individually by letter stating the purpose of the summons. All other tenants-in-chief were to be summoned generally through the king's sheriffs and bailiffs. At least forty days' notice was to be given. Thus, while the function of the council was chiefly advisory, it should provide an effective brake on too hasty royal action.

Though essentially baronial in reference, Magna Carta contained a comprehensive clause binding the tenants-in-chief, where appropriate, to grant sub-tenants the same rights conceded by the king to his barons. Just as the king exacted aids from his tenants, so those tenants customarily had collected aids from sub-tenants, either to offset taxes, or to help pay the personal debts of the barons. The charter guaranteed to prevent anyone taking an aid from his own freemen, save in the three instances previously mentioned. Two clauses referred specifically to the duties of knights. The first asserted that no one should be forced to render more service for a knight's fee, or any other freeholding, than was due from it. Since the charter failed to specify what was due, altogether avoiding the issue of foreign service, the utility of this provision was limited.

The second related to guard duties at castles. This was a sore point. The obligations attached to some holdings included

Magna Carta

a period of garrison service each year in royal castles. But the increased use of mercenaries in the king's service had left a surplus of knights owing castle guard, and these were sometimes pressed to make a money payment in lieu of their duties. The charter protected those who could not afford, or who otherwise resented this pressure, stipulating that no constable should compel a knight to pay if he preferred to stand guard or to provide a competent deputy. It was also ruled that service on the king's behalf with a military expedition should release a knight from a proportionate length of castle guard.

Among the most important portions of the charter was its judicial clauses. These made it clear that the outstanding development in legal procedure under the Angevins had been accepted by the main body of barons. There was no attempt in the document to revive the baronial courts relegated by Henry II, nor was the competence and integrity of the king's justices seriously questioned. On the contrary, while sheriffs, bailiffs, and other Crown officers tended to be condemned by implication, the silence accorded the personnel of the judicial system by Magna Carta complimented them. Its general acknowledgement of royal justice was a considerable tribute to Henry II and his lawyers, and to the tireless interest and effort with which John had advanced their achievements.

It would, however, have seemed very unusual to his subjects if a king of the times had not occasionally been influenced in his judgements by expensive gifts, or if he had not refused to hear, or postponed, certain cases to his advantage. In the charter, John, who was constantly touring the country hearing cases, promised the barons: "To no one will we sell, deny, or delay right of justice." This did not mean that access to the courts should be free. Fees were charged for writs on the basis, broadly speaking, of the duration of hearings and the trouble occasioned for the justices. But charging for writs was not regarded as selling justice, and, while

John took heavy fees from wealthy litigants, his charges for the poor who sought justice were sometimes quite nominal.

One of the most celebrated clauses of Magna Carta was that which guaranteed the king's subject immunity from imprisonment, or other punishment, save through the due process of the law of the kingdom. "No free man," it asserted, "shall be taken, or imprisoned, or disseised, or outlawed, or exiled, nor will we go or send upon him, except by the legal judgement of his peers or by the law of the land." This provision, central to the modern concept of justice, had been offered to the barons by John in his proposals of May 10. Its intention was to eliminate the long-standing royal custom of dealing arbitrarily with subjects who incurred the king's displeasure. No one could have considered it in 1215 without recalling the fate, among others, of Matilda Briouse and her family. Hundreds of thousands more were forgotten. Typically, the clause applied only to freemen: perhaps a quarter of the population. Three quarters of the people were deemed unworthy of such justice.

An adjacent provision in the charter proclaimed that no one should be put on trial on the accusation of a bailiff alone, but that the officer's complaint should be supported by the oaths of trustworthy witnesses. Only then could the accused be subjected to the ordeal. Bailiffs, it seems, were distinctly out of favour. Even the ordeal was beginning to lose way by the time of Magna Carta. In the same year, the Fourth Lateran Council forbade priests to officiate at trials by ordeal. The days of judgement by fire and water were ending; those of trial by jury approaching.

Two interesting judicial features of the charter dealt with courts of common pleas and county assizes. The peregrinations of the royal court during the reigns of John and his father had involved many of those attempting to obtain justice in a hectic, wearisome and expensive game of follow-my-leader through the kingdom. The delay and exasperation arising from this cross-country marathon prompted the realisation that many cases, being of no direct concern to the Crown, could more conveniently be held before justices at a fixed venue. These cases, known as common pleas, were originally held at Westminster, and Magna Carta confirmed their rooted nature.

The assize clause was more complex. Baronial anarchy, thriving under King Stephen, had left a multitude of disputed land claims and rights of possession to be settled by the Angevins. Henry II had out-dated the customary method of deciding such disputes by combat, in favour of the assize, an inquest resting on the sworn testimony of landholders from the pertinent neighbourhood. The charter described three types of assize: 1) the assize of novel disseisin, which was called to deal with the petitions of those who claimed to have been recently and wrongfully dispossessed of land; 2) the assize of mort d'ancestor, which heard the claims of heirs to the possession of inheritance; and 3) the assize of darrein presentment, devised to settle claims to the right of appointing clerics to vacant livings.

The procedure was to be the same in each case. Two justices were to perambulate the realm four times a year, calling at each of the shire courts. At each court, they were to be joined on the bench by four knights chosen by the freemen of the county. Verdicts were to be reached by the knights and justices on the evidence of twelve freeholders with local knowledge of the lands and rights under question.

A number of clauses in the charter dealt with sentences, particularly amercements—that is, fines imposed by the king for criminal offences. The remorseless pressure on the Angevins, especially John and Richard, to find money for defending and governing their empire, caused them to extract the largest possible sums from barons who fell into their mercy on account of misdemeanours. Even trivial offences were punished by swingeing fines. Magna Carta declared that a man should be amerced in proportion to the measure of his crime, and that in any case he should be left with sufficient resources to maintain his station or trade in society. In the charter's sole reference to the poor serf, it was here mentioned that amercement should not deprive him of his meagre livelihood. To give these well-intended, but vague directions more meaning, it was provided that amercements should be imposed in consultation with a number of the offender's honest neighbours, men able to judge what he could afford without ruin.

Earls and barons, declared Magna Carta, were to be amerced on the judgement of none but their peers, while members of the clergy should be amerced only in relation to those lands which they held by lay tenure. This last provision suggests that the authors of the charter still envisaged the trial of clerics by civil courts in some circumstances. By custom, the Crown had the right temporarily to occupy the lands of a convicted felon and dispose of anything removable. Since the king was not always in any hurry to return such lands, the charter limited the duration of their confiscation to one year and a day, at the end of which time the denuded estate was to be returned to the felon's lord if the felon were not a Crown tenant.

While generally accepting the legal procedure developed in the Angevin era, the barons still clung, in some cases, to their feudal rights to sit in judgement of their tenants. Disputes between their vassals over the possession of land were of special concern to landlords, and there was a strong feeling among the baronage that such disputes should be settled in its own courts. Henry II, in his persistent efforts to extend the power of the royal courts to the derogation of their baronial counterparts, had stopped short at ordering the wholesale removal of land-possession suits to the royal courts, employing instead an expedient known as the writ *precipe,* by which the king could intervene in a land dispute between sub-tenants.

John's passion for personal involvement in the administration of justice had encouraged the use of the writ *precipe,* with a consequent "loss of court" to his barons. Magna Carta asserted that the writ *precipe* should not be issued in any instance whereby a freeman might lose his court. There was, of course, no objection to its use when the land in dispute belonged to the royal demesne.

If this clause sought to inhibit one aspect of Angevin law reform, it was followed by another provision promoting it. Under Anglo-Saxon law, the kindred of a homicide victim were entitled to take revenge in blood; to seek a life for a life. Norman law had obliged a man accused of homicide to defend himself against his accuser in trial by combat. Such primitive customs not only offered the strong and unscrupulous a method of destroying their weaker neighbours on unfounded allegations, but also encouraged the family vendetta. Henry II had made it possible for an accused man, by contending that the accusation arose from "spite and hate," to secure a writ from the king directing a sworn jury of twelve neighbours to consider the contention. If they upheld it, the accused was dismissed and the accuser liable to prosecution for raising a false charge. Magna Carta insisted that this writ—the writ "of enquiry concerning life and limb"—should be granted freely to all who asked for it.

The position of female accusers was a special one. English tradition held that a woman's right to bring accusations of criminal behaviour was limited to two charges: the rape of her own person, and the murder of her husband. This custom seems to have relaxed somewhat with the spread of the chivalric concept, which, among other things, encouraged men of the warrior caste to seek redress of complaints laid before them by the fairer sex. The medieval period, especially those years spanned by Angevin rule in England, had produced a formidable cluster of domineering and influential women, not least, John's own mother, and his particular aversion, Matilda Briouse. That such females exploited their relationship with powerful and aggressive lords to score against those who displeased them was certain, and it appears that the consequences of their accusations had disturbed the authors of the charter, for they firmly asserted that no man was to be arrested or imprisoned, on the appeal of a woman, for the death of anyone other than her husband.

A good deal of baronial discontent originated less from the legislation of central government than from the abuses practiced by those charged to enforce it. In an age of primitive communications, regional officials were too often inadequately checked and supervised. Magna Carta abounded in provisions designed to curtail the misapplication of law in the provinces. Among the most elementary conditions in this class was a reminder that no sheriff, constable or bailiff should act as a judge over pleas of the Crown in his own county. This ruling had been made by Hubert Walter during his justiciarship at the end of the twelfth century. Its reiteration suggested that the failure of Crown officers to observe it had become a recognised issue of discontent. A sheriff acting as a judge in his own shire was plainly open to a charge of partiality, and probably of profiteering into the bargain.

That sheriffs expected to profit from office was evidenced by the large sums many paid for the appointment. One system open to exploitation was the farming out of counties. It had always been the responsibility of a sheriff to collect the Crown revenues in his territory, and the habit had evolved whereby the king farmed out the county to the sheriff in return for a fixed annual payment, leaving the sheriff to collect what he could in rents and fines. The difference between the farm, and what was actually collected, represented a profit or loss to the sheriff. Handsome profits were not infrequent. The combination of avarice on the part of the sheriffs, and an inflationary situation urging the increase of farms, resulted in a steeply mounting demand on the wealth of the counties. Magna Carta sought to check the rise in farm rates.

The laws concerning purveyance invited more abuses. Local Crown officers were empowered to requisition supplies for castles, and to hire horses and wagons for transport, when needed. They were expected to pay the going rate for goods and services, either in money or in vouchers which could be used in remittances to the treasury. Some, it seems, simply took what they wanted and pocketed the money. Supplies were seized without payment, or on the dubious promise of future reimbursement; transport was impressed without its owner's permission. Magna Carta recognised the problem by ruling that no constable of a castle, or other royal officer, should take a man's corn or provisions without an immediate money payment—unless the owner volunteered to take payment of deferred terms. Nor should "any sheriff, bailiff or other person take a free man's horses or carts for transport duties without the owner's leave."

The clauses limiting powers to requisition were directed specifically at Crown officers, and could be argued to leave open the options of the king in his own right. Indeed, the whole question of purveyance was to remain a confused and vexed issue for the monarchs of future centuries. So far as the king's personal powers to requisition were concerned, Magna Carta was content to forbid him to take timber for castle-building, or other purposes, without the consent of the owner of the wood, and regardless of compensation. This was scarcely a hardship to one whose forests ranged throughout the length of England.

The forest laws themselves received attention in the charter. Afforestation, with all the bitterness it engendered, was not of John's making. On the contrary, he had been the first king since the Normans turned the woodlands of England into their playgrounds, to arrest the trend in this direction, disdaining to create new forests and actually disafforesting some areas. He had, however, extended the boundaries of old forests in places, and the charter pledged him to restore their original frontiers. The charter also touched on the matter of forest courts.

The forests had their own courts, and freemen who lived in afforested areas were obliged to attend them, just as those outside the forests were obliged to attend the courts of common law. Men who lived outside the forests, yet close to their borders, had the ill luck to owe attendance to both the forest and ordinary courts. If they could not spare the time to meet these obligations, they were faced with being fined for nonattendance. Magna Carta provided that those living outside the forest should not be expected to attend forest courts unless directly concerned with forest offences.

On top of this, twelve knights were to be elected in each county to investigate the "evil customs" of forest officers, as well as other county officials, with a view to the total abolition of such customs. In particular, the habit of placing riverbanks "in defence" when the king intended hawking—that is, preventing anyone else enjoying the sport to the king's detriment—was to be restricted. In 1217, the forest clauses were removed from the charter, amplified, and presented in a separate document, generally known as the Forest Charter. It was the designation of the two documents in the thirteenth century as the big and little charters which led to the enduring appellation "Magna Carta."

Finally, on the subject of local government officers, an attempt was made to ensure better standards for the future. Magna Carta ruled that no justice, constable, sheriff or bailiff was to be appointed unless he was familiar with the law, and willing to observe it. This engaging provision was probably intended to eliminate foreigners from Crown offices. At all

Plate 9 Winchester Cathedral, scene of John's reconciliation with the Church

Plate 10 Rochester Castle, an important site on the old London–Dover road was successfully besieged in 1215

events, it was a hopeful one. No measurable legal qualification was established, or any authority to pronounce on the fitness of the candidates.

Many of the points in Magna Carta would not have upset the most sensitive of monarchs. Some, such as one stipulating that fish weirs should be removed from rivers to facilitate water transport, or another, providing for standard weights and measures throughout the country, may well have met with John's favour. Others, among them the assertion that the amount of work owed by men and towns on bridges should be limited, while further from the king's heart—good bridges were important to the widely roaming and road-conscious Angevins—were not of the stuff to raise his blood pressure alarmingly. Indeed, perhaps the majority of clauses in the charter, taken individually, could have been accepted by John without too much agony.

But their total was another thing. Without a doubt, it considerably weakened the armoury of arbitrary action which, under Henry II and his sons, had become an adjunct of strong central government. Moreover, among the mass of feudal technicalities and legal niceties in the document, buried well toward the end of its business, lurked a small number of provisions which, if taken in the spirit of the charter, must have gravely undermined the king's position.

The first called for the restoration of all hostages and charters held by the sovereign as security. The taking of hostages against the fulfilment of a treaty, or the good behaviour of a neighbour or subject, was a normal, if disagreeable, medieval practice. John, in the wave of suspicion which had submerged him on the loss of Normandy, had taken hostages wholesale from his English barons in an attempt to avert further treachery. He had also demanded charters pledging their loyalty, and, in some cases, had taken into his custody their deeds of tenure, leaving them without written proof of their rights to their lands and privileges. To deprive a medieval king of his hostages was to strip him of an important bulwark of security.

Two more of these critical provisions demanded the removal from the kingdom of all foreign mercenaries, and the restoration of lands, castles and liberties to those dispossessed, other than by the lawful judgement of their peers, during the reigns of John, his father, and his brother. The prospect of disbanding the most reliable arm of his forces, while returning castles to his enemies, was one the king could not have countenanced without dire misgivings.

The last clause in this potentially explosive series—one of the most sweeping in the charter—required John to remit, or submit to arbitration, all fines and amercements claimed to have been imposed unjustly on his barons. Disputed cases were to be decided by a committee of barons, joined by Langton and such others as he might wish to bring with him. While the archbishop might be relied upon to act with moderation, the provision could be seen as a means to cripple the finances of a king who was seldom exactly flush for money.

If John had cause to view the outcome of Magna Carta apprehensively, its implications were equally unsatisfactory to the rebels. Their initiative had been diverted and pruned by the authors until little of the document reflected their extreme views. Nor did it offer much joy to their allies. The merchants and wealthy citizens of London, looking to be rewarded for supporting the rebel cause, received somewhat less than they might have hoped. The condition that scutages and aids should not be imposed on the barons without the consent of the common council of the kingdom was extended to the city of London. But how far a council comprised largely of landed barons would be prepared to exert itself on behalf of London may well have struck its citizens as questionable. A further promise that their liberties and free customs would be observed was neither novel, nor more than the charter granted every other town in the country.

The Scots won little from their association with the rebellion. William the Lion's legitimate daughters, Margaret and Isabella, had been held as wards by John since their father's unfavourable peace with the English king in 1209. Magna Carta promised that John would treat their brother Alexander, the new King of the Scots, "with regard to his sisters, hostages, liberties and rights, according to the fashion in which we shall treat other barons of England, unless the charters we hold from his father, William, provide otherwise. This shall be judged by his equals in our court." Apart from being the Scottish king, Alexander was also a baron of England, with holdings in the northern counties. It is noteworthy that the authors of the charter emphasised his baronial, rather than his sovereign status, according him the dubious privilege, from a Scottish viewpoint, of having his case judged by the English barons, his peers in the sight of the charter. If Alexander had hoped to see his homage to the English Crown waived as a result of the rebellion, he was unlucky.

The Welsh princes, perhaps more feared than Alexander, fared rather better. The charter provided that John would make good to them all illegal dispossessions enacted in Wales by the Angevin monarchs, and return all hostages and charters held as securities. Among the hostages was a son of Llywelyn ap Iorwerth. What had, or had not constituted illegal disseisins, remained to be determined.

On one point, Magna Carta directly opposed the sentiments of those who had supported the rebels. English merchants, already perturbed by the privileges enjoyed by the foreign traders in their midst, found these spelt out unequivocally in the charter. All foreign merchants were to be free to come and go, to stay in the land, and to be allowed to buy and sell and travel unimpeded, except in time of war. Then merchants of a hostile country were to be detained without harm to themselves or their goods until the government could ascertain how English merchants were being treated by the enemy. Import duties levied on foreign traders, customarily about a tenth or fifteenth of cargo values, should not be unduly high, declared the charter. Since the wares brought into the land by foreign merchants were consumed, by and large, by the upper classes, it was in the interest of the barons, if not of English producers and traders, to enable imports to be sold reasonably.

When all was considered, Magna Carta offered no real prospect of enduring peace between John and his enemies. For the king, it went too far; for the rebels, not far enough. Paradoxically, what slender hopes there might otherwise have been for its survival as a moderating agent were demolished by the terms for securing its enforcement.

Chapter 16
DEMISE OF A SETTLEMENT

Saying Peace, peace; when there is no peace.

Jeremiah 6:14

John's detractors were not slow to blame the king for the failure of the treaty of Runnymede. "Everyone hoped that England would enjoy peace and liberty," wrote Matthew Paris, "but—oh shame! oh sorrow!—far otherwise was it; far differently things happened. While a smiling fortune appeared to be offering nectar, it was truly preparing draughts of gall and poison. For, behold! at the instigation of the devil, the war-loving sons of Belial whispered words of discord in the king's ear, laughing and grunting with derision." It might have been observed with less risk of contention that the rebel barons needed no prompting to further their dissidence. They had shown scant respect for the charter from its outset.

The one provision of Magna Carta which the rebels made their own, to the exclusion of more judicious and moderate barons, was that establishing the committee of twenty-five. Its members, charged with securing the enforcement of the charter and acting upon complaints against the king or his officials, were in a position of unique power. All freemen were obliged to take an oath to obey them. They were a self-perpetuating body electing their own replacements. And should their demands for redress from the sovereign not promptly be satisfied, the twenty-five were empowered to marshal his subjects and "distrain and distress him by every means possible." This sweeping sanction could be activated on the vote of a majority. The one revolutionary provision in the charter, virtually legalising rebellion and obliging the subject to support it, the enforcement clause was a crude and dangerous weapon to place in the wrong hands.

Had the committee been of a moderate or neutral complexion, the charter might have got off to a better start. Granted reasonable interpretative and administrative latitude, John might have weathered the embarrassing period immediately following the treaty, and settled down to make the peace work. It would have called, however, for co-operation on all sides, and the rebels were not bent on helping. Having failed to depose the king, or to dictate terms which in themselves would have ruined him, they resolved to dominate the enforcement committee and exploit its authority to intimidate the royal government.

So firm was their determination on this point that at least fourteen rebels, led by FitzWalter and Vesci, gained admission to the twenty-five, as opposed to a mere two of the king's supporters. The possibilities were disturbingly original: a group of reactionary and unrepentant rebels had acquired the power, at least in theory, to threaten the sovereign with his own feudal forces. Magna Carta, as the more cynical of John's captains saw it, had crowned "five-and-twenty over-kings."

In practice, the freemen of the realm were a good deal less anxious to take the oath to the twenty-five than the insurgents might have hoped. Instructions to the sheriffs concerning oath-taking had to be reinforced with an additional warning that those who failed to swear obedience were to have their lands and chattels confiscated. Even so, reluctance to take the oath remained a problem to Crown officers, and a source of frustration to the rebel leaders, many weeks after Runnymede.

The behaviour of the malcontents in the presence of the charter did little to commend their cause to men of reason. Some northern extremists had left the Thames-side conference before the sealing of the treaty. They had promptly fortified their castles and set about devastating royal manors and forests under the pretext that they had not been present at the settlement. Others actually impeded the implementation of the charter, molesting and abusing the royal agents charged with enforcing its provisions. The rationale of these dissidents seems to have been a preference for anarchy above any concordat which recognised John's government.

The more ambitious among the king's enemies, those who had acquired power by virtue of leadership, or under the terms of the treaty, soon revealed the shiftiness and bombast which not uncommonly pass for authority among men promoted beyond their capacity. The ink was scarcely dry on the parchment before they had refused to fulfil a promise to give the king security for their own observance of the charter. It had been proposed that they should place their seals to a document binding them to protect and honour the rights of the sovereign, his heirs and his realm, against his enemies. Not only John, but also Langton and his bishops, were shocked when FitzWalter and his colleagues now declined to do so—especially since the main body of rebels pointedly had failed to disperse after Runnymede, or to give up London, the key to their influence in the South.

As a cover for remaining under arms, and perhaps as a

propaganda device to win friends and discourage foes, the London-based dissidents planned to hold a grand tournament at Stamford on July 6. The outcome of this scheme illustrated the importance they attached to the city as a fortress. As the day of the tournament approached, the risk of travelling so far from London unnerved them, and they switched the venue to Hounslow, nearer their stronghold. Explained Fitz-Walter in a letter to William of Albini, a former king's man who had veered toward the side of the rebels: "You will appreciate how advantageous it is for all of us to hold the city of London, our refuge, and how damaging it would be if, by neglect, we should lose it." Albini was pressed to attend the rally and win honour with his arms and his horses. "Whoever does best will get a bear, donated by a lady," the rebel leader promised. Albini, it seems, was not overwhelmed by the inducement. To the disappointment of the "Marshal of the Army of God" and his henchmen, he stayed at home.

John appears to have embarked on a worthier endeavour to make the peace a reality. On June 19, immediately following the completion of the treaty, he sent word to his sheriffs and other officers announcing the settlement, and directing that steps should be taken to implement those provisions of the charter concerned with "evil customs" and the recognition of the committee of twenty-five. With similar alacrity, he also began to meet his obligations regarding hostages and mercenaries, releasing a fair number of the former, and dismissing many of the latter, together with the Flemish knights who had driven the rebels from Exeter. These measures were followed by the removal of a number of mercenary captains from Crown offices. Geoffrey of Martigny was relieved of his command of Northampton Castle; Peter of Cancellis was withdrawn from his office as constable of Bristol; Engelard of Cigogné was deprived of the sheriffdoms of Gloucestershire and Herefordshire.

Magna Carta provoked an immediate deluge of claims to lands and castles by those alleging their wrongful dispossession. Unable to deal with them all at once, John postponed the consideration of some, particularly the more dubious, until later that summer. Others, in the main less contentious, he granted without delay. Robert FitzWalter was given the custody of Hertford Castle, perhaps as a sweetener to the rebel leadership, for his claim was not a very strong one. Saer of Quincy was allowed possession of Mountsorrel Castle, Leicester, which, he claimed, had been detached unlawfully from his inheritance. William of Albini received the manor of Driffield, Yorkshire. Richard and John had deemed this part of the royal demesne, but William's grandfather had held it in the reign of Henry II. The Earl of Huntingdon got back Fotheringay Castle, which had been seized by the king at the time of the plot of 1212.

Among other concessions, the Earl of Clare was given the town of Buckingham to hold until his grandson, John of Briouse, an heir in wardship, came of age. Richard FitzAlan was granted the massive fortress at Richmond, of which he was hereditary constable, and which had traditionally gone to his family. Roger of Montbegon, a baron frequently out of favour with John, was given back some land taken from him in one of his periods of opprobrium . . . and so on.

Apart from lands and castles, John restored various posts and privileges to those who had opposed him. The king's officers were directed to allow Eustace of Vesci to hunt his hounds in accordance with his normal rights. Richard Montfichet was granted the office of forester in Essex, a position his family had held in past generations. Geoffrey of Mandeville was given the franchises held by his father-in-law, together with other privileges; and Robert of Vere, Earl of Oxford, was allowed a percentage of the profits from the courts of his county.

Toward the end of June, John seems to have had sufficient faith in the peace to withdraw his collection of jewelry from the religious houses in which he had placed it for safe-keeping. A receipt issued to the convent at Waltham, Essex, on the return of the king's treasure stored there, listed six brooches, six ceremonial belts and thirteen silver cups. The brooches were mainly of sapphires, garnets and pearls, interspersed with turquoises, jaspers and other stones. One contained simply six sapphires and six garnets. Another, more elaborate, had two sapphires, four garnets, two pearls and an accompaniment of turquoises. The belts were chased and decorated with precious metals and gemstones. Jewels of far greater value, it was said, were stored at other houses.

John spent the last days of June at Winchester, and was in Wiltshire early in July. Though heavily engaged with a backlog of English business, and with affairs of the charter, he had not forgotten Ireland. That summer he found time to advance the interests of many of his Irish subjects, granting privileges to towns, religious institutions and individual barons. After Runnymede, it was not until mid-July that he next met the rebels as a body, and was confronted with their continuing intransigence. At the sealing of the charter, the king and his barons had agreed to meet in Oxford on July 16 to review the progress made toward fulfilling its provisions. On the fifteenth, John crossed from Wiltshire into Berkshire and passed through Newbury on his way to the meeting place. He had suffered lately from severe gout, and his sickness made travelling difficult. Before he reached Abingdon, a few miles short of Oxford, he sent word to the barons that he would be late, but that he was sending forward in his stead the new justiciar, Hubert of Burgh, the legate Pandulf, the Earls of Pembroke, Warren and Arundel, and the Archbishop of Dublin and the Bishop of Winchester.

The king arrived at Oxford on July 17 and remained in

Demise of a Settlement

the city for six days. It was quickly apparent that the rebels intended to maintain an arrogant posture. According to one story—perhaps dubious, but reflecting the unsettled atmosphere—their representatives had declined to accept his absence on the grounds of sickness, insisting that he be carried to the meeting by any means possible. On his entry to the council, they insulted him by refusing to stand up.

When John contended that FitzWalter and his men were abusing the peace by remaining under arms in London, his enemies replied that they did not intend to leave the city until everyone had taken the oath to the twenty-five, and all demands for land, castles and privileges had been satisfied. Under such conditions, they could have stayed in London forever. Considered literally, the provision that every freeman in the land should swear obedience to the twenty-five was beyond the limits of enforcement. To persuade, even coerce, men to bind themselves to the ruling of a commitee comprised largely of barons for whom the majority had no compulsive sympathy, and many actively disliked, raised an obvious problem. On the issue of the restoration of holdings and privileges, there was not a baron in the country who could not concoct a claim of some sort. For John to have pleased all would have amounted to political suicide.

The only possible compromise was a delaying one. With the aid of the moderates, who now intervened to break the stalemate, it was agreed that FitzWalter's barons should hold London in the king's name until the Feast of the Assumption, August 15; that Stephen Langton should hold the Tower of London; and that John should not impose troops on the city or the Tower in this period. Meanwhile, every step should be taken to impose the oath to the twenty-five, all property seized from the rebels during the revolt was to be returned, and all further claims for the restoration of land, castles and privileges should be placed before the king or the twenty-five.

If the king had not met these terms by August 15, the rebels should continue to hold London.

Apart from refusing to give up the chief city of the kingdom, the insurgents continued to dishonour their promise to confirm their loyalty to the king. Among those who reproved them for their poor faith were the Archbishops of Canterbury and Dublin, the Bishops of London, Winchester, Worcester, Lincoln, Bath, Chichester and Coventry, and the pope's subdeacon, Pandulf. These dignitaries took the opportunity of issuing letters patent proclaiming that the baronial extremists had reneged on their agreement. They also issued letters asserting that all customs essential to the administration of the forests should be upheld. This was a pointed reference to the rebels, who not only sought sweeping changes in the forest laws, but, in some cases, had already fallen on the forests, felling trees for timber, and killing the king's deer.

It would be surprising had not John left the council at Oxford with a head as sore as his gout-ridden body.

How sincere was the king's approach to Magna Carta? The possibility that he might accept its provisions to silence the rebels, and then use his standing with the pope, his overlord and protector, as a get-out, had not been lost on the authors of the document. In an attempt to prevent such an eventuality, a clause had been inserted in the charter categorically forbidding the sovereign to seek the diminution or revocation of its conditions through the intercession of anyone. The fact that John was to do precisely that, invoking Innocent's aid to annul the impositions of Runnymede, has been held to demonstrate that he never intended to keep faith. The argument is not supported by the timing of the complex communications and events of that summer.

There is no evidence that John attempted to communicate with Rome between Runnymede and the council at Oxford.

Demise of a Settlement

Wendover, whose chronology is sketchy at this point, declares that "At length, after much meditation, he [the king] resolved to seek revenge on his enemies with two swords, the spiritual and the temporal, so that if he failed with one he might succeed with the other. To strike with the spiritual sword, he sent Pandulf, the pope's subdeacon, with other messengers, to the court of Rome to counteract by apostolic authority the intentions of the barons." The messengers, says Wendover, produced a copy of some articles of the charter, explaining that John had been compelled out of fear to confirm it, though protesting that the kingdom of England belonged to the Church of Rome. He had maintained, though in vain, they reported, that new arrangements should not be made without the knowledge of the pontiff.

Since Pandulf had been present at the council of Oxford, and Innocent's first response to news of Magna Carta would not be confirmed until August 25, it would seem likely that John dispatched his plea to the pope immediately after the council. This would allow a reasonable time for the journey between England and Rome, which then took something like thirty days. It is hard to believe the king would have delayed so long, or gone so far toward implementing the charter, had he intended to seek its annulment in the first place. The record of his concessions was impressive, and perhaps worth restating, for it goes some way toward refuting the notion that John killed Magna Carta.

He had dismissed his loyal but unpopular justiciar, Peter of Roches, to suit his critics. He had removed trustworthy sheriffs and other Crown officers whose foreign origins offended his subjects. He had prejudiced his security by deporting a substantial body of mercenaries and Flemish knights. He had granted the return of all property taken from the rebels, and had already reviewed and conceded a large number of claims to lands, castles and privileges. He had released hostages. He had commanded the publication of the charter throughout the country. He had authorised the establishment of county tribunals to look into "evil customs." On top of which, he had gone so far as to order his agents to seize the land and possessions of anyone who refused to take the oath to the twenty-five. He could scarcely have done more, in the time, to establish his sincerity.

Moreover, he had done as much in the face of strong rebel provocation. His enemies had little to their credit. They had abused the peace by attacking royal manors, invading the king's forests, and maintaining an armed and defiant hold on London. They had shown contempt for the charter by molesting those charged with enforcing it, and by refusing to guarantee their loyalty to the king. Those privileged with membership of the twenty-five had unashamedly betrayed the trust of their fellows by pressing their own claims to land and franchise before any others. To the restoration of goodwill, the rebel leaders had contributed not one jot. Had John despaired of Magna Carta in such circumstances, many must have sympathised. Doubtless, he had hoped to modify its provisions, to whittle down those concessions most offensive to his sovereignty, as time passed. But that was one thing—the cynical disregard for the peace by the rebel barons was another. Their truculent and insulting behaviour at Oxford was perhaps the final factor in John's decision to seek freedom from the charter.

John may also have been prompted in this intention by letters which arrived in England from Rome at about the time of the council. Although out-dated—having been penned, it seems, by Innocent on learning of the original rebel muster at Stamford—they provided a timely reassurance of the pope's continuing support for his harassed vassal. Recalling his earlier correspondence with the English barons, in which he had instructed them to observe the service they owed the king, the pope now ruled that their action in taking arms against a lord who had offered them justice was criminal. Unless they made peace with John within eight days, the Archbishop of Canterbury was to excommunicate them and place their lands under interdict.

Not surprisingly, Langton ignored these letters. It was hardly for the primate, who had flouted Innocent's orders along with the rebels, to emerge at this stage as the pontiff's bailiff. Apart from which, since the letters left Rome, the barons had indeed made peace with John in the formal sense, if not exactly in the humble manner the pope prescribed. On the contrary, their effrontery mounted. By the end of July, the danger in which the king had placed himself by dismissing his captains and running down his army, without any corresponding gesture from his enemies, must have struck him with some force. August saw the reversal of the king's policy, an unsheathing of the "temporal sword," as Wendover had it.

Once more, John's recruiting officers headed for the Continent. Hugh of Boves, having so recently organised the repatriation of the mercenaries from Dover, now had the task of enlisting fresh men from Flanders. The king's chancellor, Richard Marsh, was given a like job in Aquitaine. On August 12, John wrote to Count Peter of Brittany offering him the honour of Richmond if he would come to England "with all the speed and all the knights he could muster." No approaches were spared in bringing the royal force to strength again. According to Walter of Coventry, John even tried to obtain help from Philip Augustus, dangling "tremendous" enticements before him, but "others had been there already." The renewal of hostilities on a large scale became increasingly probable.

August 15, the day on which the rebels were to surrender London, came and passed without hint of a détente. Five days later, a further meeting of bishops and barons took place at Oxford, and John was asked to be present. He declined. Nor would he delegate anyone with the authority to negotiate, proclaiming instead that he had done enough to demonstrate his good faith, and that it was up to the rebels to move next. Meanwhile, summer advanced, and the harvest, occupying retainers on both sides, produced an uneasy lull. Langton took the opportunity to deploy moderate opinion in a final attempt to effect a rapprochement.

Unfortunately, the archbishop's authority was undermined at this moment by the arrival of a further letter from the papacy. With the Fourth Lateran Council set for November, Innocent was busy preparing a mighty programme of reform, with which he hoped to assail the world's problems. He was also planning another bid to recapture the Holy Land. Of all times, this was not one in which he could tolerate a revolt in his feudal dominion, nor the obstruction of a king he needed as a crusader. News of the rebel muster at Stamford had vexed him. Receipt of John's subsequent message of May 19, still prior to Runnymede, bringing news of continuing baronial mischief and Langton's failure to condemn the king's enemies, had more severely tested his patience. On July 7, the pope had addressed an angry response to Peter of Roches, Bishop of Winchester, the Abbot of Reading, and Pandulf. It was this letter which exploded upon an edgy England in August:

"We are compelled to express astonishment and annoyance," wrote Innocent, "that the King of England, having more than made amends to God and the Church, and particularly to the Archbishop of Canterbury and his bishops, should be accorded less esteem by some than is right and proper in the light of the Crusade, our instructions, and the oath of fealty they have taken." Since these defaulters had given the king neither help nor sympathy against the rebels, declared the pope, they could be deemed fellow-travellers, if not actual participants, of conspiracy.

"How do these bishops defend the patrimony of the Roman

Plate 11 Effigies at Fontevrault Abbey of Richard Coeur de Lion (*above*) and Eleanor of Aquitaine (*below*)

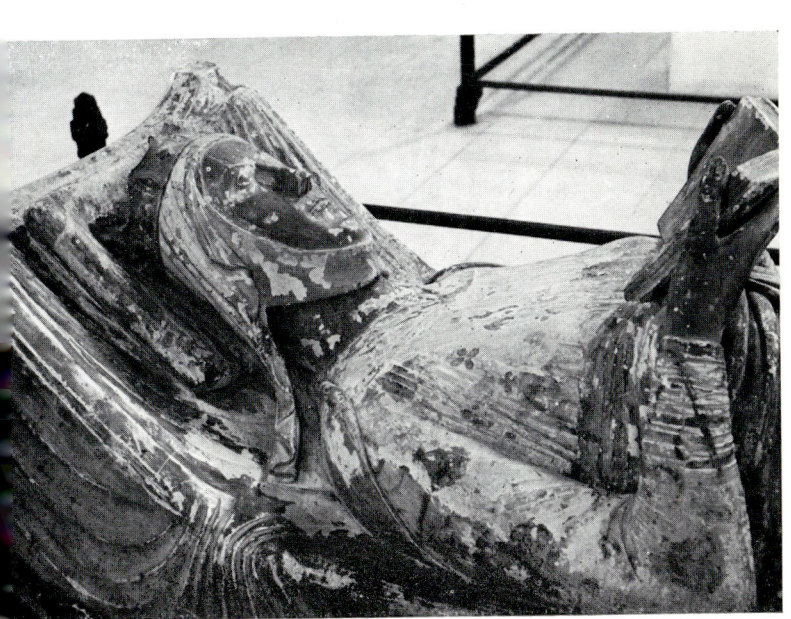

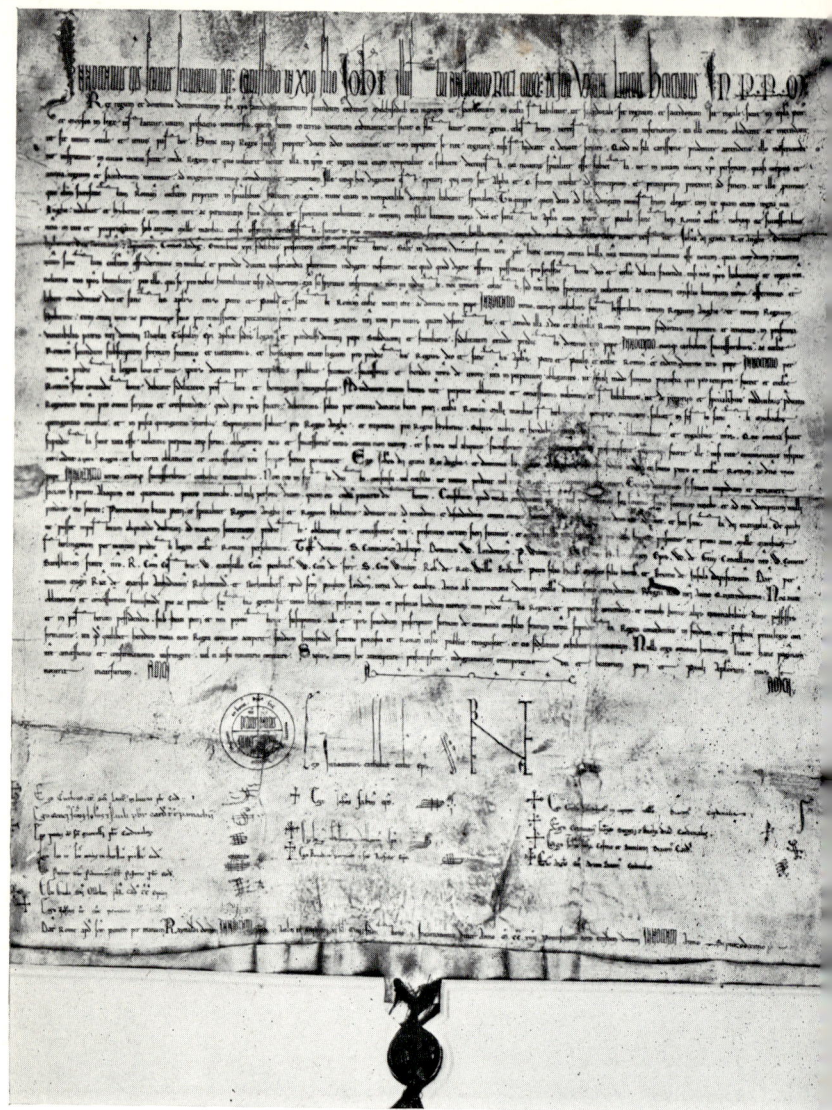

Plate 12   The Bull of Pope Innocent III accepting John's resignation of the Kingdoms of England and Ireland to the Church

Church? How do they support crusaders? Why, by attempting to overcome a king whose assistance in the Holy Land is keenly anticipated. They are worse," snapped the pope, "than the Saracens!"

Even had John's enthusiasm for the crusade been limited, continued Innocent with a touch of insight, such wickedness and presumption could not go unpunished. To prevent it endangering the realm of England, contaminating other realms and undermining the crusade, he was obliged to pass sentence: "We excommunicate all disturbers of the king and the kingdom, and all their abettors and followers, and we place their lands under interdict, rigorously commanding the archbishop and bishops to publish these sentences throughout England every Sunday and feast day." Again, Langton insisted that the pope's instructions had been out-dated by Runnymede. But this time the pope had provided against evasions. Should the prelates neglect his mandate, he added, they were to be suspended from office and the sentences enforced by his commissioners, the addressees of the letter. It was no coincidence that they had been picked from John's supporters.

While Stephen Langton faced an increasingly tricky situation, his brother Simon was under the king's fire in York. The archbishopric of that city had been vacant since the death of John's half brother Geoffrey in 1212. With the attention of much of the country on Runnymede in the unsettled June of 1215, the canons of York had gathered to elect an archbishop, perhaps hoping the king was too preoccupied to interfere. But John, characteristically well informed, was ready with a candidate. While he had conceded the right of free election to the Church, he saw nothing wrong in proposing Walter Gray, a former chancellor, now Bishop of Worcester, for the post. The canons curtly rejected him. He was, they claimed, illiterate (in fact, Gray had been educated at Oxford), and they preferred one of their own number, Simon Langton, the younger brother of Stephen.

In some respects, the appointment was a repeat of the earlier Canterbury dispute in which Langton senior had succeeded the king's choice, John Gray, coincidentally Walter Gray's brother. As John saw it, the elevation of Simon was nothing less than a rebel ploy to win the favours of Stephen Langton. The prospect of dealing with two archbishops as independent in character as the Langtons was a daunting one, and the king appealed to the pope, who, in due course, overruled the election.

In the meantime, Innocent's commissioners in England issued a carefully worded argument enjoining Stephen Langton and his bishops to obey the papal instructions of July 7. On September 5, after reminding the prelates that the pope had sent letter after letter directing them to support John against the enemies in his kingdom, the commissioners outlined their case against the rebels. Most of it was pretty familiar. It was common knowledge, they asserted, that FitzWalter, Vesci, Clare, Gloucester and the rest had conspired against their sovereign, had taken arms to defy him, and had broken the peace of a land which belonged to the patrimony of St. Peter. They had occupied London in contempt of the pope's ordinance; they had armed the city against the king; and they had maltreated the citizens who were loyal to him. One point provided the commissioners with some difficulty: the fact that John had conceded Magna Carta. They made no mention of the document, confining themselves instead to general terms. The rebels, they declared, had dispensed lands unlawfully, swept away approved customs, introduced new laws, and transmuted the decisions of the king and his advisers.

In view of the fact that the insurgents had ignored both the pope's mandates and the sanctity of the crusade, they had no option but to proclaim those barons excommunicate, place their lands under interdict and call upon the archbishop and his suffragans to publish the sentence. A number of clerics, among them Giles of Briouse, Bishop of Hereford, and his archdeacon, William FitzWalter, were included in the condemnation for their active support of the insurgents, as were the city of London and its inhabitants.

Still, Langton refused to co-operate, insisting that the papal mandate had been issued in ignorance of the changed situation in England. The commissioners, unimpressed, suspended him from office, forbidding him to enter a church or celebrate Mass. Ironically, the man who had come to England at the pope's behest to subdue John, had fallen victim of Innocent's respect for that same king. The primate was shattered. Disconsolately, he considered resigning his see and entering a monastery. But, rallying, he turned to Rome to plead his case before Innocent. He was followed closely by the king's proctors, armed with complaints against the archbishop.

The shuttle service between England and the pope's court was catching up on the major events of 1215. By now, Pandulf and John's other messengers had arrived in Italy, and Innocent was cognizant of the fact of Magna Carta. John, he was told, having placed himself and all the rights of his kingdom under the protection of the Apostolic See, had been forced to concede the unwarranted powers it granted his enemies. Pandulf handed Innocent a letter from the English king.

"Although your sincere affection for us is considered worthless by the malevolent and the presumptuous," wrote John, "God willing, it will yet bring us peace and security, confounding and striking terror in our enemies . . . We devoutly beseech that, when you have learned of the injuries inflicted upon you through our person, you will direct your fatherly concern to the government of our kingdom and the conservation of our dignity."

According to Wendover, when Innocent had perused those

provisions of the charter placed before him, he exclaimed in astonishment: "Are the barons of England trying to depose a king who has taken the crusader's cross, and who is under the protection of the holy see? Are they trying to pass to another the dominion of the Roman Church? By St. Peter, we cannot dismiss this insult without punishment!" At all events, having consulted his cardinals, Innocent took pen toward the end of August and addressed to England the most crushing of the seemingly endless stream of words to cross the Continent that summer—the letter which sealed the fate of Magna Carta.

Early in September, John went to Dover. There, and at nearby Canterbury, he spent the month preparing for the arrival of the mercenaries recruited on the Continent by Hugh of Boves and other agents. His concentration on the southeast corner of the country, plus the increasingly audacious behaviour of rebel cliques in other parts of the kingdom, gave rise to a variety of rumours. Some said that he had gone to France to raise an army; others, that he had left for the crusade. One story had it that the king had turned apostate, while a further tale reported his death at sea. Most outlandish was the gossip that he had taken refuge on the Isle of Wight, where he was living among fishermen and pirates.

In those counties where the insurgents were strong, they had begun to usurp the functions of the Crown officers, assuming judicial and administrative authority, and parcelling out the land among themselves. This was the true face of the rebellion. There was even talk of choosing a new monarch, and calling a council for that purpose. But the spree was short-lived. As John's foreign troops started to land in England, the rebel leaders had to think seriously of their safety. Overconfidence in their ability to crush John had already forced them to the compromise of Runnymede, and they could no longer plead the protection of a treaty they had ruptured at all points.

Late in September, William of Albini, who had been urged repeatedly by the rebels to join them in London, succumbed to their blandishments and entered the city. Albini, who had a reputation for capable soldiering, was "received with great joy by the barons," who immediately offered him the job of establishing a stronghold to the southeast of the city, to block a direct advance by the king. The place selected was Rochester Castle, which had fallen to the rebels on the disaffection of its custodian, Reginald of Cornhill. Rochester commanded the approach to London from Dover, and its fortress was sufficiently formidable, it was supposed, to delay the further deployment of John's foreign troops while the insurgents rallied their more distant brethren.

Albini, entering Rochester at the head of one hundred and forty knights and their retinues, found little in the way of preparations for his sojourn. Rebel organisation outside London seemed sketchy. The castle was completely bereft of supplies and armaments, even of furniture. The new garrison was obliged to ransack the town to provision it.

In Dover, John's forces were mounting. "From Poitou and Gascony came the noble and warlike Savary of Mauléon, and the brothers Geoffrey and Oliver of Buteville, with many knights and soldiers," wrote Wendover. "From Louvain and Brabant came Walter Buck, Gerard and Godeschal of Soceinne, with three companies of soldiers and cross-bow men . . . besides which, came many from Flanders to give great hopes to the monarch." But John's preparations were not without set-backs. There was one outstanding tragedy. Hugh of Boves, sailing from Calais with a sizeable army, was shipwrecked in a sudden storm. His entire contingent perished. Among those drowned were many women and children, even babies in cradles.

This gave rise to the preposterous myth that John intended to pursue a policy of genocide, repopulating the kingdom with foreigners. In fact, the rough-living routiers customarily took their families to war with them. So unpopular were they everywhere, that they hardly dared leave their kin behind unprotected. Hugh's body, with those of several knights and followers, was washed ashore near Yarmouth. Hundreds of bodies were found on the adjacent coast. "The very air was tainted by the stench," it was reported. "They were left to be devoured by the birds and beasts of the ocean."

As Stephen Langton plodded toward Rome, the pope's letter of late August crossed his path on its way to an England on the brink of civil war. Innocent, after expounding John's atonement and conversion to grace following his excommunication, held the devil responsible, in his envy, for corrupting the rebel barons. "Craftily, he perverted the situation so that the king, having earned redemption from his late faults, was attacked by those very men who had stood by him in the past against the Church." In a lengthy recapitulation of his many pleas for a settlement in England, the pope contrasted the reasonableness and forbearance of John, who had been willing to accept papal arbitration, with the excesses of the rebels.

They, declared Innocent, had rejected the directions of Rome at every step, ignored their oaths of fealty, and disregarded the sanctuary of one who had assumed the cross. By force, and through fear, John had been obliged

> to enter into an agreement which was not only vile and base, but unlawful, unjust and much to the disparagement of his rights and honour . . . We do not choose to overlook this audacious evil which embraces contempt of the apostolic see, the diminution of royal rights and the disgrace of the English nation, endangering also the cause of the crusader.
>
> Such evils would certainly thrive unless the agreement extorted from the prince (our well-beloved son in Christ, the illustrious King of England) were not revoked by our authority,

Demise of a Settlement

even were he prepared to stand by it. Accordingly, on behalf of Almighty God, the Father, Son and Holy Ghost, by the authority of the apostles Peter and Paul, and in our own name, with the guidance of our brothers, we utterly reject and condemn the charter, forbidding, under pain of excommunication, the king to observe it, or the barons and their associates to demand its observance. We annul and quash the charter unequivocally, with all securities and undertakings stemming from it, declaring them devoid of validity for ever.

In an accompanying aside to the rebels, calling on them to make reparation to the king with devotion and humility, Innocent commented pointedly: "May God, who wishes no man to perish, persuade you to accept our wholesome advice and instructions, lest, should you do otherwise, you find yourselves in dire trouble."

The warning was too late. The battle had started.

Chapter 17
THE KING STRIKES

Only the strong shall thrive.
                Robert William Service, The Law of the Yukon

Atop the massive keep of Rochester Castle, Albini's look-outs peered into the gold-laden mists of a Kentish autumn, seeking the tell-tale glint of steel, of helm and chain-mail, which would herald the advance of the royalists. The keep, a quadrangular four-storied structure flanked by turrets, had been erected by the one-time Archbishop of Canterbury, William of Corbeil, to whom the castle had been granted in 1126. It towered to a height of a hundred and twenty feet. With the rest of the fortress, built by order of William Rufus the previous century, the great pile stood on an eminence beside the river Medway, commanding a wide view of the surrounding country.

Up the estuary to the east, past neighbouring Gillingham, lay the Isle of Sheppey and the flats which separated the mouth of the waterway from the mightier mouth of the river Thames. Inland, a valley in the chalk downs led the Medway south to the Vale of Kent, where it assumed a sudden duality, one branch leading west to a bosky home in the Surrey hills, the other east to the bleak Romney marshes.

While the dominating edifice in Rochester itself was the cathedral church of St. Andrew—rebuilt by a Norman bishop, Gundulf, on an original foundation by Augustine—the structure which had given the town its primary importance was its bridge, a centuries-old crossing point of the Medway on the Roman road to London from the Kentish ports. It was by commanding Rochester Bridge that the rebels sought to deny John, with his siege train, supply wagons, and all the other encumbrances of his army, a southeasterly access to London. Apart from placing the castle in the hands of Albini, probably the ablest of the rebel captains, FitzWalter mounted a strong patrol in the Rochester area during early October.

News of the drowning of Hugh of Boves and his men encouraged the rebel leader to go further. Soon afterward, he was bold enough to lead a company of barons beyond Rochester, on the road to Canterbury and Dover. John, still awaiting reinforcements from the Continent, found himself dangerously bereft of protection. On October 2, he sent messengers to ten royal castles directing their commanders to release as many men as they could spare from garrison duty to form the nucleus of a field army. It was not an order his constables can have received with any sanguinity. Already, in some regions, rebel forces were engaged in open warfare against the king's castles. But John was impatient to take the offensive. Having finally abandoned all hope of a peace based on conciliation, he was anxious to take the step he should perhaps have taken in spring, when the rebellion was still young—an all-out bid to crush it by armed force.

Now the king lost little time through inaction. Between October 7 and October 9, the first of the foreign troops, a contingent of Flemish knights under Robert of Bethune, disembarked in England. With these, and the limited company gleaned from the castles, John immediately headed for Rochester. Even the Flemings, boastful of their intrepidity, remarked apprehensively on the king's dash. "Indeed, sire," observed one knight as they rode to meet the enemy, "you think little of your foes if you go to fight them with so slight a company."

Retorted the small king, cramped in the saddle, as he was, by the pain of his inflamed joints: "I know them too well to respect or fear them. We could safely fight them with fewer men. What grieves me, I must tell you truly, is not so much the evil these subjects of mine are doing me, as that their wickedness should be seen by strangers."

On October 12, John and his small force clattered into Gillingham, just short of Rochester. Next morning, Albini's look-outs, catching their first glimpse of the royal banner unfurled amidst distant lances, sounded the warning. Knee to knee, trailing a straggling wake of archers and retainers, the king's knights advanced along the water's edge. From the battlements of Rochester, the rebel guards watched the cavalcade approaching. One can imagine its horses snorting the briny air, their riders holding them on tight reins to maintain their battle stations. As they drew nearer, the rattle of shields and the hubbub of soldierly prattle and blasphemy would reach the town on the breeze from the estuary. Near the bridge, another company of horsemen could be made out. FitzWalter and his barons were waiting with drawn swords.

Suddenly, panic seized the townsfolk, and the streets of Rochester were filled with citizens "flying on all sides." Swept along by the multitude, Albini's garrison sought the refuge of the castle and slammed the gates. The royal force pressed forward inexorably. For a moment FitzWalter hovered undecidedly while the advance parties of the two field forces skirmished. Then the rebel leader wheeled and raced for London with his barons, consigning October 13 to anti-climax. The "Marshal of the Army of God" would fight another day.

Indeed, he would return, he promised, with an overwhelming following to succour the garrison; meanwhile, he had no doubt that the castle could hold out. As John's men took over the town, the frightened people crept back. They would grow accustomed to living among soldiers in the weeks ahead. For the present, there was one of those nice formalities of medieval warfare to be sorted out.

A rebel named Oliver of Argentan had been captured by John in the skirmish. Since Oliver's connections could not afford the ransom demanded for his release, his brother Richard, another rebel, proposed to give his service to the royalists in lieu of payment. This somewhat touching bargain was sanctioned by both sides.

John, chary of following FitzWalter while Rochester Castle remained in rebel hands astride his communications, personally supervised the siege which followed. His endeavours showed that he had lost nothing of the extraordinary energy and intensity the Plantagenets were able to bring to bear on a problem. Having swiftly surveyed the fortress, he ordered all the smiths in Canterbury to work "night and day" on tools for his sappers. Then, setting his stone-throwers and cross-bowmen to discharge a regular stream of missiles at the garrison, he began undermining the castle walls. Relays of miners hacked and scrabbled in the tunnels, boring forward like an army of hungry moles. "Not in living memory was a siege so strenuously undertaken," declared the Barnwell annalist. But, the writer added, it was resisted with equal robustness.

A great stronghold with determined defenders could not be won quickly, and John made arrangements for a long operation. As fresh drafts of mercenaries arrived from the Continent, they were sent on to Rochester to swell the siege force. Billets were allocated in the town, and lines of horses were tethered in the cathedral close. The king sent off for refreshments to help ease the thirsty work. "Be it known that we need wine," he informed a subordinate. "If you can find any for sale in Sandwich [East Kent], we direct you to buy it and forward it immediately to Rochester at our expense." Food and ordnance were imported by road and river. Through the remaining days of October and into November, William of Albini's men defended the battlements keenly, picking off many of the attackers with bolts from their crossbows.

It seems, however, that Albini had some reservations about fighting his sovereign. Perhaps mindful of the clause in Magna Carta proscribing attempts on the king's life, he passed over at least one tempting opportunity. According to the chronicler of the incident, John was inspecting the castle walls after a barrage when a rebel bowman spotted him and pointed him out to Albini.

"My lord, I have an arrow ready. Shall I kill the king, our bloody enemy?"

"No," replied the baron. "Far be it from us to slay the Lord's anointed."

Late in October, FitzWalter set out from London with a force of seven hundred men-at-arms to keep his pledge to relieve Rochester Castle. He never completed the journey. One story had it that he was turned back by a south wind—maybe a piece of figurative irony aimed at the irresolution of the insurgent leader. Another version, more credible, asserted that the "Marshal of the Army of God and the Holy Church" abandoned the expedition on learning of the numerous reinforcements John had by now received from oversea. At all events, Albini and his men were left to the mercy of the besiegers. They held out, in the end, for seven weeks.

In the first break-through, the outworks of the fortress, enclosing some four or five acres, were stormed by the attackers, recovered by the garrison, then finally seized by John's forces. Still, the lofty keep defied bombardment. Through November, the king's miners toiled laboriously to create a network of galleries under the southeastern tower of the stronghold, where the underlying chalk came close to the surface. The galleries were shored with wooden props. On November 25, John sent to his justiciar for "forty fat bacon-pigs, the least good for eating, to help fire the material we have gathered beneath the tower."

Larded with pig fat, the props in the tunnels were burned away. The corner of the keep collapsed with a rumble and a cloud of dust. But still the defenders were not beaten. The stronghold was divided by a stout party wall, and the survivors fought on from the undamaged half of the edifice. It was not until the thirtieth day of November that Albini surrendered, beaten in the end by lack of provisions. His men, faced with starvation, had eaten their horses.

Wendover proclaimed that John, whipped into a blazing fury by the stubbornness of the defenders, threatened to hang every man in the castle. He was talked out of it, asserted the scribe, by a lieutenant who argued judiciously that such a precedent might rebound against captured loyalists. It seems much more likely, both from the standpoint of medieval custom and a study of John's character, that his first consideration would have been to procure ransoms for his prisoners to offset the cost of the siege, which Ralph of Coggeshall estimated at sixty thousand marks. Walter of Coventry stated that John hanged one bowman—a man who had betrayed him after enjoying the king's support from childhood. And even this was refuted by the contemporary author of a French chronicle, who may well have been present at Rochester. According to this writer, all reports of hanging were untrue.

John had reason to be pleased with the outcome of the siege of Rochester Castle, which ranked with the relief of Mirebeau among his more spectacular military accomplishments. Nor was it the only cause for gratification in the royal camp. As the king opened his campaign against the rebels in England, his ambassadors to Rome were vying with Stephen Langton for the pope's ear. Assisted by Pandulf, who appears to have returned to Rome about the same time, they won Innocent's unstinted support for their sovereign. Langton, it seems, made no attempt to defend himself against their charges. He could hardly deny that he had failed to support the king against the rebels, and that he had refused to implement the pope's instructions. But he did plead that Innocent should lift the suspension pronounced against him in England by the pontiff's commissioners.

The pope was unmoved by the appeal of his protégé. Instead, he confirmed the sentence, reminding the suffragan bishops of the province of Canterbury that they should no longer obey their archbishop. There was no easy absolution, said Innocent, for one who had "inflicted so much injury on the King of England and the Roman Church." Turning to the matter of York, he overruled the election of Simon Langton, upholding the king's candidate for the archbishopric, Walter Gray, in whom the canons suddenly perceived shining virtues. Gray, declared the pope, was a man of chastity and purity. After all, agreed the canons, what was a little thing like illiteracy beside the triumph of preserving his virginity into manhood?

In December, Innocent sealed the case for John by issuing a letter excommunicating many of the rebel barons, not under a general heading as before, but in their own names. He also empowered his commissioners to add such other names as they wished to the black list. It was no longer possible for John's enemies to entertain the slightest doubt that, in fighting the king, they made a foe of the pope.

While John's ambassadors were rousing Rome in the king's cause, the rebels were seeking foreign aid of a more prosaic sort. Three times, during the siege at Rochester, the barons in London had made overtures of peace toward the sovereign.

The King Strikes

On October 17 and 22, and November 9, John had issued safe-conducts to various barons, including FitzWalter and the Earl of Clare, that they might attend talks with a view to negotiations. These gestures, which came to nothing, seem to have been a cover for their real intentions: to bring France into the battle on their own side, ideally before John could take Rochester Castle.

Contact between Philip Augustus and John's enemies had been almost routine since as early as 1209, but, soon after the commencement of the siege at Rochester, a rebel delegation travelled to the French court with an exceptional offer. If Philip would help them to overthrow John, they would bestow the crown of England upon Philip's son and heir, Prince Louis. Louis's legal right to the English throne was a remote one, resting on his marriage to Blanche of Castile, a granddaughter of Henry II. Assuming the throne were vacant, and John's legitimate offspring were discounted, there were still two grandsons of Henry II through his eldest daughter, Matilda —not to mention Blanche's own brother, Henry—with better claims than Louis. Nor was he a figure to command popular support. At twenty-eight, he was a strangely cold and colourless creature, a capable soldier yet with a streak of callousness which could enable him to direct one of the most brutal operations of the savage war against the Albigenses—the massacre which followed the capture of Marmande.

None of this worried FitzWalter's barons, who were now obsessed with overthrowing John at all costs. Indeed, without foreign aid their position was perilous. One advantage they might anticipate from French intervention was the inhibition of John's mounting army of mercenaries, most of whom were natural subjects of Louis or Philip. For Philip himself, the prospect of seeing his son on the throne of England must have been a seductive one, the culmination of his life's ambition to dispossess the house of Anjou. But the French king was too old a campaigner to rush into a bargain without carefully considering the drawbacks.

The most immediate was Innocent's protection for the English king. Philip had already suffered from papal interdict over his adulterous marriage, and cannot have fancied a further dose of the medicine. He had also dealt before with English traitors, particularly FitzWalter, and had little respect for them. During the Normandy campaign, he had expounded the philosophy that they were there to be used, then discarded. Certainly, the political brief they now tendered needed treating with caution. There were many imponderables. How much support, for instance, could the rebels really muster in England? What were the true dispositions of rebel and royalist forces? What reserves could they hope to draw on as hostilities progressed? How much aid did the insurgents need, and how quickly? The offer of the Crown was a dramatic one. Were they really so determined to be rid of John—or were they quite simply desperate?

Philip was wise to question the position of the English dissidents, and perhaps not unduly cautious in reaching a sceptical conclusion. None knew better than the French king that John was a formidable opponent. War or no war, he was still the crowned and anointed King of England, a fact, surrounded as it was by a deep mystique of potency, which gave him a head start on the greatest of his barons. To extend his political and psychological advantage, he was also a vassal of the pope, and a declared crusader. As a ruler in the administrative sense, he continued to control a surprisingly large portion of the country through a government machine which, while under severe duress in some areas, functioned on the whole with remarkable fluency.

The courts of law remained active, and a stream of men was tried for "intruding" on the lands of others. Anarchy had not overwhelmed the judiciary. The chancery remained as

The King Strikes

busy as ever, issuing the king's orders with a meticulous and methodical diligence which made no concessions to the state of civil war. The financial arm of the government, while obstructed to some extent by the baronial hold on Westminster, was by no means withered, even collecting a large proportion of the revenues due from rebel lands.

This last factor, coupled with John's accumulated treasure and his control of such profitable industries as the West Country tin mines, gave him an economical advantage over the rebels which would be particularly telling in the event of a protracted war. Many, if not all, the rebel forces served without pay, and, though their normal feudal contracts provided for short periods of unpaid service, those who had joined the insurgents at the beginning of October, or earlier, were already into what would have warranted overtime pay under legal conditions before the fall of Rochester Castle. Theoretically, all freemen were armed and ready for call-up at any time. In fact, the habit of commutation by payment had become so general by now that it is doubtful if the lesser military tenants spent much on the upkeep of chargers and equipment, and certain that the majority had no fighting experience.

Among the rebel leaders, FitzWalter, Quincy, the ill-fated Albini and one or two others were experienced captains, but none were generals in the sense of Salisbury, Pembroke and Chester. The only English barons who still fought as of necessity in their normal lives were those who held the Welsh Marches, and most of these were loyal to John. In short, as warriors the insurgents were unskilled, if enthusiastic, amateurs.

By contrast, John's forces were highly professional. His mercenaries made war for a living, and his leaders, when not paid men, had spent enough of their lives as soldiers to qualify as experts. Unlike his opponents, John could depend upon his troops being well equipped with what, after all, were the tools of their trade. Unlike his opponents, he seems to have been adequately provided with siege machines. And, unlike his opponents, he possessed, in Aquitaine, an oversea territory from which to draw war supplies, especially the splendid battle horses bred in southern Europe.

In terms of castles, the dominating feature of military control in any area, the rebels were similarly out-classed. Of more than two hundred fortresses which would play a part in the civil war, only fifty-three were held by the insurgents. Of these, many were little more than stockades or reinforced manor houses, and the majority, in all likelihood, were of wood. No more then twenty, it seems, could be classed as formidable strongholds. Against this, John possessed some seventy royal castles, of which fifty were first-class. He could also depend on a further sixty-five baronial or episcopal castles held by loyalists, and a dozen castles which belonged to rebels but which were held by royal officers.

Geographically, the rebel strongholds were confined to the eastern half of England, plus Cumberland, the main concentrations being London and the counties close to its north, and the far-northern areas of Yorkshire, Durham and Northumberland. Almost the entire western half of England, and elsewhere in the east, was dominated by castles and forces loyal to the sovereign.

Outside England, the insurgents might look to Wales and Scotland for assistance. The Welsh, however, were contained by two of John's most redoubtable warriors, Ranulf, Earl of Chester, and William Marshal, Earl of Pembroke. Both Chester, at the northern end of the frontier, and Pembroke, at the southern, commanded forces of tough marcher knights weaned on border warfare. Alone among the English barons, whose individual followings were seldom more than enough to man their castles and make minor forays, this mighty pair could produce field armies and sustain thoroughgoing offensives.

The King Strikes

The region immediately south of Scotland, though presenting cause for royal concern, was watched over by three capable and loyal captains. The foremost of these was Philip of Ulecotes, an experienced soldier, and sheriff of Northumberland. Ulecotes controlled sturdy castles for John at Norham, overlooking the river Tweed on the Scottish border, and at Bamborough, Newcastle and Durham, also in the northeast. Ulecotes' second-in-command was Hugh of Balliol, the greatest baron of Northumberland and Durham, and a staunch loyalist. The last of the trio, Robert of Vieuxpont, was a tested captain with a large holding and castles in what later became the county of Westmorland. During John's siege of Rochester, Alexander of Scotland laid siege to Ulecotes' border fortress at Norham. Unlike John, the Scottish king failed in his enterprise.

In all, it was hard for Philip Augustus to share the enthusiasm of the rebel ambassadors for the chances of their colleagues in England. John himself had not neglected the French king. The English monarch had wooed his continental counterpart with concessions to French merchants, and, if Ralph of Coggeshall was correct, had created some confusion at the French court by issuing forged letters, supposedly from the rebel camp, claiming that peace had been agreed in England. The outcome was that Philip stood aloof from the whole thing, leaving Louis to sort it out. Louis, with a kingdom dangled before him, evinced greater interest. While prudently deferring a personal landing in England, he sent a contingent of knights up the Thames to London late in November, and promised more help in the future.

In London, the French knights were "very well received and led a sumptuous life." Their only complaint, it seems, was that the city was short of wine, and they were forced to drink humble beer. FitzWalter and his companions had established an indulgent regime at their urban headquarters. Wendover, contemptuous of their failure to take the offensive in Kent, portrayed the rebel barons reduced to an orgy of drinking, wenching and playing dice. Be that as it may, they had handed the initiative most rashly to the sovereign, who now turned from Rochester with a powerful army of mercenaries behind him.

At this point, John was faced with two possible courses of action: 1) to attack the main body of rebels in London, and hope to end the war at a single stroke, or 2) to by-pass London, bring the full force of his authority to bear on the regional areas of rebellion, then return to deal with an isolated and landless rebel army. John has been faulted for evading a "decisive" action and taking the second, allegedly weaker course. This is to oversimplify the situation. Throughout the history of the city, London, when resolutely defended, almost always had proved impervious to attack. An assault on her walls by John's mercenaries must have galvanised FitzWalter and his barons from their martial lethargy, provoked many uncommitted citizens to join them, and, far from being decisive, probably would have resulted in a long and inconclusive siege.

The possibility of an invasion by Louis was a very grave threat to John, and one he could not afford to contemplate from a sedentary posture outside the gates of London while rebels elsewhere remained free to welcome the French prince. Moreover, Alexander of Scotland, though less formidable a foe than Louis, was the more immediate danger, having already attacked in the North, where the strength of rebel sentiment compounded the menace. John's actual decision—to divide his army, leaving one force under Salisbury, Fawkes of Bréauté, and Savary of Mauléon, to watch London, while he led the other against the rebel lands to the north—was certainly not an ill-considered one. It offered him the possibility of restoring his administration throughout the whole of the country, bar London; replenishing his coffers from fines, ransoms and the

The King Strikes

sale of rebel possessions; keeping his mercenaries happy by sharing the fruits of rebel lands; and generally disconcerting the barons in London by seizing their estates, their castles and their chattels.

On December 6, John left Rochester with his section of the royal army, skirted London to the south, paid brief visits to his strongholds in Surrey and Hampshire, where he deposited his Rochester prisoners, then passed London to the west, heading north for St. Albans. The column reached the royal castle at St. Albans on December 18. By now, the king had received the pope's confirmation of Langton's suspension, and this was read to the local clerics, with instructions that it should be copied and transmitted to all churches in England. Continuing north, John reached Northampton, the site of another royal castle, on the twenty-first, and Nottingham in time for Christmas—a day he spent not in the usual fashion but, as Wendover put it, "on the warpath."

Apart from Nottingham Castle, John's sheriff in the area, Philip Marc, a mercenary captain, commanded two other castles, Sleaford to the east, and Newark to the northeast. In the midst of these was the castle of Belvoir, the home of William of Albini. Before joining the rebels in London, Albini had entrusted the castle to his son Nicholas and two of his knights. The king now sent messengers to Nicholas demanding the surrender of the fortress. His father, they reminded him, had been captured at Rochester and imprisoned in Corfe. It would be a pity, they observed darkly, if the constable of Corfe should forget to feed his captive. Taking their point, an anguished Nicholas hastened to make the castle over to the monarch. Belvoir completed John's hold on this strategically important Midlands region, dividing the northern rebels from those of the South.

As the king continued the march north, his harrying parties fanned to right and left, destroying the manors of the rebel barons, burning their crops and villages, seizing their cattle and other valuable property. The devastation was reported with awe in the chronicles. By day, great columns of smoke blotched the grey sky; by night, the countryside was lit by the flames consuming houses and hovels. The dreaded routiers confirmed their worst reputation, exacting a cruel price in pillage and extortion. It was not only the lands and supporters of the rebels which suffered. Mercenary detachments, scouring the woodlands and villages for plunder, showed little respect for the rights of property, or the well-being of the people, wherever they found them. Nor were the king's troops the only source of robbery and injury. Unscrupulous knights and common criminals exploited the confusion to avenge old scores and fill their pockets. The scene echoed the grim excesses of Stephen's reign.

But if John could not always limit the behaviour of his soldiery, he did not condone wanton violence. His attempts to impose some standard of discipline were sometimes vehement. One man, who stole a cow from a churchyard, had a hand cut off by way of punishment. Where possible, the king preferred his familiar method of selling forgiveness to wreaking despoliation. Towns associated with rebel activity were allowed to buy his protection for sums varying from eighty marks to a thousand pounds, depending upon their size and prosperity. Knights and barons who repudiated the rebel cause and sought to resume their allegiance, were normally permitted to do so for a modest sum, sometimes as little as ten marks, perhaps with a horse or two thrown in for good measure. Indeed, the king's attitude to repentant rebels seems often to have been remarkably gracious. Money, he informed a number of them, was not all that important. It was their "good and faithful service" he coveted.

From Newark, John marched to the loyal stronghold of Doncaster, where he spent New Year's Day 1216 before pressing on to Pontefract, Yorkshire. On the approach to Pontefract, the royal army was joined by the Earl of Chester, whose constable, John Lacy, held the town as a rebel. Between them, the king and Chester persuaded Lacy to accept the pope's invalidation of Magna Carta, to revoke any oath he had made to the king's enemies, and to swear fidelity to the sovereign and his heirs by Queen Isabelle. At this, the king fully forgave the repentant lord.

Another rebel, the fickle Roger of Montbegon, whose loyalty had veered capriciously between the two camps, submitted to the king at this stage. These submissions were especially significant since both Lacy and Montbegon were members of the committee of twenty-five. The king took hostages from them to back their assurances. The offensive continued. As John and his knights plunged into the windswept Vale of York, the loping routiers strung out behind them, none stayed to offer resistance. The insurgents in their path either packed their baggage and fled, perhaps risking exposure in the wintry, wolf-infested Pennines, or promptly declared themselves for the king.

The city of York, the scene of a rising in December, immediately submitted to the sovereign, who paused only long enough to extract a handsome fine from the citizens before hastening up the valley of the Ouse to Northallerton. Somewhere in this vicinity, Chester and his men parted from the king's army to seize a rebel castle at Richmond, slightly to the west of John's line of march, which now took him over the river Tees to Darlington. From here, the scouts screening the great chain of humanity and horseflesh treading its way north—men-at-arms, bowmen, pikemen, the royal guard, court officials and servants, sumpter horses, supply wagons, baggage carts and camp-followers—stepped up their vigilance. Beasts trundling the heavy vehicles were exhorted with stick and voice to keep pace. They were entering the home of the rebellion.

On January 8, the irresistible royal army advanced from Darlington to Durham, where the king learned that Alexander of Scotland, having failed to take the frontier castle of Norham, had struck suddenly through Northumberland and burned the loyal port of Newcastle. The coastal region of Northumberland, beyond Newcastle to Berwick on the Scottish border, was strung with rebel castles, and a gathering of their lords had done homage to the marauding Alexander. Spurring forward to Newcastle, John found it in ashes, but was too late to apprehend the Scottish king, who had withdrawn toward Berwick. Swearing to "run the sandy little fox cub to his earth," John raged after Alexander and his minions. Before January was out, the English king had toppled the Northumbrian castles of Mitford, Morpeth, Warkworth and Alnwick like so many skittles.

As the rebels retired before him, they destroyed whatever they could not carry with them, hoping to deny their pursuers subsistence. But John was too resourceful to be delayed by such tactics. Cattle were driven with his army, while his foragers ranged on a wide front. At Berwick, Alexander's allies put up a short defence. On the fifteenth, after an attack of only two days, the town and castle were carried. Tragically, many of the townsfolk were butchered by the triumphant routiers, who ran amuck after victory. For a week, the royal force used Berwick as a base to support a series of raids across the Tweed and into Scotland. While the "fox cub" cowed timidly in his lair, John ranged the Lammermuir Hills, burned Dunbar and Haddington, and swept the domain of his treacherous neighbour as far as the Firth of Forth.

Finally, satisfied that Newcastle had been avenged, John put Berwick to the torch and, on January 23 or 24, started south at the head of what must have been a sore and exhausted, if

The King Strikes

grimly gratified army. Its work was not over. For two days, the king rested his men at Newcastle, granting a new charter to its loyal citizens and encouraging them to make good the depredations of Alexander. On February 7, John arrived with peremptory trumpets and unfurled banners before the rebel castle of Skelton, in the North Riding of Yorkshire. The garrison seems to have defied him at first. Within a few days, however, he had broken its resistance and was tacking south through the county, now at the loyal stronghold of Scarborough, on the coast, now inland revisiting York. Here, the rampageous monarch could take stock.

Northumberland and Durham had been forced to submission. To the west, Carlisle Castle, a possession of the rebel Robert of Ros, had surrendered to John's local captain, Robert of Vieuxpont, who now controlled all Cumberland and Westmorland. A subdued Yorkshire was handed over to the king's able and trusty chamberlain, Geoffrey Neville. John's northern campaign had ended brilliantly. Wendover, who had no interest in applauding the sovereign's achievements, stated that only one castle in the entire North, Helmsley, on the edge of the Yorkshire moors, remained in rebel hands.

John completed his march south via Lincoln and Stamford, accepting the surrender of the rebel strongholds of Fotheringay and Bedford before reaching St. Albans. His army entered the town at the end of February, less than six weeks after leaving it on the trek north. In those six weeks, the king had led his field force, with all its trappings and encumbrances, some seven hundred miles—discounting diversions and a week spent raiding in Scotland. At the same time, he had conducted sieges and assaults; had held ceremonies to accept the submission and renew the allegiance of dissidents; had exacted fines from the rebellious and granted privileges to loyal subjects; had appointed new regional officers and placed fresh captains in captured castles; and had overcome the hundred and one logistical and executive problems inherent in manoeuvring a rapacious and polyglot host from one end of his kingdom to the other, and bringing it back intact. It was a remarkable accomplishment from the ailing monarch, and a sharp reminder of the verve and energy which had once built the Angevin empire.

While John demonstrated his wrath in the North of England, the main body of rebel barons languished behind the walls of London with a lack of resolution which appears to have drawn closer to despair as the king's campaign progressed. Wendover remarked of these noble lords that they behaved "like pregnant women." Toward the end of 1215, a further delegation of barons travelled to France to implore Philip to use his influence to advance his son's aid to the rebels. Still dubious of their trustworthiness, the French king demanded two dozen hostages as an earnest of good faith before he would entertain the matter. When the hostages were delivered, Louis sent a second contingent of knights and footmen to London, but continued to delay his own arrival.

It seems that the Frenchmen were no more anxious to venture against John than were FitzWalter's barons, for they were still sitting in London when a third batch of their compatriots disembarked at the docks on February 27. More than a little of the enthusiasm faded from their welcome when the rebel Earl of Essex, Geoffrey of Mandeville, was killed by a French knight in a tournament held in their honour. But at least Louis now set a date for his personal appearance. He would be at Calais ready to cross to England, he promised, at Easter.

Meanwhile, Salisbury, Mauléon and Bréauté, the commanders John had left to watch London, had quickly surmised that the insurgents had no intention of moving. Accordingly, delegating a number of constables to guard the roads from the city, they had set forth in January to harry the king's enemies in Essex and East Anglia. While one force pursued groups of

The King Strikes

insurgents to the Isle of Ely, amidst the fenlands north of Cambridge, another laid siege to rebel-held Colchester, in Essex. Smaller royalist detachments roamed Hertfordshire, Middlesex, and neighbouring counties, plundering and ravaging.

Two of Salisbury's lieutenants, William Talbot and Robert Burgate, pressed into Lincolnshire to capture the castles of Frampton and Moulton, actually continuing north as far as Doncaster, in the south of Yorkshire. Still, the rebels in London refused to budge. Even when the royalists set fire to a suburb of the city, after carrying off valuable booty, FitzWalter's barons and their allies declined to meet the challenge.

Having spent the first week of March resting his army, John turned into the eastern counties to complete the job started there by his southern forces. On March 12, he seized Roger Bigod's castle at Framlingham, Suffolk, and on March 28 he took the surrender of Robert of Vere's castle at Hedingham, Essex, after a siege of three days. Between whiles, the king tackled Colchester Castle, which had survived an onslaught by Savary of Mauléon. Here, the garrison had been reinforced by a detachment of Frenchmen from London. Under the terms of the surrender which John quickly extracted, the French were allowed to depart unmolested to London, while the English members of the garrison were held for ransom.

If John's intention in this was to spread dissension among the rebels and their allies, he succeeded. Already upset by the killing of Mandeville, FitzWalter's barons seized the French when they arrived back from Colchester, charged them with betraying their English comrades, and threatened to execute them. Upon the intervention of the rest of the Frenchmen, it was agreed to hold the "culprits" in custody until Louis arrived from France. March ended on a note of mutual animosity between the two nationalities in the city.

John's eastern campaign, triumphantly crowning his northern successes, completed the despondency of the rebels. At the beginning of April, the whole of England, save London and one or two isolated castles, was under royal domination. Alexander's bid for conquest had been smashed. The Northumbrian barons had been shaken rudely from their dream of independence. Everywhere, rebel strongholds had been destroyed or occupied by the king's troops. Lands belonging to insurgents had been harried, and their sympathisers terrorised; their goods had been confiscated or looted; their estates had been placed in the custody of loyal Englishmen or foreign captains. The royal coffers had been enriched not only by plunder and the revenues flowing once more from the lands of the rebellious, but also from the many fines collected on John's travels.

At the end of his campaign in the east, the king was in a position to ensure the continued service of his army by the full payment of his mercenaries and the distribution of rich gifts to his officers.

During the last weeks of winter and the first weeks of spring, John issued a spate of safe-conducts to fearful rebels who now clamoured to make peace with him—to submit, as Ralph of Coggeshall had it, "to the mercy of the merciless one." Among those who demonstrated a wish to negotiate were the greatest of the rebels, the earls Robert of Vere, Richard of Clare and Roger Bigod. Suddenly, the sovereign appeared to have recovered his old authority. Where more than a year of reasoning, bargaining and compromise had failed him, three months of armed aggression had wrought wonders of persuasion. In London, the last refuge of insurrection, his disheartened enemies were squabbling among themselves. Only the prospective arrival of Prince Louis of France could save them from an outright royal victory.

Chapter 18
ENGLAND INVADED

And they embarked in six hundred ships and eighty cogs, all well equipped, sailing for Thanet, where they landed, at Stonor, on the twenty-first of May.

Roger of Wendover

The king was master; his enemies knelt to him! From the stone heart of Corfe Castle, warmed by blazing logs and hung with tapestries of rich, incandescent colouring, the queen's musicians proclaimed the message in throbbing beat and trilling overtones. The strains of festive medieval "pop" wafted over the battlements to dissolve in the sea breezes which swept the chunky promontory of Dorset they called the Isle of Purbeck. Queen Isabelle, with her children Henry, Richard, Joan, Isabelle and Eleanor, had taken refuge at Corfe when the civil war started. Henry was nine, a pretty, small-boned prince with a growing awareness of his unique station in England. His mother, though not yet thirty, was nevertheless a matron of some sixteen years standing, and her relationship with John appears to have worn well.

It is hard to see John as the awful husband legend has painted him. Henry II had neglected his queen so thoroughly that she had not only left him, but had become one of his bitterest enemies. Richard, whose marriage had been nothing but a political stratagem, had virtually ignored his spouse. John had shown altogether more affection, imagination and feeling in his wedded life. In its early days, his partnership with Isabelle had been one of passion, even infatuation, and he had never ceased, unless the dangers were too great, to take her with him on his travels and campaigns. Their mutual delight in the pleasures of the connubial bed had scandalised sanctimonious chroniclers, who labelled Isabelle a wanton. John's court, unlike that of his father, was not purgatory to a woman. The king encouraged the gaiety and liveliness which, in his youth, had been condemned by the writers, cultivating luxuriant tastes in diet, adornment and music.

Among both rich and poor in John's day, music was the language of laudation and happiness. Men were quickly moved by a brisk tune. And quick to acknowledge good fortune with melody. John's successes in the North and East Anglia must have been received in royalist circles with resonant rejoicing. The Church was powerfully equipped for such moments. Its leading temples had housed organs of formidable volume for generations. As early as the first half of the eleventh century, an organ of prodigious capacity had been installed in Winchester. Seventy men toiling at twenty-six bellows were required to fill the wind-chest, while there were no less than four hundred pipes. "Like thunder," reported one who had heard it, "the iron voice assaults the ears and drives out all other sounds. So swells the noise that you must clap hands to your ears, unable, on drawing near, to abide the brazen bellowing. All through the city the melody can be heard, and the fame and echo of it spreads throughout the land." Vicars were obliged to have musical attributes. No

England Invaded

one should fill the office, declared the Statutes of Salisbury, "unless he has a good voice."

For secular celebrations, there was no lack of instruments. Harps, gitterns (guitars), rybybes (lyres), bumbardes (oboes), recorders, clokardes (chimes), curtalls (bassoons), clappers, cymbals, nakers (kettledrums), flutes, lutes, timbrels and viols, among others, combined in the pulsating dance tunes of the epoch. The young were blithely susceptible. According to William FitzStephen, English maidens were given to cavort the night away, "free of foot at moonrise." The celebrations at Corfe, as spring approached that martial year of 1216, must have excited the queen and her children. The tempo would soon change. There were few moments of music and dancing left in John's reign.

Festivities apart, the king's work was not done. So long as an invasion by Louis remained in the offing, the rebels would not surrender London, and John now resumed his efforts to strike a friendly note with the French court. Apart from continuing to issue safe-conducts to French merchants in London and elsewhere, the king wrote to Louis signifying his readiness to come to a settlement with the prince. He also wrote to "the guardians of the truce" which existed between himself and King Philip, proposing a conference to discuss the progress of the treaty.

At the same time, he took steps to secure his kingdom against the possible consequences should these diplomatic measures fail. He ordered the coast towns to be placed in a state of alert, and he sent letters to twenty-one ports on the southern and southeastern coasts of England directing that all available ships should be manned and assembled at the mouth of the Thames, or in the Dover roads. The last time a French invasion had been threatened, John had used the naval supremacy born of his own foresight to destroy the enemy fleet before it set sail. He could take comfort from the fact that his vessels were larger and more formidable than any the French could now muster. "The little French vessels were no match for the English ships," wrote a contemporary. "One of John's ships was worth four of Louis's." If peaceful methods to avert potential danger were unproductive, he planned to repeat his earlier tactics, striking the French armada before it reached the English coast.

Other letters, aimed at those of the king's subjects who had yet to submit to him, proclaimed a general safe-conduct for all who came to make peace up to a month after Easter. Anyone failing to do so by that time would be disinherited.

While John alerted his defences and made peaceful overtures toward France, his ecclesiastical allies took steps to support him. The pope's commissioners ordered the London clergy, including the chapters of St. Martin's and St. Paul's, and the convent of Holy Trinity, to announce the excommunication of all the rebels and French troops in the city. Innocent, appraised of the ambitions of the French prince, sent a representative, Cardinal Gualo of Beccaria, to France to prevent foreign interference in the English civil war. The legate's arrival at the French court produced a further delay in Louis's plans.

If the prince's vassals were to follow him to England in good heart, Gualo could not be ignored. Neither the legate nor the French knights were likely to be impressed by a justification for invading England which rested on nothing more convincing than the invitation of a group of excommunicated English barons. The venture needed a legal framework. Accordingly, at Melun, south of Paris, toward the end of April, an elaborate charade was set up between Louis and Philip.

In public court at Melun, on April 25, Gualo was received by the French king, who assumed from the start the role of a disinterested observer of the disturbed affairs in England. An-

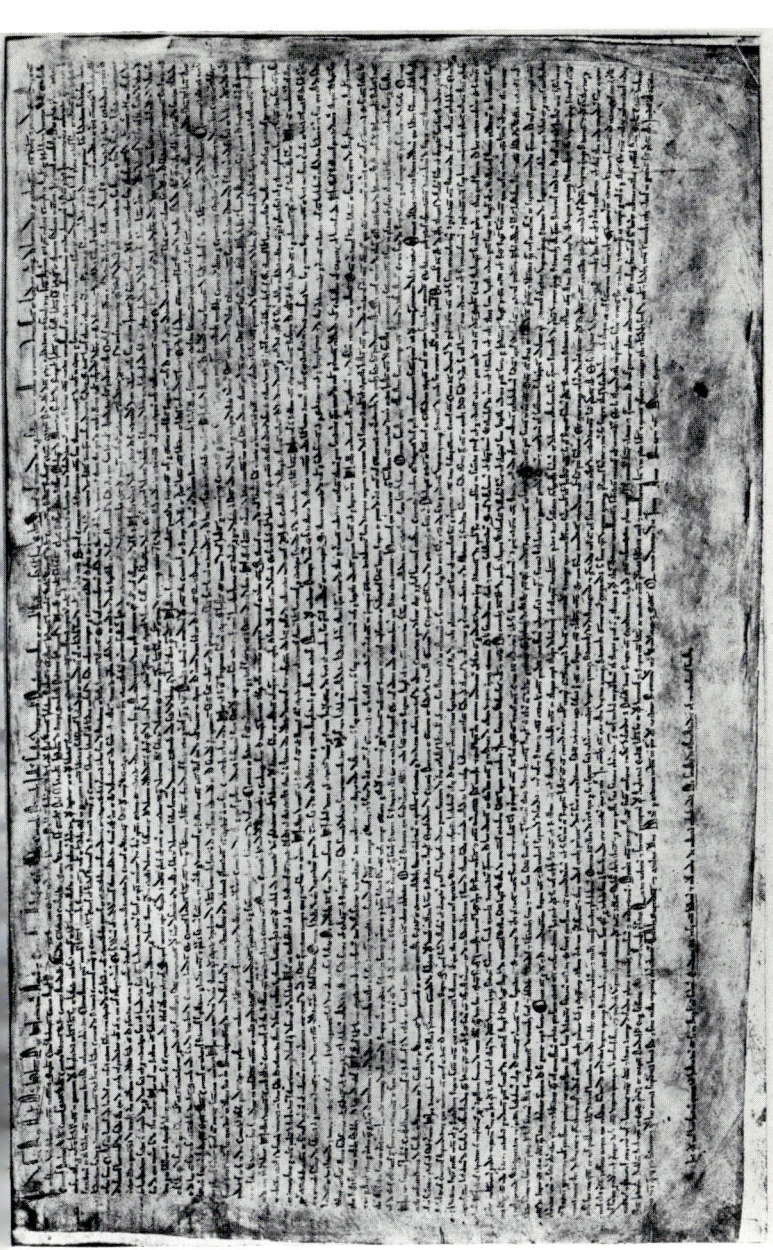

Plate 13 An Exemplification of Magna Carta, 15 June 1215

Plate 14 Corfe Castle, a frequent home of the royal family

England Invaded

swering the pope's message that England was a fief of the Holy See, and that any attack on its king was forbidden, Philip launched a studiously artless dissertation on the position of John and his kingdom. John, postulated Philip, to the delight of the French knights surrounding him, had never been the legal king of England, having been convicted of treason against his brother Richard, and condemned by Richard's court. If he were not truly king, then he had had no authority to place the kingdom under Innocent's protection. Even had John become king by right, continued Philip Augustus, he would have forfeited that right by the murder of his nephew Arthur, for which he had been condemned by a French court. Moreover, just supposing John had in fact been the true king at the time of surrendering his realm to the pontiff, then he had had no entitlement to do so without the mandate of his barons, which, the French king maintained, had not been given.

How far Gualo was in a position to confute this unexpected and specious thesis is unknown. The argument that John was disinherited by his brother's court was invalidated by Richard's clear acceptance, in the last hours of his life, of John's right to succession. The alleged conviction of John by a French court for the murder of Arthur is nowhere on record, and is generally held to be a fiction. Further, the rebels had themselves refuted the charge that John surrendered his kingdom to the pope without their consent, by later seeking Innocent's sympathy on the very grounds that they had been instrumental in forcing the king's hand. But if Gualo were not briefed to contest Philip's interpretation of history, the legate can hardly have missed the most obvious weakness in the monarch's case—the singularly late hour of its presentation. For years, Philip Augustus had treated with John without apparent doubt that he treated with the King of England.

Philip's conclusion, that the pope had no claim to dominion over England, was not aimed at converting the legate (palpably an improbability) so much as disconcerting him before the French knights. While these nobles applauded their sovereign noisily, the French king turned to Gualo confidingly. Frankly, he said, the question of England was no more his own concern than the proper concern of the pope. Personally, he had no designs on John's kingdom. But the affairs of Louis were another matter. Louis had grievances against the English king, and they should invite him to explain his position. "I have always been devoted to the pope, and faithful to the Roman Church," said Philip, "and I shall neither advise nor help my son to go against them; yet, if Louis claims rights in the realm of England, let him be heard, let justice be done to him."

Thus, having astutely ranked himself beside the legate as judge of the prince's case, Philip summoned his son before the crowded court. After listening with scant sympathy to Gualo's plea "not to invade or seize the patrimony of the Roman Church," the prince reiterated his father's hypotheses, adding a further refinement. When John had resigned his crown to the pope, argued Louis, the English king had performed two acts, one of which was legal, the other invalid. In resigning the crown, John had been entirely within his rights: his resignation, the first act, was therefore effective. On the other hand, in surrendering the crown to the pope without, as Louis insisted, the consent of the barons, John had behaved unlawfully: the transference of the crown, the second act, was nugatory. It followed that the throne of England had been vacant since John's resignation, and the barons were entitled to elect another king. Since, declared Louis, they had seen fit to elect him, bearing in mind his wife's heritage, it behove him to execute his duty.

This legalistic parcel of distortion and half-truths left Cardinal Gualo floundering. Evading it gingerly, he struck out for safer ground. John, he reminded the court, had taken the oath of a crusader, and was entitled to proceed unmolested. Not so, retorted the French prince. He, Louis, had never been party to the truce between John and Philip following the English offensive in Poitou. Since he was still legally at war with John, and since John was the original aggressor, retaliation was justified. At last, tried beyond patience, and lost in dialectic, Gualo abruptly ended the audience by bluntly forbidding Louis to invade England, threatening Philip with excommunication if he allowed it.

The French pair were prepared for the development. "On this side of the sea," observed Louis readily, "I am my father's liegeman. Concerning England, he has no hold on me. I stand by the judgement of my peers." So saying, he swept from the assembly, leaving his suave parent exonerated from blame, and an enraged cardinal with no option but to hurry on to England and warn John of the danger. Magnanimously, Philip offered him a safe-conduct to the coast. The royal show was over.

Once Gualo had gone, Louis returned to his father and received the older man's blessing for his enterprise. Philip had no objection to Louis chancing his luck in England, so long as he, Philip, remained ostensibly detached from the venture. If it failed, the French king lost nothing; if it succeeded, he gained the reward for a lifetime of struggling against the Plantagenets—an empire greater even than the Angevin empire in its heyday. Louis, for his part, was willing to risk excommunication for the English crown. All the same, he sent messengers to Rome to recite his case, probably as a delaying operation, for there can have been little hope that it would impress a lawyer of Innocent's calibre. Indeed, the pope dismissed it contemptuously. On the subject of Arthur's death, he commented merely that, as a traitor to his lord and uncle, the miserable youth had invited whatever end he might have met.

The passing of Easter, with no appearance in England by Louis, brought depression to the barons in London, and increasing confidence to the English king. Every week which passed without the sailing of the French fleet enabled John to strengthen his southern defences and watch the growth of the navy he was mustering from the English ports. As the vessels converged on their assembly point in the southeast, stoutly manned by the men of the Cinque Ports and hardy seafarers from Yarmouth, Lynn, Dunwich, and other little fishing towns, the chance of a French force reaching its destination intact seemed less and less probable. The possibility that John would be able to complete the muster of his navy, sail it to Calais, and destroy the invasion armada before it sailed, became increasingly likely.

During the end of April and the first half of May, John patrolled the Southeast, moving between the coastal stations of Sandwich, Dover, Folkestone and Romney, and his inland headquarters for the area, Canterbury. In the third week of May, when he must have been poised to mount a decisive naval offensive, catastrophe wrecked his preparations. Toward the evening of the eighteenth, in a savage repeat of the performance which had put an end to Hugh of Boves and his followers, the sky darkened, the wind rose, and a storm whipped the coastal waters of Kent with sudden and unforeseen ferocity. Throughout the night, the gale raged and howled. By morning, the English navy was broken and scattered. On the twenty-first, still awaiting reports which would enable him to assess the damage, John learned from his coastguards in Thanet, East Kent, that a fleet had appeared in the distance. Hopes that the surviving English vessels had managed to reform were short-lived.

On the night of the twentieth, regardless of still unfavourable weather, Louis had decided to embark and make the most of the disarray in the English fleet. His vessels, reputedly between six and seven hundred in number, were commanded by a well-to-do adventurer known as Eustace the Monk, a freebooter familiar with English waters, having sailed in the service of John for several years prior to 1212. Little is recorded of the French invasion army. Among the few men of rank known to have followed Louis were the Count of Holland, a hopeful opportunist; Adam Beaumont, marshal to Louis in France; the Count of Dreux, a cousin of the French prince; the Viscount of Melun, a veteran of Bouvines; and the Count of Nevers, a soldierly gentleman whose lands centred on the Loire Valley, to the east of Bourges. Simon Langton, seeking revenge for having been denied episcopal office at York, had joined the expedition as chaplain to Louis, and sailed in the same vessel as the French prince.

Due to adverse winds, the bulk of the armada did not make landfall in Thanet, Kent, until the twenty-second, a Sunday. According to one story, Louis landed alone many hours before the main fleet—a rash gesture, unless the rebels had misled him about their influence in the South. Meanwhile, Cardinal Gualo, having beaten the prince to England by a short head, had been conducted across the Romney marshes to meet John near Canterbury. Resplendent in scarlet robes, and mounted on a white horse, the legate had reached the city in time to learn that the French armada had been sighted. Somewhat breathlessly, it would seem, he pronounced the invaders excommunicate. John, deriving what comfort he might from this circumstance, now marched his assembled field force to Sandwich, from which point he could watch the arrival of Louis's fleet.

It appears that the English king meant to give battle immediately. One reads that the trumpets were sounded and the troops arrayed in readiness. But the conflict did not take place. At the last moment, the king's advisers, notably that rugged old worthy William Marshal, advocated a strategic withdrawal. Wendover attributed their caution to the unpredictability of the behaviour of John's French mercenaries when confronted with their fellow-countrymen and the son of their natural sovereign. The explanation is plausible. Should the mercenaries switch sides in any numbers, or fight half-heartedly, the result would be disastrous. Harold had lost England to William of Normandy in a single battle. For the beaten medieval army there was seldom a return match. The argument for postponing a collision with Louis until the loyalty of John's foreign troops could be tested in less critical conditions, was a sound one.

After some hesitation, John pulled off to Dover, where the castle, together with other key strongholds throughout the land, was well prepared to repel the invaders. Leaving his justiciar, Hubert of Burgh, in command of Dover Castle, the king retired west along the Sussex coast, inspecting and strengthening garrisons as he went. At length, turning inland through Hampshire, he arrived on May 28 within the familiar and comforting walls of Winchester. Here he raised the royal standard and awaited the nation's initial reaction to the French prince. It was not inconceivable that the kingdom might rise against the foreign pretender; but, as it happened, it did not. On the contrary, it soon became evident that the Frenchman's intervention was not only reactivating the rebellion, but actually gleaning some support from John's erstwhile adherents.

The forebodings of John's advisers were justified. When the French troops already in London advanced exuberantly into Kent to join the invaders, many Englishmen and mercenaries hitherto loyal to the king had second thoughts. Canterbury offered no opposition to Louis. The guardians of Rochester Castle surrendered meekly. On the second day of June, the elated French prince, still marvelling at the lack of resistance, entered London to a rapturous welcome from the rebel barons and their citizen supporters. The canons of St. Paul's, ignoring the excommunication pronounced by Gualo, received the Frenchmen with a procession in their church. Like most other

Londoners, they were only too willing to accept Louis's assurance that the legate had been corrupted by John's bribery.

On June 3, the rebel barons and other insurgents, headed by FitzWalter and the mayor of London, William Hardel, did homage and swore fealty to the French prince. Louis promised to establish "good laws" and restore "lost heritages." In a general letter to those English magnates who were elsewhere, he enjoined them to acknowledge his authority "or leave England quickly." Then, having appointed Simon Langton as his chancellor, and having filled his satchels from the treasury at Westminster (where at least the monks stood aloof from him), Louis started south with a largely French army for Winchester.

At the same time, Robert FitzWalter and William of Mandeville, the new Earl of Essex, set out with the London-based barons to recover the lost rebel hold on East Anglia. Further north, the doused rebellion sparked into new life. Alexander of Scotland, sensing a change of fortune, collected his army and once more crossed the border. England, so recently brought to order by John's tireless efforts, relapsed into chaos. Rebels who had at last made peace with their sovereign, revoked and joined FitzWalter and Louis, or reconstituted local centres of insurgency. Barons so far neutral through the civil war, warily aligned themselves against a monarch they now assumed to be facing sure defeat. As usual, the opportunists and brigands went on the rampage.

Louis left London on June 6 and reached Winchester on the fourteenth, after a virtually unimpeded march. On the seventh, he took Reigate Castle, in Surrey, which had been abandoned on his approach. Guildford Castle, in the same county, surrendered on the eighth. Farnham capitulated two days later. The complete failure of loyalist strongholds in its path to hinder the French advance on Winchester, seems to have induced something akin to panic in the royal ranks.

Further defections which resulted were not confined to barons of hitherto wavering allegiance, but included a number of the highest and most favoured of John's men, among them the Earls of Salisbury, Arundel and Warren.

The defection of William of Salisbury, the king's half brother and a senior and trusted general, was perhaps the most astonishing and humiliating of all the blows which now staggered the English king. The earl's excuse for his behaviour —the sudden and convenient discovery of grounds for offence in his brother's alleged admiration of his wife, the Countess Ela—merely compounded his dishonour. Another loss to John was the desertion of Warin FitzGerald, a chamberlain of the exchequer. At about the same time, William of Albini went over to Louis. Though less surprising than other defections, for his adhesion to either side had never seemed certain, Albini's perfidy was nevertheless an added set-back. These five men alone carried some five hundred and thirty knights to the enemy.

The defection shortly afterward of Hugh Neville, a trusted royal servant, and John FitzHugh, an intimate of the sovereign he now abandoned, must have left the king stunned and tormented. To add to his troubles, he was once again short of money. On June 8, he wrote to Richard's widow, Berengaria, concerning the pension of a thousand pounds a year he had awarded her:

"Beloved Sister, once Queen of England . . . Due to the disruption of our Kingdom by the behaviour of our Barons, whom the enemy of the human race has incited against us; and moreover to the coming of Louis, who fears neither God nor Church in his efforts to seize our realm; we have already spent most of our money . . . and every day we spend more and more. Having complete faith in your affection at this time of adversity, we earnestly seek your patience and acceptance of the delay in payment of the money we owe you, until such time as by God's will the clouds disappear and this land rejoices in peace once more."

At the end of May, Gualo had summoned a number of bishops and other clerics to Winchester, "in aid of the king and the kingdom," where he solemnly pronounced an interdict on London and the lands of Louis's adherents. As the prince approached the old capital, flames burst from its suburbs, consuming supplies and equipment the royalists could not remove from the path of the invaders. By the time Louis reached the city, John had retired cautiously northwest to Ludgershall, then to Devizes, in Wiltshire. His intention may have been to lure the French toward the royalist lands of the West Midlands, drawing them further and further from their allies in the east, and the shelter of London. If so, Louis did not fall for it. Soon after overrunning Winchester, he turned back on his tracks to Odiham, a small rural community some eight miles from the scene of his earlier success at Farnham. Things had gone better for him than he might have dared hope, but there were now signs that John's supporters were recovering from their initial shock.

At Winchester, the prince had met his first determined opposition. It came from the garrison John had left in a castle at the west end of the city to cover his withdrawal. Having defied the French and their siege engines for ten days, the defenders quit their stronghold on good terms, being allowed to withdraw unmolested.

Confirmation that the first phase of Louis's offensive, his unchecked spree through Kent to London, and through Surrey to Hampshire, was over, came at Odiham Castle. Here, camped on sloping ground which fell away to thick woods and scrubby heathland to the north, the prince spent a week besieging the garrison, before agreeing that it should march out with full honours of war. To his amazement, the force which had delayed his army for seven days comprised no more than three knights and ten men-at-arms. Winchester and Odiham were by no means great defensive actions, but they dispersed the aura of irresistibility which had wreathed the French, and marked a new stage in the hostilities—one in which John's ubiquitous castles reared defiantly above the mêlée, preserving the core of royal authority while the king manoeuvred to launch a counter-stroke.

From now on, few royal fortresses fell to Louis or his allies. While the prince was in Hampshire, FitzWalter and his barons rampaged through the long-suffering eastern counties, sacking villages, occupying Colchester and Norwich, and ravaging such places as Yarmouth, Dunwich, Ipswich and King's Lynn. But FitzWalter's rebels, "laden with inestimable booty and spoils," had little taste for determined opposition, and John's castles stood intact amidst the devastation. In the East Midlands, Gilbert of Ghent, a rebel Lincolnshire baron who had been created Earl of Lincoln by Louis, threw his forces against Lincoln Castle. Gilbert spent the rest of the war besieging the fortress, without success. It cannot have consoled him that the defence was organised by a woman, Nicola of Camville, the widow of John's old adherent Gerard.

In the North, Alexander of Scotland, marching through Northumberland and Durham, achieved no significant victories. While the Scot and the local insurgents appear to have had the run of the countryside, they beat their heads vainly against the walls of John's castles. In Northumberland, every fortress was held for the Crown. At Durham, Philip Ulecotes stood firm for the king. At Barnard Castle, Philip's loyalist colleague, Hugh Balliol, not only repelled the Scottish monarch but killed his brother-in-law, Eustace of Vesci, who had joined him.

Back South, the rebels invested Windsor Castle, commanded for John by the mercenary captain Engelard of Cigogné. Louis placed his lieutenant the Count of Nevers, in charge of the operation. But the story was repeated. Windsor, albeit handy to London and defended by an unpretentious garrison, proved too much for the attackers. The siege dragged on through the summer, as did a fruitless attempt to take Dover, where Hubert of Burgh flung defiance at the French from the battlements. Louis gave his personal attention to Dover Castle, sending to France for an exceptionally powerful stone-throwing machine known as *La Malvoisine*. The garrison, including a hundred and forty knights and many lesser troops, returned its fire with such fervour that the French scuttled for cover, henceforward blockading the fortress from a respectful distance.

John, following his retirement from Winchester, spent the rest of June and the first part of July in Wiltshire and Dorset. During this period, he visited the royal castles in these counties, issued contingency plans to Crown officers in many parts of the country, and visited Corfe for a brief reunion with his family. He also took up the matter of desertion, proclaiming a general amnesty to all defectors "who might wish to return to the king's service." On July 17, he headed north for the West Midlands and those dependable territories secured by William Marshal and Ranulf of Chester, later sending for the queen and Prince Henry to follow him.

From mid-July to mid-August, John toured the Welsh March, proceeding from Bristol to Gloucester, Tewkesbury, Hereford, Leominster and Shrewsbury. His aim appears to have been three-fold: 1) to eliminate any pockets of dissent in this region, 2) to counter rebel activity in the areas of Hereford and Worcester, and 3) to replenish his resources, physical and psychological, in the royalist heartlands, in particular to enlarge his army with good, trusty warriors.

In accord with the first of these objectives, overtures were made to Reginald of Briouse, the scion of a family with close ties to the western border and little cause to like the sovereign. Briouse was offered the restoration of his heritage in return for his loyalty. The second objective was achieved through the agency of Marshal and Chester, who combined parental admonition with armed force to expel Marshal's son, William the younger, from Worcester, which he had occupied for Louis. The third, and most important measure, involved negotiations for alliances with some of the Welsh princes, the assembly of supplies for a long-range offensive, and the enlistment of seasoned frontier fighters. Savary of Mauléon and his Poitevins, never far from John's side throughout his travels, had proved their trustworthiness. If the king still nursed doubts about the remainder of his mercenaries, it must have reassured him to brace his force with hardy English border knights and Welsh bowmen, warriors he had come to respect from long experience. In a sense, his career had turned full cycle. It was from the fastness of the Cotswolds, the highlands screening the Welsh March from the southern shires, that John had launched his first bid for power, in the days of Longchamp. Twenty-five years later, he planned to unleash his last bid for survival from those same hills.

That summer, while John struggled to reassert his hegemony, his cause faced a crisis in Italy. On July 16, at the age of fifty-five, Pope Innocent III died. Had his successor abandoned the policy of backing the English king, Philip Augustus himself might have staged an invasion to support his son. For two days, the electors in Rome debated the succession. Then, on July 18, they appointed Cencio Savelli, vice-chancellor of the Holy See, a cultivated and pious Roman, to the vacant seat. In the event, Honorius III, as the new pope became known, followed the example of his predecessor in backing John against Louis and the rebels. The messenger who brought the news of Innocent's death to England was able to inform

England Invaded

the king, and Gualo, that Rome's attitude toward the hostilities was not changed.

By the end of summer, something like a pattern was emerging from the renewed confusion precipitated in England by the invasion. As in an earlier stage of the civil war, the royalists dominated the West Country and the West Midlands. Throughout the rest of the realm, the situation was intriguing. Without a royalist army in the field to inhibit them, French, Scottish and rebel forces moved freely about the country. In the North and East, John's enemies roamed at will, plundering and imposing their will on towns and villages. Alexander actually marched unchallenged across the length of the kingdom to do homage to Louis in the South. Yet the allies were unable to consolidate their advantage, to establish any real control in the area, for at each key point stood a castle—and the castles were held firmly and defiantly by king's men.

The situation vividly illustrated the importance of castles in the strategy of medieval power-politics. Small, determined garrisons in well-placed and provisioned fortresses, though unable to venture far beyond their walls, could survive as intolerable thorns in the flesh of an enemy long after the countryside itself had been overrun. As a menace to communications, as a rallying point for partisans, as an obstruction to an alternative regional administration, such garrisons could tie up enemy forces out of all proportion to their own numbers for long periods. Louis had good cause to rue the fact. Through July and August, Dover, Windsor and Lincoln, among other strategically sited royalist strongholds, occupied the attention of major French and rebel forces in sieges which yet showed little sign of succeeding. "Long were they there," wrote a chronicler of the forces surrounding Windsor Castle, "and little did it profit them."

In some areas, resistance of a more spontaneous character had burgeoned. If Englishmen objected to John's foreign mercenaries, detestation of the foreign invaders was far greater, especially since the latter were anathematized by the Church. One William of Kensham, known familiarly as Willikin of the Weald, led a band of guerrilla fighters against the French from forest hideouts on the Kent and Sussex border. Sections of the storm-swept English fleet had reassembled and were operating against French shipping with the connivance of the Cinque Ports, which, though overrun by Louis, remained steadfastly loyal in their sympathies. Correspondence between John and others of his subjects in the French-occupied regions of the South, suggests that, though compelled to swear allegiance to the French prince, they had made it known to the king that they were for him when the time came.

John promised they would not go unrewarded. "We are most grateful to you for uniting in our service," he wrote, preparing them for his offensive, "and we ask you to persevere patiently in your loyalty, ignoring the oath you unwillingly took to Louis, the son of the French king. We do not blame you for this, and, if we felt any bitterness or anger at the time, we dismiss it completely. The time has not arrived for you to assist us, but we command you to be ready for our instructions, when you may do so in the assurance that we shall repay you with your former liberties, and with such increased benefits and rewards that you will be eternally thankful to us."

Against the picture of royalist resolution in adversity, the French and their allies had emerged from the euphoria of early success to a state of mounting disunity. The French nobles who had followed Louis to England had not been motivated by any love of the rebel barons, but by the promise of English fiefs. Clearly, these could not be wrested at the outset from their allies, whom the French prince was most anxious to please when he landed. Indeed, at the insistence of William Marshal, Junior, he deprived Adam Beaumont of the office

England Invaded

of marshal of the host and bestowed it on the Englishman. "He dared not risk alienating the English," it appears, "by doing otherwise."

The result was a somewhat contradictory situation. While Louis needed English allies, the more the English went over to the French, the less the French liked it. To the French knights, the first flush of defections from John's ranks represented so many offices and estates in England placed beyond their grasp. Faced with a proliferation of claims by their allies, not to mention a seemingly interminable vista of siege duties, it was not long before some of the invaders packed up and went home. Among the first was a disillusioned Count of Holland, soon followed by a band of knights from Artois, whose withdrawal was harried by royalist ships in the Thames estuary. In the words of a contemporary, the French host "dwindled miraculously."

Gradually, Louis forsook his endeavours to satisfy his allies. Observation of FitzWalter and his followers, who had careered from London with great bravura while the French army was between them and John, but who had displayed a poor appetite for serious action, did not impress the French prince. His attitude toward them became increasingly insolent. He taunted them with their treachery and fear of John, demonstrating his distrust of them and siding with his own nobles in their disputes with the English barons. In offering the crown to Louis, the rebels had sought, in the first place, foreign help in deposing John; in the second place, a weaker king they could manage. It began to look as if they might end up dominated by a French government. Or even worse.

One story had it that the Viscount of Melun, falling critically ill in London, made an ominous confession to FitzWalter's barons on his deathbed. "It is I who grieve for you," he said, dismissing their sympathies, "for you are ignorant of the ruin and the danger which hangs over you. Louis and sixteen other

French noblemen with him have sworn that, if he subdues England and gains the throne, he will permanently banish all those English barons who are now fighting with him. As traitors to their lord, he will drive the whole pack of them from the kingdom. Lest you doubt me, I hereby declare, at the point of death, and at risk to my soul, that I was one of those who took this oath to Louis. Heed me well: look to your safety, and keep these words a secret."

Be that as it may, the rebels had plenty to worry them. Englishmen were dropped from the prince's councils, their places taken by French advisers. Two prominent rebel leaders, Vesci and Mandeville, were already dead. Lands and honours claimed by their colleagues were given increasingly to Louis's friends. When the younger Marshal claimed Marlborough Castle, which had come into French hands through the desertion of Hugh Neville, Louis overruled him, granting it to his cousin Robert of Dreux. Not content with earlier honours, the Englishman was furious. As the summer progressed, friction intensified in the allied camp. At last, the tide of defection turned in John's favour. Marshal, Junior, flounced over to the royal camp to make peace with the king and his father. The Earls of Salisbury and York returned abashedly to their allegiance, rejoining the phalanx of royalist magnates, among them the Earls of Pembroke, Chester, Derby, Sussex, Surrey, Warwick and Devon. Lesser men, invoking John's promise of amnesty, crossed the lines to place themselves at the king's mercy.

The warmth of his welcome, at once politic and spontaneous, was unstinted. Forgiveness was one of John's special graces. He bore no grudge, it would seem, against the repentant.

At the beginning of September, then, the king's intelligence was that English and French were leaving Louis in some numbers, and that many of those still in the field for the alliance lacked resolution and unity of purpose. All the same, the

Plate 15 (*right*) The effigy of William Marshal, Earl of Pembroke. (*below*) Work on the handsome round tower of Pembroke Castle was begun when he held it for the King

Plate 16 Dover Castle (once called the key of England) was besieged by the French in

enemy was numerically daunting. He had a plurality of armies deployed in the South, and the king would have to conduct his offensive with considerable guile to be rid of them. While poor communications frequently made it difficult for medieval commanders to keep in touch with the movements of their enemies, the fronts had been static long enough for John to be conversant with the major dispositions.

Louis, with a French army, was besieging Dover. The Counts of Nevers and Dreux, with a combined French and rebel army, were investing Windsor. Gilbert of Ghent, with a rebel force, was blockading Lincoln Castle. Besides these three hosts, there were the London rebels and Alexander's army. The latter was perhaps the only substantial hostile element John could not pin down. The Scottish king, having concluded his business with Louis, was on his way home again. But he had still not left the South. John would have to allow for his movements. For the rest, the pieces were set. The time had come to act. In the first week of September, after a last farewell to Isabelle and Prince Henry, the King of England flourished a gauntletted sword arm, his knights raised an eager cheer, and the royalist cavalcade swept down from the Cotswolds.

Chapter 19
THE LONG RIDE

And of some have compassion.

Jude, 22

The corn lay ripe between the Cotswolds and the Chilterns as John descended to the basin of the upper Thames and the old frontier city of Oxford, once torn between Saxon and Danelaw England. The crops, wrote Wendover, were "white to harvest." In the riverside pastures, beasts with bellies distended by summer grass blinked placidly at trumpet and clarion. Geese cackled disapproval of the approaching army. Oxford spread invitingly amidst tall trees and water meadows on a stony terrace at the confluence of the Thames and its offshoot the Cherwell. From the anguish of repeated burnings and rebuilding in bygone days, it had survived to become not only a busy rural and river-trading centre, but a seat of education and the venue of great political gatherings.

At Oxford, King Canute had proclaimed his intention to bring all England under one law. At Oxford, King Harold had advanced his claims as a peace-maker by reconciling

The Long Ride

the warrior lords of North and South. And at Oxford, where John now paused three days with his Poitevins, his Welshmen and his English knights, the king firmly proclaimed his intention of restoring his rule throughout the country.

From Oxford, cheered on its way by well-wishing citizens, the royal force surged downstream, penants rippling, through green and tranquil landscapes so characteristic of the island realm John was bent on saving from the French prince—a land described by the monk Gildas, one of the earliest British authors, as "bedecked in the jewels and finery of mankind's chosen bride." Past Abingdon, once a river port of greater importance than Oxford, swept the cavalcade; past Wallingford and Goring, following the lush valley between the White Horse Hills and the Chilterns to the township of Reading, which it entered on September 6. Between Reading and Windsor, the latter still besieged by the Count of Nevers, the river described a wide bend to the north and back; between Windsor and London, a similar sweep to the south. By ignoring these frivolities of nature, and taking a line due east across country, John was some fifteen miles from Engelard of Cigogné's stout garrison at Windsor, and about another twenty from rebel-held London.

It looked as if the king planned to drive Nevers back on London, relieve Cigogné and his garrison, and lunge straight for the great city which had so long defied him. Instead, as so often in his military method, the objective suddenly dissolves and one is left guessing. Continuing a mile or two down-river to the village of Sonning, John pitched camp and laid up for five days. Why? Why allow his enemies time to prepare against an onslaught? It is hard to find the answer. According to some chroniclers, Nevers was secretly in John's pay, in which case the king's halt between the eighth and the thirteenth may have been the occasion of negotiations between the Frenchman and the monarch. Certainly, John eschewed a full-scale attack on Nevers, though he did deploy his Welsh bowmen in a night sortie to shoot-up the besiegers at Windsor.

It is also true that the French count shortly raised the siege voluntarily and departed to join Louis at Dover. This, however, does not inevitably point to collusion. Windsor Castle had proved a daunting target—probably beyond the resources of Nevers to crack—while the English rebels in his force were unreliable and irresolute. At all events, when John's army suddenly struck camp, skirted Windsor, and unpredictably veered north across the Chilterns, the count's men gratefully burned their siege engines, gave half-hearted pursuit, and finally dispersed to London and points south. The problem of rationalizing John's last campaign is not diminished by the paucity of information available, nor by his predilection, maintained to the bitter end, for devious and deceptive tactics.

There is a suggestion that, at this stage, Alexander of Scotland was heading north from Kent through Hertford or Essex, and that the English king meant to cut him off by a wide sweep through Aylesbury and Bedford to Cambridge. It is possible that John delayed at Sonning to await news of Alexander, deeming the Scot a better prize than Nevers. One way or the other, he recaptured Cambridge from the rebels on September 17, and struck quickly across the Gog Magog Hills against their confederates in Suffolk and Essex. Following the river Stour along the border of these counties, he pulverised Clare and Hedingham before swerving north again.

Apparently satisfied that Alexander had not passed him, the king now rimmed the flat Fen country to Stamford, in the East Midlands, from which area he set up a vigorous punitive campaign against his enemies and those who had succoured or sheltered them. To the south, many rebels had scampered for the safety of London as John's offensive gained impetus. Further north, their natural refuge lay around the soggy Fens, where secret paths and island hideouts were

The Long Ride

little known save to the monks, and other denizens of the reedy marshlands.

The people of the Fens lived quiet lives, collecting osiers (used in making baskets, eel traps and so forth) and rushes (for thatching), while supplementing their subsistence from the varied water creatures which abounded in the district. "In the eddies at the sluices of the meres," wrote a medieval visitor to the fenlands, "are netted innumerable eels, large water-wolves, and pickerels, perches, roaches, burbots and lampreys, which we call water-snakes. It is said by many that salmon, and the royal fish, the sturgeon, are taken here. As for the birds which are captured hereabouts . . . you find geese, teal, coots, didappers, water-crows, herons and ducks more than man can count."

John's troops were not on the Fens for the sporting. At places known or suspected to have rebel connections, among them the manor of Peterborough and the village of Crowland, both bordering the marshes, the royal forces burned houses, barns and crops, and drove off the cattle. As the raiding parties reported their grim work, John's trumpeters sounded general muster and the army swept north into Lincolnshire. Gilbert of Ghent was petrified. Informed of John's approach, he promptly raised the siege of Lincoln Castle and "fled from the sight of the monarch, dreading his coming as that of a thunderbolt."

Occupying Lincoln on September 22, the king spent the rest of September, and the first week of October, suppressing rebel centres in the county and re-establishing his own administration. Though now far from a fit man, he taxed his dwindling energies to the utmost, seldom out of the saddle by day, when he would ride forty or fifty miles, and sitting up through the night over matters of government.

Commencing in the north of the shire and gradually working south, John hammered his enemies systematically. The time for amnesties had passed. Rebel lands were flayed without mercy. "Never in memory was so much burning known in so short a time," declared one chronicler. Town after town was occupied for the king—now Grimsby, on the east coast; next Louth, at the foot of the Lincoln wolds; then Boston, to the south; and, finally, Spalding, at the foot of the eastern shire. It was now October, and Alexander of Scotland had slipped through Lincoln and into Yorkshire while John had been elsewhere. The king made no attempt to chase "the sandy fox," riding east instead to King's Lynn, in Norfolk—perhaps in pursuit of fleeing rebels, or to set up a garrison—before returning to Lincolnshire.

Whatever his reason for calling, the citizens of Lynn, like most townsfolk, were happy to welcome him. Rebellion, and its attendant disorder, was bad for trade in general. Business prospered in the stability of a strong sovereign, and John's arrival in the town, on October 9, was treated as a festive occasion. He was given a substantial gift of money by the burghers.

To FitzWalter and his barons, John's renewed offensive must have been profoundly depressing. Like some bobbing and swaying punch-ball, the harder the king was hit, the harder he bounced back. After the fall of Winchester, men as important as William of Salisbury had considered him beaten. To many, it had seemed certain that Louis had come to stay: that the French prince had only to take his time and reduce the royal castles one by one. Now, suddenly, the astuteness of John's strategy was evident. Contracting springlike as his enemy extended, he had awaited his moment, then unleashed his concentrated resources at the weakest links of the alliance. In just over a month, he had raised the sieges of Windsor and Lincoln almost without a fight, recaptured Cambridge and other towns, demonstrated his ability to dominate East Anglia, and demolished the rebel centres in the East Midlands, once more isolating his enemies in the far North and the southeast.

In the southwest, a contrite Earl of Salisbury, together with the dependable Fawkes of Bréauté, had routed a body of Louis's adherents at Exeter. Throughout all this, the French prince had stuck grimly to Dover. There was no reassurance for him in the knowledge that reinforcements from the Continent were obliged to run the gauntlet of the king's ships.

By the second week of October, John could afford to relax a little from his long ride and enjoy the convivial entertainment offered by the citizens of King's Lynn. He was dined and wined handsomely. On the tenth of the month, he displayed his good humour by granting Margaret, the wife of Walter Lacy, some land in the royal forest of Aconbury, Hereford, on which to erect a religious house to the memory of her parents, the luckless William and Matilda Briouse. On the morrow, he would march forward to fresh triumphs. But John's body was less willing than his spirit. Two days of resting, after a gruelling regime of endless riding and little sleep, had allowed fatigue and failing health to overtake him. He was further weakened, it seems, by dysentery, a doleful sequel to the hospitality of his Norfolk supporters. In this wretched condition, he left Lynn on October 11, heading once more for Lincolnshire and the final and most persistent legend of his troubled life.

Between the coasts of Norfolk and Lincolnshire, the North Sea floods into a gaping indentation on the eastern profile of England, some fifteen miles deep and almost as far across. Shaped somewhat like the head of a battleaxe, this marine intrusion of the low-lying East Midlands, the Wash, receives the waters of four rivers, the Witham, Welland, Nene and Great Ouse. At low tide, they flow to sea through creeks surrounded by broad banks of sand and mud. Over the centuries, these estuaries have been diminished by silting, but in John's time the largest, that of the Nene (then known as the Wellstream), stretched almost ten miles inland to Wisbech, and was four and a half miles wide between the villages of Cross Keys and Long Sutton. The most direct route from King's Lynn into Lincolnshire meant keeping close to the Wash and crossing the estuary of the Nene at low tide, when local guides could pick a footing through the treacherous quicksands. Those who wished to avoid such an adventure were obliged to take a longer inland route, crossing the river at Wisbech.

Variations on John's famed encounter with the waters of the Wash differ widely. The popular legend, based largely on Wendover, has it that the king and his army, followed by the baggage train, were crossing the Nene estuary when "the land opened in the middle of the water, creating whirlpools which sucked in everything, even men and horses." According to Wendover, John and his soldiers narrowly escaped, but "he lost all his carts, wagons, sumpter horses and treasure; everything for which he had special regard."

Another version, favoured by some historians, follows Wendover's description of the actual catastrophe, but sites it at the mouth of the Welland, the next river to the Nene. There is, indeed, some room for confusion in the similarity of the river names Welland and Wellstream, the old name for the Nene. In this account, John avoids the Nene estuary by taking his army and baggage train on the circuitous route through Wisbech. Yet a further reconstruction, minimizing the episode, sets it at Wisbech, adducing that the crossing of a ford here was disrupted by an unusually early tidal surge. By this reckoning, only part of the baggage was lost, most of which could have been recovered at low water the next day.

Wendover is not to be taken too lightly in this matter, for he probably knew the Abbot of Croxton, a Lincolnshire cleric who attended John after the incident. But the chronicler

The Long Ride

did not explain one of the few incontrovertible pieces in the puzzle: the fact that John was certainly at Wisbech the night after leaving King's Lynn. The most convincing account of the episode, now widely accepted, explains this, while giving credibility to much of the popular story. It is as follows:

On October 11, John and his army set out from Lynn to take the longer road to their destination via Wisbech, where they spent the night, continuing next morning. To avoid delaying the advance unnecessarily, however, the slow-moving baggage train was dispatched separately from Lynn by the shorter route. This was not an uncommon ploy in the line of march. Troops and baggage would diverge, to reassemble at a given point. The baggage train now proceeded to the Nene estuary. The time of the month was propitious for a crossing. Spring tide was approaching and low water was far out. Led by guides with prodding-poles to test the damp sands, the party left Cross Keys and headed for Long Sutton on the far bank.

Somewhere between these two points, disaster struck. It is not possible to say how far the waggoners had penetrated the estuary, though Wendover suggested that they were in the stream itself, therefore probably a good way from either bank. Nor is it possible to say how much time they had in hand for the crossing. Autumn is a season of dense morning mists on the Fens, and it may be that the party had been delayed, or otherwise imperilled, by poor visibility. There is also a likelihood that part of the convoy became bogged.

It is only certain, so far as the tale is in any way valid, that the incoming tide overhauled the travellers, whose accruing panic is not hard to imagine. As men and animals plunged in all directions, trapped by the fast-rising waters, many a royal servant must have perished, many a priceless cargo been lost. Administrative records, state documents, the royal wardrobe and regalia, the royal chapel and relics, all were carried in the baggage train, plus the king's treasure—jewels amassed with a collector's passion from far and wide, "dozens of gold and silver goblets, flagons, basins, candelabra, phylacteries, pendants, and ornaments, the coronation regalia, plus the regalia his grandmother had worn as Empress of Germany: the great crown, the golden wand and the sword of Tristram."

One feature has yet to be married with this story. The chroniclers believed that John was personally involved in the scene at the Wash, and that he narrowly escaped a ducking. However, since the king had crossed the river at Wisbech, and was already on the far side of the estuary, he could not have set out with the baggage train. There are two possible explanations of his presence, accepting the "separate parties" hypothesis. One is that John had arranged to meet the baggage detail on the far bank. The other is that a messenger overtook him with the news that his waggons were in trouble, and that he galloped back to the estuary. In either case, he might well have ventured on the sands in a bid to help and have been forced to flee before the water.

Whatever happened, John was much affected. Continuing disconsolately to Swineshead, between the rivers Witham and Welland, he rested on the thirteenth at the Cistercian abbey at that place. He was now a dangerously sick man. Wendover, whose catalogue of the king's sins included gluttony, claimed that he aggravated his condition by "surfeiting himself with peaches and new cider." It seems an improbable choice of diet for a man gripped with dysentery, and is certainly unnecessary as an explanation of John's distress. Already a victim of gout, the ailing king had driven himself to the point of exhaustion, exposed himself in this condition to the chill vapours of the fenlands, contracted a dysenteric sickness, probably expended the last of his physical reserves on the estuary, and further suffered the trauma of this tragedy.

On October 14, in great pain and racked with fever, he made his way to Sleaford, on the road to Lincoln. Here, he

The Long Ride

was bled, and spent a restless forty-eight hours vainly hoping to regain a little strength. Still, John determined to push on against his enemies. Barely able to mount his horse, he left Sleaford on the sixteenth and headed for Newark. His objective is not known, but this break to the west, away from Lincoln, suggests a move up the Trent Valley to Nottingham. After a few miles, John was forced to dismount and continue on a litter. If Matthew Paris can be believed, the king's companions had to hack willows from the roadside with their swords to make a bed, which they covered with a horse-cloth. It had neither cushions nor straw to soften it, and John complained miserably that his bones were breaking, that the jolts were killing him. With some relish, Paris recalled an obscure French prophesy: "John shall die, a landless king, on a litter."

Unfortunately, this graphic account of what was to be the king's last journey is put in question by the fact that Paris placed it between Swineshead and Sleaford, incorrectly locating John's death at this last place. In reality, the monarch reached the Bishop of Lincoln's castle at Newark on the afternoon of the sixteenth, where he lay, spent in body, but still lucid in mind, until the night of Tuesday, October 18. Balding and grey, aged by the almost ceaseless struggles of his reign beyond his forty-nine years, he was subjected to the alleged medical skills of the Abbot of Croxton, who had been called to attend him. Almost until the end, John continued to execute business from his bedside. Convinced of his impending death, he designated his son Henry as his heir, and ordered his companions to swear allegiance to the prince. He also sent letters to his loyal sheriffs and constables, instructing them to receive the boy as their next king.

The choice of a protector for the lad was not difficult. "Before he died, he sent word to William Marshal, the Earl of Pembroke, placing his eldest son, Henry, in God's keeping and his, and imploring him, for the sake of God, to act in

Henry's interest." Among the king's last acts was the dictation of a simple will:

> Being overtaken by grievous sickness, and therefore incapable of making a detailed disposition of my goods, I commit the ordering and execution of my will to the fidelity and discretion of my faithful men whose names are given below, and without whose counsel, were they at hand, I would not, even in health, ordain anything; and I ratify and confirm whatsoever they shall faithfully ordain and determine concerning my goods, in making satisfaction to God and Holy Church for the wrongs I have done them, in sending help to the Holy Land, in supporting my sons for the recovery and defence of their heritage, in rewarding those who have served us faithfully, and in distributing alms to the poor and to religious houses for the salvation of my soul.
>
> I pray that whoever shall give them counsel and assistance shall receive God's grace and favour; and that he who may violate their settlement shall incur the curse and wrath of God Almighty, the Blessed Mary, and all the saints. First, then, I desire that my body be buried in the church of the Blessed Mary and St. Wulfstan in Worcester. Next, I appoint as ordainers and executors of my will the following: the lord Gualo, Legate of the Apostolic See; Peter, Lord Bishop of Winchester; Richard, Lord Bishop of Chichester; Silvester, Lord Bishop of Worcester; Brother Amery of St. Maure; William Marshal, Earl of Pembroke; Ranulf, Earl of Chester; William, Earl of Ferrers; William Brewer; Walter Lacy; John of Monmouth; Savary of Mauléon; Fawkes of Bréauté.

It was said that on the night of October 18, 1216, a wild wind shrieked round the palace at Newark. The Abbot of Croxton heard John's confession and administered the last sacraments. By morning, the king was dead. Outside, messengers waited with letters from some forty rebel barons who had wished to make peace with him. The corpse was hastily embalmed by the abbot, who was perhaps better fitted to this task than to healing. Salting the intestines, and by some accounts the heart too, he made off with them to Croxton Abbey, together with a pledge for land to the value of ten pounds.

The king's enemies heaped abuse on his memory. "With John's foul deeds all England is stinking,/As does hell, to which he is now sinking," wrote an uncharitable and seemingly unimaginative poet. A great many of the king's contemporaries thought otherwise. His body, regally clad, was borne in solemn procession some ninety miles across country to the Vale of Evesham, accompanied by a glittering guard of men-at-arms in full armour. Despite fervent pleas from the monks of Beaulieu that the burial should take place at their abbey, John was interred at Worcester, as he had requested.

Bishop Silvester conducted the ceremony, and the body was accorded pride of place before the high altar of the cathedral, between the shrines of St. Oswald and St. Wulfstan. In the years to come, Worcester honoured the memory of King John with an annual feast.

Five centuries later, repairs to Worcester Cathedral offered the curious a fleeting glimpse of the physical residue of a now formidable legend. In 1797, "the venerable shrine of the Monarch," as an eyewitness described it, was opened, and the remains of the "Illustrious Personage" examined. The top of the stone coffin lay level with the church floor. Inside, the contents appeared to be undisturbed. The bones of the left arm were lying bent across the ribs. The feet were upright. The teeth were in perfect condition. A burial robe of crimson damask, though faded, was undecayed. To one side lay a sword. Most remarkably, perhaps, the skull reposed in a humble monk's cowl.

Agnostic, wanton, slothful, unjust, vindictive, cruel, cowardly —the colours sloshed on the legendary portrait of John were as dark as they were fanciful. To Matthew Paris, he was "nature's enemy." Gerald of Wales described him as "the most atrocious tyrant on record." Nearer our own time, Kate Norgate could write of his "superhuman wickedness," while Sir James Ramsay saw him as "a selfish, cruel tyrant of the worst type." As the present century has progressed, historians have come to revise the picture of King John, but it still remains largely apologetic in character. The malign tradition originated by the early Church historians was potent.

Centuries after his death, the damage inflicted to John's posthumous career by the recorded opinions of his clerical and baronial enemies was to be compounded by the glorification of the baronial rebellion as some kind of democratic movement. Had John, or for that matter his father before him, been concerned with the suppression of popular causes, in any modern sense, then his rule would indeed have been an oppressive tyranny. Instead, his struggle was with a minute and highly privileged group of his subjects, who at best sought gain and power for the aristocratic fraternity, at worst, the freedom to further individual hegemonic aspirations.

Nobody of rank cared too much about the fortunes of humble folk in John's day, but it is likely that their chances were better under an all-powerful king than under an unrestrained local lord, and certain that the anarchy which threatened to submerge a weak monarch was the last thing they wanted.

As an energetic guardian of Crown authority, with a natural disposition toward peace, John had the talent and tenacity to provide strong and beneficial government. Following a brother who ruled almost entirely in absence, and a father constantly preoccupied with the Continent, John offered the English a figure they could think of more truly as their own king. He made his presence and concern felt in areas of England for which, in the past, the Crown had seemed a remote authority indeed—a distant spectre invoked, often to its prejudice, by the local sheriff. No other ruler of the country had seen fit to know it so intimately. For the last decade of his life, the king had concentrated his efforts increasingly on the government of England, and doubtless his close supervision contributed to the resentment of the more powerful and headstrong of his subjects.

John's respect for English law, and his close interest in justice, was unquestionable. The weak benefitted from it; the strong were not unprotected. John was often unfair, but he was seldom unscrupulous. For instance, discussing the disposal of Langton's temporalities after the archbishop had left England in disgrace: These should be seized, he informed his justiciar, "if you have the power to do so by English law." And they should be kept for the Crown, "if possible by lawful process." The qualifications were characteristic.

John was both extortionate and generous. There are many instances on record of his compassion toward the underprivileged, from the hearing of lawsuits virtually free of charge, to the gift of food and drink to large numbers of the impoverished. Liberal with sick-benefits for ailing followers and servants, he gave freely for charitable purposes. One of the last considerations of his life was that the poor should benefit by his passing. Nor was his nature, in the broader sense, uncharitable. He gave public support to men who had failed him in Normandy, even when their fellows derided them, and many an erring subject benefitted from his readiness to forgive and forget past discrepancies.

The worst in John was produced by fear of treachery. Reared in an atmosphere fraught with distrust and family bitterness, he harboured a propensity to suspicion which reached chronic proportions after the betrayals in Normandy. He made servants swear to report gossip against him, and he subjected William Marshal, the most steadfast and chivalrous of his adherents, to a prolonged period of distrust and humiliation. The persecution of the Briouse family, the least defensible and most damaging of the charges against him, appears to have stemmed from something akin to paranoia. On the other hand, it must be granted that there was much to provoke the king's distrust. For the best part of his life, traitors and rivals conspired to cheat him. All too often, his vassals, English and continental, placed self-interest before their oaths of fidelity. Even Salisbury, the brother he had promoted and trusted with his armies, betrayed him in a moment of peril.

Considering all, John's restraint is more remarkable than his excesses. His ambition was not wanton; his designs were not aggressive. The theme of his statesmanship was preservation rather than aggrandisement.

The overwhelming burden in John's reign, implicit in the medieval concept of birthright, was the obligation to fight for an already doomed continental empire. Into his vain attempt —alternately stubborn, skilful and audacious—to save the crumbling structure of Angevin rule in France, he poured time which would have paid dividends invested in home policy, money which had to be paid for by discontent, and loyal lives he would have resurrected gratefully in later years. With this debilitating continental inheritance came a legacy of long-standing resentment in England. Exempt from his share of the family struggle against Philip Augustus, John might have given a more attentive ear to the grumblings of English barons, which, if drowned by the thunder on the Continent, had been ominously persistent for a long time.

Considering the assiduous attention he paid to the details of home administration, even when embroiled in foreign policy, it is remarkable that John failed to remedy the baronial unrest in his kingdom before it led to rebellion. From the very start of his rule, the danger signs were manifest, while the events of 1204–5 and 1212 raised alarms of the clearest sort. Failure to reach some reconciliation with the dissidents before Magna Carta, by which time it was too late, would seem to be the crucial blunder of John's reign. Oddly enough, he was the best equipped of his family, in many ways, to do this. He had the inclination and the imagination to embrace peace. His attempts to implement the Great Charter, by now against hopeless odds, demonstrated his belated acceptance of the need for rapport between aristocracy and monarchy.

Unfortunately for John, while it is easy to say that he should have devoted more of his ingenuity and energy to cultivating the goodwill of his vassals, and less to burdening them with his fiscal problems, it is harder to say how. From Richard he had inherited financial crisis. While the war with France remained an imperative, the demand for money was remorseless. Much of it had to come, one way or another, from the baronage. In the quest for revenue through taxes, fines and assorted feudal devices, John became, of necessity, an expert extortioner. There is no evidence, however, that he innovated any money-raising methods. The precedents were there. He was simply in no position to disavow them.

Of course, John was neither a saint nor a visionary. He accepted modes of behaviour obnoxious to a later age. He took hostages on all sides. He operated a king-sized "protection racket" in the sale of goodwill and royal indulgences. He harried the lands of his enemies and their supporters without compunction. But these were the recognised techniques of medieval kings—hard men who lived in hard times—and John must be judged in relation to his period. For all the generalised assertions of cruelty made against him, there is little evidence that he was comparatively vicious, and a strong suggestion in the inconclusiveness of specific charges that he was less barbarous than many of his predecessors. Indeed, it is one of his attractions that, for all his travail and misfortune, he refused to be soured or brutalised, but retained a wide-ranging zest for life.

Unlike his austere father, John enjoyed gaiety and ornamental splendour. Unlike the hawkish Richard, he had time for gentle, aesthetic and intellectual pleasures. In many ways, not excluding his weaknesses, this much-maligned monarch emerges from the limited data available as a more "rounded" and complete human being than his precursors; thus, contrary to myth, a more endearing character. Though hard-riding and tirelessly industrious, John enjoyed a convivial court life. Good wine, rich food and resplendent dress were lavished not only on himself and his family, but on his courtiers and his guests. Yet he was not, in general, an extravagant monarch. By the standards of his day, he indulged only moderately in the expensive pastime of sporting (hawking was his favourite recreation), and was a positively mean gambler. His gaming losses were counted in shillings and not in pounds.

John was a notably literate sovereign. He formed a library of theological and other works—including such authors as Pliny, Peter the Lombard, Augustine, and Hugh of St. Victor—and read history in the French vernacular. Even during the harassing events of 1203, he had his library with him in Normandy. He was also a connoisseur of fine jewelry and a collector of *objets d'art*.

That John was irreligious, as his detractors insisted, is hard to accept. Clearly, he was not outstandingly pious, and at times he appears to have lost patience with the protracted sermonising and ceremonial to which he was subjected by zealous ecclesiastics. But he was by no means alone in that. Where politics and religion intermixed—as they did frequently when prelates were also great secular lords with voices in the lay affairs of shire and state—John claimed the traditional right of the king to intervene as "Christ's deputy" among his subjects. For this, he spent a considerable time under papal anathema. But it is also true that, following his redemption, he was applauded and supported consistently by the Roman Church.

Like other kings, John regularly gave sums of money, or gifts of plate and furnishings, to religious houses. And, like others, he was ready to do penance when he broke the rules of the Church. Contrary to the assertions of hostile chroniclers, the king was never bereft of friendship among clerics, even through the interdict. His founding of Beaulieu Abbey as recompense to a body of monks who had been troubled by his foresters, was a spontaneous and generous gesture, while the granting of a site for a memorial to the Briouse family concluded the royal life on a note of contrition and humility. By and large, religion appears to have been neither more nor less important to John's personal philosophy than to the lives of a great many contemporaries. Following his death, chaplains at Worcester, Chichester, and elsewhere in the kingdom, said Masses for "John of blessed memory."

Altogether, John's interests were wide and positive. He reformed the coinage, developed the royal Navy, and presided over a dramatic expansion in the nation's public records, including the institution of the Charter Rolls (preserving charters granted by the king), the Patent Rolls (letters patent), the Close Rolls (private letters), the Liberate Rolls (orders for payment of money), the Prestita Rolls (advances made to public servants), the Misae Rolls (the king's household expenditure) and the Rolls of Fines and Offerings. The beginnings of a collegiate system at Oxford stemmed from John's reign. The *Universitas,* or guild of travelling scholars, was established there in Richard's time, but the boarding of students in halls under a principal was developed under John's rule, and the first mention of a chancellor comes in 1214. The king also took an active part in pressing forward the construction of

London Bridge, importing a bridge-building expert, Isambard, Master of the Schools at Saintes, to hasten its completion.

Through his interest in towns, trade and commerce, John was involved with commoners, burghers and citizens, and came to be identified with their well-being to a greater extent than most barons. As a consequence, the majority of urban communities in England, with the notable exception of London, which housed a rebel army, were for the king in the civil war.

Not the least of John's attributes was his flair for surrounding himself with officers who, unlike many of his barons, were distinguished by impeccable loyalty. In such administrators as Geoffrey FitzPeter, Hubert Walter and Peter of Roches, and such military captains as Mauléon, Bréauté and Cigogné, among others, he chose men of extraordinary fidelity and capability. He was himself an ingenious administrator and a shrewd strategist. When pugnacious barons dubbed him "John Softsword," they paid unwitting tribute to his preference for negotiation rather than violence. The inference that he was a feeble soldier is a false one. No medieval English warrior dealt so successfully with the Scots, Welsh and Irish; Mirebeau and the siege of Rochester Castle demonstrated his dash and his doggedness; Philip and Louis could have testified to the bemusing intrepidity of his generalship. Indeed, with better support from his barons, he might at last have succeeded in Poitou.

Instead, he faced a French army and the rebel host in his own kingdom. While friends despaired and enemies exulted, John picked his time, then launched a characteristically cerebral offensive. He died fighting, straining the last ounce of his failing energy toward a victory—once seemingly improbable—which had begun to look not only feasible but likely.

EPILOGUE

Unluckily for Louis, while John might have lived to beat him, the death of the English king was of little help to the Frenchman. The choice for England was now between an arrogant foreigner intent on establishing his compatriots in the kingdom, and a malleable royal child of nine years. Not surprisingly, the baronial swing toward John, apparent in his last months, considerably accelerated when Prince Henry succeeded him. At the news of his father's demise, the boy was carried from Devizes to Gloucester, where, on October 28, he was crowned in the abbey church by Peter of Roches, Bishop of Winchester. The legate Gualo directed the ceremony, and it was said that the widowed Isabelle provided a golden circlet to replace the state crown lost in the sands of the Nene estuary.

Next day, in the great hall of Gloucester Castle, an assembly of loyalist barons accepted the septuagenarian William Marshal as regent, while the Bishop of Winchester received charge of the king's person. On November 11, before a solemn gathering of lay and ecclesiastical lords at Bristol, a modified version of Magna Carta, stripped of some of its more controversial clauses, was issued as a royalist manifesto. This move, not lacking in irony, both weakened the standing of the rebels and conveniently saved the face of those who wished to change sides. That winter, they trickled across to the king's lines. Spring, and a resounding victory for Marshal and Bréauté at Lincoln, brought the turncoats flocking in. By midsummer, Louis was screaming for reinforcements. A strong body of these set sail from France in August, but were intercepted by the royal fleet off Sandwich and demolished or scattered. At last, the plans John had so carefully laid to save the kingdom at sea had been justified. In September, Louis renounced his pretensions and evacuated England.

For much of a remarkably lengthy reign of fifty-six years, Henry III cherished hopes of recovering the continental possessions lost by his father. But he lacked stability, and the tide of history had long since turned against the venture. In 1230 and 1242, he mounted expeditions to France which were repulsed, the latter disastrously for his army. Eventually, in a treaty ratified at the end of 1259, he gave up all claims to Normandy, Anjou, Touraine, Maine and Poitou.

As Henry's star described its orbit, those of his father's firmament survived their allotted spans and burned out. In 1219, William Marshal died at his manor at Caversham, near Reading, full of glory and honours. He was succeeded as regent by Hubert of Burgh, who acquired great wealth at the expense of his reputation before dying in 1243. Isabelle, neglected by her son's guardians, left England for her native Angoulême, married Hugh, Count of La Marche, to whom she had been betrothed in childhood, and increased her progeny by five sons. One, Aymer of Valence, lived to become Bishop of Winchester. In old age, Isabelle retired to the abbey at Fontevrault, where, in 1246, she died beside the graves of the in-laws of her royal marriage.

John's second son by Isabelle, Richard, became Earl of Cornwall and King of the Romans. Passing from English to German history, he eventually died within six months of his brother Henry. Joan, the eldest of their full sisters, married Alexander II of Scotland, perishing prematurely at twenty-six, supposedly of the northern climate. The second sister, Isabelle, expired in 1241, six years after marrying Emperor Frederick II, while the third girl, Eleanor, having twice married (to the younger William Marshal and the younger Simon of Montfort, Earl of Leicester), eventually outlived her brothers by three years.

Of John's illegitimate offspring, one daughter had married Llywelyn of Wales, and another an Earl of Chester. Several sons joined the ranks of the English barony. One, Richard, married an heiress of the Lucy family; two more, Geoffrey and Oliver, received lands in Kent, the latter falling on crusade; a fourth, another Richard, became sheriff of Berkshire, and gained the distinction of slaying the admiral of Louis's invasion fleet, Eustace the Monk, on his own deck. None of John's children, legitimate or otherwise, can have had much chance to get to know their bustling and ever busy father.

His mortal enemy, Philip Augustus, must have known John far better. It is a pity that the shrewd Frenchman, having pitted his wits against three Angevin monarchs, left no objective testimony to their merits before he died in 1223, three years before Louis. He would have been astonished at the low rating placed on John by posterity, for none knew better then Philip the forces arrayed against the small king. Like the victim of some epic Greek tragedy, John was doomed to adversity. He never gave up fighting. He won battle after battle. It was neither through weakness nor tardiness that he never won the war.

SELECT BIBLIOGRAPHY

Henry II and Richard I were memorably portrayed in the chronicles of writers who not only lived in their own times, but who knew them personally. Roger of Howden's chronicle of the two kings was written from the vantage point of his own service in the royal household. Ralph Diceto, Dean of St. Paul's, wrote as a familiar of royalty and court society. Gerald of Wales knew the royal family and many who surrounded it. Unfortunately for the seeker of John's image, however, the chroniclers of his own reign included no one who knew him at first hand. By 1203, Howden and Diceto were dead, and, while Gerald of Wales survived to the end of John's lifetime, his writings were recollections of earlier days. William Marshal's biographer provided an occasional glimpse of the king, but for any chronicle with pretensions to insight one is obliged to turn to scribes of a later generation. For this reason, the ready imagination and prejudice of Roger of Wendover and Matthew Paris have tended to dominate the later portraiture of King John.

Luckily, while the narrative sources dwindled, the royal archives expanded. The contents of charters, the royal itinerary, the king's orders to his officers, his letters, his accounts, items of wardrobe, jewelry, and so on, have survived to contribute to the knowledge of John's life. Among other records, the Charters of Liberties, culminating in Magna Carta, are printed in Vol. I of *Statutes of the Realm,* 1810; more royal charters of John's reign can be found in *Calendar of Charter Rolls,* 1903-27; an itinerary of King John is included in an introduction to the Patent Rolls, printed by T. Duffus Hardy for the Record Commission, *Rotuli Litteratum Patentium,* 1835; orders for treasury payments are in *Liberate Rolls,* ed. T. Duffus Hardy for Record Commission, 1844; payments for royal favours are in *Rotuli de Oblatis et Finibus,* ed. T. Duffus Hardy for Record Commission, 1835.

Records of the daily expenses of the royal court, wages and payments into the treasury can be found in *Rotuli de Liberati ac de Misis et Praestitis,* ed. T. Duffus Hardy for the Record Commission, 1844; and *Documents Illustrative of English History in the Thirteenth and Fourteenth Centuries,* ed. H. Cole for the Record Commission, 1844. Law books of the twelfth and thirteenth centuries are in *Die Gesetze der Angelsachsen,* by F. Liebermann, Halle: Max Niemeyer, 1903-16; while some notes on thirteenth-century judicial procedure by Charles Johnson appear in *English Historical Review,* lxii, London, 1947.

For a full review of material available the reader should consult *The Sources and Literature of English History* by C. Gross, London: Longmans, 1915; M. S. Giuseppe's *Guide to the Manuscripts Preserved in the Public Record Office,* London: Stationary Office, 1923-24; and A. Molinier's *Les Sources de l'histoire de France,* Paris: Picard et Fils, 1901-6.

Among original authorities for John's reign, and earlier, to whom reference is made in the preceding narrative are:

THE ANGLO-SAXON CHRONICLE. A combination of annals scripted by a series of monks working in English monasteries between the period of Alfred the Great and the second half of the twelfth century. The basic narrative authority for Anglo-Saxon history. *The Anglo-Saxon Chronicle,* tr. G. N. Garmonsway. London: Dent, 1953.

ANNALES MONASTICI. The monastic chronicles collected under this title include writings from Bermondsey, Burton, Dunstable, Tewkesbury, Waverly, Winchester and Worcester. They are of interest mainly in connection with the early years of the thirteenth century, particularly on Church matters. *Annales Monastici,* ed. H. R. Luard. London: Rolls Series, 1864–69.

THE BARNWELL CHRONICLE. The work of an anonymous canon of the Austin priory at Barnwell, near Cambridge, writing a decade or so after John's death. The Barnwell annals are perhaps the best of the early commentaries on John's reign. Though somewhat lacking in chronology, they offer a relatively impartial and balanced opinion of the king. In *Memoriale Walteri de Coventria,* ed. W. Stubbs. London: Rolls Series, 1872–73.

THE BAYEUX TAPESTRY. A picture story vitally important to the understanding of the Norman invasion of England, worked by unknown craftsmen within living memory of the battle of Hastings—possibly under the orders of Bishop Odo of Bayeux. *The Bayeux Tapestry,* by Sir F. Stenton and others. London: Phaidon Press, 1957.

GERVASE OF CANTERBURY. Gervase became a monk of Christ Church in 1163 and probably began writing his chronicle about 1188. Its scope extends from the mythical ages to about the middle of John's reign, after which the work was continued by another hand. *The Historical Works of Gervase of Canterbury,* ed. W. Stubbs, London: Rolls Series, 1879–80.

RALPH OF COGGESHALL. Abbot of the Cistercian house of Coggeshall, Essex, from 1207 to his death in 1228. Ralph recorded information gathered from knowledgeable visitors to the abbey and made notes on local events. As one of the principal narrative sources for John's reign, his chronicle is sometimes illuminating, but too often trivial and scrappy. *Chronican Anglicanum,* ed. J. Stevenson. London: Rolls Series, 1875.

WALTER OF COVENTRY. Writing at the end of the thirteenth century and the beginning of the fourteenth, Walter compiled a history from the earliest times up to 1225, using the works of earlier authors for his materials. From 1201, his history incorporates the Barnwell Chronicle. *Memoriale Walteri de Coventria,* ed. W. Stubbs. London: Rolls Series, 1872–73.

RICHARD OF DEVIZES. A Winchester monk writing in the last decade of the twelfth century. His life of Richard I is the earliest on record, and his account of events in England between 1189 and 1192 is particularly important. *De Rebus Gestis Ricardi Primi.* In Vol. III, *Chronicles of the Reigns of Stephen, Henry II and Richard I,* ed. R. Howlett. London: Rolls Series, 1884–90.

RALPH DICETO. In 1180, Diceto, a Frenchman, became Dean of St. Paul's after an earlier appointment as archdeacon of Middlesex. For the next twenty-two years—his history closes in 1202—he is a useful authority. He knew many people of importance, especially churchmen, and could write of them with familiarity. *Radulphi Diceto Opera Historica,* ed. W. Stubbs. London: Rolls Series, 1876.

WILLIAM FITZSTEPHEN. Twelfth-century itinerant justice, sheriff of Gloucestershire and biographer of Thomas Becket, whose murder he witnessed while serving in the archbishop's household. His life of Becket contains a celebrated description of social life in London at the time. *Vita S. Thomae.* In J. C. Robertson's *Materials for the History of Thomas Becket,* Vol. III. London: Rolls Series, 1877.

GERALD OF WALES. Son of a Norman-Welsh union, Gerald studied in Paris, became chaplain to Henry II and went to Ireland with John's first expedition. His social observations on the people of the British Isles are lively and colourful, but his history is marred by his venomous hostility toward Henry II (and John), whose sinfulness he expounded under the cheeky title *For the Instruction of Princes*. In *Giraldi Cambrensis Opera*, Vol. VIII, ed. G. F. Warner. London: Rolls Series, 1861–91.

EDWARD GRIM. Cleric and native of Cambridge who arrived in Canterbury on a visit to Thomas Becket in time to witness the murder of the archbishop, and later wrote his life. *Materials for the History of Thomas Becket*, ed. J. C. Robertson. London: Rolls Series, 1875–85.

HISTOIRE DES DUCS DE NORMANDIE ET DES ROIS D'ANGLETERRE. The anonymous writer responsible for the part of this work relating to John's reign appears to have been a witness to some of the events, *histoire des ducs de normandie et des rois d'angleterre*. Ed. F. Michel. Paris: Société de l'Histoire de France, 1840.

HISTOIRE DE GUILLAUME LE MARECHAL. A Norman-French metrical of the life of William Marshal written by an anonymous rhymer at the request of Marshal's son. As a study of a great man and a chivalrous knight whose influence spread over four reigns, the work is of much political and social interest. *Histoire de Guillaume le Maréchal*, ed. Paul Meyer. Paris: Société de l'Histoire de France, 1891–1901.

ROGER OF HOWDEN (or Hoveden). Educated in Durham under Bishop Hugh Puiset, Roger, who took his name from the village of Howden in the East Riding of Yorkshire, served for many years as a clerk in the royal household. His chronicle—which includes revised versions of lives of Henry II and Richard I once ascribed to Benedict of Peterborough, but now considered to be the original work of Roger himself—is a source of major importance up to its close in 1201, probably the year of Roger's death. *Chronica Magistri Rogeri de Houedene,* ed. W. Stubbs. London: Rolls Series, 1868–71.

ITINERARIUM REGIS RICARDI. A vivid record by an anonymous writer—probably a canon of Holy Trinity, Aldgate—of the third crusade. The author, who was with Richard in the Holy Land, paints a fulsome portrait of the English king, but provides some memorable incident and anecdotes. *Itinerarium Perigrinorum et Gesta Ricardi.* In *Chronicles and Memorials of the Reign of Richard I,* ed. W. Stubbs. London: Rolls Series, 1864.

WILLIAM OF MALMESBURY. Post-Conquest writer combining scholarship with literary merit whose work, reflecting the new continental influence of the Normans, attracted a wide following. For the reign of Henry I and part of that of Stephen he is a strictly contemporary authority. *Historia Regum* and *Historia Novella,* ed. W. Stubbs. London: Rolls Series, 1887–89.

WALTER MAP. Courtier and wit of the late twelfth and early thirteenth centuries. Map, the scion of a well-born Herefordshire family, studied at Paris under Girard la Pucelle before joining the royal household as a clerk to Henry II. He was also an itinerant justice and the holder of a plurality of ecclesiastical benefices. His reminiscences of court life are worldly and satirical. *De Nugis Curialum,* ed. T. Wright. London: Camden Society, 1815.

WILLIAM OF NEWBURGH. Born at Bridlington, Yorkshire, in 1136, William became canon of the Augustinian priory of St. Mary Newburgh in the North Riding, where he wrote his history, before dying around the end of the century. His work is distinguished by its literary merit and sound judgement. *Historia Rerum Anglicarum,* ed. R. Howlett. London: Rolls Series, 1884–85.

RALPH NIGER. Studied in Paris, supported Becket, and was banished from England by Henry II. His chronicles, like the works of Gerald of Wales, are remarkable for their hostility towards

Henry II. *The Chronicles of Ralph of Niger,* ed. R. Anstruther. London: Caxton Society, 1851.

MATTHEW PARIS. Born 1200, became a monk of St. Albans, Hertfordshire, at the age of seventeen, and succeeded Roger of Wendover as historiographer at that house in 1236. His history of John's reign is virtually a transcript of Wendover's *Flores,* complete with original infidelities and a good deal of imaginative elaboration. *Chronica Majora,* ed. H. R. Luard, London: Rolls Series, 1872–74.

ORDERIC VITAL. Born in England on the morrow of the Norman invasion and sent, at the age of eleven, to a Norman monastery. Orderic met many war veterans of the Conquest period and wrote shrewdly of their lives and times. *Historia Ecclesiastica,* ed. A. le Provost. Paris: Société de l'Histoire de France, 1838–55.

ROGER OF WENDOVER. A monk of St. Albans, Hertfordshire, who began to write a few years after John's death. Down to 1202, Wendover's work is seemingly a compilation of materials already available at St. Albans, but from this date it becomes original. Unfortunately, since he provided ostensibly one of the most detailed accounts of John's reign, he set no great store by accuracy, and his writing is highly prejudiced. Much of his work is parabolic rather than objective. *Flores Historiarum,* ed. H. G. Hewlett. London: Rolls Series, 1886–89.

Some collected records and other documents:

Catalogue des Actes de Philippe Auguste, ed. L. Deslisle. Paris: A. Durand, 1856.
English Historical Documents, Vol. II, 1042–1189, ed. D. C. Douglas and G. W. Greenaway. London: Eyre & Spottiswode, 1953.

English Historical Documents, Vol. III, 1189–1327, ed. H. Rothwell. London: Eyre & Spottiswode, 1961.
Magna Carta, ed. W. S. McKechnie. Glasgow: James Maclehose & Sons, 1915.
Pleas before the King or his Justices, 1198–1202, ed. D. M. Stenton. London: Selden Society, 1952–53.
Select Charters, ed. W. Stubbs. Oxford: Clarendon Press, 1921.
Selected Letters of Pope Innocent III concerning England, 1198–1216, ed. C. K. Cheney & W. H. Semple. London: Thomas Semple & Sons, 1953.

General:

Appleby, John T. *John, King of England.* New York: Alfred A. Knopf, 1959.
d'Auvergne, E. B. *John, King of England.* London: Grayson, 1934.
Barlow, F. *The Feudal Kingdom of England.* London: Longmans, 1962.
Brooke, C. N. L. *From Alfred to Henry III.* London: Nelson, 1961.
Brooks, F. W. *The English Naval Forces,* 1199–1272. London: A. Brown & Sons, 1933.
Brown, R. A. *English Medieval Castles.* London: Batsford, 1954.
Carttellieri, A. *Philip II August.* 4 vols. Leipzig: Dyksche Buchhandlung, 1899–1921.
Cazel, F. A., & Painter, S. *The Marriage of Isabelle of Angoulême.* London: *English Historical Review,* lxii, 1948; lxvii, 1952.
Chrimes, S. B. *An Introduction to the Administrative History of Medieval England.* Oxford: Basil Blackwell, 1952.

Darby, H. C. *An Historical Geography of England before A.D. 1800.* Cambridge: Cambridge University Press, 1936.

Duggan, A. *Devil's Brood, the Angevin Family.* London: Faber & Faber, 1957.

Guignebert, C. *A Short History of the French People.* Tr. F. G. Richmond. London: Allen & Unwin, 1930.

Holt, J. C. *The Barons and the Great Charter.* London: *English Historical Review,* lxx, 1955.

Holt, J. C. *The Making of Magna Carta.* London: *English Historical Review,* lxxii, 1957.

Hope, W. St. John. *The Loss of King John's Baggage Train in the Wellstream in October 1216.* London: *Archaelogia,* lx, 1906.

Hyett, F. A. *Gloucester in National History.* Gloucester: Bellows; London: Kegan & Paul, 1906.

Jolliffe, J. E. A. *Angevin Kingship.* London: Adam & Black, 1955.

Kitchen, G. W. *Winchester.* London: Longmans, 1890.

Knight, C. B. *A History of the City of York.* York and London: Herald, 1944.

Knowles, D. *The Evolution of Medieval Thought.* London: Longmans, 1962.

Knowles, M. D. *The Monastic Order in England, 943–1216.* Cambridge: Cambridge University Press, 1949.

Krehbiel, E. B. *The Interdict, Its History and Operation.* Washington: American Historical Association, 1909.

Lacroix, P. *France in the Middle Ages.* New York: Ungar, 1963.

Lot, F. *L'Art Militaire et les Armées au Moyen Age.* 2 vols. Paris: Payot, 1946.

Marriott, Sir J. *Oxford: Its Place In National History.* Oxford: Clarendon Press, 1933.

Mead, W. E. *The English Medieval Feast.* London: Allen & Unwin, 1931.

SELECT BIBLIOGRAPHY

Mitchell, S. K. *Studies in Taxation under John and Henry III*. New Haven: Yale University Press, 1914.

Moorman, J. R. H. *Church Life in England in the 13th Century*. Cambridge: Cambridge University Press, 1946.

Norgate, K. *England Under the Angevin Kings*. 2 vols. London: Macmillan, 1887.

Norgate, K. *John Lackland*. London: Macmillan, 1902.

Norgate, K. *Richard the Lionheart*. London: Macmillan, 1924.

Oman, Sir C. *A History of the Art of War in the Middle Ages*. London: Methuen, 1898.

Oman, Sir C. *England Before the Norman Conquest*. London: Methuen, 1949.

Orpen, G. H. *Ireland Under the Normans,* Vol II, 1169–1216. Oxford: Clarendon Press, 1911.

Painter, S. *William Marshal*. Baltimore: Johns Hopkins, 1933.

Painter, S. *The Reign of King John*. Baltimore: Johns Hopkins, 1949.

Poole, A. L. *Obligations of Society in the 12th and 13th Centuries*. Oxford: Clarendon Press, 1946.

Poole, A. L. *From Domesday Book to Magna Carta, 1087–1216*. Oxford: Clarendon Press, 1966.

Powicke, F. M. *The Loss of Normandy*. Manchester: at the University Press, 1913.

Powicke, F. M. *Stephen Langton*. Oxford: Clarendon Press, 1928.

Powicke, F. M. *Christian Life in the Middle Ages, and Other Essays*. Oxford: Clarendon Press, 1935.

Ramsay, Sir James H. *The Angevin Empire*. London: Swan Sonnenschein; New York: Macmillan, 1903.

Round, J. H. *Feudal England*. London: Swan Sonnenschein, 1895.

Round, J. H. *The Commune of London, and Other Studies*. London: Constable, 1899.

Stenton, D. M. *English Society in the Early Middle Ages.* London: Penguin, 1951.

Stubbs, W. *Seventeen Lectures on Medieval and Modern History.* Oxford: Clarendon Press, 1887.

Thierry, A. *The Norman Conquest.* London: Dent, 1957.

Tilley, A. (ed.) *Medieval France.* Cambridge: Cambridge University Press, 1922.

Tout, T. F. *France and England . . . in the Middle Ages and Now.* Manchester: Manchester University Press, 1922.

Toy, S. *A History of Fortifications from 3000 B.C. to A.D. 1700.* London: Heinemann, 1955.

Warren, W. L. *King John.* London: Eyre & Spottiswode, 1961.

Weymouth, A. *London and Londoners.* London: Williams & Norgate, 1951.

INDEX

Abingdon, England, 106, 319, 375
Aconbury Forest, 379
Acre, Palestine, 61–63, 64, 65, 66
Adrian IV, pope, 21
Aelfric, abbot, quoted, 88
Agnes, Queen of France, 92
Albigensian Heresy, 231, 339
Albini, Nicholas of, 345
Albini, Philip of, 289, 295
Albini, William of. *See* Aumale, William of Albini, Count of
Alençon, France, 67, 131
Alençon, John of, 75
Alexander III, pope, 10, 12, 26
Alexander, King of Scotland, 281, 311, 343, 344; border raids (1216), 348, 349, 363, 366; march across England (1216), 369, 373, 376, 378
Alexander II, King of Scotland, 395
Alfonso VIII, King of Castile, 96
Alfred the Great, 152, 222
Alice, Princess of France, 31, 33–34, 54, 61, 67
Alice of Maurienne, 12, 15
Alnwick, Northumberland, 44, 260
Amercements, 303–4, 310
Amery, master of the English Knights Templar, 289, 295
Angers, France, 84–85, 93, 97, 130; John's attack (1206) on, 161–62; English invasion (1214), 236, 237

Angevin dynasty, *xiv, xx–xxi, xxvi–xxvii,* 12–13, 14, 15, 16, 148; English resentment of, *xii–xiii,* 142, 388; forest laws of, *xx,* 187, 286, 290; Philip II of France and, 30–31, 33, 35, 66, 67, 85, 113, 127, 146, 162, 252, 339, 359, 388, 395; elective monarchy and, 80, 81, 85; government centralisation under, 109, 134, 155, 223, 252, 254, 294, 301, 304–5, 306, 309
Anglo-Saxon Chronicle, 152
Anglo-Saxons, 189–91, 271–72
Angoulême, Aymer, Count of, 101–2, 103, 108, 130
Angoulême, France, 101–2, 103, 108, 162, 233, 234, 239
Angoumois, Angoulême, 101–102, 103
Anjou, Geoffrey Plantagenet, Count of, *xx–xxiii,* 9
Anjou, France, *xii, xx, xxiv, xxvi,* 13, 15, 16, 34, 113, 117, 394; accession of John and, 80, 81–82, 85, 86, 93, 111; William of Roches as seneschal, 129–30; Normandy's loss to France and, 130, 131; French capture of, 159; John's attack (1206), 161–62; English invasion (1214) of, 236, 237
Annals of Margam, 125, 128, 129; on the interdict, 178

Annals of Southwark, 259
Anselm, archbishop, 163
Antioch, *xxv*
Antwerp, Flanders, 71
Aquitaine, William IX, Duke of, *xxiv*
Aquitaine, France, *xxiv, xxvi,* 148; Richard I and, 9, 16, 58, 61, 76; John's inheritance of, 82, 91, 101; Lusignan dispute and, 110; Philip II attacks on, 130–31, 160–62; English invasion (1214) of France and, 232; English troop recruitment (1215) in, 323, 342
Aragon, kingdom of, 101, 218, 231
Argentan, Oliver of, 335
Argentan, Richard of, 335
Argentan, Normandy, 149
Armies, 28, 29, 389; freeman service in, 24–25, 230, 232, 341; mercenary recruitment, 25, 47, 67–68, 76, 86, 89, 110, 114–15, 135, 140, 143, 144, 160, 267, 301, 310, 316, 321, 323, 329–30, 333–34, 335, 339, 341–42, 361–62; in siege warfare, 31–32, 34, 62–63, 115–16, 144, 161, 234–35, 237–38, 240–41, 334–37, 365–66, 369; guerrilla modes and, 42, 43–44, 370; crusader, 60–66; prisoner treatment in, 77, 124–25, 128, 206, 247–48, 335, 337, 345; of Arthur of Brittany, 85, 92; as royal guards, 90, 97, 101; river warfare of, 137–38; camp followers of, 139–40; national levy, 155–56, 157, 158, 159, 160, 209, 216; engineering corps, 210, 335; baronial refusals to fight, 224–25, 253–54, 255, 392; pitched battles and, 240–47; baronial revolt and, 265, 267, 268–69, 275–76, 277–79, 281–85, 315–16, 319, 323, 326, 328–30, 333–34, 341–42 344–45; limits on foreign service of, 286, 287, 290, 299; John's English campaigns (1216), 345–52, 354; French invasion (1216) of England and, 361, 362, 363–64, 365–67, 368, 369, 371–73, 375–79
Arques, Normandy, 116, 139
Arsuf, Palestine, 64
Arthur of Brittany, 31, 46, 49, 60, 232; John's accession and, 78, 79–80, 81, 84–85, 86, 91, 92–93, 97, 100; Philip II alliance, 113, 114–17, 126, 127–28; John's capture of, 116, 117, 129–30; disappearance of, 125–30, 146, 203, 206, 357, 359
Articles of the Barons, 286, 287
Arundel, William, Earl of, 89, 264, 289, 295, 318, 364
Arundel, Sussex, *xxii*
Asser, cited, 272
Assizes, 302, 303
Athée, Gerard of, 159, 202, 205, 269
Athelwold, bishop, 222, 223
Aumale, Hawise, Countess of, 184
Aumale, William of Albini, Count of, 109, 279, 316, 317, 364; Rochester and, 329, 332–33, 334, 336, 337, 341, 345
Aumale, France, 194
Austria, 61, 65, 66
Auvergne, France, *xxvii*

Bacon, Roger, quoted, 229
Baldwin, archbishop, 100
Baldwin IX of Flanders, 91, 114
Baldwin IV of Jerusalem, 18, 33
Baldwin V of Jerusalem, 33
Balliol, Hugh of, 343, 366
Balun, Maine, 92
Bangor, Wales, 199
Bar, Theobald, Count of, 194
Bardolph, Hugh, 48, 74
Barfleur, France, *xviii,* 141
Barnard Castle, 366
Barnard's Castle, London, 261, 277
Barnwell annalist, quoted, 79, 258, 259, 335

INDEX

Baronies, 88–89, 251–392. *See also* Nobles, the
Barres, William of, 245
Bassett, Alan, 285, 295
Bassett, Thomas, 82, 285, 295
Bath, Bishops of, 178, 180, 222, 289, 295, 320
Bath, England, 5
Baugé, Hugh, 116
Bayeaux tapestry, 39, 58
Bayeux, France, 111, 141, 149, 163
Baynard's Castle, London, 211–12
Beauchamp, William of, 269, 280
Beaufort-en-Vallée, France, 84
Beaulieu Abbey, 106, 182, 385, 391; abbot of, 179, 215
Beaumont, Adam, 361, 370–71
Beaumont, Robert. *See* Leicester, Robert of Beaumont, Earl of
Beaumont Palace, Oxford, 5
Beauvais, Bishop of, 77, 242, 243, 246–47
Beauvais, France, 76–77, 164
Becket, Thomas à, 9–12, 14, 22, 26, 50, 95, 128, 296
Bede, 107; quoted, 106, 271
Bedford, England, 269, 277, 278, 349, 376
Beer, 95
Bela III, King of Hungary, 65
Belvoir Castle, 345
Benedict of Peterborough, 67
Bennington Castle, 211
Berengaria of Navarre, Queen of England, 54, 61, 100–1, 148; pension of, 111, 364–65
Berkhampstead Castle, 275
Berkshire, England, 395
Berkshire Castle, 54
Berwick, Scotland, 348
Bethune, Robert of, 281, 333–34
Bible, the, 173
Bigod, Roger. *See* Norfolk, Roger Bigod, Earl of
Blanche of Castile, Queen of France, 96–97, 148, 339
Blois, France, *xx*, 31, 62

Bohun, Henry of. *See* Hereford, Henry of Bohun, Earl of
Bonmoulins, France, 33
Bonneville, France, 140
Bordeaux, Archbishop of, 160
Bordeaux, France, 97, 101, 161
Boston, England, 378
Boudicca, 271
Boulogne, Renaud of Dammartin, Count of, 91, 92, 114, 153, 158; Anglo-German alliance and, 194, 230; John's papal reconciliation and, 217, 220; at Bouvines, 242, 244, 246, 247, 248
Boulogne, France, 49, 194
Bourg-sur-Mer, France, 161
Boutavant, Normandy, 161
Boutavant, Normandy, 113
Bouvines, battle of, 240–48, 282, 361
Boves, Hugh of, 241, 242, 246, 290, 323, 328; shipwreck of, 329–30, 333, 360
Brabant, Henry, Duke of, 153, 230, 242, 246
Brabant, Flanders, 329
Brantfield, Elias of, 172
Braybrook, Henry, 269, 276
Bréauté, Fawkes of, 202, 276, 284, 379, 384, 392, 394; London occupation (1216) and, 344, 350
Brewer, William, 384
Bridgenorth, England, 104, 275
Bridges, 185, 272, 309, 333
Briouse family, 264, 302, 367, 388, 391
Briouse, Giles of, Bishop of Hereford, 263, 276, 327
Briouse, John of, 317
Briouse, Matilda of, 203–4, 205–6, 207, 208, 302, 306; memorial, 379, 391
Briouse, Reginald of, 367–68
Briouse, William of, 82, 128–29, 154, 202, 379; revolt of, 203–4, 205–7, 208, 213, 214, 263
Bristol, England, *xxii*, 5, 22, 275, 316, 367; Magna Carta manifesto of, 393–94

Brittany, Conan, Duke of, 9
Brittany, Peter, Count of, 236, 237, 323
Brittany, *xxvii*, 9, 14, 17, 58, 65, 149; John Lackland and, 79–80, 81, 82, 85, 92, 97, 115, 159; Arthur's disappearance and, 127, 129, 130; English invasion of France (1214) and, 232, 236–37
Bruneswald Forest, 3
Bruyere, William, 48
Buck, Walter, 329
Buckingham, England, 317
Burgate, Robert, 351
Burgh, Hubert of, 127, 159, 394; baronial revolt and, 282, 285; Magna Carta and, 289, 295; as justiciar, 291, 318; French invasion (1216) and, 362, 367
Burgundy, Duke of, 242, 244
Burgundy, 57
Burial, 177, 217
Burke, Edmund, quoted, 142
Bury St. Edmunds, England, 257, 259
Buteville, Geoffrey of, 329
Buteville, Oliver of, 329

Caen, Normandy, 117, 141, 149, 150
Calais, France, 329, 350, 360
Cambridge, England, 3, 351, 376, 378
Camville, Gerard of, 47, 48, 74, 366
Cambille, Nicola of, 366
Cancellis, Peter of, 316
Cantelu, Fulk, 172
Canterbury, Archbishops of: coronation privileges of, 9–10; elections of, 168–74, 175, 176, 177, 179, 217, 222–24, 226; Corbeil as, 332. *See also* Becket, Thomas à; Langton, Stephen; Walter, Hubert
Canterbury, England, 4, 10, 44, 50, 71, 90, 107, 333; Barham Down of, 216; Rochester siege and, 335; John's headquarters (1216) in, 360, 361, 362
Canterbury Cathedral, 107, 168, 174
Canute, 133, 374
Cardigan, Wales, 42, 202
Cardinan, Robert of, 264
Carew, Raymond of, 22, 23
Carlisle, England, 107, 281
Carlisle Castle, 349
Carrick, Duncan of, 205
Carrickfergus, Ireland, 197
Casamario, Abbot of, 145
Cashel Synod (1172), 26
Castile, kingdom of, 96, 97, 101
Castles: Irish, 29; under siege, 31–32, 34, 62–63, 115–16, 144, 161, 234–35, 237–38, 240–41, 334–37, 365–66, 369; Longchamp dispute over, 47, 48, 49, 52–53, 54, 55, 87; John's garrison against Richard, 68, 69, 72, 73; Norman chain of, 131, 136–37; punitive seizures of, 181, 205, 211–12; guard duties of, 300–1; baronial gifts, after Magna Carta, 317; royal strongholds (1215–1216), 342, 343, 345, 363, 365–67, 369; Northumbrian, 348, 352, 366. *See also specific castles*
Ceorls, 189–90, 191
Cerdic, Saxon king, 222
Cerisy Abbey, St.-Lô, 133
Châlus, France, 78, 82, 124
Champagne, Count of, 242, 245
Champagne, France, *xxv*, 31
Channel Islands, 134, 143, 150
Charente River, 233
Charlemagne, *xix*, 161
Charles III, King of France, 133
"Charter of Liberties" (Henry I), 255–58, 265–66, 286, 293
Château Gaillard, 131, 137, 138, 139–40; assault on, 144–45, 148, 149, 281
Châteauroux, France, 31, 32
Châtillon, Reginald of, 33
Chauvigni, Andrew of, 116

INDEX 411

Cherbourg, France, 149
Cherwell River, 374
Chester, Ranulf, Earl of, 199, 232, 367, 384; baronial revolt and, 264, 265, 341, 342, 347, 372
Chester, England, 5, 48, 73, 275
Chichester, Bishops of, 320, 384
Chichester, England, 4
Child care, 6
Chiltern Hills, 374, 375, 376
Chinon, France, xxiv, 13, 81-82, 85, 93, 111, 237; Henry's death at, 35; Isabelle of Angoulême (1203) in, 130, 131; French capture (1205) of, 159
Chivalry, xxiv-xxv, 7, 146-48; Richard and, 121-22; warfare modes and, 240-41; women and, 305-6
Christ Church Priory, Canterbury, 168, 169-70, 172
Christmas, 106-7, 192
Church, the, 6, 163-82; Henry II and, xii, 9-12, 14, 21, 26, 32, 33; John's accession and, xiii, 79, 82-84, 122-23, 357-58; Geoffrey Plantagenet and, xx-xxi; Ireland and, 19, 21, 26, 30; Longchamp and, 50; mercenary armies and, 68; Richard's ransom and, 70: Divine Right doctrine and, 87-88, 166, 173, 174; Philip II divorce and, 92, 96, 100, 340; temperance and, 94, 95; festivals of, 106-7, 164; judicial trial and, 111-12, 302; Vikings and, 133; war arbitration by, 136, 145, 248; chivalry and, 146, 147; excommunication of John, 175-82, 184, 193, 195, 200, 201, 213, 214, 215, 217, 223, 225, 227, 256, 330, 391; slavery and, 189; serfdom and, 192; English baronial revolt and, 226, 258-59, 266, 267-68, 281, 282-83, 284-85, 287-88, 289, 320-28, 330-31, 338, 340, 357-58; Albigensian heresy and, 231, 339; Henry I charter of liberties and, 256-57, 266; Anglo-Saxon conversion, 271-72; Magna Carta on, 287-88, 295-96, 299; money lending laws of, 298; inheritance and, 299; music and, 354-55; French invasion of England (1216) and, 356, 357-59, 361, 362, 365, 368-69, 370. *See also* Clergy; Crusades; *and see individual popes and churchmen*
Cigogné, Engelard of, 316, 366, 375, 392
Cinque Ports, 152-53, 360, 370
Cirencester, England, 221, 275
Cistercian Order, 105-6, 108, 114, 126, 182; Briouse family and, 129; interdict and, 178, 181; Swineshead Abbey and, 382
Clapion, Guarine of, 108
Clare, Richard. *See* Hertford, Richard of Clare, Earl of
Clare, England, 376
Class structure, xi, 154-55, 189-93, 201, 293, 300
Clement III, pope, 167
Clergy, 164-67, 188; trial rights of, 9-10, 296, 303, 304; in Ireland, 21; jesters and, 72; historiography and, 84, 85, 122-23, 125-27, 181-82, 184-85, 211, 386; land holdings of, 104, 105-6, 143, 172, 175, 178, 180-81, 227; episcopal elections and, 168-74, 175, 176, 179, 222, 225-26, 228, 258, 295, 324-26, 338; services of, 177-78, 217, 354-55; excommunication of John and, 180-81, 195, 223, 227; warriors among, 242, 244, 246-47; travel and, 296
Clifford, Rosamund, 8
Coenwalch, son of Cynegils, 222
Coggeshall, Ralph of: cited, 126, 231, 259, 337, 343; quoted, 136-37, 158, 291, 352
Colchester Castle, 351, 366
Colechurch, Peter of, 185
Cologne, Germany, 274

Committee of Twenty-Five, 290, 313–14, 316, 322, 347
Common Council, 300, 310
Communes, 155; London, 52, 53, 156, 274
Comnenus, Isaac, 61
Conches, Normandy, 135
Connaught, Ireland, 20, 22, 197
Constance, Empress of Germany, 60
Constance of Brittany, 9, 80, 85, 129; Ranulf of Chester and, 86, 93, 232; peace with John Lackland, 92–93; death of, 111
Constance of Castile, Queen of France, 10
Constitutions of Clarendon, 296
Corbeil, William of, Archbishop of Canterbury, 332
Corbeil, France, 206
Corfe Castle, Dorset, 117, 125, 206, 345, 353, 355, 367
Cork, Ireland, 19, 22
Cornhill, Reginald of, 329
Cornhill, William of, Bishop of Coventry, 277, 289, 295, 320
Cornwall, England, 15, 40, 48, 73, 188, 264
Cotswold Hills, 368, 373, 374
Courcy, John of, 27, 30, 196
Courtenay, Robert, 264
Courts, *xi–xii*, 252, 301; clergy and, 9–10, 296, 302, 303, 304; Ireland and, 20; Longchamp and, 47, 55; summonses to John, 73, 112–13, 126, 357; trial by ordeal or combat in, 111–12, 151, 202, 302, 303, 305; serfs and, 193; recourse right, 223, 224–25, 301–2, 305–6, 387; baronial power and, 262, 269, 276, 283, 301, 304–5; London, 273–74; jury trial in, 292, 302, 303, 305; land disputes in, 304–5, 317, 340, 387; forest courts, 308, 322
Coutances, Walter of, Archbishop of Rouen, 48, 49, 50, 51, 71, 85; as justiciar, 52, 54, 55, 68, 69, 75
Coutances, Normandy, 149
Coventry, Bishop of, 37, 178; Nonant as, 44, 73; Cornhill as, 277, 289, 295, 320
Coventry, Walter of, 337; quoted, 212–13, 218, 291, 323
Craon, Maurice of, 127
Cressi, Roger of, 277
Crook, Ireland, 197
Cross Keys, England, 380, 381
Crowland, England, 3, 377
Croxton, Abbot of, 380, 383, 384–85
Crusades, *xvi–xvii*, 40, 133, 146, 148, 231; Louis VII and, *xxv–xxvi;* Henry II of England and, 12, 18, 32, 33, 34, 37; costs of, 44, 66, 143, 195; Richard's conduct of the Third Crusade, 54, 57–66, 82, 102, 122, 143, 165; prospective, of John, 267, 283, 287, 324–25, 328, 330, 340, 358–59
Cumberland, 160, 280, 342, 349; Scottish claims on, 89–90, 105, 107, 195–96, 260, 281
Cumin, John, Archbishop, 29
Currency, 15, 151–52, 192–93, 391
Cyprus, 61, 62, 66

Damme, Flanders, 220, 221
Darlington, England, 347, 348
Dean, Forest of, 202
Denmark, *xiii*, 92, 132, 152, 218, 272
Derby, William Ferrers, Earl of, 87, 217, 232, 264, 372, 384
Derby, England, 40, 73
Dervorgil, Queen of Meath, 21, 22
Devizes, Richard of, quoted, 4–5, 55, 58–59
Devizes, Wiltshire, 365, 393
Devonshire, William, Earl of, 253, 264, 372
Devonshire, England, 188, 276, 281–82, 284
Diceto, Ralph of, 122

INDEX

Dol, Brittany, 14, 139
Domfront, Normandy, 194
Doncaster Castle, 346–47, 351
Dorset, England, 40, 117, 219, 280, 282, 353, 367
Dover, England, 49–50, 53, 55, 152, 217, 218, 360; mercenary troops in, 290, 323, 329, 333
Dover Castle, 362, 367 369, 373, 376, 379
Dreux, Philip of, Bishop of Beauvais, 77
Dreux, Robert, Count of, 236, 243, 361, 372, 373
Driencourt, Normandy, 108
Driffield, Yorkshire, 317
Dublin, Henry, Archbishop of, 229, 289, 295, 318, 320
Dublin, Ireland, 19, 22, 23, 24, 26, 27, 30, 197
Dudon, 132
Dunbar, Scotland, 348
Dunfermline, Scotland, 90
Dunmow Castle, London, 261
Dunstan, archbishop, 222
Dunwich, England, 360, 366
Durham, Bishops of, 10, 45, 90, 178, 226. *See also* Puiset, Hugh
Durham, England, 5, 107, 342, 343, 348, 349, 366
Dyganwy, Wales, 199

East Anglia, 263, 350, 363. *See also* Norfolk, England; Suffolk, England
Easter, 107, 192
Education, 391; of knights, 147–48; monasteries and, 164–65; apprenticeship, 274
Edward the Confessor, King of England, *xiii–xiv, xv,* 80, 87, 223; mother of, 133; navy of, 152; baronial rights and, 254–55, 256; gilds and, 274
Edward III, King of England, 123
Egbert, King of Wessex, 222
Eisteddfod, 42
Eleanor (daughter of John), 353, 395

Eleanor of Aquitaine, Queen of France, Queen of England, *xxiv–xxvi, xxvii,* 46, 54, 55, 75, 306; children by Henry II, 5–7, 8, 13, 39, 93, 148; Richard's accession and, 38, 41; Richard's captivity and, 68, 69, 71, 148; John's accession and, 82, 86, 91, 101; 101; Blanche of Castile and, 96, 97, 148; Lusignan family and, 108, 115–16
Eleanor of Brittany, 31, 65, 128, 146; English invasion of France (1214) and, 232, 236–37
Eleanor, Queen of Castile, 6, 96
Elizabeth, Queen of Norway, *xiii*
Ely, Bishops of, 45, 146, 184. *See also* Eustace, Bishop of Ely; Longchamp, William
Ely, England, 3, 5
Emma, Queen of England, 133
Epping Forest, 3
Erley, John of, 276
Essex, Geoffrey FitzPeter, Earl of, 48, 86, 88, 392; as justiciar, 143, 154, 180, 218, 229
Essex, Geoffrey of Mandeville, Earl of, 229, 262–63, 276, 317, 350, 372
Essex, William of Mandeville, Earl of, 276, 363
Essex, England, 3, 84, 88, 273; baronial revolt and, 263, 264, 317, 350–51, 376
Essex Castle, London, 261
Ethelred, King of England, 133
Eu, Ralph of Lusignan, Count of, 108, 116, 234, 235
Eugenius III, pope, *xxvi*
Eure River, 81, 133
Eustace, Bishop of Ely, 175, 177, 178, 179–80, 222, 258
Eustace the Monk, admiral, 395
Eva, Princess of Leinster, 22, 23
Evreux, Normandy, 76, 96
Ewell, England, 217, 220; Charter (1213) of, 218–19
Exeter, Bishop of, 284

Exeter, England, 5, 275, 281, 282, 316; French in, 379
Eynsham, Adam of, 181

Falaise, Normandy, 117, 125, 127, 149
Falconry, *xi,* 144, 186, 187, 390; Magna Carta on, 308
Farming, 4, 174, 185, 188; in Ireland, 19–20; monasteries and, 105–6; tenant, 189–90, 191–92
Farnham, England, 282, 363, 365
Feast of the Ass, 164
Feast of Fools, 164
Fécamp, Normandy, 134, 217
Fens, the, 273, 376–77, 379–83
Ferrers, William. See Derby, William Ferrers, Earl of
Fiefs, *xix, xx, xxiii–xxiv, xxvi–xxvii,* 9, 101, 123; of Humbert of Maurienne, 12; Irish, 15; of Innocent III, 218–19
Fishing, 309, 377
FitzAlan, Richard, 317
FitzCount, Henry, 264
FitzGerald, Maurice, 22, 23
FitzGerald, Warin, 295, 364
FitzGilbert, Richard, Earl of Pembroke. See Pembroke, Richard FitzGilbert, Earl of
FitzHenry, Meiler, 196, 197, 202, 213
FitzHerbert, Matthew, 289, 295
FitzHerbert, Peter, 289, 295
FitzHugh, John, 295, 364
FitzPeter, Geoffrey. See Essex, Geoffrey FitzPeter, Earl of
FitzRalph, William, 85
FitzRenfrew, Gilbert, 275
FitzRobert, John, 260, 277
FitzRoger, Robert, 260
FitzStephen, Robert, 22, 23
FitzStephen, William, quoted, 95, 355
FitzUrse, Reginald, 11
FitzWalter, Matilda, 211
FitzWalter, Robert, 139, 211–12, 224; baronial revolt and, 261–62, 263, 265, 268–69, 276, 277, 278, 279, 280, 326, 340, 366, 378; Magna Carta and, 288, 314, 315, 316, 319; Hertford Castle and, 317; Rochester and, 333, 334–35, 336, 339, 341; London defense (1215–1216), 343–44, 350, 351, 363, 371
FitzWalter, William, 327
Flanders, Count of, 62, 91
Flanders, Countess of, 49
Flanders, Ferrand, Count of, 194, 220, 221, 230, 242, 244–45
Flanders, 31, 71; French invasion (1213) of, 220, 231; English campaign (1214) and, 234, 237, 238, 239–40, 242, 244, 245, 248; English baronial revolt (1215) and, 276, 281–82, 316, 321, 323, 333–34
Fleet River, 272, 273
Florence of Worcester, monk, *xv*
Flowers of History (Wendover), 122–23
Folkestone, England, 360
Fontevrault Abbey, 6, 78, 82–83, 93, 182, 394; Eleanor of Aquitaine and, 97, 103, 115, 149
Food, 95–96, 150
Ford, John, abbot, 179
Forest Charter (1217), 308
Forests, *xx,* 3–4; hunting and, 187–88; Unknown Charter on, 286; Magna Carta on, 290, 307–8, 316, 320, 322
Fotheringay Castle, 212, 317, 349
Fougéres, France, 139
Fourth Lateran Council, 302, 324
Framlingham Castle, 351
Frampton Castle, 351
France, *xviii–xix, xx;* Angevin dynasty and, *xii–xiii, xxvi–xxvii* 30–31, 252; Henry II and, 10, 12, 13, 14, 15, 22, 31, 32, 33–36, 39; Acre and, 62; Richard I campaign (1195–1199) in, 75–77, 93, 389; Norman revolts against, 90–91; Church interdict (1200), 96, 100; Easter in, 107; Norman courts and, 112–13;

INDEX

Norman attack (1202) by, 113–17; Normandy capture (1203), 123, 127, 130–32, 134–41, 143, 144–46, 149–50, 158–59, 162, 200, 388; English invasion efforts (1205), 157–59, 168; excommunication of John and, 180; Anglo-German alliance against, 193–94, 214; Irish émigrés in, 197; English barons as refugees in, 206, 211; English plans (1212) to invade, 209, 214; invasion of Flanders (1213) by, 220–21, 224, 231; 228–48, 253, 359; English baronial revolt (1215) and, 281, 283, 286, 339, 343, 350, 351; English invasion by Louis (1216), 355–73, 392, 393, 394

Frederick II, Emperor of Germany and King of Sicily, 214, 395

Freemantle, Wiltshire, 281

Freemen, 191, 193, 230, 256, 341; baronial rights and, 264–65, 300, 314; due process and, 302, 305; jury duty and, 303; purveyance and, 307; forest courts and, 308; Committee of Twenty-Five and, 314–15, 319

Friuli, Italy, 65

Fulford, battle of, *xiv*

Furness Abbey, 211

Furnival, Gerard of, 82

Galloway, Alan, Lord of, 289, 295

Garonne River, 161, 233

Gascony, France, 160, 329

Geburs, 190

Geneats, 190

Genoa, Italy, 59

Geoffrey of Brittany, 6, 9, 13, 14, 16, 17, 18; death of, 30, 31, 86

Geoffrey, Bishop of Ely, 184

Gerald of Wales, 122; cited, 14, 28, 29, 51; quoted, 17, 42, 43, 95–96, 164, 386

Germany, *xviii*, 91, 394, 395; Richard in, 56, 66, 69–71, 148; Sicily and, 60, 66, 194, 214; the Church and, 166, 193–94, 214, 231; English invasion of France (1214) and, 239–40, 242, 243, 244–46, 248; London trade of, 274

Gervase of Canterbury, 195, 201

Ghent, Gilbert of, 366, 373, 377

Ghent, Flanders, 220–21

Gildas, quoted, 375

Gilds, 188, 274–75

Gillingham, England, 332, 334

Gisors, France, 40, 77

Glamorganshire, Wales, 125, 198, 202

Glanville, Ranulf, 6, 30, 44, 45, 62, 69; protegés of, 154–55

Glastonbury, Bishop of, 295

Gloucester, Earl (1215) of, 326

Gloucester, Robert, Earl of, *xxii*

Gloucester, William, Earl of, 15, 40

Gloucester, England, 104, 156, 198, 202, 210, 275, 367; serfdom in, 191–92; Henry III in, 393

Gloucestershire, England, 264, 316; John's earldom of, 15, 76, 100

Gog Magog Hills, 376

Gournay, Normandy, 114

Gracián, Baltasar, quoted, 251

Graveline, Gerard of, 276

Gray, John, Bishop of Norwich, 218, 226; episcopal election (1205) and, 169, 170, 171, 172, 173, 177, 326; interdict and, 177, 178, 180; in Ireland, 197, 213, 214, 229

Gray, Walter, Archbishop of York, 289, 295, 320, 325–26, 338

Grenoble, France, 12

Grim, Edward, quoted, 11

Grimsby, England, 378

Gruffyd ap Rhys, 105, 198, 199

Gualo, Cardinal of Beccaria, 356–57, 358–59, 361, 365, 369, 384; Henry III and, 393

Guildford, England, 104, 106, 144

Guildford Castle, 363

Guiting, Gloucestershire, 191–92

Gundulf, Bishop of Rochester, 51, 333
Gwenwynwyn, 198, 199

Haddington, Scotland, 348
Hainault Forest, 3
Hampshire, England, 74, 106, 189, 345, 362, 365, 366
Hampstead, London, 273
Harald Hardrada, King of Norway, *xii, xiv*
Harcourt, William of, 276
Hardel, William, 363
Harold Godwinson, King of England, *xiii–xv, xvii,* 65, 222, 362; oath of, 39; election of, 80; navy of, 152–153; at Oxford, 374–75
Harthacnut, King of England and Denmark, *xiii*
Hastings, battle of, *xv, xvii,* 3, 5, 24, 39, 65, 163, 362
Hastings, England, 152
Hebrides, 132
Hedingham Castle, 351, 376
Helmsley Castle, 349
Henry, Count Palatine, 193
Henry V, Emperor of Germany, *xviii*
Henry VI, Emperor of Germany, 56, 60, 66, 69–70, 71, 76, 91
Henry I, King of England, 22, 72, 74, 184, 196; accession of, *xvii–xviii,* 81–82; "Charter of liberties" of, 255–58, 265–66, 286, 293; trade gilds and, 274
Henry II, King of England, *xii, xxi,* 78, 82, 89, 122, 148, 149, 154, 280, 317, 354, 390; domain of, *xxiii–xxiv, xxvi–xxvii;* succession of, 5–6, 9–10, 13, 15, 16, 33, 35, 36, 38; Becket murder and, 11–12, 14, 22, 26, 128; government methods of, 7–8, 9, 18, 53, 74, 109, 155, 187, 200, 274, 293, 296, 301, 303, 304, 305, 309, 386; conquest of Ireland, 20–21, 22, 24–27, 28, 29; Philip II of France and, 31, 32, 33–34, 35, 39, 339; Welsh revolts and, 42, 43, 198; Scotland and, 44, 195; Church festivals and, 107; Liverpool and, 186
Henry III, King of England, 353, 367, 373, 394, 395; birth of, 183, 196; John's death and, 383–84; coronation of, 393
Henry, Prince of Castile, 339
Henry, Prince of England (b. 1155), 5, 6, 9–10, 31; rebellion of, 13–15, 16
Hereford, Bishop of, 163, 222. *See also* Briouse, Giles of, Bishop
Hereford, Henry of Bohun, Earl of, 208, 263, 276
Hereford, Herefordshire, 5, 163, 367
Herefordshire, England, 264, 316
Hertford, Richard of Clare, Earl of, 86, 89, 99, 280, 326, 339, 352; Briouse affair and, 208, 263, 317
Hertford Castle, 317
Hertfordshire, 211, 264, 351, 376
Holland, William, Count of, 230, 242, 361, 371
Holy Land, *xvi, xvii, xxv–xxvi,* 54, 61–65, 148; Christian institutions in, 12, 18, 32–33, 61–62, 102, 289; John and, 267, 324–25, 384
Holy Trinity Convent, 356
Honorius III, pope, 368–69
Hostages, 209, 210, 212, 214, 350, 389; Magna Carta on, 309–10, 311, 316, 321; in civil war (1215), 345, 347
Hounslow, England, 316
Howden, Roger of, 37, 122; quoted, 67, 70, 76, 90, 94, 97
Hrolf the Ganger, 132
Hugh of Avalon, Bishop of Lincoln (St. Hugh of Lincoln), 50, 82–83, 85; death of, 104–5, 108, 182
Humbert III of Maurienne, 12
Hungary, 65
Hunting, 186–88, 317

INDEX 417

Huntingdon, David, Earl of, 87, 212, 317
Huntingdonshire, England, 3, 73
Huntingfield, William of, 276
Hythe, England, 152

Ile de France, Paris, *xx*, 242
Ingeborg, Queen of France, 92
Innocent II, pope, *xxi*, 128
Innocent III, pope, 96, 136, 163, 166–67, 248; Canterbury episcopal election (1205) and, 169–74, 175, 176, 177, 179; excommunication of John by, 175–82, 213, 215, 217–27, 259, 330; Germany and, 194, 231; baronial revolt and, 258–59, 266, 267–68, 269, 278, 283, 287, 322–25, 326, 338, 340, 357–58; Magna Carta and, 320, 321, 326, 327–28, 330–31, 347; French invasion of England (1216) and, 356, 357–59, 368
Ipswich, England, 156, 366
Ireland, 12, 15, 38, 40, 42, 194, 200, 202, 205, 267, 318; John's mission (1185) to, 18, 27–30, 35, 43; English conquest of, 19–27, 101; taxation in, 143; trade with, 185–86; justiciarship of, 196–98, 213–14, 218, 229
Isabelle, Princess of England, 353, 395
Isabella, Princess of Scotland, 195–96, 311
Isabelle of Angoulême, Queen of England, 104, 106, 107, 110, 111, 347; Hugh the Brown and, 102, 103, 108, 234, 393, 394; clerical resentment of, 123, 150, 354; Chinon rescue of, 130, 131; as Countess of Angoulême, 162; birth of Henry III, 183–84; birth of Richard, 195; on French campaign (1214), 232, 237; at Corfe Castle (1216), 353, 355; French invasion (1216) of England and, 367, 373
Isabel of Gloucester, Queen of England, 15, 40, 99–100; Mandeville marriage of, 229, 263
Isambard, 392
Isle of Dogs, 273
Isle of Ely, 351
Isle of Purbeck, 353
Isle of Sheppy, 332
Isle of Thorney, 273
Isle of Wight, 159, 232, 328
Italy, *xxv–xxvi*, 12, 91, 194; Richard I in, 48, 51, 56, 60–61, 65, 66

Jaffa, Palestine, 64, 65
Jane, Queen of Sicily, 93
Jerusalem, 12, 18, 63–65, 133; Lusignan family and, 33, 61, 102
Jesters, 72
Jews, 41–42, 45, 47, 277, 278; the King as heir of, 184, 298–99
Joan, Queen of Scotland, 234, 235, 237, 395
Joanna, of England, 6, 61, 65
Joan of Wales, 199, 210, 353
Jocelin, Bishop of Bath, 178, 180, 222, 289, 295, 320
John, King of England, *xii–xiii*, 5–6, 8, 17, 37, 38, 121; inheritance of, 9, 12–13, 15–16, 18, 33, 35, 73, 76, 78, 101, 113; brothers' rebellion (1174) 13–15, 148; first marriage, 15, 40, 99–100, 229; knighting of, 27–28; Le Mans defeat and, 34–36; accession of Richard I and, 36, 40, 41, 46; Welsh revolts and, 43, 194, 198–99, 200, 209–10, 229, 311, 341, 367; Scotland and, 44; (*see also* Scotland); Longchamp chancellorship and, 45, 46–56, 87, 128, 368; Richard's captivity and, 66–69, 70, 71; Richard's return and, 72–73, 75–76; accession of, 78, 79–98, 102, 122, 126, 143, 181, 203, 280, 357; second marriage of, 102, 103–4, 108–17, 123, 124, 183–84, 353–54; Arthur of Brittany disap-

pearance and, 125–30, 146, 203, 357; loss of Normandy by, 123–25, 130–32, 134–35, 143, 144–46, 149–50, 152, 153, 158, 159, 162, 200, 206, 309, 387, 388; fiscal policies of, 142–44, 151, 303–4, 310, 341, 344–45, 346, 352, 388, 389, 390, 391; Church authority and, 163–82, 214–15, 390–91; excommunication of, 179–82, 184, 200, 201, 213, 214, 215, 217, 223, 225, 256, 330, 391; illegitimate children of, 184, 196, 199, 395; deposition of, 212–13, 215, 219, 257, 328, 340; papal fealty oath of, 218–19, 220, 222–27, 231, 259, 357–58; French expedition (1214) of, 228–48; barons' revolt of 1214–15 against, 251–70, 275–85, 340; Magna Carta acceptance by, 285–91, 292, 294, 295, 307–12, 314, 316, 317, 318, 319, 320, 321–22, 326, 327, 389; court procedures and, 301–302, 340, 387; war (1215–1216) against rebel barons, 323, 328–30, 331, 332–52, 374–79, 386, 392; French invasion (1216) of England and, 355–73, 379, 392; death of, 383–86, 392

Journey of the Crusaders, The, 122

Julian, saint, 84

Jumièges, France, 76, 132

Kensham, William of, 370

Kent, England, 3, 71, 217, 219, 376, 395; beer of, 95; baronial revolt (1215) and, 264, 282–83, 332–33; French invasion (1216) and, 360, 362, 365, 370

Kildare, Ireland, 21–22

King John (Shakespeare), 99, 121

King's Lynn, England, 366, 378, 379, 380, 381

Knights, 27–28, 88–89, 144, 286, 293; military service of, 25, 77, 86, 110, 156, 159, 190, 216, 224, 241, 244, 245, 247, 253–54, 255, 300, 329 342, 346, 364; armour of, 113–14; chivalry and, 146–48; gild of, 274; forests and, 290, 308

Knights Templar, 289

Lacy, Hugh of, 27, 30
Lacy, Hugh of, Earl of Ulster, 196–97
Lacy, John, 260–61, 279, 281, 347
Lacy, Margaret, 379
Lacy, Roger of, 48, 87, 260; Norman campaign, 110, 137, 139
Lacy, Walter. *See* Meath, Walter Lacy, Earl of
La Ferté-Bernard, France, 33
La Grâce-Dieu, Abbey of, 232
La Marche, Hugh IX, Count of (Hugh the Brown of Lusignan), 102, 103, 108, 115, 116, 234, 235, 394
La Marche, France, 102, 108, 159, 232, 234–35
Lammermuir Hills, 348
Lancaster, England, 40, 99, 263
Land, *xix*, 4, 191–92, 262, 310; military service and, 25, 253–54, 255; taxation of, 97, 143, 205, 208; episcopal, 104, 172, 175, 178, 179, 180–81, 227, 387; grazing rights, 105–6, 187; English holdings in Normandy, 146, 154, 157, 202; French holdings in England, 153, 154, 194, 370; freehold, 264–65; rebel land confiscations (1215), 275, 276–77, 290, 291, 317, 319, 321; inheritance rights in, 296–97, 299, 303; *precipe* and, 304–5; oath refusal and, 315, 322
Lanfranc, Archbishop, 163
Langton, Simon, 176, 325–26, 338, 361, 363
Langton, Stephen, Archbishop of Canterbury, 171–74, 175, 176, 177, 179–80, 206, 215, 231, 387; John's acceptance of, as Arch-

INDEX

bishop, 217, 218–19, 222–24, 225, 226, 228, 229, 326; baronial revolt (1215) and, 256–57, 258, 259, 265–67, 268, 282, 284–85, 320, 323, 324, 325, 327, 330, 338, 345; Charter negotiation, 287, 288, 289, 291, 296, 315; Tower of London and, 291, 319
La Réole, France, 233
La Rochelle, France, 159, 160, 162, 172; English invasion (1214) of France and, 232, 233, 235, 237, 238, 239, 248, 253
Laudabiliter (bull), 19, 21, 24
Law, 109, 255–58, 290–91, 292–312; peasantry and, *xi–xii*, 187, 191, 193, 293; Henry II and, 7, 8, 9–10, 53, 293; in Ireland, 20; maritime, 59; on royal succession, 80; Edward the Confessor and, 87, 223, 254–55, 256; price controls, 94; Church, 96, 100, 105–6, 167, 295–96, 302; land confiscation and, 104, 154, 303, 310; judicial trial and, 111–12, 301–6; conscription, 155–56; Viking, 133; coinage and, 151–52, 391; forestry and, 187–88, 290, 307–8, 316, 320, 322; slaves and, 189; due process of, 223, 224–25, 269, 293, 302, 387; on inheritance, 255, 256, 286, 296–97, 299, 303; on debt, 298–99. *See also* courts
Lecce, Tancred, Count of, 60, 66
Le Goulet Castle, 91; Treaty of, 97, 110, 114, 193
Leicester, Robert of Beaumont, Earl of, 89, 146, 154, 280
Leicester, Simon of Montfort, Earl of, 395
Leicester, England, 109, 317
Leinster, Ireland, 20, 21–22, 23, 24, 202
Le Lude, France, 162
Le Mans, Normandy, *xxi*, 34–35, 36, 115, 116, 130; accession of John and, 85, 86, 92, 93
Leofgard, Bishop of Hereford, 163

Leominster, Wales, 205, 367
Léon, Bishop of, 242
Leopold, Duke of Austria, 61, 63, 66, 70
Les Andelys, Normandy, 96, 110, 113, 131, 137–40, 144–45
Lichfield, Bishop of, 226
Limasol, Cyprus, 61
Limburg, Duke of, 230
Limerick, Ireland, 19, 202, 205
Limoges, Viscount of, 234
Limoges, France, 12, 77–78, 233
Lincoln, Hugh of, in John's will, 295
Lincoln, Bishops of, 180, 182, 222, 289, 320, 383. *See also* Hugh of Avalon, Bishop of Lincoln
Lincoln, Lincolnshire, *xxii*, 5, 39, 47, 156, 273, 284, 349; John's visit (1200), 104–6, 107
Lincoln Castle, 366, 369, 373, 377, 378, 382, 383
Lincolnshire, England, 74, 171, 378, 379, 380; baronial revolt and, 263, 264, 351, 366, 377
Lisbon, Portugal, 59, 101
Lisieux, France, 75, 149
Lisle, Brian of, 275
Liverpool, England, 186, 192
Llywelyn ap Iorwerth of Wales, 198–99, 209–10, 281, 311, 395
Loches, France, 82, 159
Lodden, bridge of, 51
Loire River and Valley, *xxiv*, 92, 93, 236, 361; Arthur of Brittany campaign in, 115, 129–30; Poitou expedition (1206), 161–62
London, Bishops of, 10. *See also* William, Bishop of London
London, England, *xxii*, 4–5, 50, 68, 95, 271–75, 355; municipal government of, 52, 53, 156, 274, 277; Richard's return from captivity 71–72; accession of John and, 86–87; papal legates in, 145, 225, 227, 228, 253, 284; Council of 1205 in, 155; Otto IV in, 193; conference (1215), 258; FitzWalter lands in, 261;

wall of, 272, 273; baronial rights revolt (1215) and, 277–79, 281, 282–83, 284, 287, 291, 310–11, 327; baronial occupation (1215) of, 315–16, 319–20, 323, 326, 329, 332–33, 334, 336, 338–39, 342, 343–44, 345, 350–52, 362–63, 375, 376, 392; French invasion (1216) and, 362–63, 365, 373

London Bridge, 185, 272, 392
London Tower, 51–52, 275, 277, 284; and, 291, 319
Longchamp, Richenda, 49–50, 55
Longchamp, William, Bishop of Ely, 45–56, 69, 74–75, 87, 128, 277, 368
Long Sutton, England, 380, 381
Lorraine, Theobald, Duke of, 230, 242
Lorraine, France, 194
Loudon, France, *xxiv,* 13
Louis VII, King of France, *xxiii, xxiv, xxv–xxvi,* 10, 13, 14, 30
Louis VIII, King of France, 96, 97, 214, 217; English invasion of 1214 and, 234, 235, 236, 237–38, 239; English crown offered to, 339, 340, 343, 356, 358, 371–72, 393; English invasion threat (1215), 343, 344, 350, 351, 352, 355, 356, 358–60; invasion campaign (1216) of, 355–73, 378, 394, 395
Louis IX, King of France, 96
Louth, England, 378
Louvre, the, 248
Low Countries, alliance against France, 193, 194, 231
Lucy family, 395
Lucy, Godfrey, bishop, 74
Luke, saint, 208
Lupescar, 135, 138, 149
Lusignan family, 102, 108–12, 124–25, 130; English invasion (1214) and, 234–35
Lusignan, Geoffrey of, 115, 116, 117, 234–35
Lusignan, Guy of, 33, 61–62

Lusignan, Hugh the Brown of. *See* La Marche, Hugh IX, Count of
Lusignan, Ralph of. *See* Eu, Ralph of Lusignan, Count of
Lynn, England, 360

McMurrough, Dermot, King of Leinster, 21–24
MacWilliam, Cuthred, 208–9
Magna Carta, 292–312, 313–31, 386; negotiation of, 285–91, 315, 389; papal annulment of, 330–31, 347; Henry III and, 393–94
Magnus, king of Norway, *xiii*
Maid Marion, 211
Maine, France, 130; Counts of Anjou and, *xx, xxiv, xxvi,* 15, 113, 117; Arthur of Brittany and, 85, 86, 92; and Normandy loss to France, 130, 131, 394; French capture of, 159, 162
Malaterra, Geoffrey, quoted, *xvi*
Mallett, William, 280
Malmesbury, William of, quoted, 95, 105, 274
Mandeville, Geoffrey. *See* Essex, Geoffrey Mandeville, Earl of
Mandeville, William of, 276, 363
Map, Walter, quoted, 8
Marc, Philip, 345
Margaret, saint, 90
Margaret, Princess of France, 10
Margaret, Princess of Scotland, 195–96, 311
Marlborough, England, 15, 40, 50, 73, 99, 104, 275, 372
Marmande, France, 339
Marque River, 240, 243
Marriage: royal permission for, *xi–xii,* 255; consanguineous, *xxvi,* 26, 27, 100; dowries, 10, 12, 38, 96–97, 256, 297; polyandrous, 21; ceremonies, 40–41, 177, 217; fines, 191, 204; serfs and, 193; Magna Carta on, 296, 297, 305–306
Marseilles, France, 59, 65
Marsh, Richard, 323
Marshal, John 289, 295

INDEX 421

Marshal, William. *See* Pembroke, William Marshal, Earl of
Marshal, William, Jr., 260, 281, 368, 370–71, 372, 395
Martigny, Geoffrey of, 269, 316
Matilda, Empress of Germany, Queen of England, *xviii, xx–xxii, xxiii,* 20–21, 382
Matilda, Princess of England, 6, 91, 339
Mauclerk, Walter, 258, 259, 267
Mauger, Bishop of Worcester, 175, 177, 178, 179–80
Mauléon, Savary of, 116, 125, 160, 368, 384, 392; baronial revolt and, 267, 275, 276, 329, 344, 350, 351
Mead, 94
Measurement standards, 309
Meath, Walter of Lacy, Earl of, 196–97, 205, 379, 384
Meath, Ireland, 20, 21–22, 24
Medway River, 332–33
Melun, Viscount of, 361, 371–72
Melun, France, 356
Melusine, *xii–xiii*
Meran, Duke of, 92
Mercadier, 76, 77, 78, 86, 96, 97
Mercians, 222
Mervent, France, 232, 234, 235
Messina, Italy, 48, 51, 60, 61
Middlesex, England, 264, 351
Milécu, France, 232, 233
Miracles, 105, 61–62
Mirebeau, France, *xxiv,* 13; battle at, 115–16, 123, 124, 129, 130, 131, 139, 149, 337, 392
Monarchy, *xii–xviii, xxvii,* 251–52; French, *xx, xxiv–xxv,* 13, 134; elective, 80–81; in Ireland, 20, 21–22, 27; death rites, 37; powers of, 87–88, 109–10, 201, 223, 293, 300, 306–7, 309–10; church power and, 9–10, 163–82, 258–59, 285; peasantry and, 189, 193; North England unrest and, 259–61, 263–64, 342, 344, 345–50; baronial revolt and, 283, 285, 292, 340, 386; constitutional, 292–93, 294; regicide and, 336
Monmouth, John of, 384
Montauban Castle, 161
Montbegon, Roger of, 317, 347
Montfichet, Richard, 317
Montigny, Galon of, 245
Montlouis, France, 15, 16
Montmorillon, France, 161
Mont St. Michel, 133
Mortain, Normandy, 40, 76, 194
Morville, Hugh of, 11
Moslems, 33, 61–63, 185
Moulton Castle, 351
Mountsorrel Castle, 317
Mowbray, William, 262, 280
Munster, Ireland, 20, 29, 197
Muret, battle of, 231
Music, 353, 354–55

Namur, Philip, Count of, 242
Nantes, France, 236, 237
Navarre, 54, 61, 100–1, 148
Navies, 152–54, 156, 157, 158, 159, 391; of Richard I, 58–59, 60, 61, 65, 75, 153; river warfare in Normandy, 137–38; Poitou expedition, 160–61; Irish expedition (1210), 197; defense plans (1213), 216, 217, 355; Ghent siege and, 220–21, 224; in invasion of France (1214), 232; in invasion of England (1216), 355, 360–61, 370, 379, 394, 395.
Nene River, 379, 380, 381, 393
Nesta, 22–23, 25, 28, 196
Nevers, Count of, 361, 366–67, 373, 375–76
Neville, Geoffrey, 349
Neville, Hugh, 285, 295, 364, 372
Newark Castle, 345, 346, 383, 384
Newburgh, William of, 122
Newcastle, England, 107, 275, 343, 348, 349
Nicholas, Cardinal of Tusculum, 225–27, 228, 231, 253, 284
Niort, Poitou, 159–60, 161, 232
Nobles, the, *xi–xii,* 154–55, 188–

89, 190, 191–92, 201; Norman, *xv–xvi, xvii, xix–xx,* 131–32, 134–35, 136, 138–39, 140, 144, 200, 265; Henry II and, 7, 15, 16, 200; Richard I and, 16, 87, 134; of Ireland, 20, 25–26, 27, 28–29, 101, 196, 197–98, 214; military service of, 24, 25, 216, 224–25, 230, 232, 238–39, 240–42, 247, 248, 253–54, 255, 268, 286, 341; Philip II and, 31, 92, 113, 134, 217, 242; castle life of, 32; accession of John and, 80, 86–87, 88–89, 101–2, 134, 280; rights demands of, 109–10, 123, 155, 156, 223, 224–25, 252, 254–59, 263–70, 275–91, 293, 310, 320–22, 386, 388–89; of Poitou, 142, 160–61, 238, 239, 248, 265, 267, 275, 276, 392; land confiscations and, 146, 154, 157, 203–5, 208, 211–12, 262, 275, 276–77, 290, 291, 304–5, 310, 317, 319, 321; Church interdict and, 175, 181, 200, 201, 213; hunting and, 186, 187; royal debts of, 204–5, 262–63, 276, 286, 298–99, 310; Briouse affair and, 208, 213–14, 263, 264, 379; conspiracy of 1212 by, 210–11, 230, 257, 262, 280, 317, 389; deposition of John and, 213, 219, 257, 328; Church intervention against, 226, 258–59, 266, 267–68, 281, 282–83, 284–85, 287–88, 289, 320–28, 330–31, 338, 340, 357–58; Magna Carta implementation and, 290–91, 293, 294, 310–12, 313–29, 389; French invasion (1216) and, 362, 363–64, 365, 366, 370, 371–72, 392; John's death and, 384, 385, 393–94

Nonant, Hugh of, Bishop of Coventry, 44, 73

Norfolk, Roger Bigod, Earl of, 89, 263, 280, 351, 352

Norfolk, England, 378, 379, 263, 264

Norgate, Kate, quoted, 386

Norham, Northumberland, 195, 343, 348

Normandy, Richard the Fearless, Duke of, 133

Normandy, Robert, Duke of, *xvi–xvii, xviii*

Normandy, Robert the Magnificent, Duke of, 133

Normandy, William, Duke of, *xiii,* 41, 117, 206; invasion and conquest of England, *xiv–xvi, xvii, xx,* 24, 39, 134, 362

Normandy, *xii–xviii, xxi, xxii–xxiii,* 94–95, 112–17, 132–34; Henry II and, *xxvi–xxvii,* 9, 10, 13, 14, 15, 35; Richard I and, 16, 40, 58, 65, 67, 70, 73, 75, 76, 78; Longchamp and, 45, 46, 47; accession of John and, 81, 85–86, 90–91, 93, 103; Lusignan family and, 108–9, 110, 124–25; English loss of, 123, 127, 130–32, 134–41, 143, 144–46, 149–50, 152, 153, 158, 159, 162, 200, 206, 309, 387, 388, 394; English invasion (1214) of, 242, 243

North Africa, Sultan of, 185

Northallerton, England, 347

Northampton, 86–87, 90, 106, 228, 268, 345; siege (1215) of, 276, 278, 284, 316

Northamptonshire, England, 3, 268–69, 284

North Sea, 379

Northumberland, 44, 45, 74; Scottish claims to, 89–90, 105, 195–96, 260; baronial revolt and, 263, 342, 343; raids (1216), 348–49, 352, 366

Norway, *xiii, xiv,* 132

Norwich, Bishops of, 146, 169. *See also* Gray, John

Norwich, England, 5, 156, 366

Nôtre Dame de Paris, 173

Nôtre Dame des Prés, Rouen, 128

Nôtre Dame du Pré, Vaudreuil, 81

Nottingham, England, 156, 210–11, 216, 225

INDEX

Nottingham Castle, 47, 48, 73, 345
Nottinghamshire, 15, 40, 76

Oaths, 38–39, 46, 49, 55, 86; of coronation, 87; of testimony, 111, 302; of fealty, 146, 148, 155, 156, 157–58, 194, 202, 213, 232, 234; of secrecy, 169; John's fealty to the pope, 218–19, 222–27, 259; John's demands for baronial liege homage (1215), 266–67; 290, 347; baronial renunciations of, 268, 279, 363; Committee of Twenty-Five and, 314–15, 319, 322
O'Brien, Donell, of Munster, 29
O'Brien, Donough, Prince of North Munster, 197
O'Connor, Cathal, King of Connaught, 197
O'Connor, Roderick, 22, 23, 24, 27
Odiham, England, 282, 365–66
Odo, Bishop of Bayeux, 163
Ordeals, 111–12, 302
Orderic (monk), quoted, *xvi*
Orford, England, 275
Orne River, 144, 149
O'Rourke, Tiernan, King of Meath, 21, 22, 23, 24
Otto IV, Emperor of Germany, 91, 96, 114, 214, 230; excommunication of, 193–94, 231, 243; English invasion of France (1214) and, 239, 240, 242, 243, 244–46, 248
Ouse River, 347, 379
Oxford, Robert of Vere, Earl of, 253, 263, 276, 317, 351, 352
Oxford, England, *xxii,* 4–5, 15, 43, 275; Councils in, 143–44, 156, 175, 229–30; Langton conference (1215) with the barons, 266–67; conference of July (1215), 318–19, 320, 321, 322; Conference of August (1215), 323–24; John's last visit, 374–75
Oxford University, 325, 391

Pages, 147
Palestine. *See* Holy Land
Pandulf, 217–18, 284, 318, 338; Magna Carta and, 289, 295, 320, 321, 324, 327
Paris, Matthew, 125; quoted, 123, 168, 184–85, 229, 271, 289, 313, 383, 386
Paris, France, *xx,* 67, 117, 134, 167; John visits in, 110, 112–13; English invasion of France (1214) and, 239, 240, 241, 248
Paris, University of, 171, 173,
Parthenay, France, 236
Pattishall, Simon, 269, 277
Paul, saint, quoted, 50
Peasants, *xi,* 25, 187, 188–93, 201–202; French, *xix–xx;* housing of, 5, 164, 186; baronial rights and, 265, 293
Pembroke, Richard FitzGilbert, Earl of, 22, 23, 24, 27, 38
Pembroke, William Marshal, Earl of, 38, 48, 50, 75, 232, 341; accession of John and, 80–81, 82, 86, 88; Norman campaigns of, 110, 116, 124, 130, 135–36, 138, 140–41; Norman lands of, 146, 154, 157–58, 202; Poitou expedition, 160; in disfavor (1206), 202–3, 204, 387–88; manifesto of loyalty, 213–14; French threats of invasion (1213) and, 216, 218, 220; baronial revolt (1215), 258, 264, 265, 268, 276, 285, 342; Magna Carta and, 289, 295; French invasion (1216) and, 361, 367, 368, 372, 394; Henry III and, 383–84, 393, 394
Pembrokeshire, Wales, 20, 88, 197
Percy, Richard, 280
Périgord, Count of, 234
Périgord, France, 101, 233
Péronne, France, 239
Peter II, King of Aragon, 231
Peter, Cardinal of Padua, 93
Peterborough, England, 3, 377
Peter of Blois, quoted, 8

Petit-Dutaillis, Charles, 124
Petronilla of Aquitaine, *xxiv–xxv*
Philip II, King of France, 30, 33, 34–36, 39, 73, 167, 252, 296; Châteauroux siege and, 31–32; Richard's crusade and, 40, 44, 54, 57–58, 60–61, 62, 63; John alliance, 66, 67, 68, 69–70, 71; Richard's campaign (1195–99) against, 76–77, 93; John's accession, 81, 85, 86, 90–92, 93, 97–98, 357; divorce of, 92, 96, 100, 174, 340; Spain and, 101; Lusignan family and, 108–9, 110, 112; Arthur of Brittany alliance, 113, 114–17, 126, 127–28, 129; Normandy victories (1203) of, 124, 130–31, 134–41, 144–46, 149–50, 153, 162; England invasion threats from, 153, 155, 157, 158, 214, 215–16, 217–18, 219–20; Aquitaine resistance to, 160–62; Langton and, 173, 215; Anglo-German alliance and, 193–94, 200, 231; Wales and, 209; Flanders invasion (1213) by, 220–21, 224; English expedition (1214) against, 228–48, 253; English baronial revolt (1215) and, 281, 323, 339–40, 343, 350, 357; English invasion (1216) by Louis, 355, 358, 359, 368; death of, 395
Philip of Swabia, 193
Picardy, 242
Plantagenet, Geoffrey, Archbishop of York, 39–40, 46, 68, 91, 96; Longchamp and, 49–50, 51, 53; land taxation and, 175; death of, 325
Plantagenet, Geoffrey (son of John), 395
Plantagenet, Hamelin, 89
Plantagenet, Oliver, 395
Plantaganet, Richard (son of John), 395
Plantagenet dynasty. *See* Angevin dynasty

Poitiers, France, *xxvi*, 13, 97, 115, 161, 236
Poitou, France, 8, 14, 17, 102, 103, 110, 142, 224, 329; English loyalty of, 157, 158, 159–62; English invasion (1214) of France and, 231, 233, 234, 235, 236, 237, 238, 239, 257, 280, 286, 287, 359, 392; Henry III and, 394
Pomeroy, Henry of, 264, 276
Pontefract, Yorkshire, 347
Pont l'Evêque, Roger of, Archbishop of York, 10
Poor, Richard, 226
Porchester, England, 156, 221
Portsmouth, England, 109, 110, 156, 159, 162, 185, 209, 231; defense plans in, 216
Portugal, 101, 103, 218
Powys, Owen Cyveiliog, Prince of, 198
Préaux, Peter of, 130, 150
Precipe, writ of, 304–5
Procopius, 211
Public office, 74, 88, 165, 204, 229, 252, 308–9, 317; class structure and, 154–55, 191; the Church and, 165–66, 167
Puiset, Hugh, Bishop of Durham, 45–46, 67, 68, 73, 74
Purveyance, 307
Pyrenees Mountains, *xxiv*, 96, 101

Quincy, Margaret, 280
Quincy, Saer of, 139, 262, 263, 280, 317, 341

Radepont, Normandy, 114, 115
Rahere, 72
Ramsay, Sir James, quoted, 386
Ramsey, England, 3
Ranulf. *See* Chester, Ranulf, Earl of
Raymond VI, of Toulouse, 231
Reading, Abbot of, 324
Reading, England, 50, 51, 375, 394
Reginald, Archbishop-elect of Canterbury, 169–70, 171, 172

INDEX

Reigate Castle, 363
Rheims, Archbishop of, 242
Rhys ap Gruffyd, 42, 43, 105, 198
Rhys ap Maelgwyn, 198, 199
Richard I, King of England, 6, 13, 14, 51, 74, 274, 303, 317, 386, 390, 391; chivalric figure of, *xii–xiii*, 121–22; inheritance of, 9, 16, 18, 33, 35; Alice of France and, 31, 33–34, 54, 61; accession of, 36, 38, 39, 40, 41–42; crusades and, 37, 40, 42, 43, 44–45, 46, 49, 53, 54, 57–66, 82, 122, 143, 153, 165, 195; revolts against, 42–44, 101–2, 198; succession of, 46, 49, 52, 55, 68, 69, 73, 78, 79–83, 88, 89, 98, 126, 203, 357; marriage of, 54, 61, 100–1, 111, 148, 354; imprisonment of, 56, 66–71, 148, 262; French campaign (1195–99), 75–77, 93, 389; death of, 78, 79–82, 88, 181–82; hostages of, 206
Richard (son of John), 195, 210, 353, 394–95; English invasion of France and, 232, 237
Richard the Breton, 11
Richmond, Constance, Countess of, 89
Richmond, England, 317, 323
Roads, 188, 221, 273, 309, 333, 350; through the Fens, 379–83
Robin Hood, 74, 211
Roches, Peter of, Bishop of Winchester, 169, 178, 180, 384, 393; as justiciar, 229, 231, 252–53, 275, 291, 321, 392; Savery of Mauléon and, 276; Innocent III and, 324; Magna Carta and, 289, 295, 318, 320, 321
Roches, William of, 92, 129–30, 237
Roches-aux-Moines, France, 237–38, 253
Rochester, Bishop of, 10, 51, 178, 180, 289, 295, 333
Rochester, Kent, 4, 71, 282–83, 284; John's attack on, 332–37, 338–39, 343, 344, 345
Rochester Castle, 329, 332–37, 339, 341, 362, 392
Rollo, 132–33, 134
Roman Empire, 94, 186, 188–89, 221, 271
Rome, Italy: papal government in, 166–68, 169, 170–74, 175, 177, 193, 215, 219, 296; English embassies to, 229, 320–21, 322–23, 327–28, 330–31, 338; French embassies to, 136, 359
Romney, England, 152, 333, 360, 361
Ropsley, Robert, 289, 295
Ros, Robert of, 260, 280, 349
Rouen, Normandy, *xxi, xxiii*, 78, 85, 90, 91, 132, 140, 215; Arthur of Brittany in, 126, 128; Philip II and, 114, 135, 137, 138, 144, 145, 149–50
Runnymede, 288–90, *see also* Magna Carta

St. Albans Abbey, London, 84, 90, 224, 261
St. Albans Castle, 345, 349
St. Andrew's Cathedral, 333
St. Clement Danes Church, 4
St. Edmund's, Adam of, 72–73
St. Edmunds, East Anglia, 90
St. James Park, London, 273
St. Martin's Priory, 50, 356
St. Maure, Amery of, 384
St. Michael's Mount, Cornwall, 73
St. Paul's Cathedral, London, 50, 52, 54, 71, 122, 212, 256; of Seberht, 271; folk-moots and, 274; French invasion (1216) and, 356, 362–63
St. Peter's, York, 173
St. Sever, France, 101
St. Stephen's Cathedral, Beauvais, 164
Saladin, 33, 61, 63–65
Salisbury, Bishop of, 10, 69, 178, 180
Salisbury, Ela, Countess of, 364

Salisbury, John of, quoted, 88
Salisbury, William, Earl of, 154, 159, 217, 387; Flemish campaigns and, 220–21, 231, 237, 239; at Bouvines, 242, 244, 246, 247, 248, 282; baronial revolt and, 264, 265, 276, 277, 282, 284, 341; Magna Carta and, 289, 295; London occupation (1216) and, 344, 350, 351; French invasion (1216) and, 364, 372, 378, 379
Salisbury, England, 221, 226
Samson, saint, 139
Sandwich, Kent, 71, 152, 336, 360, 361, 394
Satan, *xii*
Saumur, France, 130
Scarborough, England, 107, 349
Scotland, 14, 22, 107, 395; Richard I and, 43–44, 68, 73, 195; accession of John and, 89–90, 97; John's pacification of, 194, 195–96, 200, 260, 280; Lincoln conference (1200), 105; English emigrés in 205–6, 211, 280; MacWilliam and, 208–9; English baronial revolt (1215) and, 281, 311, 342, 343, 344; border raids (1216), 348–49, 363, 366, 369; John's last campaign and, 376, 378
Seberht, 271
Seez, Chapter of, *xx–xxi*
Seine River, 77, 126, 128, 131, 137, 144
Senlac, England, *xv*
Senlis, Guérin of, 242, 243, 244, 245, 247
Serfs, 191–93, 265; Magna Carta and, 293, 302, 304
Shakespeare, William, 125; quoted, 99, 121, 183
Sheriffs, 74, 151, 230, 252, 308, 387, 395; Lacy (Roger) and, 260; baronial revolt (1215), 276, 280, 281, 284, 290, 291, 316, 321; death duties and, 299; common council summons, 300; requisition powers of, 306–7

Shoreham, Sussex, 86
Shrewsbury, Robert, Bishop of Bangor, 199
Shrewsbury, England, 156, 367
Sicily, 61, 93, 218; Germany and, 60, 66, 194, 214
Silvester, bishop, 384
Skallason, Thorkil, quoted, *xvi*
Skelton Castle, 349
Slavery, 189, 190, 191
Sleaford Castle, 345, 382–83
Soceinne, Gerard of, 329
Soissons, France, 215
Somerset, England, 40, 280
Sonning, England, 375, 376
Southampton, Hampshire, 153, 221
South Wales, 42, 43, 105, 198–99
Southwark, England, 259, 272
Spain, *xxvi*, 54, 65, 96–97, 100–1
Spalding, England, 378
Squires, 147–48
Staffordshire, 86
Staines, England, 287, 288
Stamford, Lincolnshire, 268, 275, 316, 322, 324, 349, 376
Stamford Bridge, battle of, *xiv*
Statutes of Salisbury, 355
Stephen of Blois, King of England, *xxi–xxii, xxvii*, 4, 7, 45, 53, 280, 303; granddaughters of, 153
Stoke, Peter of, 82
Studland, England, 159
Stuteville, Nicholas, 262
Stuteville, William of, 90
Suetonius, 271
Suffolk, England, 264, 351, 376
Surrey, England, 89, 264, 333, 345, 363, 365
Sussex, *xv, xxii*, 3, 86, 222, 264; French invasion and, 362, 370
Swabia, 193
Sweden, 218
Swine estuary, 220, 221
Swineshead, England, 382, 383

Tacitus, 271
Talbot, William, 184, 351
Taxation, *xvii, xix*, 292; by Richard I, 70, 71, 73–75, 77, 87, 89, 134, 142–43, 165; scutage,

INDEX

96–97, 144, 253–54, 255, 259, 268, 286, 287, 300, 310; of monasteries, 106, 172, 174, 181; for continental wars, 110, 123, 143, 253, 388, 389; chattel, 143, 174–75, 178, 179, 181, 205, 276; serfs, 191–92; death duties, 204, 255, 256, 261, 262, 296–97, 299; sheriffs and, 306–7; foreign trade, 312
Thames River, 72, 272–73, 332, 355, 371
Thanet, Kent, 360, 361
Thora of Norway, *xiii*
Thouars, Amery, Viscount of, 130, 161, 230–31, 238
Thouars, Guy of, 93, 161
Thouars, Raymond, 116
Tiberias, Palestine, 33
Tickhill Castle, 47, 48, 73
Tinchebrai, battle of, *xvii–xviii*
Toulouse, Count of, 65, 93, 231
Toulouse, France, *xxvii*, 231
Touraine, France, *xx, xxiv, xxvi*, 15, 70, 76, 85, 86, 159; Normandy loss to France and, 130, 131, 157, 394
Tournai, France, 240
Tours, France, 49, 57, 91, 115–16
Tracy, William of, 11
Trade, 174, 185, 186, 188, 232, 280, 378, 392; French, 150, 343, 355; currency reform and, 151–52; in slaves, 189; London centre of, 271, 272, 273, 274, 275, 277; free, 311–12
Trenchemer, Alan, 71, 138, 153
Trent River, 104, 383
Turkey, crusades and, *xxv*, 61–65
Turnham, Robert of, 82
Tweed River, 343, 348
Twinstead, Essex, 84
Ty Bourne, 273

Ulecotes, Philip of, 275, 343, 366
Ulster, Hugh of Lacy, Earl of, 196–97
Ulster, Ireland, 20, 27, 196
Unknown Charter of Liberties, 286–87, 299

Vale of Evesham, 385
Valence, Aymer, Bishop of Winchester, 394
Valenciennes, France, 240, 246
Vaudreuil, Normandy, 81, 135, 139, 211, 262, 280
Vere, Robert of. *See* Oxford, Robert of Vere, Earl of
Vermandois, Count of, *xxv*
Vesci, Eustace of, 211–12, 224, 366, 372; baronial revolt and, 258–59, 260, 261, 262, 265, 280, 281, 314, 317, 326
Vexin, Normandy, 10, 31, 67, 91
Vezelay, Burgundy, 57, 60
Vienna, Austria, 66, 262
Vieuxpont, Robert of, 275, 343, 349
Vikings, *xiii*, 152, 186, 272; in Ireland, 19–20; in France, 132–33
Villages, 188–89; John's army in, 346, 377–78
Vitry, Cathedral of, *xxv*

Wakefield, Peter of, 212–13, 218, 219
Wales, 38, 68, 105, 125, 163, 194; Ireland and, 22–23, 24, 28, 185–86; Richard I in, 42–43; Church interdict (1207) on, 175–80; submission (1210) to John, 198–99, 200; Briouse estates in, 202, 203–4, 205–6; revolts (1212), 209–10, 229, 230; baronial revolt and, 275, 281, 284, 311, 341, 342, 368
Wall Brook, 272, 273
Wallingford Castle, 54, 68, 275
Walter, Hubert, Archbishop of Canterbury, 69, 71, 72–73, 75, 104, 107, 112, 144, 154–55, 163, 392; taxation by, 77, 165; accession of John and, 80–81, 82, 86, 87, 88, 166; Church land confiscations and, 143, 181; Norman lands of, 146, 157; death of, 160, 169, 229
Waltham, Essex, 318
Wardship laws, 296, 297, 311, 317

Wareham, Dorset, 219
Warine family, 186
Wark Castle, 260
Warren, William, Earl of, 217, 264, 269, 276, 364; Magna Carta and, 289, 295, 318
Warwick, Henry, Earl of, 264, 372
Wash, the, 379–82
Waterford, Ireland, 19, 23, 24; John in, 28–29
Weavers, 274–75, 277
Welland River, 379, 380, 382
Wendover, Roger of, 3, 84, 122–26, 129, 143, 150, 184; on episcopal elections, 172, 175–76; on Briouse family, 203–4; on plots against John, 210; on Charter of Ewell, 218; on baronial revolt, 256–57, 259, 329, 343–44, 349, 350; on Magna Carta, 321, 323; on Rochester siege, 337; on French invasion, 353, 361–62; on Wash incident, 380–81, 382
Wessex, 222
Westminster Abbey, 87, 98, 99, 104, 363
Westminster Palace, *xiii, xiv, xvii, xxvii*, 174, 272, 303, 341
Westmorland, 105, 195, 343, 349
West Saxons, 222
Wexford, Ireland, 19, 23, 24
Whitsuntide, 107
William (son of Henry I), *xviii*
William (son of Henry II), 5
William, Bishop of London, 175, 177, 178, 179–80
William the Breton, Chaplain of Philip II, 126, 247; quoted, 233, 248
William the Conqueror. *See* Normandy, William, Duke of
William of Jumièges, 132
William the Lion, King of Scotland, 43–44, 68, 73, 195–96, 210; accession of John and, 89–90, 97; in Lincoln, 105; MacWilliam and, 208–9; Vesci and, 211, 280; baronial rights and, 260; son's succession, 281, 311

William Rufus, King of England, *xvi-xvii*, 81, 332; Ireland and, 20
Wiltshire, England, 264, 268, 281; French invasion (1216) and, 318, 365, 367
Winchester, Bishops of, 44, 394. *See also* Roches, Peter of
Winchester, England, *xxii*, 10, 13, 20, 38, 82, 183, 221–24, 318; fortifications of, 275, 282; French invasion and, 365, 366, 367, 378
Winchester Minster, 222, 223, 354
Windsor, England, 287
Windsor Castle, 27, 50–51, 54, 68, 206; French siege of, 366–67, 369, 373, 375–76, 378
Wine, 94–95, 336
Wisbech, England, 380, 381, 382
Witan, 80
Witsand, Flanders, 49
Wolves, 107, 188
Women, 297, 299, 305–306. *See also* marriage
Worcester, Bishop of, 226; Mauger as, 175, 177, 178, 179–80; Magna Carta and, 289, 295, 320; John's will and, 384. *See also* Gray, Walter, Bishop of Worcester
Worcester, England, 5, 367, 368
Worcester Cathedral, 17, 384, 385
Wulfstan, Archbishop, 189
Würtzburg, Germany, 66

Yarmouth, England, 232, 330, 360, 366
York, Archbishops of, 10, 226, 361. *See also* Plantagenet, Geoffrey; Gray, Walter
York, Yorkshire, 5, 97, 273, 347; Jews of, 42, 45
Yorkshire, *xiv*, 3, 107, 122, 160, 317, 378; sheriffs of, 74, 86; baronial revolt (1215) and, 263, 342, 347, 351; John's Northern march (1216) in, 349